NOTHIN' TO LOSE

ALSO BY PAUL STANLEY AND GENE SIMMONS

KISStory

KISStory II

KISS: The Early Years

*KISS Army Worldwide!: The Ultimate KISS
Fanzine Phenomenon*

KISS Kompendium

ALSO BY KEN SHARP

KISS: Behind the Mask

*KISS Army Worldwide!: The Ultimate KISS
Fanzine Phenomenon*

NOTHIN' TO LO/E

THE MAKING OF KI// (1972-1975)

!t
itbooks
AN IMPRINT OF HARPERCOLLINS PUBLISHERS

*it***books**

HarperCollins books may be purchased for educational, business, or sales promotional use. For information please e-mail the Special Markets Department at SPsales@harpercollins.com.

A hardcover edition of this book was published in 2013 by It Books, an imprint of HarperCollins Publishers.

FIRST IT BOOKS PAPERBACK PUBLISHED 2014.

Designed by Renato Stanisic

Library of Congress Cataloging-in-Publication Data has been applied for.

ISBN 978-0-06-213173-7

19 20 21   OV/LSC   10 9 8 7 6 5 4 3

To Bill Aucoin, Neil Bogart, and Sean Delaney—
if they hadn't been there,
this story might never have been told

CONTENTS

Barnes & Noble Booksellers #2831
4300 Montgomery Road
Ellicott City, MD 21043
410-203-9001

STR:2831 REG:C04 TRN:8917 CSHR:William D

MEMBER   EXP: 03/18/2024

POP Movies: The Flash - Young Barry
   0889698655958   T1
   (1 @ 11.99) Member Card 10% (1.20)
   (1 @ 10.79)   10.79
Nothin' to Lose: The Making of KISS (197
   9780062131737   T1
   (1 @ 17.99) Member Card 10% (1.80)
   (1 @ 16.19)   16.19

Subtotal   26.98
Sales Tax T1 (6.000%)   1.62
TOTAL   28.60
CASH   30.00
CASH CHANGE   1.40-

Returns will be accepted with a receipt
within 30 days of purchase. Eligible refunds
will be made to your original form of
tender. For returns with a gift receipt, a
store credit will be issued in the form of
an electronic gift card for the purchase
price within 60 days of purchase.
Exceptions apply. Visit bn.com/returns
for full details.

MEMBER SAVINGS   3.00

059.030   08/13/2023 11:22AM

CUSTOMER COPY

INTRODUCTION

THE MEASURE OF A MAN IS WEIGHED NOT ONLY BY HOW HARD HE WORKS BUT BY HOW BIG HE DREAMS. . . .

"Before the beginning of great brilliance, there must be chaos. Before a brilliant person begins something great, they must look foolish in the crowd."
—I CHING

"Do not go where the path may lead, go instead where there is no path and leave a trail."
—RALPH WALDO EMERSON

Forty years ago, in a perfect storm of attitude, oversized ambition, and plain old dumb luck, Paul Stanley, Gene Simmons, Ace Frehley, and Peter Criss came together for the first time, and KISS was born. Outfitted in black leather and studs, lipstick, and greasepaint, the thunderous sound they created, coupled with lyrics that resonated with teenage angst, frustration, rebellion, and lust, became the mighty soundtrack for generation after generation of fans.

KISS literally changed the face of rock and roll. They invented and defined the live concert experience. You've heard it many times before: "You wanted the best, you got the best, the hottest band in the land. . . ." That was their battle cry then, and it remains their battle cry today. Blazing their own trail to superstardom, persevering despite ever-changing musical styles, fashions, and fads, KISS is truly a great American success story, built of blood, sweat, and rock-and-roll glory. Today, KISS is much more than a successful rock-and-roll band; they're part of the fabric of American pop culture, standing alongside such enduring legends as Elvis Presley, James Dean, and Marilyn Monroe.

Not only are the band and its members icons, KISS is a brand in itself. Boasting a catalog of over three thousand officially licensed products—from KISS koffins to pinball machines—the band has grossed over $500 million in merchandising and licensing fees over the past thirty-five years. Spanning the globe from Tokyo to Moscow's Red Square to New York City, KISS are universally recognized as larger-than-life music figures—a far cry from their humble beginnings.

On January 30, 1973, KISS performed their first concert at a seedy hole-in-the-wall called Coventry in Queens, New York. Tickets were a few bucks and the group was lucky that a handful of people showed up. But like the Beatles' residency at the Cavern Club in Liverpool, it was inside the cramped and peeling walls of this ratty club where KISS first came alive onstage. Stubbornly confident, the band never doubted they'd make it, playing their early gigs as if they were headlining a sold-out show at Madison Square Garden—a feat they'd achieve after a whirlwind four years. Hell-bent on making it at any cost, KISS dreamed big, and they had the drive and ambition to achieve those dreams.

Their mission was simple: they wanted to conquer the world. But the road to the top was a bumpy one. They were reviled by critics and designated public enemy number one by an army of concerned parents. Yet against all odds and enough roadblocks to frustrate lesser men, four ordinary musicians pulled off the impossible and became internationally renowned rock superstars. Long before KISS's initial rush of mega-fame that sold out multiple nights at New York's Madison Square Garden and packed outdoor stadiums in Australia and Brazil, the band's formative days playing local haunts—Coventry in Queens, the Daisy in Amityville, Long Island, and New York City's Hotel Diplomat—sowed the seeds for their emergence as one of rock and roll's most popular and enduring groups.

Think about it. The odds of becoming a big rock-and-roll star are a million to one. For a band whose members wear greasepaint and outrageous costumes and look like intergalactic aliens with guitars, the odds are even worse. KISS's extraordinary commercial breakthrough in 1975 was miraculous.

The saga of KISS is far from your classic overnight success story. Theirs is a story of struggle, of fortitude and determination, of resilience and a tireless work ethic, and of ambition and an unrelenting drive to succeed. Their success is an enduring testament to the American dream. In record speed, KISS pulled off the impossible. Denigrated by critics as a flash in the pan and viewed by many as a joke, the band soldiered on, confident that massive rock-and-roll stardom was theirs for the taking. In less than three short years, KISS went from playing to fewer than ten people in a shabby club in Queens to selling out arenas across America. Their fourth album, *KISS Alive!*, delivered on the promise of their first three studio records, selling over four million copies. The album's powerhouse single, a rousing live version of "Rock and Roll All Nite," was a smash top-10 hit and a milestone in their career. Day by day, as the number of foot soldiers in the KISS Army grew, the band solidified their hard-won status as one of rock and roll's hardest working and most successful outfits.

Understanding an artist's backstory—whether it chronicles the meteoric rise of a former Memphis truck driver named Elvis Presley or documents the Beatles' formative years honing their chops in Hamburg, Germany—lends insight into the essence of his artistry. And it's no different with KISS. Theirs is a tale of four individuals with next to nothing in common who merged fiery hard rock with stylish theatricality and were deemed outrageous, confounding, and ridiculous for doing so. Yet despite their mistakes and blunders, missed opportunities and career missteps, KISS ultimately reached the heights of global superstardom.

We spoke to the band, to manager Bill Aucoin, to producers, engineers, road crew, club owners, fellow touring acts, concert promoters, booking agents, costume and stage designers, publicity reps, photographers, art designers, music writers, and to record company, radio, management, marketing, and retail personnel who populate the narrative of the band's meteoric rise. This is their remarkable story.

By the end of the sixties, the Beatles were no more. The nightmarish residue of 1969's Altamont Music Festival, at which three hundred thousand fans witnessed the brutal stabbing of concertgoer Meredith Hunter by crazed Hell's Angels midway into the Rolling Stones' set, was the death knell of the peace-and-love generation and the beginning of a tougher, less forgiving decade. Richard Nixon was in the White House. Women's Lib swept across the nation, with Gloria Steinem out in front. The sitcom *All in the Family*—a caustic TV show that commented on societal mores via the loudmouthed and bigoted patriarch, Archie Bunker—was the top-rated show on TV.

Music had come a long way from the innocent pop exuberance of the Beatles, the protest-folk stylings of Bob Dylan, and the trippy psychedelic acid rock of Jefferson Airplane, Quicksilver Messenger Service, Moby Grape, and the Grateful Dead. Anchored by English bands like Yes, Genesis, King Crimson, and Emerson, Lake & Palmer, progressive rock was the rage, a musical crusade distinguished by virtuoso instrumental flash and complicated song structures. The sunny expanse of Southern California was ground zero for the singer/songwriter movement. The landmark multi-platinum success of Carole King's *Tapestry* album ushered in a wave of mellow acoustic troubadours like James Taylor, Cat Stevens, Joni Mitchell, Jackson Browne, Jim Croce, and Harry Chapin.

In England, a musical revolution was taking shape. Led by David Bowie, Slade, T. Rex, and Mott the Hoople, glam rock exploded, igniting a powder keg of outrageous imagery, androgynous sexuality, and futuristic songwriting. In the States, a snotty underground proto-punk movement was in full force. Acts like the New York Dolls, MC5, and Iggy & the Stooges led the charge, their musical grenades delivering a fusillade of bratty anarchy, raw rebellion, and delicious excess. Alice Cooper borrowed a page from the rich tradition of Paris's Grand Guignol theater, carving a niche all his own in the rock-and-roll universe—and dragging Middle America kicking and screaming along with him. His was music for misfits, manna for a teenage wasteland of disenfranchised youth, combining horror-inspired spectacle with rousing anthems of rebellion, frustration, and alienation.

Amid this schizophrenic musical landscape, a newly formed band called KISS was busy rehearsing seven days a week in a dilapidated loft in downtown Manhattan. Fueled by stubborn determination and faith in themselves, they had great expectations and even bigger dreams, and envisioned the day their faces would be chiseled in granite on rock and roll's Mount Rushmore, alongside the Beatles, the Rolling Stones, and the Who. But let's go back a few years, before they scaled the peaks of rock immortality.

1

MEETING OF THE MINDS

*D*ateline 1970. After the breakup of their bands, eighteen-year-old Stanley Eisen (who later changed his name to Paul Stanley) and twenty-one-year-old Gene Klein (who became Gene Simmons) were deciding upon their next musical ventures. Inside Stephen Coronel's apartment in Washington Heights, a section of Manhattan, fate intervened and brought Paul and Gene together for the first time.

GENE SIMMONS: I was best friends with Stephen Coronel. We went to school together and played in a number of bands like the Long Island Sounds, Love Bag, and Cathedral.

STEVE CORONEL (FRIEND AND FORMER BANDMATE OF GENE'S AND PAUL'S): In 1970, I got together with Gene at Brooke Ostrander's apartment in New Jersey and we talked about putting a band together. We needed a lead singer: a guy who could sing and play. I was trying to think of somebody who could complete the circle.

PAUL STANLEY: I'd been in a band with Stephen called Tree; it was me, Stephen on lead guitar, Marty Cohen on bass, and Stan Singer on drums.

Stephen Coronel, the man responsible for introducing Gene Simmons and Paul Stanley,
Americana Hotel, New York City, 1979 Ken Sharp

GENE SIMMONS: I saw them play in an underground club near Harlem and I was struck by the rhythm guitar player, a guy named Stanley Eisen. He sang "Whole Lotta Love" and "All Right Now" and was very convincing. He had the right stance onstage, looked good, and sang with a high voice like Robert Plant.

STEVE CORONEL: I thought of Stan for this new band and said to Gene, "What if I hook you up with this guy named Stan?" I called him and said, "Gene and I want to meet with you." It was late summer, circa August 1970, and I arranged for the meeting one evening at my apartment in Washington Heights. The meeting was in my living room, which I had painted gloss black. It looked kind of funky for 1970.

NEAL TEEMAN (PAUL STANLEY'S FRIEND AND BANDMATE IN UNCLE JOE): Imagine Ozzy Osbourne at his heaviest; that's what Gene looked like. He was very heavy and wore a long coat that he didn't take off.

GENE SIMMONS: I lived in South Fallsburg [New York]. I was huge—massive. I had a beard, wore overalls, and at that point I weighed two hundred and twenty-five pounds. I wasn't so much fat as much I was just big all over.

STEVE CORONEL: I remember Gene and I waiting for Stan Eisen to ring my doorbell. I'd played in bands with both of them but had yet to see if they'd like each other. When I opened the door, Stan stood poised in the doorway like people do when they visit someone's dwelling. I remember him saying hi to me and looking past me at Gene, who stood by the windows in the living room, leaning against a radiator. I had my 1964 red Gibson ES 330 guitar out and Gene was leaning against the bed, which I had elevated three-and-a-half feet off the floor because I had put it on top of two Marshall cabinets. Stan was very polite. He came in the room and walked around the bed to face Gene, who was still leaning on the windowsill.

GENE SIMMONS: Stephen said, "Gene, this is Stanley Eisen; he also writes songs." I'd never met anyone else who wrote songs. I thought I was the only one on Earth who wrote songs. I was so impressed with the fact that I taught myself how to play guitar and bass and learned how to write songs that I thought it was the first time that any human being had ever done it.

STEVE CORONEL: They smiled, shook hands, and starting talking about how they'd seen each other at gigs in the bands we were both in. I was standing facing both of them and making little comments to push it along. Stan liked the Move and Gene liked the Beatles. I was waiting to see how my Stanley recommendation went with Gene.

GENE SIMMONS: I said to him, "Show me what you got." I don't think that comment went down too well with him; he thought I was being arrogant.

STEVE CORONEL: Stan picked up a guitar and played a few originals and a song by the Move, which we weren't familiar with at all. He played one of his songs, "Sunday Driver," which was Move-influenced, and it sounded pretty darn good.

GENE SIMMONS: I liked "Sunday Driver" and was struck by how good the construction and melody was. The lyrical point of view of "Sunday Driver" sounded English, like "Eight Days a Week" or "A Hard Day's Night" by the Beatles. I also really liked his voice.

STEVE CORONEL: Stan's songs were complete and he sang them with confidence, just like Gene would when presenting an original to Seth Dogramajian and I a few years earlier. I remember looking over at Gene and seeing his arms folded in front of his chest, listening with his head cocked to one side. I thought Stan's songs sounded pretty good. Gene had a pop/fantasy quality in his writing. His melodies were major scale and kind of eclectic. Gene didn't think in terms of hard-rock bluesy vocals. Blues-rock lead singers might approach songs differently than Gene at this point, so listening to Stanley Eisen play his music was an experience for both Gene and I.

NEAL TEEMAN: Then Gene played a few songs. When he sang he shouted like the whole building should hear his song [*laughs*].

PAUL STANLEY: He played one of his songs and honestly I wasn't that impressed. Gene had a very soft, melodic voice which changed over the years. In the beginning his voice was much closer to Paul McCartney and that's who he really wanted to be; that was his idol.

STEVE CORONEL: Gene played "Stanley the Parrot" and whatever else he had at the time, which wasn't all that great.

GENE SIMMONS: Paul was not impressed at all with my songs. My writing was all over the place.

STEVE CORONEL: I think Stanley's stuff sounded a lot better. Same with the singing. When Stanley was done playing Gene said [*nonchalantly*], "Yeah, that was good." He was pissed off so he could barely muster that. He also begrudgingly admired Stan because he was good. At that point Stan was beginning to dislike Gene's manner. Gene can get a bit confrontational when he interrogates someone.

PAUL STANLEY: Gene made more of an impression with his personality, which I wasn't crazy about.

GENE SIMMONS: Paul didn't like me at all. He thought I was arrogant, kind of "Who the hell do you think you are?" I couldn't believe that anybody else would have the balls to say, "Oh, I write songs too." I wasn't being unfriendly. But I had so much confidence in myself at that point, in a very real way it numbed me to other people. My sense of self has to do with being an only child. I came from another country. I didn't have brothers and sisters to depend on. My mother lived through the Nazi German concentration camps of World War II. Early on my father left us. I had no support system and my mom was working from dawn to dusk. There are no excuses. You're gonna go somewhere if you pick yourself up off the ground and make things happen.

PAUL STANLEY: With friendships that last for a long time, initially you may have a real strong aversion to somebody. We just didn't hit it off, but it didn't matter that much to me. I didn't lose sleep over it.

STEVE CORONEL: When Stan left we discussed everything. It seemed that Gene resented Stan a bit. I didn't see much solid ground for everything he critiqued about him. I chalked it up to him being stiff competition for Gene's self-image as a musician.

NEAL TEEMAN: I remember riding home in the car with Paul after that meeting and him going, "Wow, who the fuck does he think he is?" He was really put off by him. Paul went into this meeting with good feelings and Gene acted like it was a contest, like "I could beat you" type of a thing. I think that's what bothered Paul.

PAUL STANLEY: I didn't like him and told Steve that I wasn't interested in playing with him. But at some point we started putting our stuff aside and with time you see what the other person is really about. If two stones rub against each other long enough, they smooth out and all the sharp edges disappear. That's kind of what you do. To work with somebody and have an ongoing relationship, like with your brother, you've got to know where to draw the line.

STEVE CORONEL: Paul and Gene spoke to each other a few days later and decided that there was room for both of them in the group. Neither Gene nor I played much outside of a circle of a handful of musicians, and none of them wrote songs, so meeting Stan was something new. Gene had to accept that there was someone besides him who could write, sing, and play. Until now, after the Beatles, Gene had been next in line for the most talented person in the world he knew. We called Stan and asked him to meet with us again, along with Brooke Ostrander, a keyboardist Gene knew, this time to talk and jam together.

We met at Brooke's apartment in New Jersey and were getting along really well. Stan was happy to be in a group again and have someone to sing harmony with. Gene was enjoying working with Stan and showed no ego problem. The reason they worked well together was they were both serious about making it. Their musical abilities complemented each other; one could sing lead while the other sang the harmony, and then they would switch. They worked on that interplay at the Canal Street loft. We joked a lot, too, and that was part of their developing relationship and also laughter and witty humor. That's the fun of being in a band, enjoying the creation and the trial and error that goes with it. You walk down the street and you feel you're on a close-knit team. And then there was the similar background of growing up in Queens of Jewish descent, plus the similarities in their musical tastes.

GENE SIMMONS: Paul and I shared an aesthetic, an ideal, and a work ethic, but we're as different as night and day. We're two different sides of the same coin, but when I started working with him I recognized him as being a different and important piece of the puzzle. Paul had a belief that he was going to succeed, which I connected with.

PAUL STANLEY: For both of us, succeeding was more important than anything else. Gene was bright and ambitious and willing to work hard to achieve something rather than just talk about it. Intelligence and drive will get you way farther than sheer ability and no sense of direction. He was also open to direction and input and he was very talented. Two working together and not just one plus one, it's exponentially multiplied and significantly more. It's much, much more difficult to accomplish certain goals on your own. A team is what wins a game.

2

SOMETHING WICKED THIS WAY COMES

n 1972, *two years after their first meeting, Paul Stanley and Gene Simmons were living paycheck to paycheck and no closer to achieving rock stardom.*

PAUL STANLEY: I used to spend a lot of time hanging out at a head shop located near my house called Middle Earth. They sold psychedelic paraphernalia—rolling papers, water pipes—and basically stocked all the accoutrements for the hippie of the sixties. One day I came into the store and they told me somebody from Electric Lady Studios had just been in, and I flipped because of my admiration for Jimi Hendrix and this was his new magical studio. They told me they got his number for me. On a piece of paper was scribbled a name and all I could make out was "Ron" and a phone number.

I called the studio and said, "Is Ron there?" As fate would have it the switchboard receptionist said, "Which Ron? Shaimon Ron or Ron Johnsen?" I went for the one that sounded most familiar and said "Ron Johnsen." She connected me to Ron Johnsen's secretary and I explained to her that I was in a band and would love for Ron to come see us. I called numerous times because Ron would never call me back. Finally, after a few weeks I told someone at the studio, "Tell Ron it's because of people like him that bands like mine break up." And that somehow got him to pick up the phone [*laughs*].

When I spoke to Ron I found out that he'd never been in the store Middle Earth. Shaimon Ron, who was the maintenance supervisor [*laughs*] at Electric Lady, was the one who came into the shop. So Ron Johnsen, who was an engineer at Electric Lady, wound up coming to our loft in Chinatown to see our band, Rainbow, which later changed its name to Wicked Lester. He told us, "You guys are as good as Three Dog Night" [*laughs*]. We felt that was a good thing, better than him saying we were shit. So that was our entry into Electric Lady. To get past that big security door into this mythical fabled place was magical.

After meeting with Ron it took a long time before we got into the studio to begin recording the Wicked Lester album. We were working on spec time, which means you're not paying for studio time and can only get in when the studio is vacated. If a session was supposed to end at four in the afternoon and went until nine at night, we'd be hanging around the lobby for five hours. Then you'd get into the studio once it was vacated. We would be in the studio taking advantage of any free time that we could get. Sometimes we worked literally for twenty-four hours on this crazy record that turned into the Wicked Lester album. Because the album was done on spec time, it literally took a year to complete. It was done over such a long period that if a hit record that week had a sitar on it we put a sitar on a song. So we wound up with an album with no focus or direction.

GENE SIMMONS: There was already a lot of inner turmoil within the band. We were all desperate to try and figure out how to keep the band together. You had a drummer [Tony Zarrella] who was a sweetheart but who didn't have a clue about focus and vision. Paul

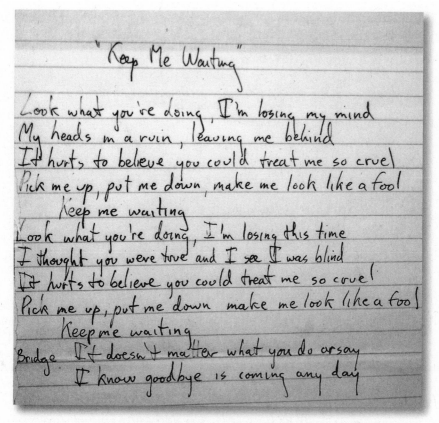

Paul Stanley's original handwritten lyrics for the Wicked Lester song "Keep Me Waiting" Courtesy of Ross Koondel

and my old school chum, Stephen Coronel, weren't getting along. Stephen had a big blowout with Paul and it had to do with a kind of "Who the fuck do you think you are? Do you think you have a fuckin' aura about you?" And Paul said, "Actually I do." Paul had a lot of self-confidence, which rubbed Steve the wrong way. The band was a straight band—no one was doing drugs. It wasn't like KISS, nothing like Ace [Frehley] and Peter [Criss], who drank and had other problems from the very beginning.

Wicked Lester only played a few live shows, and money was tight. Thanks to the intervention of Ron Johnsen, Gene and Paul were able to

Wicked Lester tape box Courtesy of Brad Estra

earn extra bread doing session work at Electric Lady Studios. This musical apprenticeship provided the two aspiring rock stars with a practical, hands-on indoctrination into the music business.

GENE /IMMON/: Wicked Lester was getting to a point where it looked like the band was going to split. One day we walked into our loft and realized all the equipment had been stolen. We were devastated. And we needed money to replace it. Ron Johnsen was the head engineer at Electric Lady Studios in Greenwich Village. He worked on hit records with artists like Lobo, who had a hit with "Me and You and a Dog Named Boo," and Little Eva, who sang "The Locomotion." He produced the Wicked Lester album, which was supposed to come out on Epic Records. Ironically enough, Ron also did some engineering with Chelsea, Peter Criss's group, who released one album on Decca. Ron Johnsen, bless him, was kind enough to say, "You guys can't just hang around here, and I'm sure you need the money. Let me give you some session work." I'd already started doing some smaller session work. I played bass on a demo by a black singer. She wasn't bad, but the song didn't do it for me. Ron was producing developing artists and he gave Paul and I some session work, which really amounted to, "Okay guys, here's the parts I want you to sing, can you do it?" Between us, Paul and I would figure out the vocal parts, sort of Everly Brothers style. He'd take the higher part, I'd take the middle part, or vice versa.

PAUL STANLEY: It was informal in the sense that it was almost like anybody who was around was in there singing. I didn't really consider that session work per se because we weren't hired for our ability or for our expertise. It was really just throwing us a bone, and throwing us a little bit of cash. And I do mean a little bit of cash [*laughs*]. It really was just a token payment.

Lyn Christopher was an artist that Ron Johnsen was working with. He was producing Wicked Lester and was involved with Lyn through her husband at the time, Lou Ragusa.

LYN CHRISTOPHER: We needed background vocals done for my album and Ron said, "I know two guys who'll be good." Gene and Paul sang on two songs, "Celebrate" and "Weddin'." They were both really sweet and had good voices. Paul was always really supportive and told me, "You're beautiful and you're gonna make it."

PAUL STANLEY: Lyn was signed to Paramount Records and her music was very soft and mellow but she was great looking. Whenever she'd walk into the studio, whether she sang or was just checking things out, I couldn't help but look at her.

LYN CHRISTOPHER: It was the first time Gene and Paul ever got paid to sing on a record. They shared my excitement to be singing on an album for a major label. I could tell it was a big deal for them.

GENE SIMMONS: When that album came out, it was the first time we were ever on a real record, and we're listed as Gene Simmons and Paul Stanley in the credits. It was an amazing experience to be on a record.

PAUL STANLEY: We also sang on a Tommy James session on a song called "Celebration." I remember playing tambourine and singing. There was a lot of music going on at that point in that studio. Tommy was coproducing it and working with the engineer Ralph Moss, who also worked with us on the Wicked Lester album.

GENE SIMMONS: We also did session work for Mr. Gee Whiz. It was very bizarre, eclectic pop. Looking back, doing sessions was fun but it was incidental. What we would get paid didn't cross our minds. We were oblivious to all of it; we didn't know what union rules were. Thinking back, for a three-hour session you were paid about $90. We were practically living, eating, and just soaking up Electric Lady Studios. For us, it was like the school of hard knocks. It wasn't even so much hard as it was a sort of baptism by fire. We were sharing space and rubbing shoulders with the people you only see in magazines, on television, and in concert halls. It really opened our eyes to a new world, a world we wanted to be a part of. Stephen Stills was working in the studio and he liked my Fender bass. It had a Gibson pickup in it which gave it a bizarre clarity. Later he paid me $300 for it. He reached into his pocket and peeled off three hundred-dollar bills. I'd never seen anything like that. Another act in there at the same time was Tonto's Expanding Headband, which was two guys, Malcolm Cecil and Bob Margouleff. It was synthesizer music way before Rick Wakeman and anybody else did it. They would go on to work extensively with Stevie Wonder.

Located at 52 West Eighth Street in Greenwich Village, Electric Lady Studios officially opened in August 1970. The studio was designed by architect/acoustician John Storyk and built for use by legendary guitarist Jimi Hendrix. Through the years, a procession of rock's elite have graced its hallowed halls, including Led Zeppelin, the Rolling Stones, John Lennon, David Bowie, Bob Dylan, AC/DC, and Rush.

GENE SIMMONS: Working at Electric Lady was bizarre because the studio was underground. For the first time in our lives we weren't aware

An Electric Lady Studios promotional ad that mentions Gene and Paul's
band Wicked Lester Courtesy of Ross Koondel

if it was day or night. It was almost like being in an ant colony—nothing
exists except feeding the queen ant. Everyone knows exactly what to do.
In the underground, there's no light, no day, everybody's only doing
one thing—music. It was a place where people aren't impressed by
stars. It was just a magical place. The house that Jimi Hendrix built had
amazing artwork on the walls. One of the murals along the walls had a
female sort of sexy astronaut in a bikini who was manning a spacecraft.
Paul and I worked in both Studio A and B. We recorded the Wicked
Lester album there and KISS would later use both studios.

PAUL STANLEY: The beauty of Electric Lady was there weren't a lot
of clocks and there were no windows. So you didn't leave until you

were ready to leave or another session was starting. Sometimes you'd be literally working around the clock through to the next day and then you'd have to vacate because another act was coming in.

GENE SIMMONS: Paul and I would hang out at Electric Lady all the time, even when we weren't working on the Wicked Lester album. We'd hang out, sit on the couch, listen, and just soak it up.

PAUL STANLEY: It was a great education. This was like the war room for the hierarchy of rock; this is where it all happened. My thrill at that time was I could come and go as I pleased. Between the two studios, which were virtually running around the clock, you could go into either one and someone who you admired or who was one of your heroes was in there working. At any given time, twenty-four hours a day, Zeppelin could be in there, the Stones could be there, Mountain, Jeff Beck, Stevie Wonder, David Crosby and Steve Stills. I remember popping into a session when Mick Jagger was doing something with Eddie Kramer and I also remember going in when they were mixing *Rockin' the Fillmore* and talking to Jimmy Page.

GENE SIMMONS: Jeff Beck was working with Stevie Wonder on a version of "Superstition." I was sitting doing a number two in the bathroom at Electric Lady Studios when Stevie was let in by an assistant who brought him in to take a piss. I was just shaking in my boots because there I am sitting on the pot and next to me is Stevie Wonder. If you would have told me then that many years later I'd be in the studio with Stevie humming him melodies for him to blow on his harp for a version of "Deuce" by Lenny Kravitz that appeared on *KISS My Ass*, I would have said that you were out of your mind.

PAUL STANLEY: I spent years at Electric Lady, from Wicked Lester days to KISS days. It was Disneyland for someone like me, and it was a great learning experience.

Despite being signed to a deal with Epic Records, Gene and Paul realized that Wicked Lester would never fulfill their musical vision. Ditching their deal with Epic, Wicked Lester called it quits.

GENE SIMMONS: Paul and I weren't happy with the record. The tunes were okay but it wasn't cool like the English bands. It had a West Coast American hippie sound and sounded like Three Dog Night and the Doobie Brothers. It was too eclectic. Groups like the Who or the Rolling Stones had a definitive sound and look. Unlike those bands, Wicked Lester lacked a definitive sound and identity.

PAUL STANLEY: The problem with Wicked Lester was it was a Frankenstein monster that evolved in the studio. We spent a year in the studio making an album under the direction of a producer who had much more experience than us but who was possibly less focused in a direction than we were. And at that point we were more than willing to try anything and the album showed that. It was all over the place. We were just aimless. It was clear that we were spinning our wheels.

GENE SIMMONS: We weren't going anywhere; it just didn't feel right. There was no direction. There was no image. Hearing back the Wicked Lester stuff, "She" had flutes on it and "Love Her All I Can" was like a dance track. We were floundering. There was a moment where Paul and I looked at each other and said, "We have to break up the band."

PAUL STANLEY: The band wasn't gonna go anywhere, so why labor over something that's flawed from the start? So in our brash naïveté we broke up the band. At first we fired all the guys. One of them, Tony [Zarrella], said, "I'm gonna honor my contract," so we said, "Then we quit [*laughs*]." One way or another, we were cutting ties with that band.

GENE SIMMONS: I honestly can't explain why we had that clarity and vision, because most people wouldn't look a gift horse in the mouth. We had a recording contract. We finished an album with a major label. . . . You have to be arrogant, delusional, or insane to walk away from a record deal. But it wasn't what we wanted and we knew it wasn't right. So Paul and I decided in this quantum leap forward to break up the band and form a new group, which was KISS. It reminds me of that scene in *2001: A Space Odyssey* where a monolith appears and apes for no reason walk up and touch it and have this great quantum leap forward in the evolutionary path.

Wicked Lester dissolved and Paul and I didn't waste any time. We still kept the Wicked Lester loft. I paid rent because everybody else was broke. Paul worked at a sandwich shop and started driving cabs through the night and slept during the day. I had a day job as assistant to the director of the Puerto Rican Interagency Council, which was a government-funded research and demonstration project. I actually made good money, $23,000 a year, which was enormous back then. I had skills. I was a Dictaphone typist and also worked on rexographs, hexographs, and mimeographs, all the various things in those days that made copies. I understood how to do that because when I was a kid I published fantasy and science fiction fanzines.

PAUL STANLEY: The first order of business was to define the music, which very quickly became guitar-driven. Humble Pie was one of the inspirations behind KISS's sound. Seeing them perform at the Fillmore and watching Steve Marriott command and preach to an audience was something that inspired me, and his approach was something that I wanted to do onstage, but in my own way. So we wanted a band that had heavy guitars but songs with strong melodies and choruses. That's the school I grew up on. It was coming more from the Brill Building kind of writers than head banging. It was more about a song with a great chorus. It's called a hook for a reason because it grabs you and doesn't let go. So I think the idea was to combine some of the old Tin Pan Alley/Brill Building sensibilities with the Beatles sensibilities and make it more guitar-driven, like Led Zeppelin or the Stones and the Who. Interestingly, most of it was about rhythm guitar, which is the foundation of everything. Without it, everything falls apart.

GENE SIMMONS: There was also a bit of Slade in our sound, too, with songs like "Gudbuy T' Jane" and "Mama Weer All Crazee Now." When you heard those songs you knew immediately that was it, two guitars, bass, drums, and those kinds of lyrics. "Mama Weer All Crazee Now" is a brother song to "Rock and Roll All Nite," with the lyrics "you drive us wild, we'll drive you crazy." It has the same language.

PAUL STANLEY: I was such a huge Anglophile and I loved everything visually and musically that was British, from the Beatles to the Who, the Rolling Stones to the Kinks, the Move to the Small Faces. There were groups that I wasn't even that fond of that piqued my curiosity. I remember listening to Dave Dee, Dozy, Beaky, Mick & Tich, who were huge in England at the time, and I didn't get most of what they were doing. But what they looked like and the camaraderie between them was appealing. It was all very Beatlesque. Most of the bands coming out of England had a sense of brotherhood. They all dressed alike. It was a club that you wanted to be a member of. We needed to focus on what we wanted to be.

GENE SIMMONS: Paul and I decided to just react to the gut. We'll know it when we hear it. We'll know it when we feel it. It's what makes us stop changing radio stations. Without verbalizing it that's exactly what Paul and I decided to do when forming KISS. Paul and I were aware that the bands we loved not only put out great music but delivered live—groups like the Who and Jimi Hendrix. We noticed that we weren't just talking about the songs but what they did live. The visual was important. It was like, "Did you see Pete Townshend jumping in the air or smashing a guitar?" We kept saying, "Did you *see* that band live?" not "Did you *hear* that band live?"

PAUL STANLEY: Quite simply, we wanted to be the band we never saw onstage.

10 EAST TWENTY-THIRD STREET

Paul and Gene swept aside the ashes of *Wicked Lester and formulated ideas for a group that would combine the musical muscle of Slade, Humble Pie, and the Who with the theatrics of Alice Cooper, David Bowie, and the Crazy World of Arthur Brown. Drummer Peter Criss placed a "Musicians Wanted" ad in the August 31, 1972, issue of* Rolling Stone *magazine ("EXPD. ROCK & roll drummer looking for orig. grp. doing soft & hard music"), which Paul and Gene answered, and was the first to join the nascent outfit.*

In 1972, Criss was a drummer in search of a band. His group, Chelsea, which had issued a self-titled album on Decca Records in 1970, had split, and he was barely making ends meet playing with a series of soon-to-be-forgotten local bands at no-name dives around New York City. Then, during a party at his home in Brooklyn, which he shared with his wife, Lydia, the phone rang.

PETER CRISS: Gene called me while I was having a wild party at my house and drinking Mateus wine—incidentally, it had a cat on the

ROLLING STONE/AUGUST 31, 1972

MUSICIANS' FREE CLASSIFIED

Free space is provided here for hungry musicians. If you need a gig with a band, or need someone to play with you, send your ad on a postcard, up to three lines of 40 characters each. Sometimes an ad is delayed an issue, so if your ad will be of no use to you after a certain date, please tell us. Be sure to indicate city and state when you mail your ad to: Musicians' Free Classified, 625 Third Street, San Francisco, California 94107.

EAST COAST

WATCH YOUR axe. There are rip off artists even in the Musicians' Free Classified.

NEW YORK CITY

WHITE SOUL female lead singer needs group. Listen. She's very good. Molly—861-7536, NYC.

SINGER-LYRICIST looking to join singer-guitarist-composer to write & perform. 683-6185, NYC.

FEMALE VOCALIST seeks to join/form rock band in NY. No exp. but lots of determination & energy. 586-0737 (eve.), 758-6200 (day), NYC.

PIANIST (ELECTRIC)/organist needed to complete band. Orig. mat., Hubbard, Allman, Davis, Zappa, Ralph—672-6236/932-1545, NYC.

POET-SINGER-skilled guitarist seeks co. of excellents-flowing within-without to new & better depths. 846-0713, Queens.

TROMBONE PLAYER wanted for NYC rock band. Horn sec. reorganizing, some wrk., rehearse in Queens. Musician—898-6738.

KEYBOARD & VOCALIST for rock band to gig in NYC area. Artie—591-8508. NYC.

LEAD GUITARIST & drummer w/orig. mat. & good equip. seeks group/other musicians. Joe—337-5623, Queens.

EXP. MALE singer/lyricist for vers. & creative grp. Everything but hard rock. Robert—734-3879, NYC.

EXPD. ROCK & roll drummer looking for orig. grp. doing soft & hard music. Peter—251-7778, Brooklyn.

LEAD GUITARIST wanted for rock band, must sing. Grp. into orig. mat. Phil—465-5371, Queens.

DRUMMER, EX-NAME grps., jazz-rock, prog. Danny—436-9597, Brooklyn.

DRUMMER, SINGLE free to travel, plays all styles, willing to wrk. Richie—652-3897, Bronx.

VOCAL, KEYBRD & bass players needed to complete band now forming. Mark—934-3117, Brooklyn.

NEW YORK STATE

LEAD SINGER: looking for wrking band. Will trav. Have PA. 893-1479, Suffolk, LI.

LEAD SINGER, trumpet, piano, composer looking for est. rock group. Alan—562-4622, Newburgh.

LEAD GUITARIST & drummer w/ultimate equip. seek "ace" mus./grp. Mike /Joe 791-1698, Nassau.

BASSIST WANTED for est. English-oriented grp. Min. equip. Van—273-4961 (bef. 5 PM, wkdays) Brentwood.

WANTED: KEYBRD lead guitar, drummer to back up female lead singer. Annie—921-1739, Syosset.

HARMONICA PLAYER (harp & chrom.) & vocalist, 10 yrs. exp., blues, C&W, R&B, Will travel. Gene—482-8545, Grt. Neck.

Musician's classified ad placed by Peter Criss in *Rolling Stone* magazine, August 31, 1972 Courtesy of Brad Estra

label—which was the big craze at the time. And he gave me this whole spiel.

GENE /IMMON/: I said, "Hi, I'm Gene Klein. We're putting together a band that's English in tone." I started asking him questions and he's repeating everything I'm saying to him to the other people at his party: "Do you have a beard? Are you fat? Are you good-looking?"

PETER CRI//: "Do I dress good? Is my hair long?"

GENE /IMMON/: He had a rock-and-roll arrogance that I liked because that's what you need to make it, because it was gonna be an uphill battle all the way. At that time, we knew image was going to be just as important as the music.

PETER CRI//: And the cool thing was that I had the newest velvets and satins because I had just gotten back from my honeymoon in England and Spain. So I went down to Electric Lady Studios with my brother, Joey.

I was wearing one of my coolest outfits, gold satin pants and turquoise boots. I looked like Jimi Hendrix's brother. And

I pass by these two guys leaning against a car wearing their mod shirts. I didn't even give them a second look. So I went inside and asked for a Gene Simmons and Paul Stanley, and the guy said they were waiting outside. I look out the window and think, "Nah, that can't be them. *These* are the guys who asked me if I was a wild dresser? They looked like bums [*laughs*].

PAUL STANLEY: Peter asked us to come see him play with a band he was playing with at the King's Lounge in Brooklyn. He certainly had a vibe about him and he really had that sense that he was playing Madison Square Garden rather than a small dive in Brooklyn.

PETER CRISS: We met at their loft to try things out. When I got there they had another drummer's drums set up. [They belonged to Tony Zarrella from Wicked Lester.] Now, anybody who's a drummer knows that you don't play well on another drummer's drums because it's such a personal thing; equipment an inch away from where you're used to can mean life and death to a drummer. Anyway, I played lousy and we were all sad about it because we wanted it to work out. So I suggested we try it again but that I bring my drums—and that was it. We played great.

PAUL STANLEY: When Peter played with us at the audition I wasn't really sold on him. We had him come back a few times because obviously there was something there. It wasn't a clear-cut no-brainer. I'm not sure Peter was initially what we were looking for in terms of style. But I think with time we wound up adapting our writing and our sound to work more with Peter's style.

GENE SIMMONS: It was loose and kind of greasy, like Charlie Watts of the Rolling Stones. Peter didn't play like other rock drummers. There was almost a big band swing to his sound but something about it worked.

PETER CRISS: I was always into Phil Spector, the Ronettes, early Stones, as well as early Motown with Marvin Gaye, the Four Tops, and all the other numerous talents. [We had] a melting pot [of influences] and [therefore] what you get is not blatantly derivative of any one area. At times we have tinges of a lot of quality music that has gone down before us. In this age, it's extremely difficult to be original—if not impossible. What you can hope for is to have the right influences predominate throughout your work.

GENE SIMMONS: When the Beatles first came out, their music was a hybrid of Motown and Chuck Berry, but they mixed it up and came up with their own thing. So even though what we did might seem retread of everything that we liked, English and American, it came out of our mouths and minds so there was something decidedly different about it. When you put records on by the Beatles they bounce with life. With English bands like Genesis and Jethro Tull starting to veer away from the meat and potatoes of rock and roll, and with Black Sabbath talking about the darkness, we centered right into the stuff that made rock and roll great, which for us was the uplifting, celebratory qualities—a "you and I against the world" sensibility.

ROBERT DUNCAN (MANAGING EDITOR, CREEM; AUTHOR OF KISS, THE FIRST BOOK ON THE BAND): Little Richard was the antecedent to anyone who was ever glam or outrageous. Also, Elvis was not hardcore macho. If you look at his pictures he was definitely a feminine man. There was some gender-bending going on. Alice Cooper picked up on that too. In many ways, I think he's the main influence on the look and sound of KISS.

It was the fall of 1972. Gene, Paul, and Peter continued to rehearse as a trio, honing their skills and fleshing out their embryonic songs in a dilapidated loft near the Flatiron Building at 10 East Twenty-third Street, above a bar called Live Bait. They had not yet ditched the name Wicked Lester.

GENE SIMMONS: It was a roach-infested fire trap with no windows. It cost $200 a month to rent the loft, which was a lot of money at the time.

PAUL STANLEY: Our loft was a little room on the fourth floor. We put egg crates on the walls to absorb the sound but that didn't work. We rehearsed constantly because we didn't want people to say, "They're

Still a trio, Paul, Peter, and Gene rehearse in the 10 East Twenty-third Street loft,
New York City, November 1972 KISS Catalog Ltd.

awful," and then later say, "Oh, they've gotten better." We wanted
to have a certain level of proficiency before we played for a paying
audience. At that point, we were still perfecting what we were doing.

RIK FOX (EARLY KISS FAN): I was one of a very small elite group
who actually got to see KISS from the ground up. I used to date
Peter Criss's sister Joanne. I'd watch the band rehearse as a three-
piece in the loft. You could see the seeds of the magic already
starting to brew. At the time the song "Stuck in the Middle
with You" by Stealers Wheel was very popular on the radio.
On numerous occasions at rehearsals and without any specific
warning Paul would start singing a line from the song, "Clowns
to the left of me," and Gene would answer, "jokers to the right,"
and they'd both sing the chorus together: "Here I am, stuck in
the middle with you." They'd pick whatever popular songs they
knew and it gave them a chance to practice their harmonies. I

also remember Gene's SVT bass cabinet had the name Jack Bruce stenciled on it.

GENE SIMMONS: I actually bought an SVT bass cabinet that was originally used by Jack Bruce of Cream. For me it was a kind of connection with greatness and that there was actually a road to Mount Olympus, it wasn't just in the clouds. Originally we were gonna be a power trio like the Who or the Jimi Hendrix Experience. As a trio we played those songs over and over again for months. We also kept writing and trying different material, like "Go Now" by the Moody Blues. We auditioned as a trio with Peter for Don Ellis [vice president of A&R] at Epic Records to try and get them to swallow this new kind of thing.

TOM WERMAN (ASSISTANT TO THE DIRECTOR OF A&R, EPIC RECORDS): I went with Don Ellis to watch them play. Having worked with Wicked Lester, seeing KISS was a real shock, but I loved it. Their performance was very young, strong, and vital. I loved the theatrics. They just wore white face and didn't have any real defined features at that point. At the end of the set, Paul threw a bucket of silver confetti at us. For a split second we thought it was water, but thankfully it turned out to be confetti [*laughs*]. It was a fantastic finish to their performance. Unfortunately, Don was completely underwhelmed. I remember walking down the stairs back to Twenty-third Street and Don said, "What the fuck was that?" [*laughs*], not in a derisive way but more out of being really confused by what he just saw. He said, "I don't get it." Don said the same thing about Lynyrd Skynyrd—"Great band, no songs." He was a great guy but he was from the Boz Scaggs school and just didn't understand rock and roll.

GENE SIMMONS: Needless to say, Epic passed.

PAUL STANLEY: Before Ace joined the band I remember spending Thanksgiving in the loft eating turkey sandwiches and drinking sherry with Peter to stay warm. It was a romanticized vision of the struggling artist but it was also, "Gee, this is what those kind of memories are made of." I always looked upon it that way. Maybe that's what helped get me through some of the tougher times.

LYDIA CRISS: They rehearsed for a few months at the loft before finding Ace.

GENE SIMMONS: I have no idea why we became a quartet other than the songs we were writing inferred another guitar for harmonies and for counter-chords.

PAUL STANLEY: I didn't want to be a lead guitar player. There was too much responsibility in doing that and it would limit some of the other things I wanted to do in terms of performing. I didn't want to shoulder the burden of coming up with solos and I wasn't adept at what I envisioned the lead player doing. So we put an ad in the *Village Voice* for a lead guitarist. [*Authors' note: The exact wording of the ad that ran in the December 14, 1972, issue of the* Village Voice *was "LEAD GUITARIST WANTED with Flash and Ability. Album Out Shortly. No time wasters please."*]

BOB KULICK (FRIEND AND GUITAR PLAYER): The *Village Voice* was always the place to locate gigs in the New York area.

BOBBY MCADAMS (FRIEND OF ACE FREHLEY): I was best friends with Ace since I was fifteen. One day back in December of '72 I brought a copy of the *Village Voice* to Ace's house—he was living at the time with his parents—and left it there. He saw an ad about a band looking for a guitar player with stage presence.

PETER CRISS: We must have auditioned close to sixty guys.

PAUL STANLEY: It really was a freak show in terms of the guitar players who came to audition for the band. We had nonstop auditions with every type, size, shape, and age of guitar players imaginable.

TOM PECK (LEAD GUITAR PLAYER WHO AUDITIONED FOR KISS): I answered an ad for a lead guitar player in the *Village Voice*. At the time I was taking jazz lessons and listening to Procol Harum. I came to the audition with my Gibson SG Les Paul and an old beat-up Marshall amplifier. I was dressed in my upstate New York cold-weather gear, and I remember they made a few snide

Ad looking for lead guitar player placed by Paul Stanley
in the *Village Voice*, **December 1972**   Courtesy of Ross Koondel

comments about the way I looked because it was anything but rock and roll [*laughs*], but I was mostly interested in being warm. At first, they played a song for me, just Gene, Paul, and Peter. Then I joined in and soloed on that song. My amp blew up during the song and stopped working. I was so embarrassed [*laughs*]. I blew the audition and the amplifier! I don't think I played very well. They told me that I didn't fit in with them but they were very diplomatic about it. To tell you the truth, I was glad to get a straight answer. Most bands tell you, "We'll call you," and you never hear from them again. Funnily enough, about a year later I was working as a roadie for Isis, who opened for KISS at Coventry. I was very impressed with how their new guitar player brought forth their sound.

GENE SIMMONS: There was a guy who was a flamenco guitarist who showed up with an acoustic guitar wearing a Spanish poncho. He auditioned with a flamenco guitar, and his wife was there and she was swooning while he was playing.

PAUL STANLEY: Another guy came in who said he was a big star in Italy, and he was awful. He had these big love beads on and a Nehru jacket. He didn't speak English and his wife interpreted for him. He never bothered to tune his guitar. Most of the people who came in were just wrong. You always have people who lack a clear sense of who they are. I remember one guy calling up and saying he'd only been playing for two months but he was amazing. That in itself is impossible. But he was insistent, and those situations are so intriguing that they invite investigation. So this guy came in, plugged in, and after he played he said, "How'd I sound?" And I said, "You sound like you've been playing for two months" [*laughs*]. But there were some guys who were pretty good. There was one guy who we decided to try working with, but after one or two rehearsals, when we talked about putting makeup on, he never came back.

ACE FREHLEY: My mom drove me down to the audition from the Bronx with my 50-watt Marshall amp in the family's big Cadillac. I was in such a rush I put on one orange and one red sneaker by accident. Before I went upstairs, I quickly chugged two 16-ounce cans of beer to relax. When I walked in, there was Bob Kulick, Bruce's brother—how weird now that I really think about it. [*Authors' note: In 1984, Bob's younger brother, Bruce, joined KISS as their lead guitarist.*]

BOB KULICK: I went down to this dark and dingy loft for the audition. They sounded like they were serious and they referenced Led Zeppelin, and that caught my attention. Being a huge Zeppelin fan, this was a gig I knew would be up my alley. I auditioned with the band and I felt it went really well. I could tell they were like, "Wow, this guy can play."

GENE SIMMONS: Bob was head-and-shoulders above all the guys we had auditioned. He was the guy we wanted.

BOB KULICK: The music was akin to what I wanted to do. Like me, they were guys from Brooklyn and Queens who loved the same bands that I loved, like Cream, Hendrix, the Who, and Led Zeppelin. After my audition I remember Gene showing me Polaroids with the ideas for the makeup and asking me what I thought. I said, "I don't know if this matters as much as the music and the band being great." Gene said, "This will be a really cool gimmick." And I said, "If you're great do you really think you need a gimmick?" Having worked with English bands like Hookfoot and Long John Baldry, I was very aware of the glam acts that wore makeup, like David Bowie and T. Rex, but I was a pompous ass [*laughs*] and could only relate to the music. They asked if I'd be interested and I said that I was up for anything. Halfway through my audition this guy showed up and it turned out to be Ace Frehley, who played right after me.

BOBBY McADAMS: Ace walked in, stumbled, and tripped. He was a real klutz. They thought he was a freak. He was a very weird-looking guy. He's half Indian and half German, and that's where he gets his look.

ACE FREHLEY: I sat in the far corner of the room to give Bob his space. After a few minutes I pulled my reverse Firebird single-pickup out of its gig bag and started to warm up. All of a sudden Gene walks over to me and asks me to put my guitar away.

GENE SIMMONS: While Bob was auditioning Ace was oblivious and kept making noise, talking really loud and laughing. Finally, I turned around after Bob was done playing one of the songs and went, "Will you shut the fuck up and let this guy audition and wait your turn?" I thought he was an asshole. I disliked him right away.

ACE FREHLEY: He said I was being rude and making Bob nervous. I never really understood that to this day. I mean, it was an audition— what was the big deal? I wasn't plugged into an amp. Anyway, after Bob left it was my turn. They told me to pay attention because after we're done we want you to try playing along with us.

GENE SIMMONS: We said, "We're gonna play you the first verse and first chorus, and when the solo comes that's when we want you to play."

ACE FREHLEY: Luckily the song was "Deuce," which would become one of my favorite KISS songs. So after I listened, I plugged in and let it rip, volume on eleven.

GENE SIMMONS: As soon as he started playing, both Paul and I looked at each other when Ace started soloing. We finally heard the sound.

PAUL STANLEY: Ace belonged in the band. He was the missing piece, the missing link. It just all jelled and made sense.

GENE SIMMONS: There was a dangerous volatility about him but also glorious playing.

ACE FREHLEY: We jammed for a few more songs and then they said, "We like the way you play a lot. We'll call you."

PETER CRISS: Gene and Paul were skeptical about him. But we were so off the wall that I thought, "What a perfect guy to join the band."

BOBBY McADAMS: It took them a little while to warm up to this strange guy.

PAUL STANLEY: It's well documented that Ace is a unique individual. His personality was certainly not what we were used to. He was very much his own person and kind of hard to get a read on. But when he plugged in it was so right. I remember it being a defining moment. Musically it was a very compatible yet combustible mixture.

ACE FREHLEY: Although they didn't ask me to join that day, I felt it was in the bag. I came back again in two weeks and the die was cast. I really wanted to be in the band. I remember coming home from the audition, walking into my house, and telling my parents, "I think I found a good band. I think this is it." I just had a feeling that this was gonna be my long-awaited chance. And it was.

PAUL STANLEY: What came out sonically when we started playing those first few songs was just ground shaking. When we started playing together I said this will take over the world.

ACE FREHLEY: I always felt I had something. I used to tell my girlfriend that I was gonna be a millionaire and be famous. I used to tell my parents when I was in high school in the Bronx. They always used to laugh at me. Everybody did. Even all my friends. When they were playing Grateful Dead music, I'd say, "Don't you know you're not gonna get anywhere copying the Grateful Dead?" I said, "If you wanna make it in rock, you gotta do something spectacular."

The one thing that pissed me off was that the ad in the *Village Voice* said "guitar player wanted for band with recording contract." Well, it turned out there *was* no recording contract. But I felt the guys were as serious as I was about putting together a theatrical rock group, and I liked the music. We rehearsed constantly, six days a week.

JOHN ALTYN (KISS FAN): I was fifteen years old in 1973 and dating Peter Criss's sister Donna. I remember my first trip to the loft. Donna, Peter's sister Joanne, Rik [Fox], and me, with Peter at the wheel, drove over the Williamsburg Bridge into Manhattan. I'd never been to a rehearsal before and didn't know what to expect. The loft was cold and drafty. The staircase was steep and we climbed to the second floor and thrust open a large, heavy factory door with a lock that extended across the entire front of it. The walls were painted white but years of dust and dirt gave them the appearance of age. The floors were dusty old wood panels like those in old sewing factories. There was a large old radiator in the loft but it was shut down at night so it was really cold in there. I remember being introduced to all of the guys, and they gave us a nod of acknowledgment and proceeded to concentrate on their music.

I sat in a chair directly in front of Ace's Marshall amp. There was nothing on the walls to absorb the sound except some paper egg cartons, which would vibrate and some would fall to the ground because they were so loud [*laughs*]. I was impressed with their songs. They had a streetwise and unpolished sound, unlike the music of the day. It wasn't pop, yet it was catchy. It wasn't metal, but it was heavy. We continued to watch KISS and I became more and more familiar with their songs. The six of us would be at rehearsal enjoying the music, but unlike the others, I usually sat there listening with a critical ear. I wasn't tapping my feet or dancing around. I think my stoic nature unnerved Paul and Gene. In fact, once Paul said to me with contempt in his voice, "Don't you like it?" I responded saying, "I'm listening." As the months went by, we became friendlier with the band and I'd occasionally bring a six-pack of Budweiser. And what's funny is every time I brought liquor, inevitably Ace would bum a beer off of me, saying in that high, squeaky voice, "Hey John, can I get a beer?" Of course, those requests multiplied through the night and he wound up drinking most of my beer [*laughs*]. But that was Ace.

A VISIT TO THE LOFT

Guitarist and resident Who freak Binky Philips, a school friend of Paul Stanley's, was a talented songwriter whose New York band, the Planets, shared the stage with KISS in July 1973.

BINKY PHILIPS (GUITARIST, THE PLANETS): Paul and I went to Fiorello La Guardia High School of Music & Art. I was a junior and he was a senior. After we graduated from high school, every few months Paul and I would call each other to catch up about our bands or talk guitars. The moment when Paul and I went from being vaguely friendly acquaintances from high school to being friends was out in front of the Academy of Music for a Jeff Beck show in the spring of '72. We were getting ready to go in for an eight o'clock show and I didn't know Paul was gonna be there. He saw me and said, "Oh, Binky, how ya doin'?" He had this guy with him that seemed like a giant, and I was wearing high heels so Gene must have really had high heels on [*laughs*]. Paul said, "Oh, Binky, this is the bass player in my band, Wicked Lester." He turns to Gene and says, "This is the guy I told you about with the Hiwatt amp."

Words can't express how unusual it was to have that amp. I literally had the only Hiwatt amp in the country. They were only available in

England. I walked into Manny's Music Store on Forty-eighth Street and there was a Hiwatt head. These were the amps that Townshend had been using exclusively for the previous four Who tours, and nobody could get them. They were like this holy grail. I was told by Manny that Blodwyn Pig had left it about an hour ago, so I traded in a Fender twin reverb for it. I now had this incredibly rare and incredibly prestigious amplifier. During one of my phone calls to Paul I must have said, "You're not gonna believe it, I gotta fuckin' Hiwatt!" Anyhow, when I met Gene for the first time, after Paul introduced me as the guy who had the Hiwatt amp, his entire demeanor changed. Gene was as cocky and self-confident back then as he is now. The thing that Gene, Paul, and I shared was the absolute determination to make it. Being in a rock band wasn't a hobby, it wasn't a way to pick up girls, it was what we had to do. Destiny had chosen that life for us.

Not that long after, Paul and I were talking and he told me that Wicked Lester was no longer. He told me he and Gene were starting a band. They'd already found a drummer. I was telling him about my band, the Planets. Sometime in late '72 he calls me up and says, "Listen, we got a lead guitarist, the lineup's complete, I really want to know what you think." So I took Andy Post, the bass player in the Planets—he'd gone to the High School of Music & Art, too, and he knew Paul, too—so we went to their next rehearsal, which I think was on a Saturday afternoon.

Andy and I show up at their loft. It was on the south side of Twenty-third Street. Their loft was located in the business building equivalent of a tenement. It was kind of a narrow, ugly six-floor building probably put up at the turn of the century. The loft was directly across from Madison [Square] Park. Also across the street from the loft was the Flatiron Building, one of the most famous buildings in the world.

There was a storefront downstairs and their loft was on the second floor. It was horrible inside. The lobby was dingy, the elevator was old. Everything was grimy and dirty. When you got out on the second floor, the hallway had one 60-watt bulb illuminating the entire hallway. The hallway was painted a mud brown. It was one of those paint jobs where you could tell there were nine coats of paint underneath it. Inside the loft it was a room maybe fifteen by fifteen. There were some old dirty quilts on the wall. There was a section with egg cartons glued or nailed to the wall, very rudimentary soundproofing. Three of the band members were there—Paul, Gene, and Peter.

Paul sheepishly explained that their lead guitarist wasn't there yet but he should be coming any minute so we hung around and made small talk. At some point Gene went, "This is kind of silly, we ought to play something for these guys." So Andy and I sat down on the floor against the wall and they strapped on their instruments and did three songs. They started with "Deuce," then they played "Strutter" and ended with "Firehouse."

As for what I thought of them, you have to understand that I was a terrible snob in terms of playing. One of my favorite jokes of all time is, "How many lead guitarists does it take to change a lightbulb? Six. One to change the bulb and five to stand around going, 'This guy sucks'" [*laughs*]. I was listening with a very critical ear. They were certainly better than the New York Dolls. While this snobby competitive musician was listening to their playing and coming to the conclusion that I was a better guitar player [*laughs*], the other issue that was sinking into my brain almost begrudgingly was, damn, these riffs are good. They were well-crafted songs. "Boy, that's a good chord change." "What the fuck did he just do? That's interesting how he went from that chord to this one." By the end of the three songs, I remember saying to them, "Those are good songs."

So we talked about the three songs for a bit. Things started getting awkward as we ran out of things to say. Andy and I were kind of looking at each other like, how much longer are we gonna hang around? When they weren't playing we had the front door open because the room had no ventilation whatsoever. Then we hear the sound of the elevator and the door opening. We hear someone making grumbling noises, and in walks Ace. He had that weird off-kilter walk. He was leaning 20 degrees to one side, and I look at his feet and he's got on one red Converse sneaker and one orange Converse sneaker. In 1972, that was really different. I think Paul said, "Man, you're an hour late." Ace's answer was, "I had to do some shit." No apologies, no explanations. He takes a Les Paul Junior out of his case, which at the time was the lowest-budget Gibson guitar. Now they're a very sought-after instrument. But when he took it out of the case I was like, "That's what the guy plays?" You could get those things for $80 back then. He walks over to an amp, plugs in, and turns around and says, "What are we doin'?" He really did have an air of "I've been here for four minutes, what the fuck are you guys doin'? What are you guys wasting my time for?" I remember thinking this guy has some fuckin' balls on him. Gene shot a really pissed-off look at Paul, like, if Binky and Andy weren't here I'd take this guy's fuckin' head off. So they do the same songs in the same order with Ace, and it sounded so much better. Ace had an attack that complemented Paul's guitar style. Paul's playing had a rawness to it and Ace had the same kind of an attack but had a smoothness to it, so the rawness and the smoothness mixed nicely.

Ace's lead playing was simplistic compared to my playing. I was racing all over the frets à la Jimi Hendrix and Jeff Beck. Like a lot of us, we were hugely influenced by Paul Kossoff of Free and how he bent notes. You could tell that Ace was influenced by him in his style of lead playing. Ace sounded like a big-time lead guitarist, his tone and attack were really powerful. He was the perfect guitar player for KISS. Everything about their sound was lowest common denominator. Everything was geared toward being as easy to digest as possible. And it worked.

I was very impressed with their tunes and once Ace came in and played with them the sound was really big and full. So they did the three songs again and Andy and I clapped and I told Ace, "Great tone on your guitar." Paul immediately put his guitar down and said, "Hey, let's step out in the hallway." Paul goes, "We have to yell at this guy and tear his head off but we just can't do it with you here. I wanted you to hear some more songs but with this guy showing up an hour late Gene and I are gonna read him the riot act." A day or two later Paul called me to pick my brain. I told him that I thought the material was really good and if Ace was gonna straighten up and be reliable that his style fit the songs. KISS was on their way.

LARGER THAN LIFE

By December 1972, the original lineup of KISS was in place. But in the beginning of their career, KISS were still more Clark Kents than superheroes. It would take months of trial and error and constant reinvention and reconfiguration of their look and sound before Superman was ready to walk out of that phone booth.

PETER CRISS: Me, Gene, and Paul rehearsed seven days a week, eight hours a day.

RIK FOX: Watching them play at the loft, I could see that even without the makeup their onstage personas and body language dictated who they would eventually be. The makeup was just the icing on the cake as far as the power they put forth in their rehearsals.

PETER CRISS: Before KISS, I played every club in New York—Arthur's, Harlows, Trudy Heller's, the Metropole. I played bar mitzvahs. I played strip joints. But [in] every band I was in I wanted to do originals. I kept saying, "We gotta dress, man, we gotta wear makeup, we gotta put on a show." I would just keep leaving these bands. Leaving them and leaving them, saying, "I gotta find the right guys."

EDDIE SOLAN (EARLY KISS ROADIE AND SOUNDMAN): I was a good friend of Ace's long before he joined KISS. In fact, I used to stop at his parents' house in the Bronx and pick him up and drive him down to rehearsals at the loft in my little Volkswagen Beetle 'cause I had a car and he didn't. I was there at the loft every night. At the time I was building them a PA. They really didn't have a lot of money. I sold these speakers that they had and took the money and bought four big speaker cabinets for the PA. It was always Paul and Gene's band but after a while they started to realize that it was Ace and Peter that were gonna make it work. Gene and Paul had a good thing going. They had a good business head on their shoulders. They were very creative and focused but they didn't have the rock-and-roll looseness that Ace and Peter provided. There was a determination with Paul and Gene. They had this attitude, "We're gonna make it, don't even doubt it." That attitude was very infectious to Ace and Peter. Ace was emboldened by their enthusiasm and sense of determination. For Ace, everything before was a bar band; this group had a different feel about it and it was infectious for me, too. I believed in them and wanted to do what I could to help things get going.

RON JOHNSEN (PRODUCER, WICKED LESTER): I saw them at their loft and they were just outrageous, a lot of high energy, a lot of wild playing. They were just hitting the walls. They were a very physical act, rough and rowdy. A lot of their vision came from groups like the New York Dolls and the Brats.

PETER CRISS: We copied a lot of things. A lot of our ideas, the art of what we did came from the Beatles, Alice Cooper, and the New York Dolls. We sat down and said, "What if all that was rolled into one?" And it worked. It was brilliant.

GENE SIMMONS: Like the Beatles, we wanted to have a band where you had four distinct individuals. You could be a fan of the band and a fan of a different persona as well.

We are an extension of everything that came before us. We're children of the last generation of rock. All my idols—the Stones, the

Who, and the Kinks—had a profound influence on my outlook on the world. When I saw Peter Townshend perform live I knew the kind of excitement that could be attained and we've tried to live up to that kind of an archetypal image.

We started wearing makeup when Alice [Cooper] took it off, when David Bowie left it—when Genesis thought it was uncool to wear it. We were really enchanted with the concept of being able to immerse yourself into your own fantasies and come out of it a completely different person, and yet the same person. It's like when you're five or six years old and you and your sister stand in front of a mirror wearing your parents' clothes, you start making believe you're somebody else, but you're really the same person. When you're invited to a masquerade party, you're most likely to wear a costume that really reflects your own personality.

LEW LINET (FIRST KISS MANAGER): Every time I'd come by rehearsals I began to notice little compacts of makeup. First thing I noticed [was that] they were wearing eyeliner, then a little bit of rouge, then a little bit of an eyebrow pencil, and it took off from there. Every rehearsal became a little bit louder and the band wore a bit more makeup. They were putting together what their dream was—a loud, old-fashioned hard rock band, kind of a Rolling Stones–David Bowie–Alice Cooper amalgamation.

GENE SIMMONS: In the beginning, it was the glitter period and a lot of bands had that androgynous look, so we tried it. Paul was very convincing but I just looked like a football player in a tutu. The look evolved as the band went along.

When we first toyed with the idea of makeup it happened very fast. Paul and I went to a department store down the street and bought two four-foot-high mirrors for $15. As we leaned them up against the walls in the loft, they slightly bent because they were cheap. When we looked at our faces in the mirror they had this freak-house effect. All I remember is we started putting makeup on. Our first gig was a week away. Between the time I called the club and the time we went onstage at Coventry, we'd changed the name of the band to KISS and changed our look.

When we first put on the makeup, we just put makeup on our faces. No one had put on the whiteface except me. I plunged into it all the way. It was cathartic. For the rest of the guys it was like, "Let's play dress up and be in a band." I remember at one of the early shows, Ace kept looking at his reflection on Peter's drum kit, which had Mylar on it, and would start cracking up. He'd get off on how bizarre it all was. But in the beginning there was no connection for the other guys between the makeup and who they were. It was like Doctor Jekyll hadn't quite become Mr. Hyde. For me the change happened immediately, inside and out. When I look back at some of the photos and see how I'm standing on the stage, it looks the same as the guy who later put on the full war paint and the outfits.

EDDIE SOLAN: Paul and Gene told Ace, "Look, we're not the best band in the world but we're gonna do something to get attention." They were convinced it was gonna happen. There was no looking back. I'd pick up Paul Stanley on Friday nights at his parents' house and we'd go out looking for gigs for the band.

TOMMY RAMONE (DRUMMER, THE RAMONES): At the time there were only three places to play original material in New York City—Max's Kansas City, the Mercer Arts Center, and Coventry. New York was totally dead. There were some cover band clubs, but as far as original music there weren't many places to play.

GENE SIMMONS: We couldn't get jobs because we didn't play top-40 songs. We wanted to play our own songs but clubs didn't want bands that played original material. But for us, the idea was to go into a small club and figure out who and what we are live.

With no money but a lot of ingenuity, KISS cobbled together rudimentary costumes and stage gear from the most unlikely sources.

PAUL STANLEY: It's not by coincidence or chance that our early outfits were made by S&M stores. We went into parts of the city and buildings that I didn't know existed. We saw strange things like a hood with a hose coming out of the mouth. We were buying pieces and they were also making us things, too. There was an S&M gay biker's clothing store called the Eagle's Nest who were making us clothes. What did we want? Black leather and studs. What did they have? Black leather and studs. We got our original studded leather belts and collars from pet stores—something that might have been used for a Great Dane—and S&M shops in the West Village. Our outfits were predominantly black. I was wearing real high heels, skintight Lurex pants, black knee socks, and a black T-shirt that said "KISS." My costume cost about $45 for the shoes, $3 for the T-shirt, and about $5 worth of Lurex for the pants.

JOEY CRISCUOLA (PETER CRISS'S BROTHER AND EARLY KISS ROADIE): My mother used to embroider KISS T-shirts for Peter. He wore one for that first show at Coventry. She used to put glue on the shirt, sprinkle glitter on the glue, and do the KISS logo in glitter. It would come out really cool. She'd also embroider drums on his T-shirts. My brother used to wear shorts with studs on the sides with black leotards.

ANNEMARIE HUGHES (EARLY KISS FAN): Me, Lydia [Criss], and Peter's sisters Donna and Joanne would also chip in and help make the T-shirts, not just for Peter but for the whole band and any fan who wanted to buy one. I remember one time the band gave Ace money to go out and buy some T-shirts but he never made it to the store. He blew all the money on booze [*laughs*]. That was Ace.

ACE FREHLEY: I started laughing the other day 'cause I saw an old photo from that time and Gene was wearing a shirt with a silver skull and crossbones and I was wearing a shirt with silver wings and I realized that my mom had sewn both of those shirts by hand.

PAUL STANLEY: All the bands on the New York scene who could afford it bought clothes at stores like Granny Takes a Trip and Jumpin' Jack Flash, which were the stores that sold the cool clothes that came out of England. I sure as hell couldn't, so I decided I'd make them myself [*laughs*]. I went out and bought the material and then my father said,

"Well, nice try but I'll buy you the pants. I admire you for wanting to make the pants, but you can't, you've never done it before." I said, "Oh yeah?" So I took my best pair of jeans apart, cut the Lurex like the jeans, asked my mother to show me how the sewing machine worked, and made myself a pair of pants. I wore them at the Daisy and they were so tight they ultimately tore onstage, right up the crotch, from stem to stem. I was the hit of the evening. I made Gene a pair of pants too, and he still has them.

GENE /IMMON/: We must have looked like dinosaurs at the time. By 1973, everybody had stopped wearing high heels. We had these six-inch boots with studs on them and it looked like an S&M thing. They were the strangest things you ever saw and they looked like they weighed a ton.

With hardly anything in common but an allegiance to the life-affirming power of loud rock and roll, KISS were four disparate personalities joined at the hip in an uphill battle to conquer the world.

PAUL /TANLEY: When the four of us first got together and played, it was undeniable. As soon as you heard it, it was world-class, and not in a virtuoso sense. It had something of an international appeal and importance, and along with that went four distinct personalities. There was a combustibility about the original band, and combustibility isn't necessarily a bad thing. That's how cars win a race. It's combustibility in an engine that makes it fast. It's harnessing that which is the key to it. It was always an effort to keep the band on track. But there was something in the beginning that was undeniable.

There were a lot of concessions made to make it work and most of them had to do with either people's limitations or wanting to sabotage a direction to give them a sense of empowerment. It almost became more important to sabotage than to succeed. That was happening since the very beginning. Peter quit the band early on in a Chinese restaurant and Ace refused to carry a piece of equipment. But at the beginning of the day or the end of the day it was always Gene and I who were there. Whether it was renting and driving a truck or hauling equipment or borrowing gear or drawing posters, ultimately that was Gene and I. That said, both the image of the band and how people perceived the band was what made it so special.

NOTHIN' TO LO/E

On January 30, 1973, KISS performed their first show ever at Coventry, a seedy club in the Flushing neighborhood of Queens, New York.

PAUL /UB (OWNER, COVENTRY): Coventry opened in the early seventies. It was located on Queens Boulevard and Forty-seventh Street in Queens.

PAUL /TANLEY: It was originally a Masonic hall or a Polish veterans hall.

PAUL /UB: The club was originally called Popcorn Pub, and I later renamed it Coventry after a town in England.

PAUL /TANLEY: When we played Coventry, it was called Popcorn, and they were trying to change their image. It was a perfect relationship in that we brought a certain New York credibility to the club so other bands started coming across the water and playing there, too. Once the word got out about KISS, it was a very rock-and-roll clientele. It was years later that I found out that the big tall guy watching us in the back with the specs on was Joey Ramone.

JOEY RAMONE (LEAD VOCALI/T, THE RAMONE/): I was at their first show ever; I was also at the show at Coventry where they got signed to Casablanca Records. KISS and the Ramones both grew up in Queens.

MARKY RAMONE (DRUMMER, THE RAMONES): We all hung out at the same places—Max's Kansas City, the Coventry. We all liked the same music—the Kinks, the early Phil Spector stuff, the Beatles, and the Who. Their music was straight-ahead rock. You didn't have to be a Juilliard-trained musician to appreciate them. They had a really good vocal style, which I think blended very well together.

JOEY RAMONE: At the time I think they were the loudest band I ever heard. I liked a lot of their stuff. They were fun and had great songs. I saw them when they first started out and they just had dry ice; Gene had a skull and crossbones T-shirt. This was way before their image and show came together.

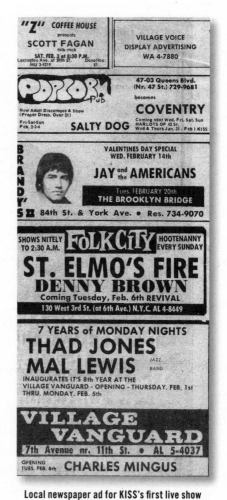

Local newspaper ad for KISS's first live show at the Queens club Coventry
Courtesy of Brad Estra

TOMMY RAMONE: I saw KISS at Coventry, and it was a great show. I didn't know what to expect but they were really, really good. I was impressed with what a strong and unique sound they had and how professional they were. They had their own direct, solid, short, quick kind of compact song structures. I don't think they sounded like any other band except maybe Slade. Slade was an influence to a certain extent on the Ramones, too.

ACE FREHLEY: Coventry was a fun hole-in-the-wall. I remember going there to see the New York Dolls. It was a happening place. At the time everybody in the New York scene played that joint—bands like the New York Dolls, the Brats, and Teenage Lust were performing there. It was also a place to be seen and mingle with other musicians at the time and, of course, meet girls.

JOEY CRISCUOLA: The band worked hard to promote that show. They took to the streets and put up advertisements throughout Brooklyn, Queens, and Manhattan. It was the hip place to play. KISS was proud to play Coventry because a lot of the hot New York bands would play there.

RIK FOX: All the big New York bands were coming across the Queensboro Bridge to play at Coventry. That club was a jumping-off point for the burgeoning New York scene. I was still in high school and underage but I found a way to fudge my ID so I could get in. When I first walked into Coventry it was like walking into a big toy store and I had a pocketful of money [*laughs*]. I found a world of my own that I could identify with.

HAROLD C. BLACK (TEENAGE LUST): Coventry was closer to a New York City club than what you'd expect in Queens. If you wanted to see bands your parents didn't like or approve of, you went to Coventry.

PAUL SUB: It was a big club—around five thousand square feet—and it held around seven hundred people. Everyone from KISS, the New York Dolls, the Ramones, Blondie, Sam & Dave, the Dictators, and Elephant's Memory played there. I'd put on ten acts a week, both local and national. Aerosmith was the only act we turned down because we didn't want to spend $300 [*laughs*]. The New York Dolls were the ones that kept Coventry going. They played once a month, and whenever they played seven hundred people would show up. They had the main following of all the bands who played there. The Dolls really helped pay my rent. All the other groups who played there, from KISS to the Ramones, didn't really bring in that many people.

STAN MIESES (WRITER, NEW YORK DAILY NEWS): In '73, outside of Manhattan, the only clubs that were of any value were the burgeoning discos. Disco was just beginning to happen at a club called Le Jardin. This was pre–Studio 54. So in the boroughs it was the dawning of the *Saturday Night Fever* era. There weren't many rock-and-roll clubs outside of Manhattan. Coventry was very similar to Kenny's Castaways on Bleecker Street in the Village. It looked like it had been a big Irish pub.

JIMI LALUMIA (WRITER, *WORDS & MUSIC* MAGAZINE): Coventry was a real nexus for rock and roll 'cause there were no strings attached. Max's Kansas City had strings attached because it was associated with the Warhol crowd and the glitter/glam rock scene that was happening with the Dolls and Wayne County. The Mercer Arts Center in downtown Manhattan was also not considered rock and roll, it was considered an art center which made itself available to rock and roll after all else had failed. Coventry was viewed as a real nuts-and-bolts rock-and-roll joint. It felt like a real rock-and-roll room. It was a perfect venue for KISS to get their act together.

GENE SIMMONS: Coventry was located in a downtrodden industrial area. Two stories above the building was a subway, so when we played the trains would be going by and it was loud. It was owned by the boys [*imitates tough-guy accent*] "who kind of talked like this."

JOEY CRISCUOLA: Coventry had seen better days. It was pretty funky.

SHAYNE HARRIS (DRUMS, LUGER): Coventry was located in an Irish/German neighborhood surrounded by restaurants and coffee shops. The El subway was right in front of the club, running the entire way down Queens Boulevard. You could take it all the way into Times Square.

MARK POLOTT (CONCERT ATTENDEE, COVENTRY): The outside of Coventry had a nondescript sign with old English letters. You'd park your car underneath the elevated subway and walk into the club.

ANDY DOBACK (CONCERT ATTENDEE, COVENTRY): It was normally two or three bucks to get into Coventry. You had a two-drink minimum. The beers were a buck apiece. They had a big jukebox with all the latest hits and they had a single by a local band, the Harlots of 42nd Street.

PAUL SUB: When you walked into the club there was the bar area on the right-hand side. It was a regular restaurant setting with tables and chairs and a big dance floor. There was also a basement with a dressing room where the bands would change.

KEITH WEST (THE BRATS): There were a lot of sexual escapades happening in the basement of the Coventry. The dressing room was where everybody would hang out—all the chicks, drugs, everything was going on downstairs. All these hot girls got passed around through all of the bands. You'd run into a guy and you'd see him with this girl and you'd be like, "Hey, I fucked her," and then someone else in my band would also be thinking the same thing [*laughs*].

RICK RIVETS (THE BRATS): It was a much bigger club than CBGB's and Max's, and it was a great-sounding place. The stage wasn't that high and the ceiling was really low. If you lifted your guitar high enough the neck would go through the ceiling.

EDDIE SOLAN: The club had stages on opposite ends of the room. So one band could be setting up and getting everything ready while the other band was playing. When they stopped and ended their set, the band on the opposite stage could start right away. KISS was loud but not ear-splitting loud. We always tried to be as loud as we could. Coming through the PA was mostly vocals and drums, and we tried to keep everything in balance with the amps so there wasn't a lot of noise. Some of the other bands sounded like such a mess of noise that you couldn't understand their songs. We had a small crew, just me, Joey Criscuola—Peter's brother—and Bobby McAdams. But everybody helped. Paul used to drive a bread truck with all of the band's gear [*laughs*]. It was filled to the ceiling with equipment.

PETER "MOOSE" ORECKINTO (KISS ROADIE, PYROTECHNICS, AND SOUND MIXER): Coventry was a typical run-down CBGB's kind of New York club. There was no PA and you had an owner who didn't give a shit—all he wanted to do was sell watered-down alcohol.

BILL AUCOIN (KISS MANAGER): It used to be the dungeon of rock-and-roll clubs. It was a hole-in-the-wall but you could be really free and play as loud as you wanted.

BINKY PHILIPS: Coventry was truly a generic dump. CBGB's was a dump, but it had tons of character. As soon as you walked into CBGBS's you felt it was someplace that was funky and unique. It was so awful it was great. Coventry consisted of two rooms that were painted flat black. It was blatantly obvious that the guys running the club didn't give a shit about rock and roll. It was also pretty obvious that it was a mob front. They didn't give a shit if you played originals or covers. The booking policy there was so lax. You could see such awful bands. You could tell nobody gave a shit; it was like a money-laundering joint.

MARK POLOTT: The vibe of Coventry felt like a Manhattan vibe. It rocked. A lot of the people that went there were in the same clique of people you'd see at Max's Kansas City. There were also a lot of beautiful girls there, which brought out all the rock guys. It was the place in Queens to see and be seen. In those days, everyone knew each other; it was a smaller music scene. The Dolls had really broken through and that opened it up for a lot of bands to follow.

KEITH WEST: When KISS came together, it was a small glitter scene in New York City with about ten bands that were popular—the Dolls, the Brats, Eric Emerson & the Magic Tramps, Teenage Lust, Harlots of 42nd Street, Ruby & the Rednecks, the Planets, Luger, and Street Punk. Every band in the glitter rock scene in New York City had their own gimmick. KISS wore the kabuki makeup, Jayne County was the transsexual, the Dolls had this gender-bending look, and the Brats were into bands like the Faces. Everybody was into the glam/glitter/pop stuff like Sweet, David Bowie, T. Rex, Mott the Hoople, and the Raspberries. But it was Bowie who led that scene for all of us.

HAROLD C. BLACK: There was definitely a rivalry between all the local New York bands as far as the music. There was also a rivalry over the women—who got who, and who got who first.

MARK POLOTT: KISS separated themselves from other bands. They had a certain charisma. In a lot of ways they weren't part of the scene; they were their own entity and they cultivated this mysterious vibe. So many guys I knew in bands were from Queens. You had Paul Stanley and Gene Simmons from KISS, you had the Ramones, Johnny Thunders from the Dolls, Ricky Byrd from Joan Jett & the Blackhearts, the Brats, Murder Inc., Rags, and Street Punk.

Fueled by a burning hunger to make it big, the members of KISS had been determined to do whatever it took to promote the band from day one.

PETER CRISS: I used to go around Brooklyn in the early morning and hammer these ads for our shows all over town. Ace would do the same thing in the Bronx. Gene worked in an office and had access to write a bio and print up things. We were all very resourceful; it was great.

PAUL STANLEY: At night we would put up flyers and posters advertising our gigs, which is interesting because that became the norm later for bands.

GENE SIMMONS: Paul did the artwork for our concert ads and placed them in the *Village Voice*.

PAUL STANLEY: It was very hands-on. One of our early ads had a drawing I did of a naked girl. I knew if anything was going to get someone's attention, it would be a naked girl. Sex has always sold, so whether it's rock and roll or toothpaste, the chances are you're gonna do better [*laughing*] if you have a picture of somebody without their clothes on. I was drawing pubescent nymphs. It was very funny because the *Village Voice*—the progressive paper in New York—made me put a bathing suit on the girl. It ran once with the naked girl, and the second time it got masked. There's a poster I designed for a Hotel Diplomat show we did with Street Punk and Luger, and I wound up designing logos for some of the bands that were on the bill with us because I wanted the posters advertising our shows to look good [*laughs*].

GENE SIMMONS: I was always the asshole who decided to pick up the phone and bother people and get us to where we wanted to go. On my way into work in the city I used to pass by this club in Queens. I called the club, got the manager on the phone, and started selling, which is what I've always done my entire life. I said to him, "We've got a band called Wicked Lester and I'm really excited about it. You should book us because we're terrific." So he agreed to put us on for three nights during the middle of the week when nobody went there. The money we made just about covered the rental of the equipment truck. We had yet to name ourselves KISS. That first night we changed the name of the band from Wicked Lester to KISS. Ace took out a magic marker and hand-drew the logo on the poster. We came up with the name KISS one day when Paul, Peter, and I were in Paul's car and he was driving.

PAUL STANLEY: I was on the Long Island Expressway coming back from the city with Gene and Peter in my Plymouth Fury and we were throwing around all these names for the group.

GENE SIMMONS: I mentioned "Crimson Harpoon" and "Fuck." I thought "Fuck" was genius. The name of the first record could be "You," the name of the second could be "It." You'd have people at your shows screaming, "Fuck, fuck, fuck!" It's the ultimate band name.

PAUL STANLEY: I came up with the name KISS. When something's right, you *know* it's right. All I could do was hold my breath and say, "I hope these guys are smart enough and put whatever ego aside because this is the right name."

GENE SIMMONS: As soon as I heard it, I said, "That's it." It clicked right away.

PAUL STANLEY: When I said "KISS" it was such a relief to have everybody go, "Yeah, that's good."

GENE SIMMONS: We talked about it. It could be the kiss of death. It's also romantic and sexy and kind of English.

PAUL STANLEY: I thought of the name KISS because it just seemed like a name everybody was familiar with. And it was universal. No matter where you go people know that word. Even then we were thinking of ourselves as an international act. KISS had a magic from the beginning that was wonderful and very strong. There are moments in our career that are so undeniable and that was one of them. You couldn't argue with it. And not because I came up with it, but because it was right.

Having decided upon a name, next on the agenda was to create a distinctive logo that would communicate instantly the essence of the group.

ACE FREHLEY: I've always been a graphic artist. When I was sixteen years old, my guidance counselor said, "You have no business being in this school. You belong in an art school developing your talents." My specialty is logos. I designed the KISS logo in about three minutes. I do my best stuff quickly. I drew the KISS logo with a felt-tip pen. Paul cleaned up my artwork with a Rapidograph pen; he always had steadier hands.

PAUL STANLEY: Ace came up with the initial design for the logo. I thought it was a great idea but not fully realized. What it evolved into was mine. I remember fleshing out the logo with a straight-edged ruler on my parents' coffee table. I turned it into something more like a car emblem and refined it for the poster for our show coming up at the Diplomat. If you look at the two *S*'s they're not identical and not completely parallel because I basically did it freehand. When we got our record deal the art department said, "Do you want us to redraft it?" And it had gotten us that far so we said, "No, leave it just the way it is," and that's our logo to this day.

In their first year, the group's makeup was a work in progress. Paul, Gene, Ace, and Peter experimented and refined their look from gig to gig.

GENE SIMMONS: We did a photo session as Wicked Lester. One of Ace's friends took the photo in the staircase at our loft on 10 East Twenty-third Street. The early photos of us didn't have

Ace, Paul, Gene, and Peter posed in the stairwell of the 10 East Twenty-third Street loft, New York City KISS Catalog Ltd.

the KISS makeup on. We looked like grade-B drag queens, a New York Dolls kind of a band. We had yet to commit to the makeup, although we tried out a primitive version of it as a trio with Paul, Peter, and I. It looks like I have silver hair in the photo, but it was gray color spray. We didn't know who we were at the time but we knew we had the musical goods. That photo showed us looking like a New York glitter band. Everyone had pouty lips and was doing that "look at me, I'm neither straight or gay" androgynous thing. By the time we played that first show at Coventry we decided to call ourselves KISS. We blew up that photo into a

Early promo photo of KISS taken in the stairwell of their 10 East Twenty-third Street loft, New York City Ken Sharp Collection

poster about three feet high, which was put into the window of the club.

PETER CRISS: We looked like four guys in drag. Gene looks like a transvestite, Paul looks like some whore, and Ace looked like Shirley MacLaine [laughs]. We would all kid him about this.

BOBBY McADAMS: In those days, Alice Cooper, David Bowie, and the Dolls wore makeup, but it was more drag makeup. And at the beginning KISS was wearing drag makeup, too, lots of red lipstick and rouge.

PAUL SUB: The New York Dolls were a drag band wearing makeup, so when KISS came in with makeup and costumes it didn't surprise me too much. But their look was completely different from the Dolls.

GENE SIMMONS: I had a primitive version of my makeup on for that first show at Coventry. I put on whiteface, put my hair up, kind of had that batlike thing, but no black lipstick. I had the design. Ace had his little exploding design, but no whiteface. Paul didn't wear any makeup and Peter had only rouge on his cheeks and red lipstick. By our second appearance at Coventry we had a prototype of the KISS makeup on and had a real sense of who we were gonna be.

ACE FREHLEY: The first night at Coventry, I painted my face silver. The second night, I thought, "That's boring. I'll have to think up something more imaginative," and then I started painting stars on my eyes.

PAUL STANLEY: The makeup was always basically the same, but what was on my eye kept changing.

ACE FREHLEY: People don't know that I designed Paul's makeup.

PAUL STANLEY: Ace thought of the star, and it fit because when I was a kid I loved drawing stars.

GENE SIMMONS: The first time we were putting makeup on, Paul had two stars, one star on each eye. My reaction was it was a little close to Ace's design because they both had those kinds of spikes at the end. When it was time to do the first Daisy show, Paul left one star on his eye. I said, "Where's the other star?" And he said, "Nah, I'm lazy, I don't want to do another star." My makeup design was a combination of Batman and the Phantom of the Opera. I was inspired by a distinct image of Lon Chaney Sr. as the Phantom of the Opera that I saw in [the magazine] *Famous Monsters of Filmland*, where the shadow hit it really hard and it lent it this batlike quality. During that first show at Coventry my hair kept falling down and getting caught on my makeup. That's why I took all the hair on top and tied it into a ball so it could stay out of my face. Everybody thought I did it because it was like kabuki. Not true.

Early KISS promo photo KISS Catalog Ltd.

PETER CRISS: We did some soul-searching and became the characters. We knew Gene was always into monsters. Paul was a true rock star and Ace was definitely from another planet, and I was the cat. Being an emotional guy, an independent person, and a loner, one minute I'm loving and cuddling next to you, and the next minute I'm going to tear your eyes out. When cats want to be bothered they love to come over and be petted, and when they don't want to be fucked with they'll scratch ya. Gene said, "Oh shit, you couldn't pick a more perfect character." I have this attitude of a lion, a friggin' feline, a cat, so that's where the idea for my makeup came from.

QUEENS BOULEVARD

Grand expectations turned into severe disappointment in the band's first-ever live performance. By all accounts, opening night at Coventry was anything but a success, a sobering reminder that the group's rise to stardom could be a bumpy ride.

PAUL STANLEY: First time we played there it was virtually empty.

PETER CRISS: Nobody was there [*laughs*]. It was a nightmare. We killed ourselves for six people.

LYDIA CRISS: I remember it was a really cold winter night. The only people who showed up at that first Coventry show were me, Gene's girlfriend and her friend, plus the road crew—Eddie Solan, Joey Criscuola, and Bobby McAdams—and the people who worked at the club.

PAUL STANLEY: Whether there were four people at the first gig or forty thousand, it didn't matter. Our path was already predetermined. I was completely oblivious to anything other than we were gonna be the biggest band around. Nothing ever seemed like a setback or a detour from that path. To me everything just seemed like days

LEFT: Dressed in a sailor suit, Gene performs at Coventry, January 30, 1973
RIGHT: Paul and Ace, Coventry, January 30, 1973 KISS Catalog Ltd.

that I would look back on with nostalgia and a sense of awe. I was convinced that this was the road to world domination.

GENE SIMMONS: We played a Tuesday, Wednesday, and Thursday and were paid $30.

LEW LINET: Coventry was a toilet. Those gigs were awful. Nobody liked them, nobody clapped.

PAUL SUB: Nobody knew KISS at the time; they didn't have a following.

LYDIA CRISS: Even though there wasn't anybody there, they weren't discouraged. They were just happy to play and played their hearts out. The band made $30 that night but all the money went to the road crew.

RICK RIVETS: Paul Sub, the owner of the club, wasn't cheap, but he wouldn't pay bands up front. All the bands split the door. But he'd give the bands a lot of drink tickets and you can't argue with that [*laughs*].

GENE SIMMONS: Our show itself was straight ahead, real raw, real short, real good rock and roll. That night at Coventry, I wore velour bell bottoms with cuffs, a pair of high heels that I put studs on, and a white sailor shirt for the first show. It was a holdover from Wicked Lester's audition for the head of Metromedia Records.

BOBBY McADAMS: Ace would get pretty blitzed for the shows. But to his credit, he could play well when he was blind drunk.

PETER CRISS: We still put on the makeup, went onstage, and played. We kicked ass for nobody, and that's what I respected about them guys from day one. We always stuck to what we practiced and what we worked on no matter what was out there. We still gave it our all. When we got to the Daisy my conception was that it's a bar but that we should look at it as the Garden [Madison Square]. And I remember when we finally got to play the Garden, Gene says, "You little son of a bitch, now we're really playing there!"

PAUL STANLEY: In 1972, I remember driving people to the Garden to see Elvis Presley. I thought, "Someday people will be driving to the Garden to see me," and five years later KISS was headlining there. It may be blind, idiotic self-belief, but it will get you very far if there's some talent to go along with it. If you're dead set in where you're going you don't let anything get in the way.

GENE SIMMONS: We'd read about all those bobby-soxers for Frank Sinatra and how Elvis Presley's manager, Colonel Tom Parker, literally created the excitement that people thought was natural. The show wasn't only onstage, it also went into the audience. We had to create our own vibe because we were no one at that point. We'd invite our girlfriends and our friends to the shows. So you had people getting up and dancing to a band nobody ever heard of. If you just walked in you'd go, "Hey, what's going on here? They already have fans."

PETER CRISS: We eventually played at Coventry enough times. I remember pulling up one night in the car with the boys and there was a line down the block. We went, "Holy shit. Wow, this is cool!"

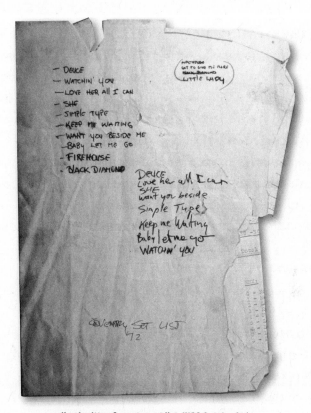

Handwritten Coventry set list KISS Catalog Ltd.

We had to go through the crowd and they were all patting us on the back, and we made it to the basement and we said, "Fuck!" It was cool.

JOEY CRISCUOLA: After the first show, word spread about this wild act, and for the few more times they played Coventry they'd built a small following.

PAUL SUB: From then on KISS would normally draw between 100 to 150 people a night.

EDDIE SOLAN: People would sit there with their mouths open [*laughs*] because they were so different. We played the Daisy a lot, too, and one night people were sitting there thinking, "Who the hell are these guys?" But word got around that little town, and the next night the club was packed.

GENE SIMMONS: We refused to play top 40. We had brass balls. We said, "We're not gonna do 'Hang On Sloopy' or 'Midnight Hour,' we're gonna go on and do our own tunes." We were taking a really big risk doing that. We did two sets at Coventry for that first show. All originals. We still had the same musical arsenal we use today— "She," "Watchin' You," "Deuce," "Strutter," and "Black Diamond." Those songs wound up on the first two or three KISS albums, with one notable exception: "Life in the Woods" was one of the all-time bombs. Paul wrote it.

EDDIE SOLAN: "Life in the Woods" was different from any other rock song they were doing at the time.

PAUL STANLEY: It was more like a riff, and the lyrics just came afterwards. They were very bizarre—just kind of spat out so we had something to sing.

EDDIE SOLAN: [*Reciting lyrics*] "Life in the woods would be easy, living with the birds and the trees. . . ." It was a strange song [*laughs*].

GENE SIMMONS: We never recorded it. [*Reciting lyrics*] " . . . Keeping in tune with the city, singing along with the breeze." The lyrics were bizarre but the riff was outstanding. It reminds me of a song by the group Detroit with Mitch Ryder.

PAUL STANLEY: I nicked a little bit of the guitar and verse feel from a song by the Buddy Miles Express called "Dreams." "Life in the Woods" was a song we played in our club days and served as a time-filler. We had a limited number of songs and we had to play *X* amount of sets a night. It was more a vamp, just something to stretch out and kill time. There was never a thought about recording it in the studio.

RIK FOX: Back in those club days they used to do a song called "Acrobat," which was an extended jam. When it got to the heavy section, it epitomized heavy metal in my mind.

GENE SIMMONS: "Acrobat" was originally seven minutes long. It started off with an instrumental and then went into another section called "You're Much Too Young." "Acrobat" became "Love Theme from Kiss," and then it went off into a "Detroit Rock City" riff, which Paul ripped off from me but never gave me credit for.

Our show had no talking, just bang-bang-bang song-song-song and off the stage. We didn't have any real effects at the time.

EDDIE SOLAN: We had to look more professional so I started building a primitive light system. I bought some dimmer switches, built these Radio Shack towers, and mounted some colored spotlights on it with some dimmer switches that I could mount on the mixing console. Other bands didn't have this so it made us appear more professional. For "Firehouse" we had this idea to use these red revolving beacon lights. They had a magnetic base so a fireman or cop could just reach out and put it on the roof of his car and plug it into the cigarette lighter. They wanted to have flashing red lights for "Firehouse." I worked for a company called Lafayette Radio, an electronics retail store in Scarsdale, New York, and we sold those kinds of lights. I made a box out of a car battery charger to turn on the red lights. We had three of them on top of the amps. We used to use it at the end of "Firehouse" and at the end of the show, too, to build excitement. That whole thing stuck with them for a long time. Even when they were on the road playing big places, they always had the revolving red lights.

I also made lights for the band from a TV antenna stand. I made these tripod stands that would be used to support TV antennas on a roof and attached colored lights to it. Back then we had a little PA system with a Peavey twelve-channel mixing board that Gene and Paul had left over from Wicked Lester, and I'd have the lightbox on the console that I'd turn on and off [*laughs*]. It was primitive but it worked. We did a lot with a little bit of ingenuity and very little money.

ANDY DOBACK: Coventry had a Christmas light color wheel that was mounted on the ceiling. Someone would stand on a chair from the club and rotate the wheel to change the colors lighting the stage. We always got a big laugh out of that.

LEW LINET: After the show, even though only a few people showed up, the band was in high spirits. They were very young and naive and they were on the road to success. They had a gig, and they were very impressed with themselves and happy with what they were doing. They didn't second-guess themselves or question their journey. They did what they loved to do. They didn't understand how difficult it would be to achieve success. They didn't know how high the mountain was to climb. When we're very young we're not frightened of working toward success because we don't know that it's difficult. It's the same syndrome as children picking up a second language. They don't know that picking up a second language is hard. They just do it. So in many ways KISS were babies in rock and roll, bright-eyed and bushy-tailed and ready to take on the world.

JTAN MIEJEJ: Back in 1973, I was twenty years old and working as a copy boy at the *Daily News*. Hanging around, I impressed a couple of the editors with my enthusiasm for rock and roll. I'd gotten a couple of assignments to review rock shows. Then this guy Paul [Sub] wrote me from Queens—he must have seen my byline. He said, "You're the *Daily News*, you guys should really cover clubs in Queens." So I went out to this guy's club, the Coventry, sat down, and this group named KISS came on. I looked at them and thought this was like comic book or kabuki, something I'd never seen. They looked great. Musically, it sounded like cement mixing. It was not my style of music—my style leaned more to the Velvet Underground—but I thought their stage show was very impressive. The club was half full, but they were enthusiastic. The substance of my review, which ran in the *Daily News,* was how they looked. I described the band in detail and not so much the sound. They had clearly defined characters, and that's something I hadn't seen since the Beatles. Each member of the band was individualized. The makeup made all four guys distinct. The behavior onstage was also very distinct. I thought these guys had a shot at making it because at the very least the next day people would say, "You should see what I saw!"

Five years later, I was the rock-and-roll reviewer and Sunday pop music columnist for the *Daily News*. I got a call from their publicist inviting me to join KISS on their first tour of Japan. We were all sitting in first class and they were rotating journalists on this junket in and out of the seats of the band members. I got to sit next to Gene for a while. I introduced myself and he turned to me and gave me this really curious look. He reaches into his pocket and pulls out this clipping from his wallet. He said, "You're the guy who wrote this review!" It was my 1973 review of KISS's show at the Coventry. And we just bonded after that.

7

DAISY DAZE

Perhaps even more than their shows at Coventry, it was KISS's performances at the Daisy, a small club in Amityville, Long Island, that shaped their sound and stage show and set them on the path to stardom.

LEW LINET: At the time, in Manhattan there was no place for an act like KISS. This was a tremendously loud, raunchy band and I had a hard time getting them gigs so I had to go to other places, like Long Island. I was managing a band called J.F. Murphy & Salt who'd played a place out in Amityville, Long Island, called the Daisy. It was run by this nice guy named Sid Benjamin, who was a paperhanger, and his wife. I went to Sid and booked KISS there.

SID BENJAMIN (OWNER, THE DAISY): I trusted Lew's taste and I wasn't wrong. The audience reaction was great.

RICHARD BENJAMIN (SON OF SID BENJAMIN): Originally it was a Rexall drugstore. The name of the club was a play on hippie flower power. The Daisy first opened in the late sixties and closed about ten years later. Everyone from KISS to Attila [Billy Joel's early band] to the Stray Cats played there early in their career.

Original site of the Daisy, Amityville, New York, circa mid '60s
Courtesy of the Amityville Historical Society

LEW LINET: The Daisy was a casual teenage-to-early-twenties joint. It was much nicer than Coventry. It was clean and located in a nice area. It was just a bar with a little bandstand at one end. The kids would crowd in there on the weekends.

PATTY BENJAMIN (DAUGHTER OF SID BENJAMIN): In its heyday, the Daisy was the biggest club on Long Island. The entrance to the club was around the back, which was situated close to a quiet residential neighborhood. Because of the noise from inside the club and from the crowd who'd hang out in the parking lot and get rowdy, the neighbors would regularly call the police. They clearly didn't like the "rock-and-roll element." The police would often come and harass the kids because the place was so packed and noisy. My father was always worried they'd shut him down permanently.

The club's tongue-in-cheek manifesto, printed on the back of a recently discovered matchbook from the Daisy, says it all: "Long Island's Strangest Nite Club–Warm Beer–Rotten Food–Lousy Bands–Crazy Bartenders–Cheap Booze."

Original Daisy matchbooks Courtesy of Richard Benjamin

CAROL GULOTTA SOTTILI (CONCERT ATTENDEE, THE DAISY): We were going to the Daisy for some time before KISS started playing there. It was a local dive bar with lots of personality. I remember it as being very dark with black-light accents—a place where hippies who liked to drink too much felt at home. We punched in "S3" on the jukebox to play our favorite song—"You Really Got Me" by the Kinks. I basically lived at the Daisy—I was there just about every day for a chunk of my life back in 1972–'73. Much of that had to do with Sid, who was what I'd call a "den father." He cared about us. If we didn't have any money, he'd buy a few rounds. He knew a lot about music, and we looked up to him.

RICHARD BENJAMIN: KISS was having a hard time finding gigs. Nobody wanted to hire them. My father took a chance on them and booked them. My rock band, Children of the Night, was a costume act that dressed as monster characters. We had a Wolfman on drums, Dracula on guitar, Phantom of the Opera on keyboard, a Mummy on sax, and a Frankenstein on bass. We used dry ice and Dracula would come out in a coffin. So my dad was no stranger to a theatrical act; I think that's why he embraced them. My dad was ahead of his time having a club that booked bands that played original music.

PATTY BENJAMIN: The legal capacity of the Daisy was 144. But we didn't pay much attention to that. Sometimes we'd pack in over three hundred people. Initially, my dad booked KISS mid-week. Bands that had a local name were booked on the weekends because they already had a fan base. They quickly went from a curiosity to building a real following.

We advertised the shows using a hand-operated ditto machine in the basement of our home. My mom would make the master ad by hand and then we'd run off a ream of paper, which was five hundred copies. My friends and I would drive over to places like Jones Beach, Farmingdale College, C. W. Post College, and various shopping centers and put them on the windshields of the cars. My mom ran a record store and she'd stuff a flyer into every bag. My dad also paid an artist to make huge signs that we'd place in the club to advertise upcoming shows.

GENE SIMMONS: We'd put on our makeup and costumes in Sid's office, which we used as our dressing room.

PAUL STANLEY: It was always fun because when the phone would ring and we would answer it, people would say, "Who's playing tonight?" and we'd say, "This amazing band called KISS, you've just gotta come see them."

EDDIE SOLAN: There was more pressure on them playing at Coventry. There was more competition with all the other New York bands plus there was always something breaking that needed to be fixed. Out at the Daisy there *was* no competition. We were out in Amityville, Long Island, which is in the sticks. They were looser and more relaxed playing there.

GENE SIMMONS: It's interesting that the crowds coming to see us at the Daisy connected with KISS faster than those in New York City. KISS broke in the same town where *Jaws* and *The Amityville Horror* were filmed. We were embraced by people that weren't affected by style and don't care what's happening anywhere else. They either like it or they don't. KISS was a respite and a way to go off and see the Wizard on the Yellow Brick Road, not just another band.

PAUL STANLEY: We weren't interested in playing some of the hipper clubs in Manhattan like Max's Kansas City. Max's was a place for poseurs. It was more about the soundtrack for a fashion show, with people dressing the part rather than being it. The Daisy was us going to the salt of the earth, blue-collar people, and rockin' and rollin'. It wasn't a chic affair; it wasn't "who's the hippest guy in the room?"

PATTY BENJAMIN: My dad let KISS rehearse in the club during the day for free. I was still in high school and my dad had me work the door. There were no tickets. You paid a buck to get in. KISS was paid a $100 guarantee against 50 percent of the door plus free drinks. Ace was happy with the free drinks clause [*laughs*]. I remember he drank a lot of beer [*laughs*].

PAUL STANLEY: The Daisy was a really cheap place—drinks were 35 cents. Most bands playing there were doing four sets a night and we came in like big stars and told them we'd play twice a night for a weekend's worth of work. They gave us $100 for two nights. After expenses I think the four of us walked away with $3.50 per man.

CAROL GULOTTA SOTTILI: The first time they played, there weren't many people there. We initially just sat at the bar and listened politely.

EDDIE SOLAN: People looked at them like, "Who the hell are these guys?"

CAROL GULOTTA SOTTILI: We were a little skeptical. We were used to the typical bar band, and a bunch of guys wearing makeup was a first. But we all came around really fast. We knew they had something that was different and good and raw and real. I don't know how long it took for us to hit the dance floor, but I don't think they played for very long before we were hooked.

LOU GABRIELSON (CONCERT ATTENDEE, THE DAISY): We looked at each other and said, "Sid got us a good band for a change." After that first show we told everyone we knew about them.

EDDIE SOLAN: Word got around town and then the next night there were ten times as many people.

CAROL GULOTTA SOTTILI: I saw every show they played there, which wasn't much of a stretch, since I was there most nights anyway. But I made a special point of being there when KISS played.

PAUL STANLEY: We wore makeup then but it was not as sophisticated as it is now. The rest of the band pretty much looked the same, but I didn't. I wore just eye makeup and rouge.

PATTY BENJAMIN: The first time they played there the customers thought they were a transvestite act because the makeup was more feminine looking. I can still see them in my dad's office tinkering with their makeup and asking me, "How do you think this looks?"

EDDIE SOLAN: There was this girl named Roni who was a friend of the club owner, Sid Benjamin, and she helped us a lot. The second time we played there she let the band go to her parents' house and put on their makeup and costumes.

RONI ASHTON (EMPLOYEE, THE DAISY): I remember KISS putting on their makeup in the office while I was counting money. We became friendly. From talking to Gene, you knew how bright he was. To this day, Gene Simmons is probably the brightest person I ever met in my life.

CAROL GULOTTA SOTTILI: I remember Patty helping them put their makeup on in the back room and making suggestions about how they could fine-tune their looks.

EDDIE SOLAN: One night we were in the office at the Daisy and they were putting on their makeup. Gene said, "Give me my bass, I wanna tune it." Little did he know, but the night before Paul took all the guitars home, put Gene's bass under his bed, and never brought it back [*laughs*]. So I had to go into the club and ask if anybody played bass. The band were all onstage and they were stalling. We met this girl named Roni, and she knew somebody who played bass. He went home and this guy comes back and opens up this case and it's a blue Hagstrom bass with nylon strings. Gene's face went pale [*laughs*]. But he got through the first set. Then we found somebody else who played bass and he brought his bass and it was something better. Gene used that for the band's second set. We were a hundred miles from home—it wasn't like we could run home and get his bass.

PAUL $TANLEY: From the time we first got to the Daisy this big bouncer wanted to kill us.

PATTY BENJAMIN: His name was Brian and he was a massive guy with long hair, a full beard, and moustache. He wore a denim vest, had lots of tattoos, and looked like the scariest Hell's Angel you'd ever seen.

RICHARD BENJAMIN: You didn't want to mess with Brian; he wouldn't take crap from anybody. He'd crush you. Multiple times I saw him remove people from the premises by picking them up with one hand around their neck, kind of like Popeye, and throwing them into the parking lot cartoon-style.

PATTY BENJAMIN: Brian really didn't like KISS [*laughs*]. Before KISS came to play their first show at the Daisy, I remember him picking up a photo of the band, looking at it, dropping it on the desk, and walking away in disgust.

PAUL $TANLEY: He didn't like the whole vibe of the band. You could hear him screaming by the back door, "I'm gonna kill them!" We were terrified.

GENE $IMMON$: We'd lock ourselves up in the back office and only come out as a group.

PATTY BENJAMIN: Brian thought KISS was a transvestite band. Paul had an androgynous look at the time and that really didn't go over very well with Brian.

PAUL $TANLEY: But once we played he became a big, big fan of the band. No matter how bad someone's feelings were about the band, as soon as we played we had won them over.

With money exceedingly tight, the group served as their own road crew for those early gigs at Coventry and the Daisy.

PAUL STANLEY: We'd bring our equipment into clubs in the afternoon so nobody could see that we didn't have a road crew. We were basically hauling our own equipment.

BOBBY McADAMS: One time we'd rented an old square box-shaped milk truck to carry their equipment. Paul was driving with the makeup on and we got lost in Long Island somewhere on our way to the Daisy. Paul walked into a gas station wearing the full makeup, costume, and platform boots and asked for directions to Amityville. We thought he was gonna get killed [*laughs*]. We were ready to go in and save his life with baseball bats but everything turned out okay. Very few bands had the balls to dress that outrageously.

KISS was always acutely aware that perception was reality. That knowledge led them to limit their appearances on the local club circuit.

PAUL STANLEY: Once KISS started playing clubs we were careful not to play too many shows. We didn't want people to think we were hanging around the city; we wanted people to think we were out playing outside of the New York area. So we were literally sitting in our loft counting down the days before we could play again. We had a rule that we would only play X amount in the New York area. Literally, when we'd go onstage I'd lie and say, "We just got back from playing . . ." and I'd make up some place.

In their early club days, KISS's live show was very much a work in progress. The band experimented with pacing, stage banter, and song selections. And there was the dilemma of choosing a song to close their set with.

GENE SIMMONS: We couldn't figure out how to finish our set. We tried to write a "Thanks for coming, good night" kind of song. [Producer] Bob Ezrin figured out all those things for Alice Cooper [*sings part of "Hello Hooray"*].

EDDIE SOLAN: "Go Now" by the Moody Blues was the only cover song they did as a club act, which they used as their closing song.

GENE SIMMONS: Paul sang lead and we all jumped in on the harmonies. It sounded like the original Moody Blues version crossed with the Allman Brothers—the middle section of it breaks into dual guitar.

EDDIE SOLAN: It had a very strong riff [*imitates descending chord line*]. They used it as their closing song. "Go Now" went over well but only lasted in the set for a few gigs.

GENE SIMMONS: We never recorded it in the studio. It was one of the things considered for the first album but somehow never wound up on it. But we came up with a really good version.

Unlike the slate of local bands that trod the boards at the Daisy, KISS brought a solid professionalism to both their live performances and stage presentation that invariably elicited polarizing reactions among the patrons.

RICHARD BENJAMIN: A lot of the cool local musicians looked down on KISS because they weren't the greatest players. The power and potency of the band pushed them over the top.

BILLY LOURIE (CONCERT ATTENDEE, THE DAISY): They were more packaged and polished than the bands that typically played at the Daisy. Watching them you could tell pretty quickly they were going places.

RICHARD BENJAMIN: KISS had a real attitude onstage, like "Let's have a good time and party—if not, get the fuck out" [*laughs*]. If you were sitting out in the audience like an emotionless schlump, Gene would come out to your table and encourage you to participate in the festivities, and that's putting it delicately.

GENE SIMMONS: In order for the audience to start clapping along, you've gotta force 'em. This pregnant girl was sitting in front of the stage, and during our song "Life in the Woods" we'd get off the stage and get people to clap along. This poor woman was holding on to her stomach so not too much noise would get to her baby. I remember running off the stage at the Daisy to a pregnant woman who was drinking. I remember putting her drink down and forcing her to clap her hands. When I ran back onstage I was thinking, "I hope she doesn't have a heart attack or a miscarriage," because we were playing *loud*. I hope the baby came out okay and not with two heads.

PATTY BENJAMIN: One time I remember a conga train happening during their show. Gene jumped into the crowd and people followed him in a line dancing and clapping around the whole bar, and then he jumped back on the stage.

CAROL GULOTTA SOTTILI: I have no idea who started the conga line thing but it was a big part of at least a couple of nights. And this was before conga lines were a thing at every kid's bar mitzvah and every couple's cheesy wedding.

RONI ASHTON: KISS was so different from the bands that played at the club. They became popular really quickly. The crowds at the Daisy embraced KISS because it was so alien to the other bands that played there. Word spread that this was the band you had to see. They stopped playing there because they became too big for the venue.

CAROL GULOTTA SOTTILI: By the time they played their last gig, the place was rocking. It was packed to the gills, with long lines around the building. Because we were regulars, we got to go around the crowd—I can still remember the grousing as we cut in front of everyone.

GENE SIMMONS: The Daisy was important, not just for the people that saw KISS but for a mindset that we got. We were putting on makeup in the back office and Peter said, "Let's go out there and kick their asses like we're on the stage of Madison Square Garden," and he was right. It was a mission statement, and Peter got it. That was the right vibe. Whether you're playing to ten people or a hundred thousand people, you pour your heart out and always give it your all.

PATTY BENJAMIN: From the first song to the last song, KISS had so much energy and excitement. I remember they'd throw our candy kisses to the crowd. After they made it, a lot of the Daisy regulars were so thrilled for them. Some of them would say, "Oh my God, I used to do shots with Ace and now he's a big star!"

PAUL STANLEY: The last time we played there people were breaking the windows on the street trying to get into the club. It was a phenomenal rise. We saw something go from literally twenty people in a club wondering who the hell we were to hundreds of people trying to get in, all in a matter of a few months. We played the Daisy about five times—five weekend gigs. That was the plan, to play the Daisy until we were ready.

CAROL GULOTTA SOTTILI: KISS got too big for the Daisy in very short order. I don't know if we knew then how lucky we were to be a part of that short moment. But I do remember having a fucking great time.

When KISS first appeared on the music scene, club owners frowned on bands that played original material and booked cover bands instead. KISS quickly caught on that landing gigs in New York City was going to be an uphill battle.

EDDIE SOLAN: Besides the shows at Coventry and the Daisy we were running out of places for the band to play. There were a limited number of clubs wanting to book bands playing original material. The band decided to put together a press kit to try and attract club owners to book them. I brought my tape recorder to the second Daisy gig, took it back home, made a crude mix, and made some cassettes. I think Lydia or Gene put that press kit together. We got some envelopes and put in a cassette, which had a couple of songs from their live set, a photo, and a little bio.

So I drove off to Paul Stanley's family's house on Jewel Avenue in Queens. I picked up Paul and we went back to Westchester and I took him around to some of the clubs I knew of to see if we could get more gigs for the band. We went to the Fore n' Aft club in White Plains and dropped off the press kit. Then we went to the Rising Sun in Yonkers. I knew the owners there and they said they'd book KISS if they had a following in Queens or Brooklyn and could get people in the door. But the band didn't really have a following at that point and that's why they didn't book them. That night Paul stayed at my parents' house and I drove him home the next day. He wasn't demoralized because he always had this feeling that no matter how small the steps were, things were moving forward. You'd look Paul or Gene in the eye and knew that it was gonna work—KISS were gonna be a big band.

LIP/TICK KILLER/

n the spring of 1973, while KISS was still dreaming about making it
to the big leagues, the New York Dolls were the rock-and-roll kings
(and queens) of New York City. These mascara misfits were the "it"
band, pushing the boundaries of androgyny and, in the process, building
a loyal fan base. Signed to Mercury Records in March 1973, the band,
armed with an arsenal of raunchy Rolling Stones–meets–girl-group–styled
material, recorded their debut record with producer Todd Rundgren. The
eponymously titled album was released in late summer. But despite rave
notices from the pop cognoscenti, it sold modestly outside of their hometown.

BINKY PHILIPS: Musical prowess and technical ability had gotten
completely skewed in New York. This was the era of Genesis, King
Crimson, ELP, Yes. All those very highly convoluted bands that
stressed virtuosity. That summer of '72, every musician in a band
made a trip to the Mercer Arts Center to see the New York Dolls
because there was a huge buzz about them. Just the name alone made
you want to go see them. And the Dolls were absurdly rudimentary.
Between Johnny [Thunders] and Syl [Sylvain] I doubt they knew
more than eight or nine chords. The drummer sped up and slowed

down. They were terrible on a musical level but every band who saw the Dolls wanted to be them. Aerosmith came down from Boston and saw the Dolls and went back home wanting to be the Dolls. Months before, Jeff Beck [had been] their guitar hero, and now, all of sudden, they all wanted to be like Johnny Thunders.

BOB GRUEN (PHOTOGRAPHER): One night after KISS was rehearsing they went to see the Dolls at the Diplomat Hotel. The Dolls were the best-looking band around, and KISS couldn't compete with the Dolls in terms of trying to be better-looking. So they did something completely opposite, which was to be monsters instead of trying to be attractive. The Dolls were very rhythm-and-blues oriented, where KISS had much more of a metal, hard rock sound.

PAUL STANLEY: You couldn't be from New York and not be aware of the Dolls. If you were in a rock band, just because of where you were from, there had to be some attention given to the Dolls.

GENE SIMMONS: Paul and I went to see the Dolls at the Diplomat a few months before we played there, and it was packed.

PAUL STANLEY: The Dolls had a very big following and pulled a big crowd as an unsigned band. We wanted to see what all the buzz was about and hadn't seen them play at the Mercer Arts Center. They showed up a good hour late.

GENE SIMMONS: The Dolls walked in with the glitter, big hair, and big shoes. As soon as they hit the stage Paul and I looked at each other and said, "Wow. They look incredible. They look like stars."

PAUL STANLEY: Man, they looked just great. They were dressed in the coolest Lurex, a fabric with metallic threads. Also, there was a real sense of camaraderie onstage. They had that vibe which made you feel, "I wish I could be a member of *that* club." That's what great bands have.

GENE SIMMONS: Then they started playing, and we turned to each other and said, "We'll kill 'em."

TOMMY RAMONE: KISS was nothing like the Dolls. This was the glam/glitter era. Everybody was wearing platform shoes, and some bands were wearing makeup, like the New York Dolls, Twisted Sister, and the Fast. If anything, in some of their earlier ads, KISS looked like they might have been inspired by the Fast. At the time I thought KISS's look was just a gimmick. I was more impressed by KISS's music and showmanship than their costumes and makeup.

EDDIE SOLAN: You couldn't compare KISS to anyone else. If you were a glitter band you'd be compared to the Dolls or the Brats. But KISS was so different. There was no category for them. Paul and I saw the Dolls together. Paul liked them and got inspired after seeing them.

PAUL STANLEY: The Dolls were the biggest band in New York and we wanted to be the biggest band in the world. I think they were scared shitless of us.

BOB "NITEBOB" CZAYKOWSKI (NEW YORK DOLLS SOUND ENGINEER): I remember Johnny Thunders of the Dolls saying, "Man, these guys are really huge, they're like football players!" The front three guys in KISS were all over six feet tall without the big boots, and most of the Dolls were little guys.

PAUL STANLEY: There was no way to compete with them visually. Early photos of KISS will attest to the fact that we looked like linebackers dressed in drag for a masquerade party. By the time we left that night after seeing the Dolls we said, "Let's get rid of all the color and let's go black and white." And then it became black and white and silver. Once we saw them we realized we weren't gonna beat the Dolls at their game so we had to find another way to look.

They were cool, they looked cool, and they had an amazing vibe, but they would never play with us in the beginning. I remember talking in the bathroom of the Diplomat to Sylvain, their rhythm player. I said, "We should do a show together." And he said, "We won't play with you—you'll kill us." They weren't stupid.

SYLVAIN SYLVAIN (RHYTHM GUITAR, NEW YORK DOLLS): The Dolls were an underground, subterranean, sleazoid rock band. America could bank on something like KISS but not on the Dolls. To

America, we were gay, we were drag queens. We were disgusting, we were diseased and drug addicts. In my own Brooklyn way I describe the Dolls as club kids. We were sexy and weren't trying to look like women. It was all done tongue in cheek and campy. We were just having a blast and living our lives to the fullest. This wasn't a job to us, it was our lives. Compared to KISS we were a lot more dangerous. Every idea they ever fuckin' got was from the Dolls. If you had two groups of people, strippers or club kids, they would become the Dolls, and if you had a bunch of truck drivers that toyed with makeup they'd be KISS. They were looking at it like, "Okay, I see what's going on today—makeup [*laughs*]. That's what the kids want and so let's give 'em a show." Our mentality of show business came from *The Little Rascals*, it was like, "We're bored. What are we gonna do? Why don't we put on a show?"

The Dolls were a reflection of what was going on and the industry didn't want to touch us. We were the first and helped break down that door and KISS were part of what followed. I love what KISS did and think it's incredible how huge they got but I have to say I missed the blues in them, which is something the Dolls had. But I've always respected that they were talented enough to change everything and be more successful than David Bowie, myself, Iggy Pop, and the Velvet Underground.

DAVID JOHANSEN (LEAD VOCALIST, NEW YORK DOLLS): What you've got to admire KISS for is staying power. They put on the same drag every night and come out in it, and boom, eventually the world caught up with them because they saw them so many times in pictures, TV, advertising, whatever. Finally they were immediately identifiable as KISS because who dresses like that?

GENE SIMMONS: It's easier to be a Stones-inspired band: you get your nice shag haircut, put on some scarves and your fancy clothes, and the girls will like you and the guys will think that you're just like an English band. And here we are completely turning our backs on that and going our way. We weren't convincing as androgynous guys. The Dolls were pivotal and important, but c'mon—they were a Rolling Stones–inspired band. There's David Johansen, a guy with big lips that looks like Mick Jagger, and Johnny Thunders, a guy who looks like Keith Richards. It was sort of an iconic model. They were the American Stones. There isn't much of a difference between the Dolls, Aerosmith, and the Stones. Don't get me wrong, they're all great bands, but KISS had a unique identity.

KEITH WEST: KISS sounded great. But a lot of other bands were also really good. We didn't expect KISS to be the breakout group. Everyone was banking on the Dolls to be as huge as Bowie, but it never happened.

BINKY PHILIPS: KISS were viewed as outsiders by the other New York bands. Most people thought the makeup was ridiculous. There was a certain clique of New York bands like Teenage Lust that circled around the Dolls like planets around the sun, and those bands were the cool ones. If you played the Mercer Arts Center, you were part of that clique, and KISS never played that venue. The fact that [KISS's] songs owed something to a band like Humble Pie, who were never considered hip or groovy in the new world of the New York Dolls, KISS's general stage act, and their sound made them outsiders. They didn't get much respect from the other bands. It was a very small scene. You had KISS, the Planets, the Dolls, and the Brats. That's like four of a total of fifteen bands on the scene. The problem with KISS is that they were significantly better musicians than most of the bands in New York. Probably the only band that had better musicianship was the Planets. I think a lot of people were grumpy about them because everybody hates anyone that's better than them.

GOTHAM CITY

On March 13, 1973, KISS entered New York City's Electric Lady Studios and recorded a five-song demo with producer Eddie Kramer of Jimi Hendrix and Led Zeppelin fame.

GENE SIMMONS: Our manager at the time, Lew Linet, also managed a singer/songwriter named Diana Markovich, who sounded like Laura Nyro, and J. F. Murphy and Free-Flowing Salt, who were signed to Elektra Records. They played at Max's Kansas City and did a version of the Leonard Bernstein *West Side Story* song [*sings* "When you're a Jet, you're a Jet all the way . . ."], which we thought was the corniest thing we'd ever heard except for the fact that Eddie Kramer was the engineer on that record. We said, "Yeah, Eddie Kramer, he's the guy who engineered Jimi Hendrix, and Humble Pie, Led Zeppelin—a lot of cool stuff." We thought that guy was cool. We later found out he engineered "Baby, You're a Rich Man" by the Beatles as well. He was highly respected at the time. Ron Johnsen had produced Wicked Lester and it was clear that our sensibilities were less pop and more aligned with the British rock bands like the Who, Cream, and the Stones, more in line with what Eddie Kramer was doing. We liked

Original tape box for the KISS demo produced by Eddie Kramer in March 1973
Courtesy of Eddie Solan

listening to pop music like Strawberry Alarm Clock and Three Dog Night—they had good songs but they didn't have that grand guitar English sound. Eddie Kramer understood that; he was from that school.

Paul and I had been owed money from doing sessions at Electric Lady—about a thousand between us. Ron said he could pay us in cash or that we could use the money to come in and do a demo.

PAUL STANLEY: We said, "Give us some time in the studio and get Eddie Kramer to produce our demo."

RON JOHNSEN: I called Eddie Kramer and said I had this wild, almost heavy metal–type of act that really needed some consideration. I told him I had lost their deal with CBS and I needed to find them a new record deal. Knowing of his work with Jimi Hendrix and Led Zeppelin, I told him he was the strongest hard rock engineer/ producer and that I knew he could do this.

EDDIE KRAMER (KISS PRODUCER): I remember saying to Ron, "Tell the band we're gonna do this the old-fashioned way. We're gonna do this as a four-track demo, no messing around. They play, and whatever comes out goes on that four-track demo. Drums, bass, guitar, vocals. We mix it and that's it." I felt if they were capable of playing and making it sound cool then I would capture it and it would stand up.

DAVE WITTMAN (KISS ENGINEER): The first KISS demo was done on four-track, the same way that the Beatles did *Sgt. Pepper*. It was done pretty much live except for the vocals and solos. The demo was good—they were really tight.

EDDIE KRAMER: We recorded it in Studio B, which is a tiny studio. It's a tribute to them as performers that even though they were fairly primitive musically in the beginning of their career they played in a fairly tight manner. KISS had obviously done their homework and rehearsed. We did it very quickly in a matter of a couple of days. Ace impressed me as a player. Right off the bat I could tell he was a pretty talented guitar player. Peter Criss's enthusiasm was tremendous. Gene had the concept and Paul was the rock star singer. My game plan was to capture the spirit of the band. It's like a time capsule in a way. You grab that moment when the energy is at its raw peak and try not to overembellish. You want to capture the vibe. And that's the trick. I was very fortunate I was able to do that with KISS on that demo.

PAUL STANLEY: We put down pretty much who we were. It was like a musical manifesto. The demo is much rawer than the first album. In many ways I don't think anything captured the magnitude of what we were doing just in terms of its sonic scope.

GENE SIMMONS: If you capture that innocence without thinking too much about it there's an honesty there. The first Beatles and Zeppelin albums were done really quickly, no real thinking, just get in and do it, and the first KISS demo was done like that too. It still stands up today. At the time it was the most advanced demo I'd ever heard. By some standards it sounded as good as the English records that were coming out at the time.

EDDIE KRAMER: To this day Gene, Paul, and Ace think it's one of the best things they've ever done. The demo has five songs—"Deuce," "Cold Gin," "Strutter," "Watching You," and "Black Diamond."

GENE /IMMON/: The Eddie Kramer demos of those songs are better than what turned up on the first KISS album. With all due respect, our producers Kenny Kerner and Richie Wise tried to calm it down a little bit. They'd come from producing Stories, Gladys Knight & the Pips. Some of the tempos were brought down. We were told the energy was a little too high for a record. Maybe that's why the demos have more energy—we just sort of went, "This is who we are."

EDDIE KRAMER: It was a very powerful demo. It was undeniable. With songs like "Strutter" and "Black Diamond," it was the central core material of KISS.

EDDIE /OLAN: I have the original reel-to-reel of those Eddie Kramer KISS demos. It was recorded live except for the vocals. The songs were cut dry—no reverb, no effects. On the tape box it says, "Boost right channel on ¼." I told the engineer I was the only one with a reel-to-reel tape recorder so I'd be the only one making cassettes for labels and press. He wrote that note on there to tell me how to handle the copies on my regular home reel-to-reel player.

GENE /IMMON/: That was our first KISS demo, which later got us the deal with Neil Bogart and Casablanca Records.

Following their first shows at Coventry and the Daisy, KISS ventured into the Big Apple on May 4, 1973, to play a Bleecker Street loft party, their first show in New York City.

RICK RIVET/: Paul used to come into the Music Box, a record store in Queens owned by Keith West of the Brats. He started talking to Keith and he said, "Yeah, I'm in a band and we wanna play in the city." Keith said, "Well, we have these loft parties every month, maybe you

Paul Stanley's hand-drawn Bleecker Street loft party ad,
June 1, 1973 KISS Catalog Ltd.

can do one of those with us as long as you don't mind going on first."
And Paul said, "We don't care, we just wanna play in the city."

PAUL STANLEY: We did that show with Wayne County and the Brats.
I think one of the guys in the Brats [David Leeds] worked there, and
after five o'clock it was closed. The loft was on the eighth floor and it
was a machine shop that the Brats were renting to rehearse.

EDDIE KRAMER: I went with Ron Johnsen and his wife, Joyce, to see
KISS perform at the loft on Bleecker Street.

PAUL STANLEY: Literally, there were stationary tables that workers
used during the day and those couldn't be moved for the show.

EDDIE SOLAN: There was no stage—it was just a big open space and they put a rope around where the band played. I brought my sound system and my lights made from Radio Shack parts.

PAUL STANLEY: We showed up in the afternoon and set up our gear. I was friends with Keith from the Brats but a couple of guys in the band had a chip on their shoulder. We said hello to them and a couple of the guys were a little standoffish until we played "Strutter" and "Deuce." After we played those songs we had new friends.

RICK RIVETS: At sound check KISS asked us, "We need to know exactly what time you want us to go on. We rented a hotel room and need to get dressed." So it's getting closer to showtime and all of a sudden the elevator opens and they come in and they're all in makeup and costumes, and our jaws dropped [*laughs*]. I thought, "Holy shit, what is this?" I remember telling our drummer, Sparky Donovan, "Shit, we gotta go on *after* them? We're dead. They're gonna blow us off the stage." And they did. They killed us.

DEE DEE RAMONE (BASS PLAYER, THE RAMONES): The first time I saw KISS was at a loft with Wayne County. Everybody was sort of afraid of them. KISS acted like a tough band that had already been touring for a while.

GENE SIMMONS: By the end of the first song, which was "Deuce," everybody just stopped and said, "What the fuck is this? This is not kid stuff." The difference between us and all the glitter bands in New York was we rehearsed seven days a week. If you put in enough time you're going to become very good.

RICK RIVETS: All of the Dolls came to the loft party. They didn't know what to make of KISS. There were also a lot of people there that you'd see in the back room at Max's; some Andy Warhol people were there too, like Jackie Curtis, Taylor Meade, and Eric Emerson.

GENE SIMMONS: The loft was packed because Wayne County and the Brats were becoming a force.

RICK RIVETS: It was brutally hot inside and we couldn't open the windows because tenants that lived in other lofts nearby were complaining to the police about the noise. You could hear it from three blocks away. KISS were super loud, they had two Marshall stacks and Ampeg SVT bass amps.

RON JOHNSEN: Eddie and Joyce ended up having to put cotton in their ears because it was so intensely loud. At one point I turned around and my wife collapsed—she had fainted from the heat. Eddie and I had to take her down the stairs to get her some air.

EDDIE SOLAN: Ace was playing a Les Paul copy made by this company called Univox. It was a cheap guitar but it was heavy. So I took the back off, routed out all the extra wood, and put a black piece of cardboard over it. He was more comfortable playing that. This was the main guitar he used in their club days. Back in those days he used to play at home through an old tape recorder. He'd plug the guitar into the tape recorder and it would overdrive really nicely. He just loved the sound of it.

Paul and Gene had brown matching custom-made bass and guitar, which was made by a Manhattan guitar maker named Charlie LoBue. Somebody stole Paul's guitar that night and he was devastated.

PAUL STANLEY: It was a shock but not a big setback. We had all guns blazing at the time. It didn't matter, your guitar was gone, buy another one and keep rockin'.

EDDIE SOLAN: Thankfully, he had another guitar with him, a black Gibson Les Paul.

RICK RIVETS: KISS wasn't the only outrageous act on the bill. Queen Elizabeth with Wayne County was also quite outrageous. During their show, Wayne got on top of a girl and put whipped cream on her and licked it off.

GENE SIMMONS: Wayne County's set ended with him putting his head in a toilet and eating what looked like shit.

PAUL STANLEY: We saw him do that and thought, hey, everybody's got to have a calling card if that's your gimmick [*laughs*].

RICK RIVETS: After seeing KISS perform at the loft party I felt these guys were gonna be really big. They were on their way.

Poster for library benefit, Palisades, New York,
May 26, 1973 Courtesy of Brad Estra

A little over three weeks later, KISS played what might be their strangest gig ever, a benefit for a local library in Palisades, New York, on May 26, 1973.

VIRGINIA BARRETT (LIBRARY EVENT CO-ORGANIZER): It was a fundraiser for the Palisades Free Library, which was a very tiny structure in town. Palisades, New York, is a small hamlet on the border of New Jersey and New York on the Hudson River. For years they'd put on a yearly fundraiser in either a country club or local restaurant. For that year's event we wanted to up the ante.

RON JOHNSEN: We had the function in the Lamont Hall at the Lamont-Doherty Geological Observatory, which was part of Columbia University. They did seismographic studies for earthquakes.

VIRGINIA BARRETT: Ron Johnsen was our neighbor and he worked at Electric Lady Studios. Ron had done some work with Blood,

Sweat & Tears and he was going to try to get them, but there was nothing definite.

PAUL STANLEY: Ron Johnsen, the guy who was producing us in Wicked Lester, lived near Snedens Landing, and asked us if we could do this fundraiser for the local library. Sneden's Landing is a very exclusive, quiet, and beautiful rustic area on the other side of the George Washington Bridge—about fifteen minutes from New York City but thousands of miles away. It was a very small, close-knit community, almost like a village unto itself, where a lot of well-known or well-to-do people lived.

JOYCE SACCO (RON JOHNSEN'S EX-WIFE): People who resided there included the famous theater producer and choreographer Jerome Robbins, Morley Safer and Mike Wallace from *60 Minutes*, and actresses Ellen Burstyn and Dixie Carter.

RON JOHNSEN: I booked the event through my neighbors, Bob and Virginia Barrett. Virginia was putting together this benefit and she knew I was involved in music. She asked Joyce, my wife at the time, if I could get a band to play for the affair, so I helped bring in two bands, the Pat Rebillot Quintet, who were a contemporary jazz band, and KISS.

VIRGINIA BARRETT: We constructed a tent behind the Lamont Hall overlooking the Hudson River, and KISS showed up in the afternoon to help set up chairs and tables. Then they went back to Ron Johnsen's house, which was located right on the Hudson River, to put on their makeup and costumes. As I recall, the Pat Rebillot Quintet went on first during cocktails and hors d'oeuvres.

PAT REBILLOT (PIANO, PAT REBILLOT QUINTET): That gig at the observatory was so much fun for us because we had total freedom. It was classy and relaxed. We were a five-piece group with a female vocalist. I loved to play for crowds that wanted to dance and I'd make up tunes on the spot. That night we performed standards in a jazz vein, songs like "You Do Something to Me" and "I Can't Get Started."

JOYCE SACCO: It was a very formal event. One of the neighbors, Joe Hyde, was a well-known chef and he provided dinner for the guests outside in the garden and we also held a raffle.

ROBERT BARRETT (LIBRARY BENEFIT ATTENDEE): Lamont Hall was a huge old mansion and the party ran through the entire house and outside in a big tent. The show was held in a large library within the building, and it was a beautiful room with floor-to-ceiling windows.

ANN TONETTI (LIBRARY BENEFIT CO-ORGANIZER): It was a warm night and all the big French doors were opened so guests outside could hear the music—and I'm sure across the Hudson River as well [*laughs*].

GENE SIMMONS: We looked forward to turning up the amps and doing what we did because it's not as much fun as playing for people who get it. We wanted to get a rise out of them.

LYN CHRISTOPHER: Before they got into their costumes and makeup, they were spending time at the party mingling with us. My sister Roseanne was dancing with Paul and I was dancing with Gene. Then they left to get ready for the show, and when they came out I pointed at Paul, who was now wearing makeup and a costume, and said nonchalantly to my sister, "That's the guy you were just dancing with." And she said with great surprise in her voice, "That's Paul?" She couldn't put it together in her mind; it was just too surreal [*laughs*].

VIRGINIA BARRETT: These people who'd helped us set up chairs and tables in jeans and T-shirts now all of a sudden appeared in these wild costumes and wearing makeup and looked spectacular. Most people were standing watching the show but there were a few tables set up close for the older folks to sit and watch. The band came on around 10:30, 11 p.m., and I remember Paul Stanley grabbed the microphone and yelled, "Okay baby, move your ass!" [*laughs*].

ROBERT BARRETT: It was a wild and unbelievable scene. People were astonished.

ANN TONETTI: I looked around and saw the shock on the faces of some of the older grande dames. They didn't know what to make of the band.

EDDIE SOLAN: After taking a look at KISS they thought the Martians had landed.

VIRGINIA BARRETT: I was standing next to the table with all the older people. One of them was Anne Tonetti Gugler, who was an elegant old lady in her late seventies. She looked at the spectacle in front of her and said with great delight, "Oh my!" It just set the tone and it was party time even for the over-eighties crowd [*laughs*].

GENE SIMMONS: I remember a couple of these old folks stood up on their seats.

ANN TONETTI: They got into it and some of them even got up and started dancing a little bit. They loved the outfits and the makeup and were amazed at their platform boots. For them it was like theater.

GENE SIMMONS: The crowd was nothing like a KISS crowd. They were old, but it was a hip crowd.

JOYCE SACCO: There were doctors, lawyers, authors, actors, architects, and people in the entertainment field.

ROBERT BARRETT: Morley Safer was there as a guest and he thought KISS were exciting. He told me he thought they were splendid.

VIRGINIA BARRETT: People were dancing like crazy and having a ball.

ANN TONETTI: Teenagers in the little village knew something was up, so many of them sneaked into the event. It was a big crowd, almost three hundred people. Prior to this event we'd have thirty or forty people show up, so this was an amazing occurrence. The band took breaks during their show and mingled with the crowd in their costumes [*laughs*].

RON JOHNSEN: The band had fun because it was so wild and extreme. Still, nobody knew who the heck this crazy band was. Their music was loud and abrasive and definitely not the appropriate kind of music for an event like this [*laughs*].

EDDIE SOLAN: The band did a set, and surprisingly, the people didn't freak out and run away. It was like a show to them, and most of them stayed for the whole set. It was a reaction we didn't quite expect.

PAT REBILLOT: Of course, my group and KISS had quite different styles but we were both accepted by the crowd. It didn't hurt that there was a lot of drinking going on—that might have made the crowd more amenable to the shock of when KISS came on [*laughs*].

ROBERT BARRETT: The party went on until all hours of the night.

VIRGINIA BARRETT: The library committee had promised the Lamont organization that we'd clean up after the event. So the next day we all returned at an unearthly early hour to clean up and what's funny is the band joined us picking up all the debris, which shows what a class act they are.

ANN TONETTI: After the cleanup, the band and many of the people on the committee went back to Ron Johnsen's house and played volleyball. Both KISS and the Pat Rebillot Quintet did the benefit for free. The event raised over $3,000, which at that time was a lot of money. We'd lose money every year on the library benefit and this was one of the few times we made money, which was delightful.

ROBERT BARRETT: It was touted as the best library party ever. There are old Rockland County residents that still talk about it, saying, "When are you gonna do another one like that?" [*laughs*].

PAUL STANLEY: For me the coolest thing about that library show was that the drummer in one of the other bands was Joe Butler from the Lovin' Spoonful. We never had one day of adversity or a setback that I didn't go through at that time thinking, "Boy, this will be something great to look back on." The belief was always that these will be great memories and part of the building blocks of what we were doing.

In July and August of 1973, KISS played to the biggest crowds they'd ever had at the Hotel Diplomat in New York City.

Hotel Diplomat

ABOVE, LEFT: Paul Stanley's hand-drawn ad for a KISS show at Hotel Diplomat, New York City, July 13, 1973. ABOVE AND LEFT: Vintage Hotel Diplomat postcard and Diplomat coaster. Courtesy of Brad Estra

PAUL STANLEY: We did the Diplomat shows to build a following and also to try and attract industry interest in the band.

BOBBY McADAMS: They played Coventry a bunch of times; not that many people came to see them there. They were much more successful at the Daisy and the Diplomat Hotel.

JON MONTGOMERY (LEAD VOCALIST, STREET PUNK): At one time the Diplomat was a world-famous hotel, but it had clearly seen better days when we played there.

BOBBY McADAMS: The Diplomat was a dump. It was located near Times Square, in an area teeming with drug addicts, adult bookstores, X-rated movie theaters, and hookers walking up and down the street.

BINKY PHILIPS: The Diplomat was located on Forty-third Street and was basically a flophouse—very run-down and sleazy, a notch above skid row. It was dilapidated and sad and filled with old people just waiting to die. I don't think many tourists rented rooms there. I think most of the rooms were old people living on some pathetic pension. There are still a few side streets off of Times Square where you see these little funky old hotels.

PAUL STANLEY: The Diplomat was a fully operational hotel. They also had long-term housing there. It was scary in the sense that there were some pretty forbidding people in there. They had a few ballrooms. One up on the second floor was called the Crystal Room. Those ballrooms could be rented out for functions, for parties, weddings, whatever. The Diplomat was the place the Dolls had graduated to after playing Mercer Arts Center.

BINKY PHILIPS: Inside the Crystal Room everything was dark red, dark maroon. The columns had mirrors on them. It had a low ceiling for a ballroom.

SHAYNE HARRIS: The Diplomat was in shambles. The stage was in bad shape because of the rotted floors. Because of the Diplomat's horrific condition, people were able to rent out the Crystal Room for cheap. Before the show started, Peter and I were in the men's room. We were standing at the latrine and a goddamn rat ran behind us and the thing was the size of a small cat.

GENE SIMMONS: Paul and I knew about the Diplomat Hotel from back when we went to see the Dolls play there. We set up the show at the Diplomat because we knew we had to get to the next step. We needed a manager and a record label.

PAUL STANLEY: We put on shows at the Diplomat because clubs wouldn't hire us. You couldn't get a gig unless you were playing three or four sets a night of covers. In a club situation we would tell them we'd do two sets and they'll probably be the same set [*laughs*]. The shows at the Diplomat were really pretty packed. We would put these shows together without the thought of headlining. What we were trying to do was grab the audiences that these other bands had, like the Dolls and the Brats. So we'd get bands that were better known than us. Putting other bands on the bill wasn't us being nice—we needed bands that could draw people.

KEITH WEST: The Brats were friends with KISS and we used to play together a lot. It's funny but at the beginning KISS couldn't get proper gigs in New York City. We booked our own opening acts and had KISS play with us at the Hotel Diplomat.

BOBBY McADAMS: When KISS played the Hotel Diplomat, the Brats headlined, KISS was the middle act, and the Planets opened. The band made up posters and put them up all around town. Word of mouth spread like wildfire.

BINKY PHILIPS: Paul called me up and said, "Look, we're gonna rent the Crystal Room at the Diplomat with the Brats, do you want to be on the bill?" The Dolls had already played both a Valentine's Day show at the Diplomat and a St. Patrick's Day show. Wherever the New York Dolls played instantly became a legitimate venue. The original schedule was KISS as the headliner, the Brats were in the middle, and my band, the Planets, were the opening act. A couple of weeks before the gig, Keith West, the lead singer for the Brats, got very huffy and insisted that they were the best-known band on the bill, which was questionable, and they had to go on last. It was either Paul or Ace who had to at the last minute take a razor blade and cut the ad that they did for the *Village Voice* and put KISS in the middle and the Brats on top.

GENE SIMMONS: I was working during the day at the Puerto Rican Interagency Council and because I had access to stamps and postage, I physically put together the bio kit and invited people to our show.

Original tickets for KISS's two Hotel Diplomat shows KISS Catalog Ltd.

I think I came up with the term "heavy metal masters." I got the year-end issues of *Record World*, *Billboard*, and *Cashbox*, which listed every music industry figure, record company, and manager, and did a mass mailing. Paul and I designed the package and we included a ticket for our show at the Diplomat. Paul and Peter stayed up the night before the show and put glue in the design of the KISS logo on black T-shirts and poured glitter on them. They gave those T-shirts to Peter's sisters and some of their friends. So when industry people showed up they saw a packed house, KISS onstage, and girls in KISS T-shirts.

BOBBY McADAMS: Inside the hotel it was a huge room, kind of like a high school auditorium. I collected money at the door, and the place was completely packed.

GENE SIMMONS: We were keeping track of the industry people who came in because while they didn't have to pay to get in, they had to sign their name at the door when they presented their ticket. We only had a few industry people come down. The genius of the system was we didn't even mention any of the other bands on the bill when in point of fact they were the ones drawing the crowd because KISS was unknown in New York.

BINKY PHILIPS: KISS didn't sound dramatically better than when I saw them in the loft. But they were powerful. The arrangements were very simple and uncluttered, which gave them power. I remember being totally hooked on the guitar riff for "Deuce"—I just loved it. As for the makeup, except for Paul, these guys weren't really that good-looking so I thought maybe it was smart that they were wearing makeup. I also vividly remember while they were playing thinking to myself, with Alice Cooper retiring there's a hole in the market for this kind of theatrical presentation. There was nothing to indicate that these guys were gonna be gigantic, but people liked them.

Paul and Ace rock the house at Hotel Diplomat, New York City, July 13, 1973 Gavino Abaya III

RIK FOX: Seeing KISS play at the Hotel Diplomat was like being in *Alice in Wonderland*. You'd walk through the crowd and see all these different colorful characters. For me, as a kid in high school, it was all new and exciting, almost like I'd opened a door and fell through a hole and was being exposed to this scene I never realized existed.

I remember coming to the show with my then girlfriend Joanne, Peter Criss's sister, Peter's younger sister Donna, and several other kids from the neighborhood. I went out and bought a bag of balloons and inflated each one, drew the KISS logo and their faces on the balloon, and then deflated them and carefully placed them within a box. We commandeered the entire front row and just before KISS came on I handed out the balloons and we blew them up. We carefully held them in our arms like one would hold a child, taking care not to smear the ink. When the lights came up and KISS came

Gene and Peter in performance at Hotel Diplomat, New York City, July 13, 1973 Gavino Abaya III

Gene, Ace, and Paul, Hotel Diplomat, New York City, July 13, 1973 Gavino Abaya III

onstage, they found themselves inundated by hundreds of balloons with their logo and faces. You had to see the look of surprise and shock on their faces. They were in total awe of this unexpected fusillade of KISS publicity. It was like a shower of KISS balloons. Gene began to playfully stomp on the balloons while Paul kicked as many as he could into the crowd like soccer balls. This stunt gave their show that much more of a wow factor. Going from watching KISS in rehearsals and early performances at Coventry to seeing them onstage with the fully fleshed-out makeup and rudimentary costumes completely blew my mind—the energy was amped up exponentially.

BINKY PHILIPS: Gene stood out. He was already doing a milder version of the monster, sticking out his tongue, shaking his head like a lizard, and stomping around.

GENE SIMMONS: I have no idea how and why I started moving onstage the way I did except my references were not rock and roll. Instead they were influenced by the stop-motion animator Ray Harryhausen. He's the same guy who did *Mighty Joe Young, Son of Kong*, and *Jason and the Argonauts*. There was a movie called *20 Million Miles to Earth*, which was about an aircraft that comes back from Mars with an egg. Out of the egg pops a Martian called an Ymir. It was a serpentine creature the size of King Kong with an awkward gait that threw its weight from one side to the next because it wasn't sure about the gravity of the Earth. The weird way it moved always fascinated me. I remember studying the way it walked and the way its legs kept picking up high. When I walked on stage I was doing the Ymir from *20 Million Miles to Earth*. I realized I couldn't copy the movements of Mick Jagger or the Beatles because I didn't have a little boy's body, but I could be a monster.

EDDIE KRAMER: It was very off-the-wall stuff, wearing makeup and high boots. For some people it was revolting but to me it was very interesting because nobody was doing the full makeup trip. They had a lot to learn. They weren't great musicians. However, they did have a great stage act and they were very organized.

BINKY PHILIPS: When I first saw them in the kabuki stage makeup at the Hotel Diplomat they reminded me of a more macho, more cartoon version of the Hello People, a New York band produced by Todd Rundgren. They wore whiteface although their look was more like the classic Marcel Marceau mime look.

KEITH WEST: The minute I first saw KISS play I thought they sounded fantastic. Their chords were so crisp and heavy. They had a really good sound. They were very tight and well-rehearsed and had good anthem songs. If you had good songs you'd have longevity.

GENE SIMMONS: Our equipment was A-level standard and we had a much better sound than the other bands. We had a complete look so we were much more advanced than the other bands.

RICK RIVETS: When I first walked into the Diplomat that night

I said, "Holy shit, this place is packed." But my excitement at the turnout changed later in the night because after KISS played most of the crowd left. And when the Brats went on the place was pretty empty.

BINKY PHILIPS: At the end of the night on July 13, 1973, once all the glam kids and girlfriends had gone, all three bands were loading out of the Hotel Diplomat. Marshall stacks and drum cases were strewn around the sidewalk of West Forty-third Street waiting to be loaded into rented vans. The two guys who were sort of assigned to watch the equipment outside while other band members brought the rest of the gear down from the ballroom were me and Peter Criss. While we weren't really pals, he, of course, knew me from my connection to Paul and Gene. As we stood outside the hotel at midnight, Peter turned to me and confessed that he really, really hoped something would happen with this new band he was in. "Man, I have to make it soon," and then he lowered his voice, "I'm twenty-eight." I was stunned. Holy crap—twenty-eight? I had turned twenty a few months earlier and could barely fathom being that old.

GAVINO ABAYA III (CONCERT ATTENDEE, HOTEL DIPLOMAT): I was a fifteen-year-old kid from the Philippines. We moved to America in 1972. I'd become friendly with Keith West of the Brats who ran the Music Box record store. He said, "Bojie,"—which was my nickname—"we're playing a show at the Diplomat Hotel. Why don't you come see us?" I decided to go, and my dad drove me there. It turned out to be my first rock concert. I stood right in front of the stage when KISS performed. It was love at first hearing. The songs were really catchy and their image was totally new and exciting. Keith took me backstage to meet the band. It was a crowded scene backstage but the band was really friendly. I asked Ace if he thought KISS would play a show in the Philippines and he answered in that funny squeaky voice of his, "I don't know, it's so hot over there our makeup might melt before we even get onstage" [*laughs*]. It's just amazing to me that I was present at such an historic show in the band's career and witnessed a group that have since gone on to become icons.

Less than two months after the band's first shows at the Diplomat Hotel I ran into Paul Stanley at the Music Box, a record store in Queens. I told him, "You guys were great and in fact I took some photos that night on a little Instamatic camera." He got excited and said, "Really? Can I get some copies?" I told him I had copies of them at home and if he wanted to drop by some time I could give them to him. He said, "Why don't I drop you off when you're ready?" So he drove me home and I ran in and brought him the photos. He said, "Oh wow, these are great!" At that time so early in their career no one was taking many photos of them so he was really excited. A year or two later I ran into Paul at a Brats show and he remembered me and called me "Mr. Music Box" [*laughs*].

By the early seventies, Alice Cooper was being hailed as the king of shock rock. Racking up a flurry of hit albums (Love It to Death, Killer, *and* Billion Dollar Babies) *and smash singles like "School's Out," "I'm Eighteen," "No More Mr. Nice Guy," and "Elected," his stage shows were legendary spectacles combining horror tropes—guillotines, slithering boa constrictors, and a giant cyclops—with a thunderous metallic rock power. Having performed their first gig less than six months earlier, Paul, Ace, and Peter checked out the reigning competition on June 3, 1973, attending a sold-out Alice Cooper show at Madison Square Garden.*

EDDIE SOLAN: Not long after a Bleecker Street loft party show, I treated the band to tickets to see Alice Cooper at Madison Square Garden [in June 1973]. They were starting to be compared to Alice

Cooper and we wanted them to see a professional concert with theatrics. They dressed up like rock stars and went as a band. People looked at them and were wondering, "Who are these guys? They must be somebody." Peter Criss and I were drinking scotch in a flask and they caught Peter trying to sneak in the flask and confiscated it. But I was able to sneak mine in.

PETER CRISS: I sat in the back and Paul and Ace literally ran all the way down the stairs to be right up in front of the stage. That's how impressed they were. I'll never forget it.

PAUL STANLEY: Seeing that show was stunning. I still remember him walking down these stairs when the show began with "Hello Hooray" and it was godlike. The crowd was just going crazy. Much like other things I saw that were great, I wanted to be that guy. What Alice was doing was perfect for him and I wanted to do my version of that.

GENE SIMMONS: I didn't go to the show; I had to work. But the guys reported back and told me, "You've gotta see this show." It was all about the presentation and what you saw with your eyes.

PETER CRISS: We got back to our loft that night and we played and said, "Wait a minute, what if there was four Alice Coopers?" We thought the idea was pretty hot. We did some soul-searching and became the characters we are today.

BOB EZRIN (PRODUCER, DESTROYER, MUSIC FROM "THE ELDER," AND REVENGE): Alice was the forerunner of over-the-top theatrical rock, and KISS were inspired by his success. Having worked with both Alice Cooper and KISS, I don't think KISS was thinking about filling a hole that Alice Cooper left. They looked at Alice Cooper and went, "Theatrical rock, holy moly! We can do that and we can do it better." KISS always thought of themselves as the best band in the world.

EDDIE SOLAN: Seeing Alice onstage performing this very theatrical show gave them the reassurance that they could pull this off. And they were right. Four short years later KISS would be headlining the Garden.

10

ROCK STEADY

On August 10, 1973, veteran TV director Bill Aucoin walked into the Crystal Room at the Hotel Diplomat, where he saw KISS perform for the very first time. Fellow New York bands Luger and Street Punk were also on the bill.

IVAN KRAL (GUITAR, LUGER): We played the same clubs in Queens as KISS. I saw them a few times at Coventry, and that's how my band, Luger, became friends with them. I remember that Diplomat show as being very important for them. They knew it would be the biggest crowd they'd ever played in front of and they told me that important industry people would be there.

BILL AUCOIN: KISS was sending me notes every week saying, "Would you come to see us?" and there would be a hand-painted pass to the Diplomat Hotel.

GENE SIMMONS: I was the one who sent him the promo package with the bio and invitation to the Hotel Diplomat show. I wanted somebody who wasn't just going to manage the band but somebody who had a point of view who understood visuals, television, and promotion.

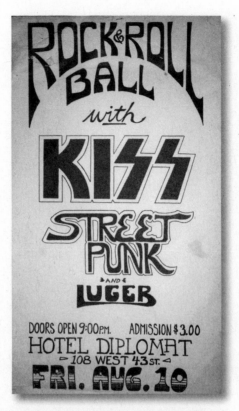

Paul Stanley's hand-drawn poster for the band's August 10,
1973, show at Hotel Diplomat KISS Catalog Ltd.

PETER CRISS: Bill came down and sat between my two sisters [Joanne and Donna], which was perfect, and they were going, "Oh, they're going to be great!"

ANNEMARIE HUGHES: I was sitting up front with Joanne and Donna and we were wearing our homemade KISS T-shirts. I told him, "Wait until you see them, you're not gonna believe it, they're just incredible." Once they came on we were screaming and going crazy. That definitely got his attention.

BILL AUCOIN: When I first saw KISS at the Hotel Diplomat in 1973 they didn't have much of a show. They had the red beacons, a couple of amps. They were wearing black jeans—no one could afford

Gene, Hotel Diplomat, New York City, August 10, 1973 Dina Regine/dinareginephotography.com

leather. The show was just a regular rock-and-roll show except they had spontaneity. They wanted to do something different and they wanted it very badly. That kind of devotion is worth more than anything. It's so special, and you start picking up on it. I saw that magic in them.

JON MONTGOMERY (LEAD VOCALIST, STREET PUNK): We shared the bill with KISS the second time they played the Hotel Diplomat. We knew Gene and Paul, and they liked the band. They did their research to see what New York bands were drawing and whose music was closer to their style. All of my songs had this huge anthemic chorus. In fact, KISS later purchased the publishing for one of my Street Punk songs, "The Master of Flash," but they never recorded it. So KISS asked Street Punk to appear with them at the Hotel Diplomat because we could draw between two hundred to three hundred people in New York City and they were basically unknown in the city; they were more of a Queens/Coventry band.

DONNIE NOSSOV (BASSIST, STREET PUNK): I remember they showed up at the Diplomat in full KISS drag. Even though they were listed as the headliner they matter-of-factly said, "We're going on second." They wanted the 10 p.m. slot so they could have the biggest audience. Plus they didn't want the suits, especially Bill Aucoin, to wait around through two bands to see them.

DINA REGINE (FRIEND AND PHOTOGRAPHER): Since the early seventies I'd been shooting big bands like Led Zeppelin and the Rolling Stones, but I wasn't shooting many local bands. KISS were friends of mine and that's why I brought my camera to their show at the Diplomat. They banded together to put on a rock-and-roll ball. It wasn't like going to a concert or a club. It was really a creative way to do it because no other bands were doing that sort of thing. Compared to other local New York bands, KISS in its infancy was really professional and organized. Everybody else played and daydreamed, but [KISS] had a plan and it worked. The band was fearless back then. I had a gut feeling that they were gonna make it; I knew it that night.

SHAYNE HARRIS: Their performance was tremendous. I looked at Ivan [Kral] and said, "Here we are a glitter band and look at them!" They were so explosive and really took command of the stage, letting you know in no uncertain terms, "This is our show." They floored everybody.

DONNIE NOSSOV: KISS brought the house down. No one had seen anything like that before. As it turns out, after they were done, 80 percent of the audience left and we did our show to an almost empty

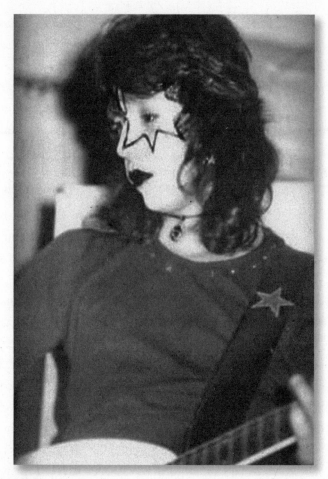

Ace, Hotel Diplomat, New York City, August 10, 1973 Dina Regine/dinareginephotography.com

Crystal Room. I recently located a tape of our Diplomat performance and you can tell that there was hardly anyone left in the audience after KISS's show.

JON MONTGOMERY: Their performance didn't knock me out personally but I recognized their appeal right away and knew that the young kids would go for the painted faces. All young musicians are attracted to music in its simplest form and KISS was able to deliver something accessible to the teenage masses. It was much easier for garage bands to learn how to play a KISS song like "Strutter" or

"Deuce" than a Led Zeppelin song. And they had a plan for success. They were determined to do it at any cost, and they got there.

IVAN KRAL: Many of the New York bands would mock KISS and say they were horrible, and it was a snobbery that I didn't appreciate. Like Alice Cooper, the New York Dolls, and Iggy Pop, KISS was about having a good time, and nothing deeper. They were also very serious and committed. They knew something that I didn't know as far as how to market themselves.

DONNIE NOSSOV: There was a little bit of indifference about KISS among the New York bands. Those of us who took ourselves way too seriously thought they were a joke and dismissed them as a cartoon. I guess the joke was on us. Little did we know that that cartoon would work on such a massive scale.

JON MONTGOMERY: We respected their ambition more than the music itself. I give them all the credit in the world for their success and I'm proud to say that they came out of our city.

SYLVAIN SYLVAIN: [The New York Dolls] used to play the Hotel Diplomat all the time, way before KISS. I remember the first time I saw KISS playing there—Peter Criss was sitting down with his mother in the back room and she was going, "Peter, why this? This is weird." He was going, "No, no, Ma, this is great! The New York Dolls did it. This is like the Dolls in a way. You saw how popular they got."

GENE SIMMONS: Eddie Kramer came down, Ron Johnsen, CBS Records, and Rich Totoian from Windfall Records, who had Mountain.

RICH TOTOIAN (NATIONAL PROMOTION DIRECTOR, WINDFALL RECORDS): During the early seventies, when glitter bands were fading and theatrical bands were taking the stage, I was working at Windfall Music with Bud Prager, Gary Kurfirst, and Felix Pappalardi, who had produced albums by Cream and Mountain. Every night we would get a pile of demo tapes, listen to the tapes, and discuss them. I came across a tape that really impressed me. This band was hungry to get signed with my company and be produced by Felix Pappalardi.

They felt he would be a great producer for them. The band shopped their music around to the major labels and they invited Don Ellis of Epic Records to come see them play. I was also invited to see them and brought Gary Kurfirst. Gary called me the next day and asked me what I thought. I told them we should sign them immediately, [that their] music was incredible. The stage makeup the band wore was just a hint of what would come later, taking the theatrical band show to a whole new level.

Gary was lukewarm on them and he couldn't figure out what market to fit them into and wanted to pass. I had two or three meetings with the band in my office at Windfall. They gave me an acetate record in hopes it would still meet the ears of Bud and Felix. As fate would have it, they never heard it and had to go on Gary's word. Without Felix's vote Windfall Music would end up passing on the deal. Whenever I see Paul Stanley, he always thanks me for my interest and passion for their music and how badly I wanted to sign them.

PETER CRISS: We were a young band really fucking becoming something. I wish people could have seen what it was like then because it was like the roots of metal. Everybody was starting to sprout from New York. The New York scene was very hot.

EDDIE SOLAN: For the second Diplomat show, we had to move a step ahead with stage presentation. I talked Gene and Paul into selling their two PA speakers. We sold them and they gave me the money. In the Lafayette Radio Electronics store where I worked in Scarsdale, New York, there was a warehouse in the back and I spent a week building four Altec Lansing speakers for the band. They looked imposing because they were big and I painted them black. Paul and Gene drove up to Scarsdale in a bread truck. We loaded up the speakers and drove to the Diplomat show. Now we had a PA system that looked professional.

Eddie Kramer came to the show and he came up to me at the mixing board and said, "We gotta hear the snare drum more and bring up the kick drum." He told me, "Take a microphone and put it on the snare drum," so we did that right in the middle of the set.

I was out in the audience doing the sound and this mustachioed guy came up to me at the soundboard and told me he was Bill Aucoin. He said, "These guys knocked me out, I want to meet them." I took him backstage after the set and introduced him to the band. He told them, "I love what you guys do. I'm new at this too but give me a month to make things happen." With his TV background, he proved to be the perfect manager for the band. He was so enthusiastic about them. That's what everybody was impressed with. Also, their manager at the time, Lew Linet, was losing interest in them because he had another band he was working with called J.F. Murphy & Salt.

LEW LINET: In that period I had to make a decision. I just didn't care for that genre of music. I told them, "With all due respect, I think you need a manager who is committed to what you do." They would tell me, "Lew, mark our words, we are going to be the biggest band in America." I said that I hoped it was true but I didn't think they'd become that big because what they did was derivative of bands like the Who. But they did it. Gene and Paul are the epitome of American entrepreneurial spirit. They are the epitome of drive, commitment, and persistence.

GENE SIMMONS: When we came off the stage after our Diplomat performance, Bill cornered me. I still had my makeup on. As soon as I saw him, he invited me over to talk to him. He wasn't a manager, he was a director and producer of a TV show called *Flipside*. I remember specifically watching that show and seeing the end credits and writing his name down.

At that point KISS were looking to get on board with anyone with industry clout, and Simmons admired Bill's television work, which also appealed to his sense of theatricality.

GENE SIMMONS: While [Bill Aucoin] was talking to me I motioned for a girl who I had been with the night before to come over. She was very well endowed and dressed very sexy and I had her sit on my lap. While Bill and I were talking, I was bouncing her on my knee, to kind of demonstrate that we were already on our way—we have our fan base, the girls love us, and we're happening. So he thought, "My God, something's going on!" He was very enticed by the whole notion and he was the one who pitched to manage us. Bill said, "This is quite something. I'd like you to come up and meet me at my office."

BILL AUCOIN: The guy who came with me to see the Diplomat show thought I was out of my mind. He said, "You've flipped; you're not going to do this." People thought I was an idiot for wanting to manage KISS. What I liked about them in the first place was that wonderful determination. They wanted to do something different and they wanted it very badly. That kind of devotion is worth more than anything. Aside from being such fantastically exciting musicians,

BILL AUCOIN SUITE 805 75 EAST 55 STREET NEW YORK NY 10022 TEL 212 752 7455

Bill Aucoin's Direction Plus business card Courtesy of Brad Estra they were super showmen. The energy they put out rocked the room whenever they played.

PAUL STANLEY: Right after the show Bill gave Gene his card. I couldn't figure out who Bill was. I'd heard of his TV show, *Flipside*, and thought it was a *16* magazine–type of teeny-bopper show. Then Gene and I went up and met with Bill at his office. He told us, "If you guys don't want to be the biggest band in the world I don't wanna get involved." And that's interesting coming from a guy who wasn't a manager. But then again we weren't a normal band. So it made sense that we'd be working with a guy who had no real history or experience as a manager.

GENE SIMMONS: Bill said, "If I can't get you a deal in thirty days, then I won't be your manager." Paul and I left the office and discussed it. And we decided to give him a chance.

Certain bands seem to have an added advantage if the manager is gay. The Beatles had Brian Epstein, the Who had Kit Lambert, and we had Bill Aucoin. And it has to do with flamboyance: the more open you are emotionally, visually, and conceptually to the idea of flamboyance and going over the top visually onstage, the better it is for you if that's intrinsically who and what you are. And KISS was over the top, flamboyant, and visual onstage.

PAUL STANLEY: Thinking theatrically, Bill obviously saw this on levels that some people couldn't or didn't.

GENE SIMMONS: Bill was different. He had a lot of style and was very well spoken and had a visual sense, and we immediately connected. We liked him immensely.

PAUL STANLEY: Bill was very much about presentation. He dressed impeccably. He was fastidious about the way that he looked, so much so that it was very obvious to me that he wasn't heterosexual. He wasn't effeminate, he was just so perfect. Perfectly groomed, perfectly dressed.

GENE SIMMONS: Bill's sexuality actually added something to the band. Bill's close friend, business-wise and socially, was Sean Delaney, who also was gay. He was our first road manager. Sean's sexuality also contributed greatly to the band because he would point out what worked onstage and what didn't.

PAUL STANLEY: Bill brought Sean in and he was another important piece of the puzzle in the beginning. I remember being in an apartment on Eleventh Street with the whole band dyeing our hair blue-black in the bathtub. That was Sean's idea. He was dyeing our hair blue-black like Superman. Sean had great ideas.

SEAN DELANEY (KISS ROAD MANAGER/CHOREOGRAPHER): In the beginning, I dyed everyone's hair blue-black just to put everybody on an equal level, so no matter where they went, they were connected.

GENE SIMMONS: It gave us a uniformity of look. In fact we had to force Ace and Peter to dye their hair blue-black like ours. Bands like the Beatles and the Temptations looked like they came from the same mother. They could never be in another band. They wore the same hairstyles and the same suits so you knew they were in the same band, and that's what we tried to do with KISS.

PAUL STANLEY: Once in rehearsal Sean saw us swaying together, doing that rocking back and forth move, which is now a signature part of our shows. We did it impromptu, just spur of the moment. After the song was done Sean said, "That move you did, you have to do that in your show." We were like, "We're not gonna do choreography. What are we, Paul Revere & the Raiders?" And he said, "No, it's really cool, you've gotta do it." And he was right. Sean had very good ideas.

GENE SIMMONS: Whatever came naturally to us he'd point out and we'd wind up doing it consciously. I used to raise my one index finger in the air onstage and he said, "You're too big and too strong to use one finger." He said, "You should use fists or full hands." Both Bill and Sean contributed immensely to the concept that became KISS.

Like the Beatles' manager, Brian Epstein, Bill Aucoin was a creative visionary who inspired KISS to think BIG.

PETER CRISS: I knew Bill had something. He had energy and he had a great eye for art and for what was right and wrong. He was a force. He was very bright and had a great way around people.

PAUL STANLEY: In the beginning Bill was very much a fifth member of the band in more ways than I can possibly emphasize. He really was a partner and also somebody to bounce ideas off of and get ideas from. He was a father figure to us, a mentor and a mirror. And he was the overall leader. We couldn't have done it without him.

Sharing the band's fierce determination to make it, Bill Aucoin systematically dismantled every roadblock that lay in front of them. With his background in television, Aucoin intuitively understood the explosive potential of spectacular visuals colliding with tight, exciting rock and roll; it was he who transformed the four ordinary New York City musicians into international superstars.

BILL AUCOIN: I was always interested in television. When I was eight years old I built a little television studio in my home out of cardboard boxes and cans. I also got involved in electronics and built a radio station when I was fourteen—illegally of course. We used to broadcast the games for my junior and senior high school. That ran for three years. We started getting sponsors and doing dances and everything else.

One day I was in a class in junior high school and I got a call to go to the principal's office. I went in there and the FCC [Federal Communications Commission] was there. They looked at me and went, "Oh, no!" [*laughs*]. I think they really wanted this to be a big bust. They went to all the advertisers and threatened to put my dad into jail. We got past that and then a radio station gave me my own show, which was called *Teenage Hop*, on WEIM in Fishbury, Massachusetts.

I went to college in Boston at Northeastern University and knew I wanted to go into television. I remember going to WGBH, the top public broadcasting educational network, and begged for a job. I told them I'd work for free and they hired me. My first job was sweeping the studios and driving a scenery truck. They finally allowed me to work one of the cameras and liked my work. From there I moved from floor manager to assistant director to director to producer. Later I worked for Teletape Productions and worked on some PBS specials in New York, including some Barbra Streisand shows. Then I got a job on a TV show called *Supermarket Sweep*. After that I began directing commercials but I was really antsy to work on television shows. In 1968 I came up with a late-night show called *Saturday Night at the Movement*, which was the precursor to *Saturday Night Live*. But I couldn't get it off the ground because people just wouldn't go for late-night television. Basically, after *The Tonight Show* everything on TV closed down.

Then in the early seventies I came up with a show called *Flipside*. The idea for *Flipside* came out of what I learned doing the pilot for *Saturday Night at the Movement*. Most artists hated doing television because it has lousy sound and they always came across terribly. I came up with the idea of doing shows at recording studios where the artists did their albums. Along with the artists you'd see the producers and engineers in action, along with record company presidents. So you'd meet these different people every week. We did shows with Stevie Wonder, John Lennon, Yoko Ono, the Raspberries, Judy Collins, and Seals & Crofts. Back in '68, '69, Joyce Biawitz became my partner in a company called Direction Plus.

JOYCE BOGART-TRABULU∫ (KI∫∫ COMANAGER): Direction Plus was an advertising company and we did commercials and television pilots. [*Authors' note: While comanaging KISS, Joyce went by the last name of Biawitz. She later married Casablanca Records founder Neil Bogart. After his death, Joyce Bogart would go on to marry a man named Joshua Trabulus. Throughout the text, when she is quoted she is referred to by the last name of Bogart-Trabulus.*]

BILL AUCOIN: More than commercials, Joyce and I always believed in videos for rock-and-roll artists. Neil Bogart liked the idea and

Bill Aucoin and Joyce Biawitz, KISS's future comanagers, early 1970s
Courtesy of Joyce Bogart-Trabulus

gave us some money to do videos for some of his acts on Buddah Records, like Charlie Daniels and Gladys Knight & the Pips.

JOYCE BOGART-TRABULUS: Nobody was doing this back then. Neil was always thinking ahead. He foresaw MTV.

BILL AUCOIN: Joyce was really bright and I loved her. I said, "Why don't we start working together in management?"

JOYCE BOGART-TRABULUS: When Bill and I started working with KISS we opened a management company called Rock Steady. Bill said to me, "We need a company name that's respected by the banks." One of my favorite songs was "Rock Steady" by Aretha Franklin, so I said to Bill, "Let's use the name 'Rock Steady'—it's stable and says to the music acts, 'This is where we're at.'"

BILL AUCOIN: Because of my background in television, I always believed that a visual band could make it big. That band turned out to be KISS. I like things that are bigger than life. I always think if you see things in your mind's eye then you go for it. My idea of management is you don't try to get an act to do what you want. What you do is get to know an act, see what's inside of them, and you take something that's special and embellish it and give it back to the act. With KISS we did a lot of crazy things and got away with them about 80 percent of the time. We were really lucky. We got away with an awful lot.

PAUL STANLEY: We did what Bill told us. Fairly early on in the band's career we were supposed to do an in-store when we were on tour and we decided we weren't gonna do it. Bill came walking into the hotel room where we were supposed to be getting ready and we told him, "We're not doing it." And he really put us in our place. We wouldn't take it from anybody other than him. He said, "You guys think you're too big for this and you think you've made it? But you're not even in the semifinals, and you'll be forgotten tomorrow." We all just kind of gulped [*laughs*] and shook our heads and silently put on our makeup and did the in-store. And Bill was right. I spoke to Bill every day back then. He was the driving force of the band.

CAROL ROSS (DIRECTOR OF THE MUSIC DIVISION, ROGERS & COWAN): Bill came from a theatrical background and saw the band as a theatrical experience. No other rock band was doing that. Alice Cooper was one person in makeup. These were four larger-than-life characters. Bill was so futuristic in his thinking.

MARK RAVITZ (STAGE DESIGNER): I always thought Bill was an alchemist; he could turn shit into gold.

BILL AUCOIN: There were two reasons why I got involved with KISS: being a hard rock band and being into theatrics. Alice was really, in my mind, peaking. He was at the top of the ladder, and I knew Shep [Gordon, Alice Cooper's manager] wanted to take him off the road to become an actor. Now that meant Alice had built up that audience and no one was really out there to fulfill their needs. I don't think they wanted another Alice Cooper, but they wanted more of that showmanship. But beyond that, there was another reason. Hard rock in my mind today has the strongest fans. They don't go from band to band—they really decide, "This is my group, this is my music." That's important when you're developing an artist. And I found when I investigated that probably the groups who sold the most music around the world were the hard rock bands.

KENNY KERNER (COPRODUCER, KISS): Bill was one of the only managers that I've ever known who was really artist-oriented. If Gene and Paul came to him and said, "We have this idea for a big live show that no one's ever done before. We want the drums to levitate and move out into the audience," Bill would just laugh and [say], "Let's find out if we can do it." He never said no. He had a vision, and he wanted KISS to be the biggest band in the world. He always encouraged Gene and Paul to come up with new ideas to make the band more spectacular and more special. He totally thought out of the box. Bill brought a belief to the band that against all odds you could succeed.

PETER CRISS: He had the belief that we could do it and that nothing could stop us. He took our self-esteem as high as it could go.

JOYCE BOGART-TRABULUS: They had a concept and vision, and we loved vision. KISS understood that people wanted to go and see a concert that was fun and [that] the audience wanted to be part of it and [see] fantasies . . . acted out onstage.

BILL AUCOIN: I don't think they expected I would move so quickly. I first met them in August, got them a record deal in September, signed with them in October [October 15, 1973], they recorded an album in November, and by December the first KISS album was finished.

With Bill and Joyce onboard as managers, things began to fall into place.

BINKY PHILIPS: Paul called me and told me they'd signed with this new manager. He said, "We haven't even signed papers with him and he's already got us a record deal with Neil Bogart." He told me he was starting a label and it was gonna be distributed by Warner Brothers. I asked him what the label was called and he said, "Well, they're still having to decide that; it's either gonna be called Emerald City or Casablanca." Paul was telling me about all the different things being planned. Gene was gonna spit fire and they were making outfits for them. I was very excited for them. I think Paul and Gene will both agree that most New York musicians very quickly turned their backs on KISS out of sheer, raw jealousy. The competitiveness and insecurity of most musicians meant they lost friends left and right. I had such confidence that I was also gonna be rich and famous that I looked at it as my friends Paul and Gene are six months ahead of me. I thought it was great.

CAROL ROSS: Bill knew KISS would be a hard sell and everyone told him he was crazy to work with a band like KISS. He just loved the challenge and knew the sky was the limit for this band. Bill and Neil [Bogart] were determined to make it happen.

JOYCE BOGART-TRABULUS: Neil and I and Bill were very involved in putting together what today PR people would call their "branding." We worked with them to develop their makeup, which was not the same as it is now. We worked on their costumes as well—hiring a designer, going over sketches. I lived around the corner to a shop near my house in the West Village called the Pleasure Chest. One day I stopped and looked in the window and said, "Wow, look at those big dog collars with those spikes coming out." I went in there and they were inexpensive. I told Neil and said, "Let's bring this to the guys and make this part of their costumes."

GENE SIMMONS: Paul and I went to gay S&M shops in the Village to look at what things we could wear that would get people's attention. We noticed all the S&M shops had studs and leather, which we thought looked cool. So we started putting studs on dog collars and guitar straps.

JOYCE BOGART-TRABULUS: We looked for ways to develop their act. . . . We went to magic stores, the one on Broadway that all the pros went to [Tannen's Magic], and bought them the drum riser, flash paper, and flash pots. Their audience had never seen a disco ball. When that disco ball got hit with light and zoomed around, the crowd went nuts. I had seen this before because I'd been going to all the underground discos in New York City. I thought it was cool and brought it in to be used in their shows.

MARIA CONTESSA (COSTUME DESIGNER): I started working with KISS in late 1973 making costumes. I had a store in the Village with my ex-husband called Jermaine Leather. We made the first professional costumes the band ever wore. One of the first costumes we made for them was Gene's costume with the bat wings and leather. The band knew exactly what they wanted. They would speak with us and just sketch out the costumes. I can still see Gene sitting in my office by the fabric-cutting table drawing costumes. He used to tell me they were going to be famous and I was going to be famous with them. And I went, "Yeah, yeah, yeah," but he turned out to be right.

I'd also give them costume ideas and they would say, "How about a zipper here or stud there or rhinestone here?" It was a group of people with the same aim: to create something unique. Gene's costumes were always the most difficult to make—too many details, lots of studs, leather, bat wings, and codpieces [*laughs*]. They were also extremely heavy. His costume weighed over thirty pounds.

At the beginning of their career we used a lot of leather—leather bat wings, leather belts. But later we used a bathing suit fabric called Lycra because it looks like leather, [but] Lycra shines. The band's costumes took quite a while to make—from the drawing board to fittings to the final costume took about a month. Their boots were made by an old Italian shoemaker in New York. I remember when Gene appeared on *The Mike Douglas Show* in Philadelphia and one of the wardrobe people took his boots but they made a mistake. They took two of the same foot [*laughs*]. But I think he wore them anyway [*laughs*].

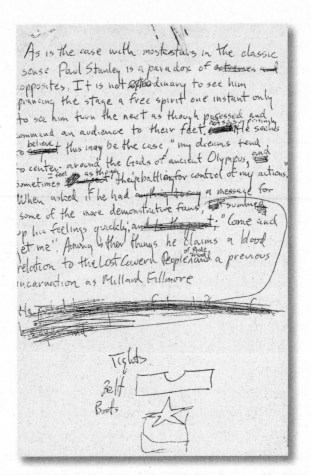

As is the case with most stars in the classic sense Paul Stanley is a paradox of ~~extremes and~~ opposites. It is not ~~extr~~ordinary to see him prancing the stage a free spirit one instant only to see him turn the next as though possessed and command an audience to their feet, ~~not spsi~~ surprisingly He seems to ~~believe~~ this may be the case. "my dreams tend to center around the Gods of ancient Olympus, ~~and~~ sometimes ~~I feel~~ as they ~~post~~ their battle for control of my actions. When asked if he had ~~anything to say~~ a message for some of the more demonstrative fans, ~~I summed~~ up his feelings quickly; and ~~the point~~ "Come and get me". Among other things he claims a blood relation to the Lost Cavern People, and a previous incarnation as Millard Fillmore

Tights
Belt
Boots

Paul Stanley's handwritten bio for the first KISS album Courtesy of Brad Estra

JAY "HOT SAM" BARTH (FRONT-OF-HOUSE SOUND ENGINEER): We were with KISS in the early days, when it was leather and studs—before it became spandex and sequins. After the band got done with a show you'd put their sweaty leather costumes in a trunk and travel to the next gig. Then the first thing you'd have to do when you arrived at the next venue was pull out the costumes and put them somewhere outside the building because they smelled so bad [*laughs*]. You'd need to leave them outside all day to air them out.

JOYCE BOGART-TRABULUS: KISS had worked out their initial concept, their logo, their sound, and even some of their merchandising with the KISS T-shirts. The ultimate KISS T-shirt was the first one we made with the rhinestones. They knew where they wanted to go from the beginning with us. They wanted to take it as big as it could go, but we really enhanced all the details. We grounded the concept and gave some backstory to their concept. Susan Munao, our PR person, and I sat them down and said, "Okay, we're gonna put together a press kit and tell who you are, just like you'd do with an actor explaining a role." They thought it was nuts at first but then they got into it. Because of our film backgrounds we had them write their stories. Who were each of these characters? Who was the cat? Where was he from? Why was Peter the cat and Ace the spaceman? (The latter was easy.) We incorporated this into their PR kits and their interview stories in magazines. It gave them a mysterious aura—a larger-than-life essence—and a kind of comic book quality. We gave them the resources and added our ideas to theirs to make the possibilities larger than life and more professional. We worked together as a team on every aspect of their careers. One idea would lead to another, and Neil was game enough to pay for it and make it happen. And we had a great time doing it. We loved working with each other. Like Bill, Neil, and I, KISS always had a sense of adventure—"Let's see what controlled chaos we can create."

11

ALL THE WAY

n the fall of 1973, Bill Aucoin and Joyce Biawitz were on board as managers. KISS continued to fine-tune their stage show and added new special effects and gimmicks.

JOYCE BOGART-TRABULUS: Howards Marks had an advertising company and had given us office space when we were doing our show *Flipside.* He'd just painted the offices white. Bill, Neil, and I hired this magician called Presto who came to my freshly painted white office to teach one of the band members to spit fire. He did his fire-breathing trick and I still remember the shocked expression on the faces of the group, "Oh my God, what's this?" [*laughs*].

GENE SIMMONS: Bill Aucoin said, "One of you guys should be breathing fire. Which one of you guys doesn't want to do it?" And everybody raised their hand. I thought he said, "Which one of you guys *wants* to breathe fire?" I thought, fuck, I don't wanna breathe fire. It was a negative question and I forgot to raise my hand so I was stuck. Bill said, "Okay, Simmons, you're gonna do it."

BILL AUCOIN: I didn't plan for Gene to do the fire-breathing; originally I had Paul in mind to do it.

PAUL STANLEY: Bill tried to come up with some stuff for me to do but I wasn't about to fill my mouth with kerosene [*laughs*]. So I didn't do it.

BILL AUCOIN: Gene had this kind of "I'll do anything" attitude, so he went along with it.

JOYCE BOGART-TRABULUS: The first time Gene breathed fire he blew so hard that he scorched all my newly painted white walls black and I had to call the painter back in. He could have burnt the place down [*laughs*].

Along with his fire-breathing stunt, Gene introduced a blood-spitting routine—another show-stopping gimmick that fast-tracked the show's evolution.

GENE SIMMONS: I was always a fan of horror movies and remember being profoundly struck seeing Christopher Lee as Dracula in one of the Hammer films, either *Blood of Dracula* or *Horror of Dracula*. I remember the audience shrieking when his fangs came out and he bit into the neck of a woman and you saw red blood pouring down his face. And in full color! I thought, wouldn't it be cool to do that onstage?

PETER "MOOSE" ORECKINTO: There have been many rumors through the years that the blood Gene used was a combination of actual pig's blood and flour. That's not true. Gene used a product made by DuPont called Simulated Blood. I'd buy a case or two for each tour at City Chemical in Lower Manhattan. It was designed for theatrical stage performances and use in movies. It had the same appearance and consistency as blood. I tasted it once and it had a cardboard kind of taste, the type of thing you'd want to spit out right away, so it was perfect for the blood-spitting routine.

BILL AUCOIN: KISS wanted to be different so they started playing off what they loved in their own life. Ace loved space, Gene loved horror movies, Paul always wanted to be a rock star, and Peter loved cats.

GENE SIMMONS: Onstage, we did a lot of ménage à trois kind of stuff. I'd put one leg out and Ace would kind of wrap around my leg and

Paul would get in back of Ace, and we'd all move around, back and forth. And remember, this was in the days when nobody except Alice Cooper moved. All rock bands stood still. When we did the song "Firehouse," Paul had a bucketful of confetti that said "Water—In Case of Fire." And at the end of the song he took the bucket and threw it into the audience and everyone went, "Oooh!" But there was no fire-breathing or any pyrotechnics. Just a lot of gyrating, a lot of jumping up and down. We'd tune offstage, walk through the crowd wearing these high heels, and go right up there and play.

On a mission to perfect their stage act, manager Bill Aucoin set up a video camera and began taping band rehearsals.

BILL AUCOIN: We filmed rehearsals in a little basement that we rented off Canal Street that had roaches the size of cats.

GENE SIMMONS: Bill Aucoin had a primitive version of a video camera set up in our rehearsal hall that Sean Delaney arranged.

PAUL STANLEY: We set up a video camera just so we could see how we moved and check ourselves out.

PETER CRISS: That impressed me about Bill Aucoin. Here we are in 1973 in a basement with video cameras on us. He had four videos running on us all of the time, getting our moves together, getting our choreography together. After we were done, we'd watch ourselves to see how stupid or how cool we looked. Whatever's cool, keep; whatever's stupid, lose.

SEAN DELANEY: Gene, Paul, Peter, and Ace always had a very strong idea of who they thought they were. But when I'd say, "Can you try this?" they'd say no and get mad. So what I did was I took a video camera and I said, "Look, I've got an idea. Why don't we try it both ways and see what you think?" So the moment that we did that, they sat down and saw that it's not running around real quick and crazy that works onstage; they could see that when something is choreographed it really works.

When all the makeup got on their faces, the only one that looked close to human was Paul Stanley. He had the star on his face, but everyone else was like a creature from another world and we had to convince them to inhabit the persona in that way. . . . Do demons talk to you? No, they growl, but they don't talk. Ace would have opened his mouth and went, "Ha! How you doing?" Peter was way back at the drums—cats don't talk to you. Paul, on the other hand, had to learn exact lines. I used to work with him on "How ya' doin'?"

A jack of all trades, Sean Delaney could move mountains through hard work and sheer force of will. Sean was a gifted singer/songwriter who would go on to cowrite many classic KISS songs with Paul, Gene, and Ace and coproduce Double Platinum *and Gene's 1978 solo album.*

BILL AUCOIN: Sean had a great theatrical sense. He could always tell when something wasn't right. He was a very strong-willed and creative person, and he would correct any weak points in the show. He went on tour with them and was a very strong part of making sure it all happened, even if they didn't understand or were a little afraid. He wouldn't even allow them to think there were weaknesses. He'd just say, "Let's do it." His attitude was, "We're going to do it no matter what." And it worked.

ACE FREHLEY: Sean did so much for the band. In the early days Sean had more input on the choreography than Paul and Gene. Sean was a major player with KISS. He came up with a lot of moves and was a major part in getting our show together.

GENE SIMMONS: Sean played a very important role in the beginning of the band. He was a road manager, he would suggest moves. He cowrote songs with the band. He was an idea guy.

SEAN DELANEY: I knew what they wanted and they learned to trust me. Gene would come out walking like a monster and he'd walk back like a human and I'd go, "You can't do that! You have to *be* this thing." So I was their mirror and I did that twenty-four hours a day.

PETER CRISS: He would stay on our ass morning, noon, and night at rehearsals until we really got it right.

SEAN DELANEY: In the beginning, the whole band and I got close real quick, because unlike Neil Bogart and Bill Aucoin, I was a musician. I looked at them differently. They were like my babies. I wasn't going to let anything bad happen to these guys that happened to me because I had been through it before. I was prepared for it: lies from record companies [and] managers. I wanted them to succeed.

PETER "MOOSE" ORECKINTO: Sean gave KISS the personalities that he wanted to see. I can still picture him standing in front of them down in the loft, and he's got that Charlie Manson look in his eye, that intense fuckin' look, and he's going, "Gene, you're the monster, you've gotta act this way!" He solidified their stage personas and wanted them to come across larger than life.

SEAN DELANEY: Paul Stanley got an itchy scalp, so when he'd be playing in rehearsal, he'd reach up and scratch his head, and I'd say, "What are you doing? You can't be up there and do that." He said, "Well, what am I supposed to do? My scalp hurts." I said, "Paul, instead of just scratching it, really scratch it!" And that's one of his big moves. He'll stop and say, "How ya' doing?," scratch his head, and throw his arms out.

ACE FREHLEY: In the beginning we used to critique stuff we did but after a while it came pretty natural. In the beginning, Sean would help us with our choreography. But after a while we did it ourselves.

Bill Aucoin made good on a big promise and landed KISS a record deal with a new label called Casablanca, which would release records by Donna Summer, Parliament-Funkadelic, the Village People, and Angel.

KENNY KERNER: I used to go to Neil's office every week or two and pick up a box of all the tapes that came in the mail, and I'd take them home. I'd listen to them one at a time, and two or three weeks later I'd bring home another batch. In one of the boxes that I brought home one blisteringly cold winter afternoon was a demo reel-to-reel tape from KISS, with a black-and-white photo. They looked like some kind of kabuki act in makeup. I instantly got what they were trying to do. I put the tape on and thought it was great.

RICHIE WISE (COPRODUCER, KISS): KISS's music was a throwback to simpler rock and roll. I thought the material was very simple and raw, and I wasn't into simple and raw. I liked progressive rock bands like Yes. I wasn't sophisticated enough at the time to see that KISS had a really narrow view and that their narrow view is what ultimately made them successful. They were gonna do one thing and do it really well, which was play loud, simple rock and roll with real suggestive lyrics.

KENNY KERNER: The songs were raw and youthful and very well structured. The demo had "Deuce" and "Strutter" on it and some other really good songs. This was on a Friday. I didn't even listen to the rest of the stuff. Monday morning I took the tape and picture back to Neil at Buddah Records and said, "Neil, this is a great tape; I think we should sign these guys." And he said, "I can't sign them to Buddah but I'm starting a brand-new label called Casablanca. Let me listen to the tape." And he listened to the tape and the next day he said, "You're right. We're going to sign them as the first act on Casablanca."

Founded in the late sixties, American Talent International, also known as ATI, was a concert booking agency that specialized in hard rock acts. Jeff Franklin, the owner of ATI, was a longtime friend and industry colleague of Neil Bogart's and helped fund KISS's initial recording contract.

JEFF FRANKLIN (OWNER, ATI): Neil grew up in Brooklyn. His real name was Neil Bogatz.

NEIL BOGART (PRESIDENT, CASABLANCA RECORDS): I always wanted to be an entertainer . . . all my life. I started off my career as an actor doing a lot of off-Broadway summer stock, television, commercials, that sort of thing. When I was eighteen or nineteen I became a part of a song-and-dance team, and I worked on a lot of the Bermuda cruise ships with that act. When I was about twenty, we were playing a club in New York, and a fellow named Bill Darnell saw me and asked me if I'd like to make a record. His exact words, in fact, were, "Your voice is bad enough to sound good on this song that we have." I recorded my first record, "Bobby," on the Portrait label. That was the age of all the "sickie" records [1961], and the song was about a girl dying in a hospital. I recorded it under the name Neil Scott. It sold something like two hundred thousand records and went top 40 in *Cashbox* and *Billboard*. After that, I released about five bombs in a row and my career went immediately downward. I really wanted to be an entertainer at the time but realized that in order to make a living, I'd have to get into the other end of the business.

JEFF FRANKLIN: His recording career as Neil Scott went nowhere. Then he went to work for *Cashbox* doing ad sales. From there he lied to Allen Klein who owned [the record company] Cameo-Parkway and got the job to run the company. He told him he'd been doing marketing and promotion for years and Allen Klein didn't care, he just needed somebody to babysit it. The first big hit he had on Cameo-Parkway was "96 Tears" by Question Mark & the Mysterians.

NEIL BOGART: We had about twenty chart records that year: the Rationals, Bob Seger. When Allen Klein bought Cameo-Parkway, he probably did me the greatest favor of my life. He told me he didn't care whether I stayed or left. My pride was a little bit hurt so I went seeking greener pastures. I ran into Art Kass, who is now president of Buddah Records. Art was vice president at the time, and Artie Ripp was president. Artie asked me to join the label and to bring my whole staff with me. So Cecil Holmes, Marty Thau, a few secretaries, and I all joined the new company. The most important thing that I had to do at Buddah initially, since the company was just barely making it financially, was to have hit records. And the only way I knew how to have hit records was to reach back to my days in Brooklyn and come up with simple rock-and-roll records.

Formed in 1967, Buddah Records was home to a diverse array of artists, including Lou Christie, Melanie, and the Edwin Hawkins Singers. However, the label is best known for originating bubblegum music. In the years 1968 and 1969, Buddah's mighty bubblegum factory pumped out a string of sticky AM radio blockbusters by the Lemon Pipers ("Green Tambourine"), 1910 Fruitgum Company ("1, 2, 3, Red Light"), and the Ohio Express ("Yummy Yummy Yummy"). The label was headed by Bogart, whom Time *magazine dubbed "the bubblegum king of America" in an article titled "Tunes for Teeny-Weenies" dated July 19, 1968.*

NEIL BOGART: I tried to live that down for a few years. Now, though, looking back, I'm really proud of it. I think that the simplicity of bubblegum was a great step to getting back to rock-and-roll music, and I think a lot has come out of it since then.

LARRY HARRIS (CO-OWNER, SENIOR VICE PRESIDENT, AND MANAGING DIRECTOR, CASABLANCA RECORDS): While at Buddah, Neil was mostly known for bubblegum and R&B artists like Gladys Knight & the Pips and Bill Withers. We also signed the Charlie Daniels Band. None of those acts were over the top like KISS. The only act we had at Buddah that compared with KISS was Sha Na Na, because they put on an incredible show.

JEFF FRANKLIN: So Neil had some success at Buddah with all the bubblegum music, Curtis Mayfield, and others. Viewlex owned Buddah and Neil wasn't making the kind of money he wanted, so when his contract was over he left and started Casablanca.

NEIL BOGART: I had Casablanca in my head. I left a note for the people at Buddah saying, "This is something I have to do, and here's looking at you, kids."

Casablanca Records president Neil Bogart Courtesy of Ross Koondel

Splitting from Buddah Records in September 1973, Neil Bogart fashioned the label of his dreams.

NEIL BOGART: I got myself a business manager and I told him I wanted to make a deal with Warner Brothers. They [were] the only company in the world that I would have changed for—I think that their executive talent is the finest in the world. My business manager called and set up a meeting, and from the moment I walked in, the attitude of Joe [Smith], Mo [Ostin], and Ed West and the rest of the people I dealt with was, "Yes, we'd like to make a deal, let's just figure out how to do it." I told them the direction I wanted to take was to create another kind of Buddah Records, a much smaller company that would really devote itself to building a few acts; I figured that our spread [would] be basically what it was at Buddah—about 50 percent black, maybe 20 percent hard singles, and 30 percent heavier rock acts.

JEFF FRANKLIN: The label was originally gonna be called Evergreen and later Emerald City Records, but we couldn't clear the name.

GENE SIMMONS: I hated the name and told Neil to his face that the name sucked. "We're off to see the Wizard" was the idea, and I thought it was weak.

JEFF FRANKLIN: Neil came up with the name Casablanca, which fit his image and everything that was going on.

NEIL BOGART: I was really into *Casablanca*. It's one of those movies that just keeps coming back to you. I must've seen it about eighty times. *Casablanca* represented a whole revolutionary freedom to me ever since I was a kid. The more I got into *Casablanca*, the more I got into Bogart. But there was no connection between Bogart and *Casablanca* when I chose the name. The path just seemed to lead to one night me laying in bed thinking, "Well, I'm gonna start my new record company. What should the name be? Maybe Emerald City? That's where the Wizard of Oz lived. Or maybe Paradise Records? Because I really wanna build my own new paradise. But, Bogart. . . . Where does Bogart belong?" Then, all of a sudden: "Bogart! Bogart belongs in Casablanca!" It all came together that night.

JOYCE BOGART-TRABULUS: Think about the film *Casablanca*— the drama, the excitement, and the mystery of *Casablanca*. That's something that Neil, who was theatrical and visionary, could connect to.

JEFF FRANKLIN: Neil and I had met when he was at Buddah Records. I had done a record deal with him on Jack Wild and I took his eyeballs out and he was mad at me. Then he came to me and said, "I want to start my own record company." I said, "Why do you want me to be involved in this?" and he said, "'Cause you're the best." Initially, I negotiated for Neil to take over Bell Records, which at the last minute didn't happen—they went with Clive Davis. I made a deal with Mo Ostin and Joe Smith at Warner Brothers to start Casablanca.

JOE /MITH (PRE/IDENT, WARNER BROTHER/ RECORD/): Mo and I took a calculated risk that Neil Bogart and his crew could come up with something we wouldn't come up with ourselves. Warner Brothers was one of the great record companies of all time, but we didn't handle every kind of music. We weren't looking for bands like KISS. We were mostly into bands that had real musical value. I knew Neil back in his days working at Buddah. He was a wild guy, but he made things happen. He spent money like crazy but we felt if we could control that we'd get some good results out of the partnership.

BILL AUCOIN: Warner Brothers gave Neil $750,000 to start his own label. They were the money and distributor behind Casablanca. They saw Neil as the up-and-coming wonder kid of the record industry.

NEIL BOGART: People ask me what kind of music I'm looking for, and I say "hit music." I really believe that there should be music for every kind of audience. I'm really interested in music that appeals to an audience—*whatever* that audience might be.

NANCY /AIN (NATIONAL /ECONDARY POP PROMOTION DIRECTOR, CA/ABLANCA RECORD/): He had a knack for making hits, and Warner Brothers thought they could make money with him.

JOE /MITH: In addition to getting Neil and the crazy guys that worked with him, we brought Casablanca into the fold because he was able to provide an element we didn't have at Warner's, a kind of "fly by the seat of your pants" philosophy. That was part of Casablanca's methodology—to do something crazy and flashy.

BUCK REINGOLD (VICE PRE/IDENT OF NATIONAL PROMOTION, CA/ABLANCA RECORD/): Neil never had the big money to sign a band like the Stones. He had to take things from scratch and make them happen because he didn't have the bucks that Columbia, Atlantic, or RCA had to give big advances.

STAN CORNYN (EXECUTIVE VICE PRESIDENT, WARNER BROTHERS RECORDS): Neil Bogart was fairly well known as a wonderful hustler—and *hustler* is a complimentary word. Warner Brothers was very interested in getting into the company someone who had done bubblegum and all kinds of stuff that we didn't do. Between Mo Ostin and Joe Smith at Warner Brothers, we made a distribution label deal with Casablanca. That entailed money for Casablanca in exchange for the distribution rights, manufacturing, and marketing. We didn't have anything to do with the talent. Neil would deliver the masters and packages to us and we would take it into the commercial world. As is typical of these deals, we would split the profits fifty-fifty. Neil was attractive to the boss, Mo Ostin, because Bogart had a sense of "light" recordings—quickies, singles, teen-cute—and Warner's concentrated on album types. Hits for Warner Brothers this same year ranged from hot albums by acts such as Black Sabbath, Alice Cooper, Deep Purple, the Doobie Brothers, Little Feat, Van Morrison, James Taylor, Tower of Power; and on Reprise we had Gordon Lightfoot, Randy Newman, and Neil Young, among others. My point being Warner Brothers Records had plenty of hit acts to handle. So Casablanca was a bit different, singles-inclined, and a "why not?" for us.

Neil Bogart signed acts that were trailblazers and didn't conform to cookie-cutter expectations. KISS fit the bill.

KENNY KERNER: Neil was always into hype. If you could hype it, it was perfect for Neil. So he immediately saw that. I said, "Who's managing the band?" And he said they're working with Bill Aucoin, some guy who directed some off-Broadway plays and has a production company called Direction Plus, which he runs with his partner Joyce Biawitz.

JOYCE BOGART-TRABULUS: Neil was knocked out and loved their music. I think we told him about their stage act and makeup but he really thought they were a group he wanted to sign based on the music alone. He asked if we would bring them to him when he started Casablanca.

DENNIS ELSAS (MUSIC DIRECTOR, WNEW-FM): Larry Harris called me and said, "Neil's looking at this new band he's thinking about signing and he wants you to come see them."

GENE SIMMONS: What's interesting is Neil didn't know we wore makeup. He thought Eddie Kramer's demo was great and his staff producers told him he should sign us.

PAUL STANLEY: We needed a place where we could showcase and there really weren't music rehearsal studios in the city. Some of them wanted nothing to do with you because they didn't want loud music, but LeTang's was game. It was a dance studio located in midtown Manhattan that was owned by a photographer named Henry LeTang.

GENE SIMMONS: It was a small room with a small stage and mirrors all over the walls. You'd fit maybe forty people in there.

PAUL STANLEY: Neil brought some people with him. I think he wanted some feedback from other people and he also wanted to see what we were all about.

KENNY KERNER: Bill [Aucoin], myself, Joyce [Biawitz], Richie [Wise], Neil, Bucky Reingold, Larry Harris, and the Kama Sutra/Casablanca promotion staff went into this little rehearsal studio. The room was as big as a shoebox, literally from the back of the stage to the front door couldn't have been more than thirty feet. The group came in and they looked twelve feet tall. They had platform shoes that had to be a foot high and the stage was about a foot off the ground so they looked like skyscrapers.

DENNIS WOLOCH (ART DIRECTOR/DESIGNER, HOWARD MARKS ADVERTISING): They were so close to us you could reach out and pluck their guitar strings.

KENNY KERNER: They all wore black outfits and their faces were painted. Gene had his tongue going. They came on in such a demonic way—Gene especially looked really demonic—that I was

KISS performing an industry showcase at LeTang's ballet studio, New York City, September 1973. Casablanca Records president Neil Bogart and producers Kenny Kerner and Richie Wise are among those in attendance Eddie Solan/KISS Catalog Ltd.

scared shitless. They were just bigger than life. I could see kids just going nuts for this stuff.

DENNIS ELSAS: My impression was that they were a little strange—I'd never seen anything like it.

DENNIS WOLOCH: I sat next to Jeanette, who later became Ace's wife, and I remember they gave us earplugs [*laughs*]. They almost killed us with how loud it was.

RICHIE WISE: They were very loud and I always loved loud music. But to be truthful, I didn't get it.

JOYCE BOGART-TRABULUS: The music was beyond loud and Neil sat in the first row. This was the first time he saw KISS perform.

GENE SIMMONS: Bill was sitting next to Neil Bogart and was talking to him while we were onstage. I was incensed that they were talking while we were singing our songs. We were playing "Nothin' to Lose" and there's a section where we encouraged the audience to clap their hands. I stepped off stage and put my nose up in front of Neil's nose to get him to stop talking. Bogart's eyes are popping, like "What the fuck's going on?" I took his hands and literally forced him to start clapping.

SEAN DELANEY: Neil started applauding because he was scared to death. And I said to myself at that moment, "I wanna be involved in this" because that's the kind of balls you have to have to do anything.

GENE SIMMONS: I thought for sure we lost the deal but Neil liked it. He responded to that arrogance and fearless quality. And that's what I saw in Paul, Ace, and Peter. You had to have that.

BUCK REINGOLD: I told Neil, "Visually they're amazing but it ain't gonna be easy to get them played on the radio."

JOYCE BOGART-TRABULUS: Neil connected with their fire-in-the-belly enthusiasm and their willingness to do anything to make it.

NEIL BOGART: When I first saw them their music hit me like a bolt of lightning. Their sound, their image was something I had waited seven years to find. Here was a group whose music and visuals came together in perfect harmony.

They're everything I've been looking for in a band.

JOYCE BOGART-TRABULUS: After the show, the group, Bill, Neil, and I met in a tiny room, maybe a supply closet. We stood in a small circle, the group in full costume and makeup, as Neil told KISS he wanted them to be his first signing for Casablanca. When he finished his speech outlining their future and telling them how excited he was, that he thought they were stars, Peter Criss fell down. He just fell off his high heels and landed with great force on his rear. We all roared, including Peter. You might say it sealed the deal. And then the hard work began.

12

ON THE ROAD TO CASABLANCA

O n November 1, 1973, KISS signed a deal with Casablanca Records. With Bogart at the helm, the team included industry veterans Larry Harris (artist relations and national album promotion), Buck Reingold (top-40 promotion), and Cecil Holmes (national R&B promotion).

NEIL BOGART: Casablanca is a company that is owned by myself—totally—and that Warner Brothers distributes. In terms of organizational structure, we're a promotion company. I promote. I call radio stations. I go on the road to visit radio stations. I love to promote. Promotion is the name of the game, and that's what we have: a promotion company. There are no A&R people at Casablanca—I don't believe in it. The promotion people are going to have to sell the product; they should be the ones to choose it.

We run the promotion of a record the same way you would an army going to war. You have to have a war plan. You have to know exactly how you want to promote it, where you want to advertise, when you want the record to break, when you are going after certain stations, when you're going to advertise on those stations. You really run a whole war game.

KENNY KERNER: The band was ecstatic to be signed because it was with a new label. Whenever you're with a new label you know you're going to get a push.

NEIL BOGART: KISS was the first group we signed. When we signed them we affirmed that KISS *was* Casablanca. We put everything we had into it. We undertook what has become one of the most exciting promotions of my career.

PAUL STANLEY: I'm pretty sure we signed a three-album deal with Casablanca. Back then you were nurtured by the record company and your creativity and your artistry was built over the course of albums. Back then bands were expected to do three albums before they might break. If you didn't make it by your third album, you were out. But it wasn't unheard of for bands to need three albums to make it. When we signed with Casablanca, it felt really good and new. There was the feeling back then that they needed us because KISS *was* Casablanca. I think a lot of creativity comes from when you want something very badly or when it's new and there's a certain amount of excitement. Neil wanted his record company to be great and he needed to devote everything to whomever he signed to the label. That fit in with all of our plans.

NEIL BOGART: I've never been into hard rock until recently. But I can honestly say that KISS is the first band I've devoted myself 100 percent to. Their visual show, which features a drum set that levitates six feet in the air, a lead singer who blows fire out of his mouth, and their wonderful use of makeup, is just a shatteringly satisfying experience. Even more important is the fact that they're probably one of the best rock-and-roll bands I've ever heard in my life.

JOYCE BOGART-TRABULUS: Neil was a man who lived to invent the next trend. He was fiercely loyal to the artists he chose, making them family, as he did his staff, many of whom traveled with him from Cameo-Parkway to Buddah to Casablanca and then Boardwalk afterwards. He was the first to create a twelve-inch with Donna Summer's "Love to Love You Baby" and the first to do disco promotion, to have a promo department to sell records through club play as an alternative to radio. Most of the great disco music came from Casablanca. He was a master promoter and the king of the art of independent promotion and distribution. So many of his acts are still around today, as is the music his companies recorded.

Neil got the KISS concept right away. It was a match made in heaven—a natural—as KISS was a high-concept act and he was a promoter. I don't think any other music executive then or today would have seen all the possibilities for promotion and merchandising so clearly. Neil loved fun and he loved nothing more than creating something that was fun for other people to enjoy. He saw this possibility in KISS immediately. He had been a singer, a musician, an actor, and a producer. KISS provided him with a matrix to play, to use the synthesis of all his talent and experience.

NEIL BOGART: When we started with KISS people thought we were crazy.

JOYCE BOGART-TRABULUS: And the fact that everyone else thought he was crazy for signing them only made it more of a delicious challenge. When the world told Neil it would never work, he knew he was on the right track. He was looking to create something new, not to follow trends.

GENE SIMMONS: Casablanca bet the store on a new act who didn't write singles, didn't sing about heartbreak or love, and didn't look or sound like the Partridge Family. And all of that had to do with Neil Bogart, a man with a vision. Casablanca was unlike other labels. We could walk in, sit down, and have a heart-to-heart with Neil Bogart. Casablanca was the last of its kind.

BOBBI COWAN (PUBLICIST, GIBSON & STROMBERG): Money was never an object with Neil. He spent money like he had it, and most of the time he did—and there were times he didn't and you'd never know it. While he was getting Casablanca rolling, if things were getting rough he had his building painted on the outside. He said, "People think if you're painting your building you're doing really well. Nobody paints their building if they're broke." Neil was magical in that he could create a perception that would inevitably become reality. He created the perception that KISS was gonna be the biggest act in America and eventually it happened.

JOYCE BOGART-TRABULUS: He was willing to stick his neck out and put his money and all his contacts and influence behind making the band a success. To financially launch the band, there were large advances from Neil, ATI, and from us. We put all our money into this. Everyone pooled their resources. Neil was responsible for getting the band booked on tours, which was no small feat. No one wanted to tour with them. All the agents told us to leave the equipment home as it was too expensive to tour. They didn't get it. He insisted with his friends at ATI that they book the band. Jeff Franklin was very important here and was Neil's very good friend. He would loan us money we needed to stay on the road. We couldn't have had that if it wasn't for Neil. He used his long-term friendships to get KISS television exposure on every show that featured music, from Dick Clark's specials to *The Mike Douglas Show*.

GENE SIMMONS: Neil Bogart was the last of his kind. He was a showman like P. T. Barnum.

LARRY HARRIS: Neil believed in making something as entertaining as possible, which would in turn sell product.

DENNIS ELSAS: Neil's approach to things was bigger than life. Neil was a showman from day one. Whether it was the 1910 Fruitgum Company or the hipper stuff like Curtis Mayfield, he just went for broke with everything.

PETER CRISS: Neil Bogart was the Barnum and Bailey of rock and roll. He would spend a thousand dollars to make a dollar. He would spend a ton of money to make the biggest, grandest something and if he even made a buck out of it he didn't even give a fuck.

LARRY HARRIS: When it comes to spending, two dollars to make one dollar is bullshit. Neil believed he had to back his artists up and spend a lot of money to get them to a certain level. Even though we spent a lot of money on KISS, we made a ton of profit on them as well. It wasn't like he was spending two dollars to make one dollar; he was spending two dollars and he made four.

JEFF FRANKLIN: Neil was a marketer and promotion man. He believed he could sell a refrigerator to an Eskimo. So if you gave people something different he could sell it. That was his philosophy.

PETER CRISS: I loved him. I wish he was still here. There was nobody like him. He was the last breed of those kinds of men. He was a visionary who thought outside of the box. Think of all the crazy acts he signed, whether it was us or the Village People or Donna Summer, they were all home runs.

DONNA SUMMER: Neil was a very unusual guy. He was one of those kinds of people who wouldn't take no for an answer when he believed in something. Neil thought without limits. Very often in my career when I'm doing something and I feel that people are putting limits on me, I think of Neil. I go, "What would Neil do now?" And he would say, "If you can't go over it, go around it. If you can't go around it, go through it. If you can't go through it, go around the other side. Whatever it is, just find a way." Neil was a man who always found the way. He didn't allow the obstacles to be an obstacle. He allowed it to be a challenge, and the challenge was he was going to overcome it.

JOYCE BOGART-TRABULUS: Neil was involved in every aspect of their career. He worked with me, Bill, and the group to choose the artwork for their covers, the photographs; to design the radio promotional campaign; to create a PR campaign with both an outside and internal PR department. And everything was the best he could afford to provide. They worked with all the best—from photographers to producers. And when we were all out of money, he advanced us the money to continue when any other label would say that we had already used up our advance.

GENE SIMMONS: Neil was really one of KISS's true early believers to the extent of whatever it cost, he reached, he went for it. It was Neil Bogart who came up with the idea of "Why not have the drum platforms levitate?" He also came up with the idea of Peter's exploding drumsticks.

RICHIE WISE: Neil was the most unhip guy in the world as far as I was concerned. He was the bubblegum "Yummy Yummy Yummy" guy. Casablanca wasn't a rock label, Buddah wasn't a rock label, and Neil wasn't a rock guy. Good rock bands were on Atlantic and Warner Brothers. I didn't think Casablanca was the right label for KISS.

KENNY KERNER: He wanted a serious label and he was looking for serious artists but Neil always wound up with artists that were really talented but were driven by singles—artists like Donna Summer and the Village People. He was brilliant at promotion and marketing but not very good at developing artists. Neil was a really bright and sweet guy and he really knew the record business. To be honest, I'm not sure he liked anybody's music. I think he approached it from, Is this gonna sell? Is this marketable? Does this song have a chorus people are gonna want to sing? I think he was out of his niche with hard rock and was at home with singles.

PAUL STANLEY: Neil was very into salesmanship. When he believed in something he sold it. However, the down side to that was I don't think Neil was very concerned with the long-term success. He would do anything to have a hit regardless of the impact it might have on your career. Neil wasn't used to long-term because I think Neil was not used to careers lasting. So the name of the game was to have a hit.

GENE SIMMONS: So here's a guy who was all about singles and yet the first band he signs to Casablanca Records doesn't have any singles. He was all about very stylized, beat-driven [music] and we had nothing to do with it. He was very much a guy who wanted to be in charge—do it my way or the highway. And yet he met a group of guys who basically said the same thing. What he was best at was believing in something if *you* believed in it. He was able to put his own beliefs aside if he saw passion. And when he did it he did it with all his heart.

ACE FREHLEY: I thought he was a genius. Neil wasn't afraid to take chances. He rolled the dice with us when a lot of other companies didn't want to touch us.

PAUL STANLEY: Things happened quickly after we got signed. It was virtually overnight that we were in the studio recording our first album.

After signing with Casablanca, KISS entered Bell Sound Studios in November 1973 to record their debut album. Kenny Kerner and Richie Wise were enlisted to produce the label's inaugural act. Their credits included Gladys Knight & the Pips, Badfinger, and Stories, who scored a number-one single with "Brother Louie."

KENNY KERNER: Kerner and Wise were really hot as producers and [Neil] Bogart wanted somebody fresh and into rock and roll. So he assigned us to produce the first KISS album.

Bell Sound Studios acetate album jacket Courtesy of Ross Koondel

Located at 237 West Fifty-fourth Street in Midtown Manhattan, Bell Sound Studios was one of the top studios in New York City. Established in 1953, the studio's alumni included doo-wop pioneers Frankie Lymon & the Teenagers, Little Anthony & the Imperials, Pat Boone, Frankie Avalon, Paul Anka, and Roberta Flack.

KENNY KERNER: The studio was located close to the Brill Building, where all of the music publishers would hang out with songwriters like Gerry Goffin, Carole King, and Neil Sedaka. Bell Sound was one of the studios they'd use to record. We wanted to record at Bell Sound because we'd worked there before with a great studio engineer named Harry Yarmark. He worked with Frank Sinatra and did a lot of Four Seasons records.

WARREN DEWEY (ENGINEER, *KISS* AND *HOTTER THAN HELL*): In those days most studios had resident geniuses who built their mixing consoles in-house. Bell had just installed a new console made by an outside company and it was really complex, flakey, and unreliable compared to the old homebrew technology. The room was very seventies-looking and was big enough to record a full orchestra. The studio was situated on three floors of an old parking garage and still had the giant elevator that lifted the cars up and down, which was handy for moving drums and amps. The studio was up on the fifth floor. There was a dedicated phone on the wall that was a hotline direct to the Carnegie Deli.

RICHIE WISE: Bell Sound was owned by a company called Viewlex, which also owned Buddah Records. Having cut a lot of hits at Bell while heading Buddah, Neil cut a good deal with the studio for the making of KISS's first album.

KENNY KERNER: When I first listened to KISS's original demo, what impressed me was not only the song structure but the rawness and the realness of the music. In going in to do the album we didn't want to lose that. We knew there'd be a huge backlash because of the makeup and also because KISS would be perceived as a Neil

Bogart gimmick band. We didn't want people to think the band is a gimmick and that they brought in Kerner and Wise to slick it up and make it look like the band can really play. The rap on a lot of the bubblegum records was there were no such groups as the 1910 Fruitgum Company or Ohio Express. After watching KISS play live at LeTang's and Coventry, we decided that this had to be a real street album, a real raw album. I wanted the album to sound like the band live so when people saw them in concert they'd go, "Yeah, that sounds just like the record!" That's what Casablanca were lacking—an authentic rock-and-roll band. Not slick. No production tricks. I think we were able to capture a real, raw sound on the first KISS album. That album had a spontaneity and immediacy to it. We didn't want it to be perfect. We felt the songs were so strong and they'd jump out of the speakers.

RICHIE WISE: As producers, our roles were well defined: Kenny was more the business guy and I was the music guy. The first KISS album took six days to record and seven days to mix. We would cut three basic tracks in a day—drums, bass, and two rhythm guitars. Ace would overdub his solos not long after we cut the tracks. Then we would spend the last three days of the recording doing the vocals.

KENNY KERNER: It was that quick. They'd worked hard in preproduction. They'd been playing the songs live for many months and they knew the songs. The longer we stayed in the studio the more chance that someone would say, "Can we double this guitar?" and it would have gotten farther and farther away from KISS.

RICHIE WISE: KISS came in the studio well prepared but I probably rearranged all of the songs so they worked great on record. The songs on the album were good, solid rock and roll. I did simple things like making sure the choruses came in at the right time and also making sure that the verses weren't too long. I listened for the things that I felt would make a more interesting album, and the band were always open to my suggestions.

KENNY KERNER: One of the top talents we had as producers was

Paul laying down a rhythm track on his Gibson Les Paul for KISS's
debut album, Bell Sound Studios, November 1973 Eddie Solan/KISS Catalog Ltd.

we were able to create a fun atmosphere in the studio. There was
no pressure. We worked at a great pace. We laughed. There was no
screaming, "You missed a note!" KISS were adequate musicians.
Nobody in the band was a spectacular virtuoso.

RICHIE WISE: Paul was a really great rhythm guitar player who never
wanted to be anything more than a Pete Townshend kind of rhythm
player. He knew his role. Ace played some great solos on the album
in that [Eric] Clapton/[Jimmy] Page style.

KENNY KERNER: There was a timing problem with Peter. We always
used to joke that "The Peter Time" was the name of a magazine.

So it took a little extra time to nail down Peter's drum parts. Ace wasn't an Eric Clapton and Peter couldn't play like Ginger Baker [the drummer with Cream and Blind Faith]. But to become successful, they didn't need to be virtuosos. That was immaterial. I'd say the same thing about the Rolling Stones. They're not virtuoso musicians, but they're perfect for what they do, and KISS was perfect for what they did as well. They took direction well. They knew exactly who they were. They knew they weren't great musicians but they got the most out of their talents. What made KISS great was their determination and drive. Gene always understood that he was in the entertainment business, not the music business. They were showmen.

RICHIE WISE: I remember having a discussion with Gene about the Grateful Dead. He hated bands like that who'd go onstage with beards and street clothes. Gene, more than anybody else, had blinders on, and laser beam focus that they were gonna do something that no one had ever done before. They were gonna get onstage and look different than all the other bands and play louder than everybody. During the making of the first album they'd draw pictures of what they wanted their costumes to look like.

EDDIE SOLAN: KISS acted like they belonged there. That was always their attitude. This is the next logical step.

RICHIE WISE: While working on that first album I remember walking down the street with Gene and he said, "Do you see this building? It's not enough for me to own this building, I have to own the whole block" [*laughs*]. Looking back, he was the most focused guy I ever worked with.

GENE SIMMONS: The recording sessions for the first album were almost surreal. We knew the songs forwards and backwards, and we had already broken our cherry with Eddie Kramer, who produced our first demo. The recording process was simple and direct.

PAUL STANLEY: I remember being very intimidated by the studio. Although I had recorded at Columbia Studios when I was fifteen, I never spent enough time doing it to see that the studio was your friend.

Gene Simmons's handwritten lyrics for "Deuce" and "Let Me Go, Rock 'N Roll" KISS Catalog Ltd.

It actually seemed like a foreboding monster and at any moment if a mic got moved the result would be catastrophic. Recording those songs on the first album was pretty effortless but we didn't have final say. Kenny and Richie were calling the shots. The songs on that album are great. It's always funny to think when that album came out you either got it or you didn't. People liked it or they didn't think of it as real music. Real music was Emerson, Lake & Palmer, and the irony of it is you put on some of the stuff that [is] considered real music today and [then] put on our first album, and tell me which one sounds contemporary. It came down to the songs. There were great tunes on that album and they were well crafted, with catchy melodies and catchy hooks.

ACE FREHLEY: It was the first time I ever did a real album. The songs on the first album are good. We knew those songs backwards and forwards. It was one of our best records because it had that spontaneity and that tough kind of sound. We were all very hungry at that point in our lives. I think we put in 110 percent on that record.

KENNY KERNER: The guys were jazzed to do the record. Paul and Gene gave the direction and watched over everything. They seemed to have the most camaraderie so it was only natural that they would lead the band.

EDDIE SOLAN: During their shows, at the end of "Firehouse" we used a crank siren. They wanted that effect on the song "Firehouse," so I set up the siren in the studio and cranked it, and it's on the record. They credit me on the album as "Firehouse Fire Engine driven by the magnificent Eddie Solan" [*laughs*].

KENNY KERNER: Gene still took the subway to the studio. I remember meeting Gene one day on the subway on our way to the studio. We were standing on the D train and I said to Gene, "You just signed a deal with Casablanca and you got an advance—why are you still taking the subway?" He looked at me seriously and said, "Do you

Ace kickin' out the jams during sessions for KISS's debut album, Bell Sound Studios, November 1973 Eddie Solan/KISS Catalog Ltd.

know how many records the first album is going to sell?" And I said no. And he said, "Well, neither do I, so I'm taking the subway." And he was right. Gene felt that nothing was guaranteed. He said, "We're doing an album but so what—97 percent of the albums released fail, so the album comes out and God forbid it bombs and I'm broke." He was always a very frugal businessman. He recognized that if the first album bombed he'd need that money to live on.

RICHIE WISE: Paul was truly professional. Gene was always focused. Ace was a blast; he was a big beer drinker and a fun guy. He called everybody "Curly." Peter was a great guy to work with.

WARREN DEWEY: Once we were doing a vocal with Peter and he was sitting on a stool on the other side of the studio glass facing Richie and me. "What the hell is that?" I asked. Richie was like, "Holy shit!" He hit the talkback and said, "Peter, have you got a sock in your pants?" And Peter, completely deadpan, said, "Oh, no. I have

Paul and Gene clowning around during a background vocals take during sessions for KISS's debut album, Bell Sound Studios, November 1973 Eddie Solan/KISS Catalog Ltd.

Paul, Ace, and Gene team up to supply background vocals during sessions for the band's first KISS album, Bell Sound Studios, November 1973 Eddie Solan/KISS Catalog Ltd.

a thirteen-inch penis," which I guess was true, and probably still is. And this was years before *Spinal Tap* [*laughs*].

I also remember Paul once did this pantomime thing in the studio that was amazingly funny. He said something like, "Look! Look!" and turned his back on us, miming like he was wildly jerking off.

EDDIE SOLAN: I took almost a hundred photos at those sessions, and they haven't been seen in over thirty-five years. Photos of Gene and Paul singing around the vocal mic, a great picture of Ace with a few days' growth with headphones on laying down a solo on a white Ovation Breadwinner electric guitar, Peter behind the drum kit, Ace singing background with a beer bottle in his hand, all kinds of stuff.

PAUL STANLEY: Looking at the photos of us recording the first album, besides the wonderment and excitement we all had at being in the studio, I was also struck by the fact that we were all very, very different as individuals. The only common bond we had was our passion for the band and the hunger for success. I think we all had different thoughts about how each one of us would participate in that success.

GENE SIMMONS: Everybody got along great in the early days. Ace and Peter were a joy to work with. They felt very fortunate and appreciative of having the chance to record an album. They were very good team players and never came to work drunk or high during the recording of the first record.

PETER CRISS: At that point we were all on the same page and were really together—one for all and all for one. We were all new to each other and everything was beautiful working on that album. When we finished that first album I was elated. I felt, "Finally I got into a creative situation!" I had experience in the recording studio with Chelsea, who released an album with Decca Records in the early seventies. I got to work on that album with Lewis Merenstein, who worked on Van Morrison's *Astral Weeks* and with John Cale of the Velvet Underground. But I have to say, KISS was always more of the band I wanted to be in.

BRUCE STEPHEN FOSTER (PIANO, KISS): I'd recently worked with Richie Wise on my album *Reality Game*, and he asked me to play on an album by a newly signed band he was producing called KISS. Richie wanted me to come up with a pounding rock piano part à la Jerry Lee Lewis for a track called "Nothin' to Lose." After a few hours of refining the part, my fingers were raw and bleeding from the stiff action and frayed keys of the old Steinway piano. Gene and Paul came in after I finished and gave me an instant nod of approval and a satisfied smile when they saw the blood splattered all over the piano keys. Since that day, every time I see Gene he always jokingly checks to see if my fingers are still bleeding [*laughs*]. I'm grateful to have recorded, performed, and composed with some of the greatest artists in pop history, but after people read my bio, inevitably the one thing they always say is, "Oh my God, you played with KISS!"

An acetate disc for KISS's first album, which includes the unreleased song "Acrobat"
Courtesy of Ross Koondel

GENE SIMMONS: We had a song called "Acrobat" that had a slow section and then went into a faster section that sounded like the beginning of "Detroit Rock City." Richie Wise cut that out and wanted to make the song into an instrumental and give it a love theme title. We thought "Love Theme from KISS" was a horrible idea. But we didn't rock the boat and thought maybe he was right.

RICHIE WISE: KISS was such an easy band to record, the songs fell together so quickly. The desire to be huge, the desire to hit the grand slam right out of the box was the foundation that KISS was built on. Nothing was gonna stop them from becoming the biggest band in the world. I never sensed that KISS was about making musical magic; they wanted to make rock-and-roll history.

PAUL STANLEY: As a collection of songs, the first KISS album totally stands up. Musically it's timeless. Those songs sound as current as anything else.

WARREN DEWEY: Gene and Paul wrote songs that worked great. They were creative and smart and didn't hold back or self-censor. I think it's basically a rock thing—kids that never got any heavy music training could often do great work; it didn't require a complex skill set. And to me, the real strength of that first album was in the writing.

GENE SIMMONS: From day one starting with our first album, our lyrics were a celebration of life. The lyrics we wrote weren't deep and didn't talk about the secret of life and what it all meant. They didn't preach or proselytize, and that was all done on purpose. It was all about enjoying yourself and being alive.

PAUL STANLEY: Recording the first album was the culmination of everything I'd worked for up to that point. It was exciting because we were doing an album, but pretty early on I thought that the sound was lacking in terms of what I wanted it to be. I don't think it's a competitive-sounding album in terms of our contemporaries at that point. That became a familiar story every time we went into the studio. We didn't have the experience or the knowledge to articulate what we were looking for or what was lacking in terms of the sound. I always thought that the material we had was much better than the recordings that represented them. I always felt that we missed the boat in terms of being competitive on a world level with some of the other bands who had albums out. I thought our songs were every bit as good if not better than many but that sonically, our albums were pretty tame.

GENE SIMMONS: At times we felt disappointed that the producing team of Kerner and Wise didn't get a better handle on our sound. [Eddie] Kramer understood it better.

PETER CRISS: Kerner and Wise were the wrong producers to work on that album. We should have stayed with Eddie Kramer. Eddie produced our demos, which got us the deal with Casablanca, and they were so much rawer and kick-ass than the album we did with Kerner and Wise. Eddie made Paul give up "Black Diamond" and had me sing it because he thought I could do it better.

RICHIE WISE: In hindsight, the first KISS album is fabulous. But at the time I thought it sounded wimpy. I didn't think the guitars

Paul playing an Ovation Breadwinner guitar during the recording of the first KISS album,
Bell Sound Studios, November 1973 Eddie Solan/KISS Catalog Ltd.

were distorted enough. I didn't think that the album was aggressive enough.

WARREN DEWEY: I remember some struggles with amp volume in the studio, especially with Gene. This was normal with bands that hadn't recorded much. They thought that turning their amps up loud will automatically sound powerful on tape, but that's usually not the case. When I recorded Jimi Hendrix, he always provided an exciting, powerful sound and I just tried to record it accurately. But with most players' guitar or bass turned up to stage volume, it usually became just pure distortion and not powerful when recorded. The blast of air pressure could knock you over, but most people just do not play their home stereos that loud. You wanted to create the illusion of volume, which may not be achievable just by playing loud. It took me years to get to the point where I got really knowledgeable about portraying

Peter on drums during the recording sessions for KISS's debut album, Bell Sound Studios, November 1973. Eddie Solan/KISS Catalog Ltd.

the power of a loud electric guitar and helping musicians get there in a confident way. Keith Richards often recorded through a crummy little cassette machine and the sound was pretty amazing, but it wasn't loud. I worked with Boston on their first album, and with the band's lead guitarist, Tom Scholz, I rounded up every obtainable Marshall amp in Hollywood, and out of about twelve amps we found only two that actually were usable. I'm sure that the modern CD of the first KISS album sounds better than the vinyl pressings from that era. Aficionados like the analog sound of vinyl, but we were always fighting the medium because producers and labels wanted maximum level on the disc. But at some point you just ran out of room and the disc would start to skip or sound distorted. This got worse as the needle approached the inside grooves. Digital gives you more flexibility. Like anything that was done a long time ago, in a way I think it would really be fun to do that album over. Listening to it now, I can hear how the music could easily sound more powerful.

PETER CRISS: I put my heart and soul into it, which I didn't do with every one of our albums. I was just so amazed that we were in a studio and signed to a real record contract even though it was a nobody contract at the time. But we did it, we really did it.

GENE SIMMONS: Recording the first album was a dream come true. We had a ball and we actually made $75 per week salary! We weren't thinking about Rolls-Royces. We were just happy we had enough money to go to any hot dog stand and order a hot dog, sauerkraut, and mustard, or being able to go to Tad's Steakhouse where for $1.29 you could get ground beef, a baked potato, diet Coke, and a piece of apple pie. That was heaven. We didn't have to work for a living anymore, and we thought we had made it.

PAUL STANLEY: Everyone else is working nine to five and we're recording an album? It felt like we were living the dream.

Ready to launch his new label, Neil Bogart sought a designer to capture the visual flair of his new enterprise. Graphic artist, designer, and illustrator David Edward Byrd, who'd designed posters for Bill Graham's Fillmore East for the likes of Jimi Hendrix and the Who—in addition to creating the artwork for the Rolling Stones' 1969 world tour—was tapped to design the memorable logo for his new record label.

DAVID EDWARD BYRD (GRAPHIC ARTIST, DESIGNER, AND ILLUSTRATOR): I knew Neil Bogart when he ran Buddah Records. He called me into his office one day and said, "I'm starting this new record label called Casablanca Records and I'd like you to do a logo for me." So I did a sketch and later a painting. I came up with neon letters for Casablanca, which was inspired by Rick's Café in the film *Casablanca*. Neil wanted to look like Humphrey Bogart with the hat and smoking a cigarette, so I drew that as well. Behind that was an outline of a desert building and palm trees. Neil loved it. That logo was used for the first few years of the label.

David Edward Byrd's original Casablanca Records logo, pencil drawing   Courtesy of David Edward Byrd

After recording was completed, the band's management hired photographer Joel Brodsky to shoot the cover of their debut album.

JOEL BRODSKY (PHOTOGRAPHER, KISS): I [had] shot between five hundred and a thousand album covers, including the Doors' *Strange Days* and Van Morrison's *Astral Weeks*. I was given the assignment to shoot the KISS album cover by Casablanca. I had done a lot of stuff for Buddah Records with Neil Bogart. The shoot was done in New York City at my studio on Fifty-seventh Street. The makeup was unique at the time; it was the beginning of glitter.

PAUL STANLEY: Joel Brodsky was so appealing to us because the stuff he did with the Doors was pretty cool and surreal.

DENNIS WOLOCH: I worked as the art director at Howard Marks Advertising, and Bill Aucoin shared office space with us. We knew Bill before he managed KISS. He came to me and said, "Will you come down to the photo shoot for the album cover? I'm concerned it won't look good enough and I want to make sure their makeup looks perfect. Could you help them put the makeup on neater or help them fix it?" And I said, "Okay." Then I thought about it and my art director mode kicked in. When you're an art director you want to hire the best people for the job. In essence, you become the conductor of the orchestra. So I said, "You know who would really be good for this? A guy named David Byrd." David was a very talented and well-known illustrator and designer. He designed the posters for the original Broadway shows of *Godspell* and *Jesus Christ Superstar*. I thought he'd be attracted to the show biz aspect of it and I was right. David said, "Great. I'm in."

DAVID EDWARD BYRD: I remember there was a big party the night before and we all got very drunk, so everyone at the photo session had hangovers except for Paul and Gene, who didn't drink. I was there to help refine their makeup and make it look better. Mostly I remember working with Peter Criss. I didn't think his makeup looked terribly catlike at first. We talked about it and I made some suggestions to make it more catlike, and it ended up looking good. The other guys' makeup was more stylized. I didn't have anything to do with their makeup.

GENE SIMMONS: We had no concept for our first album cover and we didn't even understand what concept was. We simply showed up at a photographer's studio and took our places.

JOEL BRODSKY: It was a basic four heads on a square picture, a little like the *Meet the Beatles* cover. They were draped in black velvet with a black background. I've done that kind of cover a number of other times with other acts like Nazz, Todd Rundgren's band. My philosophy of album covers is if people knew the music, they were gonna buy it in a brown paper bag. If you were brand new like KISS and you needed to attract attention, the cover did it. And that's a cover that attracted attention.

PAUL STANLEY: When we were going to do a photo shoot for the cover of the first album with Joel Brodsky, Neil said, "Why don't you take some pictures without the makeup?" and we refused.

JOEL BRODSKY: The photo session lasted a little less than an hour but the makeup session probably lasted three hours. It was really Simmons and Stanley who were most concerned with the visuals of the shoot. KISS were reasonably cooperative. I remember the other guys were all on the set and we were all waiting for Gene Simmons to come out. I couldn't get Simmons out of the dressing room and I was getting more and more aggravated. He wanted his makeup to be perfect. I told him, "If you're not out in fifteen minutes there's not going to be anyone here to *take* this picture" [*laughs*].

GENE SIMMONS: After we put on our makeup and outfits, Joel Brodsky said something like, "Oh, I get it, you guys are like clowns. Wait, let me get some balloons." We told him we were serious about this and he didn't get it.

JOEL BRODSKY: The story about me wanting to put balloons behind them, thinking they were circus clowns, is not true. That's someone's imagination.

PAUL STANLEY: We had no input into that album cover. First time I saw that cover was in Bill's office on Fifty-fifth Street and they had the test printing of the cover. I was a bit disappointed because I thought we were so much more over the top. I didn't go, "Gee, this is a great cover!" It wasn't the cover of the first King Crimson album. It wasn't *Led Zeppelin II*, it wasn't *Disraeli Gears*. It was just a photo slapped on a cover. But I couldn't have cared less if it [had been] *your* picture on the cover, I was just thrilled to have an album.

GENE SIMMONS: The first album cover was unapologetic and simply said, "This is KISS. Take it or leave it."

On December 4, 1973, Larry Harris, Casablanca's senior vice president and managing director, arranged to bring the band down to the Spectrum in Philadelphia to witness one of the group's major influences in concert.

LARRY HARRIS: I brought them down from New York to see the Who in Philadelphia for two reasons: one was to get a little closer to the guys, but even more importantly, for them to see what I considered the greatest band in the world at the time. On the ride back from Philadelphia we talked about, "Wouldn't it be great if we could break a guitar onstage like Pete Townshend?" or "Wouldn't it be great if something could happen with the drums?" because of the way Keith Moon played. We spoke about certain aspects of the Who's live show and trying to incorporate it into KISS's show. Early in their career I worked out an endorsement deal with Gibson guitars and they provided free guitars that Paul could smash. In exchange we'd put Gibson on the back of their album covers.

13

THREE, TWO, ONE, LIFTOFF!

*B*efore embarking on their first national tour, KISS returned to play two last shows at Coventry on December 21 and 22, 1973.

PAUL STANLEY: At the time we did the show at Coventry in December of '73, we knew that we were on the verge of the next step toward world domination.

ACE FREHLEY: We had a record deal and management in place plus brand new equipment and costumes, so it was really a special gig for us. As usual, we were well received by a gracious audience.

GENE SIMMONS: When we played there in December of '73, there may have been eighty to a hundred people. But there was a special excitement within the band because we had just signed to Casablanca Records and we were the first artists on the label. For all we knew we were about to become big stars. In the beginning you dream big.

TOMMY RAMONE: When KISS made it, it was a good thing. We felt like if a band like KISS got signed from Queens, maybe we have a shot, too.

BILL AUCOIN: After the Fillmore East closed no one was using it. So we hired the venue to rehearse the KISS show on a bigger stage. They were used to small clubs and we knew we were coming up to

Local newspaper ad for KISS's last shows at Coventry, December 1973 *Courtesy of Ross Koondel*

their first big live show on New Year's Eve. That was the reason for playing Coventry in December of '73.

GENE SIMMONS: That would be the last time we'd play a New York club. We had full outfits, we had the candelabra.

BILL AUCOIN: I wanted to develop a *stage show* and Neil was all for it. He thought, "The bigger, the better."

PETER "MOOSE" ORECKINTO: I started working with KISS in September of 1973. They wanted someone with roadie skills who knew how to move equipment and also how to handle special effects. I was working at the Theater of the Lost Continent in the West Village doing fog machines, flash pots, and 16-millimeter and 35-millimeter projection. I had the experience for what they needed. That night at Coventry we were short on effects. I think we had the fog machine and Peter had the hand shooters. The hand shooter was a device that looked like a drumstick but you'd put flash paper in it. You pressed a switch and it would shoot out a little starburst and it would disintegrate. It would burn and leave no ash. It would be a quick flash and then it was gone. Money had just come in from Casablanca and the major effects were being built. They were building the flash pots. They were building the levitation machine. All of their original stage show was under construction. I remember Sean Delaney counting the number of people that went through the door at the Coventry. The band had a percentage of the door and he didn't want them to get rooked [*laughs*]. They played very well that night because they were hungry. There was a fantastic energy among the band. The music was tight. They were out to make it roll.

KENNY KERNER: They were too big for the club. It was a small dive and they looked huge. The music was powerful and *so* loud. They were a supergroup waiting to happen. They were a supergroup in search of an audience.

STEVE CORONEL: Gene invited me to come see them at the Coventry. The material was good; I thought "Black Diamond" was a great song.

NEAL TEEMAN: Paul called me and asked me to come down to the Coventry to see his new band. When the lights came up and they came out it was like, "Holy shit." I didn't know anything about the makeup or outrageous outfits. They were loud enough for the Garden but in a little club I thought the glasses were gonna come off the racks from the bar and break [*laughs*].

STEVE CORONEL: They looked very scary and intimidating. They were all six feet tall to begin with, and they had these heels and you're looking up at these huge people and you're going, "Wow." It had a lot of presence to it as opposed to a bunch of cute-looking Frampton guys. They looked like big monsters.

BINKY PHILIPS: I went with my girlfriend at the time and I walked in and there were four absolutely brand-new out-of-the-box Marshall stacks. The drum set looked like it had been unpacked from the shipping crate a week earlier. These guys were having money spent on them. There might have been fifty people there. [The band] came out and their outfits were all black leather, expensive and custom made. The makeup was more stylized and read better from further away. They were much better rehearsed and impressed me much more than when I first saw them in the loft and later at the Hotel Diplomat. Just the sound of the new equipment made it sound so much better. They were tight. It sounded like they were playing four or five days a week. I remember turning to my girlfriend and going, "Oh my God, America is gonna eat this up."

TOP: **Ace and Paul perform at Coventry, December 1973** Rik Fox
ABOVE: **KISS at Coventry, December 1973** Rik Fox

MARK POLOTT: KISS played two sets a night and their sets were really strong, especially "Deuce," "Strutter," "Firehouse," and "Black Diamond."

RIK FOX: At one point in their show Gene used to go out into the audience and physically grab people and make them clap their hands. When Bill Aucoin saw him do this, he advised Gene to just keep the act onstage.

MARK POLOTT: The theatrics were beginning. KISS was very impressive. In that era, most of the other bands' material was a little shaky. It was glitter/punk, and these guys were a hard rock band. They were much more polished, and they could play. They weren't the greatest musicians but they really played strong. They really had something. You could tell everything was very thought out and calculated, but in a good way. These guys were smart. They weren't drugged out. You had to respect them. They knew exactly what they were doing every step of the way. They had stage moves, and they had choreography in certain parts of their songs. You didn't see that with other local bands. Maybe you saw it on TV with Paul Revere & the Raiders years before, but not then. Visually and sonically, KISS were exciting.

PAUL STANLEY: We could barely afford amps to play through so I purchased a bunch of speaker cabinets that didn't have speakers in them, which were made by a Dutch company called Marquis. From the beginning it was more important for me to have cabinets than the speakers [*laughs*]. I couldn't afford all the speakers, but I *could* afford the cabinets. This store wanted to get rid of them for cheap and so I bought them and they looked great. These were really cheaply made. Marshall amps are made out of solid wood but these were made out of fiberboard. I can't even imagine how they would have sounded with speakers in them. But even though they weren't Marshalls, they were the right color and they looked cool.

GENE SIMMONS: Paul and I knew that size mattered and that if you saw a new band with a bunch of Marshall stacks, it's the real deal, like Cream and Hendrix.

KISS in action at Coventry, December 1973 Rik Fox

PAUL STANLEY: In the truest sense, how people perceive you ultimately becomes reality; it becomes the truth. They looked great and they gave us a wall of amplifiers, which was very impressive and something all the big bands had. The order to the guy who worked the lights was, "Don't put lights on the speaker cabinets" because as soon as you put lights on the speaker cabinets you could see through 'em [*laughs*].

TOMMY RAMONE: The Ramones liked the equipment KISS used—Marshall stacks and SVT cabinets—and we ended up using the same equipment when we got some money.

RICK RIVETS: Me and the drummer from the Brats, Sparky Donovan, knew KISS were gonna make it and make it big. They reminded me of a futuristic Beatles. You had four guys who could sing, they all had the same look with the black leather and studs, although they each had their own individual characteristics. Musically, Ace impressed me the most. His style was unique. There weren't many guitar players who played like him. He had that arena sound like a Jimmy Page or Jeff Beck. He wasn't a Johnny Thunders type of guitar player. He was also the fun one in the band. He was quite a prankster. You could hear him coming tables away when you heard that laugh of his. Nobody laughed like Ace.

PAUL STANLEY: Coventry was a study in contrasts. The first time we played there, there was nobody there. The last time we played there you could barely get in the door. It was very cool. It was the first place we played when we got a record deal.

On December 21 and 22, 1973, KISS played their final shows at Coventry on a bill that included the all-girl band Isis as well as Rags, City Slicker, and Flaming Youth.

NYDIA "LIBERTY" MATA (LATIN PERCUSSION, ISIS): There was a heated conversation between our managers as to who would open the show. From my recollection, we opened for them.

JOYCE BOGART-TRABULUS: You got paid based on a percentage of the amount of people that were there. So I stood at the door with a clicker and clicked everybody in so the band wouldn't get ripped off. This is how management begins [*laughs*].

EDDIE SOLAN: That night Gene broke a bass string, which is rare. He was amazed he broke a string. He asked me for a new string but I think he knew we didn't have any. But I had some old strings that I used to use to tie up wires and PA cables [*laughs*]. They looked like they were the same thickness so I ran back to the stage with this old string in my hand and he couldn't believe that I found a bass string. He grabbed it, put it on, and it worked.

LYDIA CRISS: The Dolls were in the audience. It was a wild show. It was all starting to happen for them and you could sense the momentum building. Spirits were high.

NYDIA "LIBERTY" MATA: I watched their set and could not believe what I was seeing. No one was doing this kind of an act. Watching them that night you could tell their act was way too big for a small club like Coventry. KISS was meant to be experienced on a big concert stage. And they got there in lightning speed.

JOE VALENTINE (GUITARIST, RAGS): Their music was so good, to be honest, I thought they didn't even need the makeup. I said to myself, "These guys are gonna be big." The Dolls were struggling at the time; their asexual look was a tough sell to Middle America. KISS were the next New York band in line poised to conquer the world.

BILL AUCOIN: Back then the Dolls were still much more popular than KISS was. Where the Dolls used to be able to pack the Coventry, KISS would bring in twenty-five to fifty people. They really weren't that well known and didn't have a tremendous following at that point. KISS had been out of commission for a while, all those months since the summer. So while there were people there for their December show, it wasn't packed.

The group's nine-song Coventry set was captured on a primitive video camera and is included as a bonus on the DVD KISSology Volume Three, 1992–2000.

BILL AUCOIN: I shot the footage of KISS's show that night at Coventry on a half-inch Sony reel-to-reel recorder with a Sony black-and-white video camera. We shot the footage not to preserve a show per se but more to see if they did anything wrong that we could fix before their big show on New Year's Eve at the Academy of Music. Unfortunately, that same reel of videotape held some wonderful moments in their rehearsals in this dungeon down in the Bowery, but I taped over it when I shot the Coventry show.

I always knew I had the footage, and a few years back I finally had it transferred. I came out to LA and showed Gene and Paul the Coventry footage and they were both quite amazed. Gene said, "Gee, we really were together then." At that point they'd rehearsed so much they were really tight. They were thinking of themselves as not being that tight and focused, but the truth of the matter is yes, they were. Watching the video you can sense what I believed from the first moment that I worked with them: KISS were really on a mission. They were driven to make this happen. And a lot of artists aren't, they expect it to happen or they dream about the money, but they don't necessarily have the drive. But KISS had it. At that time, they were very excited. They had their album coming out. They were doing their first tour. This was a dream for any artist and you can see the excitement in their performance at Coventry.

GENE SIMMONS: What people are seeing is early videotape of our show at Coventry, December of 1973. The band is pretty well rehearsed, pretty tight, and the sound quality is pretty damn good. I always knew the footage existed and went after Bill, and it took me years to convince him to let us put it out. I negotiated the deal with Bill and eventually we came to an agreement. He was very kind about it. The fans deserve to see this. I hadn't seen the tape for over thirty years.

PAUL STANLEY: Seeing the footage of us at Coventry only reaffirmed for me how great this band was just in terms of the commitment we had to what we did and the sheer balls to be who we were at that time. There we are basically with no frills in terms of what people would consider a stage show today. The footage is great, the songs are great. It was a thrill to see the footage. You're seeing a band on the verge of exploding into a world force. And again, it only pointed out to me what I always believed, which was that you could either go with us or we'd roll right over you, but you couldn't stay in the way. The band live, even in such a raw state as it is in that Coventry footage, it's undeniable the sheer power and force that we were putting out. And the commitment we had to what we were doing. Commitment is a word that always comes out in terms of referring to KISS. Everything we do and everything we've always done has been done with 100 percent commitment.

GENE SIMMONS: The most impressive thing about it was you saw a *band*. Peter and Ace especially were really into it. They were clear-headed, really committed, and their playing was really solid. Both Ace and Peter played in tune and had great live energy. They rocked. You could see that everybody felt proud of being onstage together. It really was a four-wheel-drive vehicle in the early days. What was most impressive to me was how tight it was. I thought because the band was playing in a club right before we went off on tour we would be loose. Actually, it wasn't loose at all, it was pretty tight. Onstage it was a real band. Offstage it was a dysfunctional family. Ace and Peter had their own demons that continue to this day, unfortunately. When you watch the video of us at Coventry, you can see Peter is playing his heart out. While he was onstage with us, there was nothing bad you could say about him. It was only later that the dysfunction offstage crawled its way into Peter onstage, where drumsticks would be thrown or he'd stop in the middle of a song because he was angry. Ace was very professional onstage but when he was offstage he would drink whatever was around and numb himself. But with all the dysfunction, in some bizarre way we did care for each other.

EDDIE SOLAN: From the first time they played Coventry to the last time they played there, you could sense a big difference in their performance. KISS constantly took a step forward. Every show they did was a constant build. They had a vision. That made them a little more serious than the other local New York bands. Nobody doubted that they'd make it eventually.

BINKY PHILIPS: Here was Paul playing a club with twelve-foot ceilings, a complete dump with shabby tables, a stage covered with torn carpeting, and maybe fifty people, and Paul's screaming, *"Awright New York!"* like he was playing the Garden. We were having a ball and enjoyed how completely over the top they were. It was obvious—[whether] you took this out to Rochester, New York, or Knoxville, Tennessee, that kids were gonna eat it up.

JOE VALENTINE: KISS were a well-thought-out machine. They had their act together in every way. They were a phenomenon waiting to happen.

RIK FOX: Seeing KISS at Coventry you could tell they were a concert arena act squeezed onto a little club stage. The buzz was almost immediate. They were like gods to us. No one had ever seen a band like this before. It was thunder and lightning, just the most awesome thing we'd seen up to that time. They were like a locomotive and nothing was gonna stop them.

BOBBY McADAMS: More than anyone else in KISS, Gene knew the band was gonna make it, and that rubbed off on the rest of the guys. He had that determination and drive to make it happen. I also remember thinking if Ace didn't become a rock star, I didn't know what he was gonna do with his life.

JOEY CRISCUOLA: KISS had a real ballsy attitude. Even back in their club days they had a sense they were something special. Gene always had that ego and so did Paul, Ace, and my brother. They always felt they were stars, whether they played for one person or twenty thousand.

GENE SIMMONS: I was a nobody and KISS were nobodies and we probably were only gonna get one chance, so I wasn't gonna do this half-assed. To me, if you're gonna make an impression you need to make a complete spectacle of yourself. Each of us were trying to make a lasting impression immediately because there might not be a second time. Fuck confidence, fuck everything. You must stick your neck out there. There's no choice. It's a dog-eat-dog world.

PAUL STANLEY: We needed a place that could be ours and Coventry was a place in Queens that was just on the other side of the East River. It gave people in New York access to come see us and it also set us a little apart from the New York glitter bands. Coventry was a place where we really cut our teeth and it was the first place we ever played.

GENE SIMMONS: For us, playing at the Coventry was magic. Coventry defined who and what we are. We felt like we belonged together and believed it was us against the world. There was definitely something there. By our last show at Coventry, we had gotten a real sense of who we were. By that point, we became comfortable in our skin. We were not like the rest of the bands. We didn't care about hit singles. For some bizarre, delusional notion we knew who we were and how we had to do it, and that was going to be our way. [*Singing*] "I did it my way. . . ." "My Way" is a song that should have been written about KISS.

14

GREAT EXPECTATIONS

By the end of their first full year on the rock-and-roll battlefield, KISS were hardened metal warriors fueled by big ambition and even bigger dreams. Under the guidance of manager Bill Aucoin and his creative foil, Sean Delaney, the band had worked tirelessly to perfect their makeup, costumes, and stage show. But on the cusp of the release of their debut album, Warner Brothers Records suddenly got cold feet over KISS's unconventional image and openly expressed their concern.

BILL AUCOIN: In late '73 Warner Brothers called Neil and said, "Can you ask KISS to take the makeup off? We don't believe in it." At that point Alice Cooper's records were starting to sell less, and his makeup was nowhere near as extravagant as KISS's makeup, so I guess that scared them off. We were at the Fillmore East after a dress rehearsal in preparation for the Academy of Music show and Neil [Bogart] called me personally and said, "I know this is gonna be a tough one, Bill, but can you please just ask the band if they'd take their makeup off?" I went up to the dressing room and said, "I just got a call from Neil. He asked me whether or not you guys would consider taking off the makeup. Warner's isn't buying it." They had real puzzled looks on their faces. Then the band asked me what I thought and I told them we should stick with the makeup no matter what and they wholeheartedly agreed. I called him back and told him in no uncertain terms, "You tell Warner Brothers we're not gonna do that—the makeup's staying on," and to his credit, Neil didn't fight me on it.

GENE SIMMONS: We said, "All or nothing. You get the makeup and the band or you get nothing." We told them it was our way or the highway. This is the line in the sand [and] you may not cross it.

KISS won the battle with Warner Brothers and wrapped up the year in grand style. Then on December 31, 1973, the band played their biggest gig to that point, landing the opening slot on a four-act bill at New York's Academy of Music—KISS, Teenage Lust, Iggy & the Stooges, and Blue Öyster Cult.

BINKY PHILIPS: The Academy of Music was a classic old theater from the vaudeville days. It was located on East Fourteenth Street in the Village and was one of the main venues in New York. They later changed its name to the Palladium.

PETER CRISS: The first time I really felt like a star was at that Academy of Music show. They always called me "the complainer." I was going, "I don't know if we're gonna make it. We ain't going nowhere." At the time we were riding around in milk trucks and beat-up station wagons. And all of a sudden up pulls this stretch Mercedes, and I went, "Wow, this is cool [*laughs*], this is what the big guys must feel like." We wanted to make a grand entrance to the gig—and nobody was there when we pulled up! But it lifted my spirits. I knew then that these guys had style. They thought bigger than life, and I liked that. Even though it meant spending whatever last buck they had, they were willing to do that just because it was important.

PAUL STANLEY: Typical of our bravado or sense of importance, I remember thinking there were other bands in New York who were doing better than us or were bigger than us, and all I wanted to do was get on a bill with them. I knew we'd blow them away.

HAROLD C. BLACK (MULTI-INSTRUMENTALIST, TEENAGE LUST): A few weeks after their last show at Coventry, KISS opened for us at the Academy of Music on New Year's Eve. Unlike all the other local New York bands, they had money behind them, plus publicity and a label—all the things you needed to get ahead. KISS was well prepared for the show but none of the bands on the bill knew they were gonna open. They weren't even included in the ads for the show.

ERIC BLOOM (LEAD VOCALIST/GUITARIST, BLUE ÖYSTER CULT): KISS was not originally on the bill. I was told by our management that a new band had been shoved in as an opener at the last minute.

PAUL STANLEY: We were very excited about the Academy of Music show even though we were fourth on the bill. We were excited to show people what we could do and also take the next step and write the next chapter in our career.

GENE SIMMONS: Without sounding too big-headed, we punished them severely and we knew that we had arrived.

BOB GRUEN: I did a lot of work for Buddah Records, from Sha Na Na to George Burns, so that's how I got the job to photograph KISS. I took photos of the band with Neil Bogart before the show in the back alley behind the Academy of Music. Neil came down in makeup to kid around with them—[he was] handcuffed to the record contract.

EDDIE SOLAN: We got to the show and there was no PA system. It was in a trailer truck coming from Denver, Colorado, and because of inclement weather it got there really late. Since we were the opening act we'd be the first to use the PA. We had no time for a sound check. I was up on the mixing platform and Gene's mic wouldn't work. One of the stagehands grabbed a microphone off Peter's drums, set it up in front of the stage, and that worked.

BUCK DHARMA (LEAD GUITARIST, BLUE ÖYSTER CULT): My wife walked into their dressing room by mistake and saw them putting on their makeup, and she didn't know what to make of it [*laughs*].

PAUL STANLEY: I remember walking out onstage, and I'd never seen anything that big before. We'd played clubs a few weeks prior to that and now we were playing a place with a 4,800-seat capacity.

IVAN KRAL: Seeing them on this big stage I felt, "This is where they belonged." I shot about a minute of Super 8 footage of their set.

PAUL STANLEY: I thought the stage was huge and the audience was enormous. I remember busting the snap off the top of my pants and being afraid that if I didn't keep the guitar pressed against it I was gonna lose them.

ERIC BLOOM: Somebody told me, "You gotta catch this new band KISS." Normally I wouldn't be at the venue early, but I was intrigued so I showed up early.

EDDIE SOLAN: I was up on the mixing platform and Bill Aucoin was sitting next to me. KISS comes out and does a few songs.

DEE DEE RAMONE: Everybody there must have been a Stooges fan, and KISS took over the whole night. Nobody could believe what they were seeing. They had ten Marshall stacks on each side. It was a real show.

SCOTT ASHETON (DRUMMER, IGGY & THE STOOGES): No one had ever heard of KISS. I thought, "Wow, this band is totally different." Where Iggy could be outrageous onstage, it was nothing compared to KISS. They were pure entertainment. The crowd was diggin' it but there was also an element of "what the hell is this?" [laughs].

JAMES WILLIAMSON (LEAD GUITARIST, IGGY & THE STOOGES): In those days there were so many novelty bands that nothing surprised me. I caught a little of KISS's set and remember doing a double take upon first seeing these guys in makeup and crazy costumes [laughs]. It was over the top. I'd never seen anybody take the makeup thing to that extreme before. A lot of guys were wearing makeup in those days, but it was more subtle than [KISS's]. They wore white clown makeup with painted-on faces, and it was extraordinary.

TODD RUNDGREN: When I saw KISS that night I didn't think, "This is revolutionary" or "This is going to be the biggest thing ever." I remember thinking they didn't play very well, which is probably why they had to wear the makeup [*laughs*]. A band like KISS that wore makeup wasn't unusual to me. New York had a lot of funny stuff going on then. Half of the bands dressed in drag, with the New York Dolls leading the way. Alice Cooper dressed up in half-drag and wore dark raccoon makeup. It was an English tradition, too; a lot of English bands wore makeup prior to KISS, like the Alex Harvey Band.

PAUL STANLEY: There were a few mishaps that night. This magician had come up with this idea where Gene would light flash paper, which had flash powder inside of it, throw it up in the air over the audience, and there would be a burst of fire and then an explosion.

GENE SIMMONS: Presto, the magician who had taught me how to breathe fire, also taught me this trick with flash paper. It was designed to fit in your palm like a Hershey's kiss. I practiced that trick so many times. There'd be an explosion and flash over people's heads in total darkness.

EDDIE SOLAN: So it comes to the point in the show where Gene would throw fireballs from his hand. He had a candelabra and he lit the flash paper with that. Every time we practiced it the flash paper would burn instantly.

GENE SIMMONS: That night my aim wasn't so good and some guy was standing on his chair and that flash went off in his face. I saw it explode in his face, and he fell over like a pin in a bowling alley.

EDDIE SOLAN: Bill Aucoin and I looked at each other with both of our mouths open. We were thinking, "This is the beginning, and now this is the end of KISS."

JOYCE BOGART-TRABULUS: I'm trying to keep things light and said to the kid, "Come and sit here, let me put something on your face. Maybe we should take you to a doctor." I'm doing all of this while Bill is getting a release form dictated to him by our attorney so this kid could sign it, and he did.

GENE SIMMONS: The guy came backstage and it looked like Velveeta cheese had melted over the left side of his face. He looked like someone from a Hammer Films horror movie.

PAUL STANLEY: Through the blisters on his face he said, "You guys are awesome!"

GENE SIMMONS: He was saying, "Wow, that was the coolest show I've ever seen."

PAUL STANLEY: Thankfully he was a huge fan. We could have been in a lot of trouble, but it worked out great.

BOB GRUEN: He wasn't angry or pissed off. I remember before he got into the ambulance he told a reporter, "KISS is my favorite band" [*laughs*].

GENE SIMMONS: Needless to say, I never did that trick again.

PAUL STANLEY: And that wasn't the only mishap that night. Gene's hair also caught fire.

GENE SIMMONS: That was the first time I breathed fire onstage. That night we wanted to make a big impression. We were excited that we were actually playing the Academy of Music where we went to see bands like Slade, Argent, and Fleetwood Mac. We wanted to be impressive so I used extra amounts of hairspray to make my hair as big as possible. On the can of hairspray it says, "Warning: Do not get near flame." By the third song we're playing "Firehouse," and as soon as I breathed fire the right side of my hair just went up.

EDDIE SOLAN: He took a mouthful of kerosene, held out a dagger with the flame on it, blew fire, and that went great. There was a block of foam on the stage that he could stick the dagger in when he finished. So he bent down with his hair falling forward and it went into the flame and set his hair on fire. Bill Aucoin and I looked at each other again and said, "What else can go wrong?"

GENE SIMMONS: I didn't know my hair had caught fire; all I remember is feeling some warmth, but I thought it was the lights. Sean Delaney came out with a wet towel to put out the flames. I didn't realize what

KISS performs in the opening slot on a four-act bill at New York's Academy of Music on December 31, 1973. Note Gene's smeared makeup design. During his fire-breathing stunt, Gene's hair accidentally caught fire; the errant flames were extinguished with a wet towel by choreographer Sean Delaney. Dagmar/www.dagmarfoto.com

had happened until the end of the show when I started to smell something. I looked in the mirror and saw my hair on one side was two inches shorter than the other.

PAUL STANLEY: When you see four guys onstage in white makeup, black leather studs, and seven-inch heels with big amplifiers and all hell's breaking loose, if somebody's hair did catch fire you might not even notice it. And if you did notice it you might think it's part of the show. I once got hit in the face with a bottle and I was bleeding onstage and I'm sure there were people in the front row going, "How does he do that?" [*laughs*].

ERIC BLOOM: I was on the side of the stage behind the curtain watching them and they blew me away. I liked KISS's coordinated, rhythmic side-to-side swaying and all the pyro. I like shtick and they had plenty of it. They also had quality songwriting to back it up, with songs like "Deuce" and "Strutter." I thought they were outrageous. They were young and hungry.

BUCK DHARMA: Just the sheer spectacle of KISS was amazing. I also was struck by how physically large they were compared to us. They were big guys and they had those big platform boots on so they looked unearthly to me. Then I saw all the fire and explosions, the big KISS sign, and their drum riser go ten feet in the air and I went, "Wow! This is something I never expected to see." It was just a level of production that you didn't see coming from a fledgling act.

JOYCE BOGART-TRABULUS: We surprised the band with the KISS sign at that show. Nobody had ever seen anything like it at that point. That sign would forever brand them with an audience.

IGGY POP (LEAD VOCALIST, IGGY & THE STOOGES): I saw KISS come out onstage and from above them lowered the most gi-fucking-normous neon lightbulb–adorned sign that said "KISS." I thought, "Jesus fucking Christ, these guys have got some dough behind them." It did look cool—in a crude and very vulgar way. It was the largest piece of production I have ever seen used by a third-bill act in a run-down theater in my entire career. It obviously worked for them.

HAROLD C. BLACK: That night was the first time they used the KISS sign, which lit up like a movie marquee. It was so huge it wouldn't have fit into Coventry.

PAUL STANLEY: The KISS sign was Bill Aucoin's idea. It was very heavy and made out of wood that was covered with silver vinyl.

MARK RAVITZ: They needed us to build it so it could be premiered at that show. At the time they were into sequins and glitter. They showed me a photo of their logo made out of sequins, so our objective was to build a stage sign that lit up and looked like their sequined logo. The sign was four feet high and made out of plywood, which we painted black. The letters that spelled out K-I-S-S were three-dimensional, probably a foot deep.

GENE ƧIMMONƧ: When the stage would go dark the KISS sign would come on and it was so bright that it would burn the imagery of KISS in your eyes. When you closed your eyes you still saw "KISS" in your head.

PAUL ƧTANLEY: Productions were in their infancy at that point. So first of all, to put a sign up was ballsy and nobody thought to say, "Take it down."

BILL AUCOIN: They let us get away with it because they didn't know what this damn opening act was gonna do. Everyone who walked into the theater saw the KISS logo already set up. So the hour before the show all you saw was the KISS logo.

PAUL ƧTANLEY: Literally the sign would be hanging while someone else played. Nobody had anything like it.

BILL AUCOIN: From there we learned a lot of lessons that we got away with all the way through their career.

PAUL ƧTANLEY: We got away with a lot of things. People were just baffled and stymied by what we were doing because no one else had done it. You can't get away with that now because it's been done. Nobody was there to say you can't hang a KISS sign up, because no band had a sign.

HAROLD C. BLACK: Between the big KISS sign and Gene's hair catching fire during their show, I wondered, "What the hell can we do to top this?" [*laughs*]. Everyone had a hard time following KISS that night.

EDDIE ƧOLAN: The band viewed the Academy of Music gig as a real triumph. They played with three other acts on the bill and blew everybody away. All the bands that followed seemed dull.

On January 8, 1974, more than a month before the release of the band's first album, KISS took part in a Warner Brothers/Casablanca joint press showcase held at the site of the now-shuttered Fillmore East. A former Yiddish theater, the Greenwich Village venue, owned by famed rock promoter Bill Graham, officially opened on March 8, 1968. Led Zeppelin, the Who, Jimi

Hendrix, the Doors, Janis Joplin, Pink Floyd, the Beach Boys, Frank Zappa & the Mothers of Invention, and countless other rock legends performed at this historic venue until it closed its doors in June 1971. A string of classic albums were also recorded there, including Humble Pie's Performance Rockin' the Fillmore, *the Allman Brothers Band's* At Fillmore East, *and Jimi Hendrix's* Band of Gypsys.

MARK RAVITZ: At that point the Fillmore East was lying dormant. Apparently, it had been ransacked, and the Hell's Angels were using it. The idea was to take advantage of that as a texture. For that event we made up a big spiderweb backdrop twenty feet wide and about ten feet high because it seemed to fit their image and work within the environment. That was only used for the Fillmore East press launch. It was made out of clothesline rope and we just tied it together.

I created a simple stage set for the band. There was an amp line behind them. The pyro was in the front and the sides so it could circle them. Flash pots added to the atmosphere. It was a little metal box with explosive material that gets a charge and goes off and creates a big puff of smoke and a little bit of flash. In terms of lighting, it was very simple. I wanted to create a mysterious mood and capture the gritty feel inside the Fillmore East. This added to the excitement. They didn't have a wall of amps at that point. At that time they didn't have the money to mount a big show so we took advantage of all these elements to create a simple but effective presentation. Funnily enough, I was involved in the design of two major theatrical rock presentations around that time, with KISS and David Bowie's *Diamond Dogs* stage set.

GENE SIMMONS: We were gonna go off on this short tour in Canada and used the Fillmore East to rehearse.

EDDIE SOLAN: I remember the moment we walked in you could feel the vibes of all the legendary artists that stood on that stage: Led Zeppelin, Jimi Hendrix, Jim Morrison.

TOP: Fillmore East rehearsal, New York City, December 26, 1973
ABOVE: Fillmore East rehearsal sans makeup, New York City,
December 26, 1973 Photos by Eddie Solan/KISS Catalog Ltd.

GENE SIMMONS: Here we are rehearsing there and our minds were blown to be on the same stage as the Who or Led Zeppelin.

BOB MERLIS (PUBLICITY MANAGER, WARNER BROTHERS RECORDS): KISS made their New York City press launch at the Fillmore East. We invited music journalists to the show, people who worked for the Warner branch, and people from retail as well.

GENE SIMMONS: My mother came down, and friends and family.

EDDIE SOLAN: During the afternoon before their press launch, I took photos of the band posing with Neil Bogart in full makeup and their managers Bill Aucoin and Joyce Biawitz. Neil was wearing handcuffs with one end ceremoniously handcuffed to their record contract.

A close look at Paul Stanley in those photos reveals he is sporting a different makeup design from his trademark star.

PAUL STANLEY: Neil Bogart didn't like my makeup design and didn't like my prancing around onstage. He thought it was effeminate and wasn't masculine and was afraid of us being lumped in with other bands like that. So he wanted me to change it. Being a team player, I said, "Okay." In five minutes I came up with an alternative bandit design that had no rhyme or reason. It meant absolutely nothing and that's probably why it didn't work. If KISS were just a matter of putting paint on your face then there would be a lot of other bands still doing it. I had that bandit makeup design for about a month and then said, "Screw this, Neil will just have to live with it" and went back to what felt right and *was* right, and that was the star.

On hand to cover their hometown press launch was Warner Brothers publicity manager Bob Merlis.

BOB MERLIS: I was at the show in the capacity of a reporter, as I [had been] enlisted to write the blurb about their launch for *Circular*, the weekly Warner Brothers in-house newspaper, so it wasn't gonna be anything negative. Before KISS came on I remember Neil Bogart came out and said, "My Puerto Rican numerologist told me that this band was gonna be a sure thing." They did their whole show and it was pretty powerful. I seem to remember the reaction to the band was pretty positive because it was quite a spectacle.

An excerpt from the *Circular* review:

"The band comes on strong and we were struck with the fact that KISS play like the demons they resemble (rather than four villains from a vintage Batman comic). Their music is the hardest of hard rock—macho glitter, if you can get through the apparent ambiguity. Some call it thunder rock. . . . Their repertoire is 100 percent up-tempo killer stuff. . . . Theirs is a kind of mood music, if you happen to be in the mood to blow up buildings or wreck cars. You'll either love or hate KISS but the odds are that they're going to be a big act whether you like them or not."

—Bob Merlis

RIK FOX: I was in the front row and shot some photos during the show. They were fantastic. Each level of seeing the band was exciting and new. They progressed really quickly from the shows at Coventry and the Hotel Diplomat. Now at the Fillmore East launch they were pulling out the big guns with the fire-breathing, smoke, bombs, and the big KISS sign. It took it to another whole level that I hadn't seen before.

GENE SIMMONS: We only did eight songs. We got a great reaction. We had the musical goods and the vibes. After the show we came back out onstage to greet press, friends, and family. One of the first guys who came up was a guy named Fred Kirby from *Variety*,

ABOVE, LEFT: **Paul and Ace, press launch, Fillmore East, New York City, January 8, 1974** Rik Fox

ABOVE, RIGHT: **Gene, Paul, and Peter, press launch, Fillmore East, New York City, January 8, 1974** Rik Fox

LEFT: **Paul, press launch, Fillmore East, New York City, January 8, 1974** Rik Fox

who wrote a great piece about us. Then I see my mother coming up to the stage. I was on the right-hand side of the stage and Paul was on the left meeting his family and his friends. I remember my mother turning to her right and going to Paul's side. I was going, "Mom! Mom! Over here!" She couldn't hear me because of all the noise and the talking and she walks up to Paul thinking it's me.

PAUL $TANLEY: Gene's mom came up to me with that accent of hers and said [*imitating her Israeli accent*], "Stan, I very much like your orchestra, which one were you?" [*laughs*].

DICK CLARK: I remember Neil Bogart telling me about the idea of presenting a rock-and-roll band in clown makeup. The idea sounded ridiculous! In 1974, I recall having dinner with Neil and his wife at the Century Plaza Hotel. Immediately after the bite to eat, we adjourned to a moderate-sized room in the hotel where KISS, in full makeup and dressed in their outlandish costumes complete with giant, oversized high-heeled boots, presented an abbreviated concert. Mind you, their audience was only the four of us. I recall, even back then, Gene Simmons's tongue was already part of the act. The presentation was mind-boggling and most memorable. I had never seen anything like it before in my life. Obviously, if Neil was going to pursue the development of this band, it was going to be unique and challenging.

With his background in hype and promotion, Neil Bogart always thought big. On February 18, 1974, Bogart threw a lavish coming-out party for his new label at the Century Plaza Hotel in Los Angeles. Adorned with the colorful red neon Casablanca logo, the circular invitation read:

Casablanca Records launch party invitation, February 1974   Courtesy of Ross Koondel

Times are tough. The only things left are Victor Laszlo and the underground band KISS. Bring someone you trust and join them at the last outpost of freedom, Rick's Café Americain (Los Angeles Room, Century Plaza Hotel), Monday, February 18, 8:30–11pm. Got it, sweetheart? Rick will have his gaming tables running, and nothing is going to stop him. Feel lucky? Want to forget the bad times? If you can take it so can he. The time is the early 1940s—so Rick wants you to dress accordingly.

PAUL STANLEY: We were told there was going to be a press party in Los Angeles. The label flew us out and put us up at the Chateau Marmont.

JEFF FRANKLIN: The economy was totally in the gutter, and here's Neil spending a ton of money on a party.

GARY STROMBERG (CO-OWNER, GIBSON & STROMBERG PUBLIC RELATIONS): Neil Bogart hired our office to help build a buzz around their Century Plaza launch. Neil understood theater, and that was just a wonderful, theatrical event. Neil was a publicist's dream because he really understood how to get media attention. In the rock-and-roll world you had to be flamboyant, and Neil fit the bill.

JOE SMITH: Neil told us he had this great band but it would require an enormous kickoff. That party cost us a fortune.

BOBBI COWAN: He was starting his label and he was doing it, as he did everything, in completely over-the-top fashion. Neil's idea was to re-create Rick's Café from the film *Casablanca*. It was a very exotic Moroccan décor.

JOE SMITH: We turned Neil loose on the Warner Brothers film prop department. They brought in all kinds of props that fit the theme.

STAN CORNYN: Bob Regehr at Warner Brothers had created a *Casablanca* theme to the room. There was a Humphrey Bogart lookalike wandering around in a white tux jacket. There was also a Maltese falcon there and a roulette table.

LARRY HARRIS: There was a live camel. Palm trees were brought in—real and fake. People were gambling for door prizes.

JOYCE BOGART-TRABULUS: Everybody was in costume. Neil was wearing Humphrey Bogart's suit from *Casablanca*. People that worked at the event were wearing props from the movie. Some wore these little legionnaire hats that were part of Claude Rains's costume from the movie.

GARY STROMBERG: I wore a Moroccan robe and a fez. One of my good friends, the musician Hugh Masekela, came dressed as a Nazi officer. He had an authentic SS uniform with the high boots. It was just so crazy, this black guy dressed up as a Nazi. This was keeping in line with the *Casablanca* theme of the event, Rick's Café.

The event drew hordes of industry bigwigs, radio and retail, press, and its fair share of Hollywood glitterati, including actors Ted Knight from The Mary Tyler Moore Show, *David Janssen, Dick Clark of* American Bandstand *fame, soft-pop crooner Bobby Goldsboro, punk rock anarchist Iggy Pop, and Burton Cummings, lead vocalist of seventies hitmakers the* Guess Who.

BURTON CUMMINGS (LEAD VOCALIST, THE GUESS WHO): KISS freaked me out completely. I felt like quitting. There was no way I was gonna go that route. That's why I wrote a song called "Glamour Boy," which was about KISS and David Bowie. It all became makeup and costumes, and the music became fourth or fifth in importance. I was depressed after seeing KISS and I remember that I went and got drunk after that show. I didn't dig it. It was so shocking to me that these guys were there looking like that. I don't remember anything about the music.

MARK PARENTEAU (MUSIC DIRECTOR AND DJ, WABX-FM): The event was way over the top, like everything that Neil Bogart did. The actor David Janssen was married to Neil Bogart's wife's sister, and his TV show, *The Fugitive*, was one of the biggest TV shows ever. I remember walking backstage with Neil and his wife, Larry Harris, and David Janssen and his wife, and we found some little corner to put something up our noses. At that moment I was going, "Wow, I'm snorting blow with David Janssen, that's pretty interesting" [*laughs*].

A roulette table had been set up, and some serious gambling ensued. Whoever racked up the most winning chips scored first prize: a reproduction of the original Maltese falcon from the classic film of the same name. The second-prize winner walked away with a giant stuffed camel.

JOYCE BOGART-TRABULUS: Alice Cooper and David Janssen won the prizes in the gambling stakes.

BOBBI COWAN: The launch was very well attended. Everybody knew that Neil Bogart was the genius of the music business and nobody wanted to miss anything that he was gonna do.

JOYCE BOGART-TRABULUS: The Century Plaza Casablanca party was the biggest party the town had seen. It was to introduce the record company, not the band, which was secondary, really.

NEIL BOGART: As a new company we didn't have much time to break them. But within five months we had everybody talking about KISS. The hype was ready to start. KISS was the next coming.

STAN CORNYN: Hype is part of any label that wanted to make hits. It's a four-letter word for promotion, for exposure, for recognition. Warner Brothers did its own brand of hype, too, particularly in our startling ads for Randy Newman with the headline "Once You Get Used to It, His Voice Is Really Something." For Joni Mitchell, an ad headlined "Joni Mitchell is 90% Virgin." That, you might say, is hippie hype. But yes, Bogart was to records back then what today World Wrestling Entertainment is to sports.

With a towering wall of Marshall amps cranked to ear-splitting levels, KISS showcased their new spectacle of sound and wild theatrics. Reps in attendance from Warner Brothers Records, the distributor of Casablanca, were wholly unprepared—and frankly, underwhelmed—by the band's music and image. Hard rock kingpin Alice Cooper was also in attendance, no doubt to witness first-hand his new competition and the potential inheritors of his shock-rock throne. After seeing the band perform, he famously deadpanned, "What they need is a gimmick."

STAN CORNYN: This anonymous ballroom had a stage at one end. I was having cocktails and dinner with my fellow executives and then KISS came on to perform.

RICHIE WISE: I was helping the band with the live sound that night. The ballroom was not the right place to present KISS.

MARK PARENTEAU: It was a jaded Hollywood audience. It wasn't kids in Detroit. I remember the explosions and the big KISS sign coming on, and I thought it was interesting theater but I wasn't impressed with their music.

STAN CORNYN: Gene had the longest tongue I've ever seen. The band was an assault on your visual senses as well as your ears.

GARY STROMBERG: The party itself was the star. The party had too much energy, and it overwhelmed the performance. The band came on and it was anticlimactic.

JOYCE BOGART-TRABULUS: The party was extremely successful on every level, except for the reaction to KISS. It was a theme party with lookalikes from the movie and *tout de* Hollywood in costumes of the era, but a disaster for the band. Neil had told them to play full throttle, to not hold back. But a hotel ballroom is no place for a rock band with a sound like KISS.

GENE SIMMONS: We went out there to try and blow this place up and put on a full-on performance.

JOE SMITH: When KISS came onstage it was shocking. Our staff was underwhelmed. They had kind of an elitist attitude. If it wasn't what they considered music with artistic flair like Randy Newman, Neil Young, or Joni Mitchell, it didn't count.

GENE SIMMONS: We did the whole show. By the third song the ballroom was filled with smoke from our bombs. People were coughing and running out.

PAUL STANLEY: Literally as soon as we started playing the room pretty much cleared out.

GENE SIMMONS: It was a disaster.

PAUL STANLEY: It was obviously not our audience. It showed us that we were the people's band, we weren't the elitists' band.

JOYCE BOGART-TRABULUS: The Warner Brothers people hated them.

GENE SIMMONS: Neil Bogart came to our defense. He was telling the Warner Brothers people, "This is what they do; this ain't Lawrence Welk. KISS doesn't change for nobody."

JOYCE BOGART-TRABULUS: Of all the guests that night, I think only Alice Cooper got it.

ALICE COOPER: I had no problem with KISS for one reason: it never touched on what Alice did. I always said that KISS were comic book heroes whereas Alice was much more *Phantom of the Opera*. KISS was another band that had a couple of good special effects. I thought the breathing of fire was a very good idea and some of the costumes were over the top. And I liked their music.

LARRY HARRIS: I viewed the party as more of a success for launching the label than a success for launching KISS. What it did do for the record distributors that walked out was ingrain KISS's name in their head, and that was important.

STAN CORNYN: I remember we all thought KISS was amusing, fun, but we were people who had seen Jimi Hendrix in a boa lighting his guitar on fire in Monterey, so KISS seemed like a variation, not an epiphany. When you saw the drummer's drumsticks explode, not to mention Gene Simmons blowing fire, his lizard tongue, all the makeup, and the sort of drag king outfits they would wear, one of the perceptions at Warner Brothers was perhaps maybe there's not much music under it [*laughs*]. It was and is the job of label personnel, certainly in 1974, to avoid making personal judgments about acts that the label has signed. Our job was to do our best promotion and selling job on each act, whether it's Debby Boone or the Fugs. Our

"Open up and say aah . . ." **Gene Simmons's legendary tongue** Fin Costello/KISS Catalog Ltd.

criterion, like any label's, was getting airplay that made listeners want to buy a copy of this song or album. Publicity was a natural for KISS, with the makeup. But not many people buy an album because one of its singers can stick out his tongue notoriously.

Urban legends have always been a part of the fabric of rock and roll. During concerts or in photo sessions, Gene Simmons had a hard time keeping his tongue in cheek. Flopping out of his mouth like a swollen alien appendage, his tongue is almost as famous as the band itself. As a result of its almost supernatural length, Gene's tongue has been the source of many wild rumors and urban myths through the years.

GENE SIMMONS: I remember being in seventh grade and the girls kept asking me to stick my tongue out. I'd wiggle it and they'd giggle like chickens being led to slaughter, never imagining what they wanted me to do with it. Even in the first bands I was in, like the Long Island Sounds and Cathedral, I would stick my tongue out at various girls in the audience. By then I knew what the fascination with my tongue was all about. For some reason when I started playing onstage with KISS I began sticking my tongue out and it caught on. Later, there were a lot of rumors and urban myths going around in the seventies about my tongue—crazy stuff like how I'd had a cow tongue transplant or that I had the flap under my tongue surgically cut to make it longer. None of it was true.

15

"PUT YOUR TWO LIPS TOGETHER..."

n February 1974, a little over a year after the group's debut performance at Coventry, KISS was unleashed on the world as their big major-label debut. Almost forty years since its release, KISS is championed as a watershed in hard rock history, boasting such signature classics as "Deuce," "Strutter," "Firehouse," "Cold Gin," and "Nothin' to Lose." Their striking album was reminiscent of the cover of Meet the Beatles, the perfect introduction to this outrageous new rock outfit.

RICHIE WISE: We turned the record into the label and everybody loved it, but I think Neil realized it would take a long time to break KISS. They weren't gonna break on radio—it had to come from their live performances.

KENNY KERNER: The album wasn't getting much airplay and did not sell well. It wasn't reviewed favorably. The media looked at it like "Here was Neil's attempt at a rock band." The makeup made the press look at it as a rock-and-roll gimmick, not a bubblegum gimmick. It hurt the band that they weren't being taken seriously. I remember Richie and I spoke to them and said, "Don't worry about the reviews, don't worry about the sales, let your live show do the talking. Get them to the show and you can build a career from there." And they did.

In preparation for their first tour, KISS signed with the powerful booking agency ATI (American Talent International).

IRA BLACKER (CO-OWNER, ATI BOOKING AGENCY): ATI was an international rock-and-roll talent booking agency. We would handle tours, individual concert dates—basically anywhere the artists worked, and that included television, too.

JEFF FRANKLIN: When I started ATI, I didn't have superstars. I had acts like the 1910 Fruitgum Company and the Lemon Pipers, although I also represented some bigger acts like the Beach Boys. So we started packaging shows. We'd take Rod Stewart, Deep Purple, and Savoy Brown and put them all on a show and we'd sell out across the country, and none of them at that point were big stars. We did the same thing with KISS. We put them on the bottom of the bill with two other decent-sized acts like Savoy Brown and Manfred Mann's Earth Band. Ninety percent of the artists that ever played with KISS were our clients.

IRA BLACKER: Most of KISS's early shows were part of packages. ATI repped acts like Blue Öyster Cult, Manfred Mann's Earth Band, REO Speedwagon, Nazareth, Uriah Heep, and Rory Gallagher, and we'd pair KISS up with these acts. I placed them on a bill with Savoy Brown, an act I signed to ATI, and that was one of the first big tours they did. KISS was going down great. Their music wasn't amazing but their presentation was extremely original both in the exaggerated performance, the makeup, the theatricality, the levitating drum kit. They were in essence the P. T. Barnum of rock and roll. They were larger than life.

RICK MUNROE (KISS LIGHTING DIRECTOR): Back in the early days, even though we were the opening act and there were two acts ahead of us—a special guest and headliner—KISS really made an impression on audiences. People would leave after KISS played.

PAUL CHAVARRIA (KISS ROADIE AND BASS TECH): When the band was an opening act, it didn't matter if they were playing for twenty people or twenty thousand people. They came out with the intention of kicking the headliner's ass. That was their attitude from day one.

STEVE SYBESMA (CONCERT PROMOTER AND CO-OWNER, SUNSHINE PROMOTIONS): ATI tipped us off about this hot up-and-coming band that they were representing. We always tried to help out the booking agencies, so we put them on shows.

DAVE LUCAS (CONCERT PROMOTER AND CO-OWNER, SUNSHINE PROMOTIONS): We believed in investing in the future with artists and working with them from the ground up. Our very first date promoting KISS was in August of '74. Blue Öyster Cult and James Gang were co-headliners and KISS was the special guest. They made a whopping $2,000 that night [*laughs*].

STEVE SYBESMA: That year we promoted four shows with KISS as either the opening act or special guest. Early on KISS started to build a die-hard following and word-of-mouth started to spread about the band from the press, fans, and other promoters. KISS broke very quickly as a concert act.

IRA BLACKER: I knew KISS was gonna make it big when I began getting reports from promoters following their dates that they were willing to take them back on their own afterwards. Pretty quickly into KISS's career they began headlining smaller venues.

DAVE LUCAS: We went from doing that date in August '74 with KISS as special guests to them headlining and selling out the Indianapolis Convention Center less than a year later.

It became a common occurrence for KISS to blow away the headlining act. But the band's ferocity as an opening act presented its own problems for their booking agency.

GENE *S*IMMON*S*: ATI was getting worried because they were having a hard time booking us because we were so good and no one wanted to play with us.

JEFF FRANKLIN: The show was so powerful it made it difficult for other acts to follow. They were blowing bands off the stage and because of that it was murder getting shows for them.

PAUL *S*TANLEY: There was a meeting held at Casablanca between the band, Jeff, and Neil. At some point Jeff said, "We really can't get you any gigs; there's nobody left to play with. Can you guys tone it down and not be so good?" And my jaw dropped. Isn't that what we're supposed to be doing? It was like going into the ring and boxing with one hand behind your back.

GENE *S*IMMON*S*: We were incredulous. "What do you mean 'not be as good'? That's nuts. We're gonna do what we always do, go out there and try and blow everybody off the stage." But he was adamant. "No. Listen to me, you've got to tone it down, otherwise I can't book you on any tours." I remember Neil Bogart coming to our defense and telling him, "I've been listening and I know it's tough but I can't have our band do that. We've gotta fight our way through this and they've gotta be who they are."

ERIC WEIN*S*TEIN (KI*SS* ROADIE): KISS opened a bunch of shows for Manfred Mann and Savoy Brown and blew them away every night. You've got Savoy Brown who play boogie blues and Manfred Mann doing "Blinded by the Light," and both bands were really good but they just couldn't compete with a spectacle like KISS. I mean, how do you follow a band like KISS, who blow up the stage every night? You just can't do it.

NEIL BOGART: No matter where the group went, they never had an audience that didn't get on its feet.

JEFF FRANKLIN: They started headlining shows in smaller buildings because we didn't have a choice—we couldn't get other bands to play with them as headliners. They weren't selling many records but they were doing good live business. I used every favor I could. Neil kept covering the touring deficits because the losses were massive on a weekly basis. I had a lot to lose as well. I was representing KISS and I was also an equity participant in Casablanca. I think we were losing $50,000 a week, maybe more. KISS couldn't generate enough money to cover it because the show was expensive to move around the country. I had horrifying fights with Neil about this. From the beginning, KISS wanted to take out their whole show even though they were an opening act. There was a constant war with the other bands over KISS's enormous staging.

JOYCE BOGART-TRABULUS: Ira Blacker at ATI and I would have these fights. He'd say, "I can't give you an advance, you're spending too much money on equipment. Leave the equipment at home; it's too expensive." I said, "You don't understand, it's not just the music, it's the show. We're creating an experience."

BILL AUCOIN: We were pouring a lot of money into the band based on a true belief that they could do it. I mean, you always know *inside* whether it's there; it's just when it's going to break, when it's going to happen. I'd say we spent a quarter of a million dollars before the band started breaking.

ALEX COOLEY (CONCERT PROMOTER, ALEX COOLEY PRESENTS): One of the first shows I ever promoted was Ted Nugent at the old City Auditorium in Atlanta. There'd been a play there the night before and they left two light trees. Back then they used to light [rock] shows from the side. Just for the hell of it, the stage manager who owned the lights said, "Do you want to use these tonight?" And I said, "Yeah." Before that, in terms of lighting, all we did was use a spotlight and wash the stage with different colors. From that point forward I saw rock and roll getting more theatrical and believed the time had come for a truly theatrical group like KISS.

16

THE GREAT WHITE NORTH

I n early February 1974, KISS descended upon the frozen terrain of Canada for their first tour, a brief three-date jaunt through Edmonton, Calgary, and Winnipeg. Treading the boards in the dead of winter, the band's first taste of life on the road was anything but glamorous and proved to be a harsh wake-up call. Yet despite brutally freezing temperatures and less than favorable working conditions, the band were up for the challenge and remained focused on the herculean task at hand: building an audience, one fan at a time.

PAUL STANLEY: Our parents drove us to the airport. I think our parents thought they were sending us off to summer camp when they were actually sending us off to a whorehouse [*laughs*]. No sooner did we land than all hell broke loose.

JOYCE BOGART-TRABULUS: Ace didn't have a suitcase so he showed up at the airport with a shopping bag with his clothes [*laughs*]. I remember Gene's mom called me when they went on the road for those first shows in Canada and she was all concerned: "Are you sure he has a sweater?" [*laughs*].

PAUL STANLEY: We went on our first tour, which was as a replacement for a group called the Michael Quatro Band. That Canadian tour was a grand adventure. We were taking Michael Quatro's place, who was Suzi Quatro's brother. Michael canceled a bunch of shows, which were basically a bunch of school lunchrooms in Canada, and we wound up doing the shows.

GENE SIMMONS: We'd never gone off on tour. I remember being on the flight to Canada and writing my girlfriend a postcard. Paul saw me writing it and looked at me like I was from Mars. I wrote, "We've made it." We hadn't even played our first show but to me if you go off on tour you've made it.

PAUL STANLEY: We were primed for success, but success was going to take a little bit of time to come. We really built our foundation by being a grassroots band, a band that would go anywhere and also play a lot of places other people wouldn't. In the beginning, we played bars, clubs, libraries, you name it. It was a matter of getting out there and having word of mouth spread.

MICHAEL WHITE (CONCERT PROMOTER, SCENEMAKER PRODUCTIONS): Earlier in the fall of '73, I was at a college conference in Hamilton, Ontario, and I saw the Michael Quatro Band in concert. This show absolutely knocked me out. It was very theatrical. They started out with dry ice and you saw this stepladder moving around the stage. They had a dwarf with an oversized mad-scientist overcoat turning on the amps. The show opened with the group doing the full-on album version of "In the Court of the Crimson King" by King Crimson. It was great theatrics, and I wanted to bring the band to Edmonton and Calgary. I was dealing with Carol, a woman who worked for ATI. I booked two halls—February 5, 1974, in Edmonton at the University of Alberta in the Dinwoodie Lounge, which was a cafeteria in the student's residence complex on the third floor, and February 6 in Calgary at the Southern Alberta Institute of Technology in the school gymnasium.

I'm already into January of '74 and I get a call from Carol at ATI who said, "Michael Quatro turned down your offer of $1,500 a show because he's now being managed by the Belkin brothers out of Cleveland. They'll only do it if you're willing to up your offer to $5,000 a show." I was the only one who knew who Quatro was but at five grand a show it wasn't gonna work so I turned it down. Carol calls me back a day later and asked if I still had the halls on hold. I said, "I haven't had a chance to cancel them yet." She said, "I've got a band for you. They're going to be absolutely huge. The record is not out in America yet but they sound like this. . . ." I heard her drop the needle onto a record and I'm listening to it and go, "That's Status Quo." She said, "KISS sort of sounds like that but they dress up like Halloween, wear full-on makeup, and the show is outrageous, plus they're harder and edgier than that." And then she added, "They're only gonna cost you $500 a night." So she's telling me about a band I've never heard of, playing me a record by Status Quo, and she wants $500 a night. She told me, "They're trying to get some dates outside of New York City and they're on their way to play Dick Clark's *In Concert*." I said, "Give me a day to think about it."

My office was based out of Calgary at that time. About two o'clock in the afternoon there's a delivery company at my door and I'm handed a box from Casablanca Records. I open up the box and inside it are copies of KISS's first album and two KISS T-shirts with the KISS letters done in rhinestones, some press kits with a one-page bio and glossy photo. I see the album cover and go, "Oh my God." I take one of the records out and put it on my turntable and noticed it was warm. I wondered if it had been freshly pressed. I put it on and I'm listening to "Deuce" and "Firehouse" and go, "This might work." Not twenty minutes later the phone rings and it's Neil Bogart, president of Casablanca Records. He's telling me to really consider booking the band, they need these two shows and they're gonna be a huge band. I called Carol back and said, "All right, I'm gonna give it a shot." Listen, I'm a little schmuck from Calgary, Alberta, and I get a phone call from a record company president? I'm thinking, this group has weight. I called Warner Brothers, the local record company, to tell them about the shows and they said, "This group is not on our release sheet." I said, "Well, I'm bringing the band in." They said, "White, you always bring in bands we've never heard of, you always lose money, and we all look bad." But my mind was made up so I booked KISS for the shows.

I was told there would be a rush release of the first KISS album in Canada and Warner Brothers would support the shows as much as they could. In those days AM radio ruled the airwaves, but AM radio wouldn't even play Queen, let alone a band like KISS. So I knew I was dead in the water with radio. I sent a record to the one newspaper in Edmonton and another to the one in Calgary, along with the press kit. The record company said they'd try and get some newspaper ads and build street buzz with the record stores, which was where kids were finding new bands. Not long before the first show, I'd received another box from the record company with a hundred copies of the first KISS album, and I was handing them out like popcorn to my friends and at bars trying to draw interest.

In the mail comes the contract and I'm looking at KISS's rider which details what they'll need for the show. They wanted four hundred pounds of dry ice, scaffolding, a forklift, and a three-ton truck to haul all their gear, plus they wanted to be met at the airport. To me all of this was excessive for the rooms we were playing. The Dinwoodie Lounge jammed might have held 350 people and the gymnasium in Calgary never even put on a show before. It was a single basketball court.

I only had one guy to help me—Peter Sookie, my stage manager. Peter and I drove up to Edmonton the day before the show and checked into the Holiday Inn. The record company guy was also told to meet the band at the airport. So off we go to the airport to pick up KISS at around seven o'clock. While at the airport we get information that the band had to change planes in Toronto and they weren't gonna arrive until eleven p.m. The record company guy takes off and goes back to the hotel. Peter and I wait for the band at the airport. Then the band comes through the departure area, and it's only them. I found out the plane that they flew into Canada with was not acceptable for Canadian airspace so they chartered a small Air Canada jet to fly to Edmonton. When we saw all the gear come out of the hold I had to send Peter off to get a bigger truck.

Their road manager [Mike McGurl] was totally tricked out in black leather. He came up to me, introduced himself, and said, "Where's the record company guy?" I told him the plane was delayed and that the record company guy was back in the hotel lounge and he'd meet you there. He goes off to make a phone call. I've got my rental car and they've got a limousine. We travel forty-five minutes to downtown Edmonton. I get out of the vehicle, the band goes to the front desk to check in, and the record company guy comes up to me and said, "What did you tell these people?" And I said, "The truth. You were at the airport, you didn't want to wait four hours, and that you'd meet them at the hotel." He told me, "They fired me."

You have to understand, this plane landed at eleven o'clock at night. The road manager got ahold of Bogart, who got a hold of Warner Brothers Canada, who got ahold of the branch manager in Calgary, who got ahold of the guy in the lounge at the Holiday Inn and fired him. All this happened in the time that it took for us to get to the hotel. I went, "Holy shit."

There were a lot of Chinese students that were supposed to have a function going on the evening of KISS's show in the Dinwoodie Lounge. But I was told I could rent that room as long as I put down the deposit, plus they added the stipulation that these Chinese students could get into the show for free. The morning of the first show in Edmonton, right across the street from the Holiday Inn, was CHED radio, 640 AM. The record company had somehow arranged a 9 a.m. interview just before the morning show ended. KISS got fully tricked out in the makeup and gear, didn't even go to the corner and cross at the crosswalk, they jaywalked straight across the street to CHED radio. When the group walked in the receptionist screamed. The DJ was totally flummoxed about what to ask the band because

Gene, Paul, and Peter posed in their 10 E. Twenty-third Street loft displaying their primitive early makeup design, New York City, November 1972

A unique image capturing Paul sans makeup and Ace in full makeup, Coventry, August 31, 1973

KISS poses in the Daisy office with club owner Sid Benjamin, March 10, 1973, Amityville, New York. The band's makeup design is still evolving. Note: Though he is wearing a little rouge, eyeliner, and lipstick, Paul has not as yet come up with his trademark "star" design.

Less than a month and a half since they played their first show, KISS performs at the Daisy, March 10, 1973

Gene, The Daisy,
March 10, 1973

Lydia Criss—*Sealed with a Kiss*/www.lydiacriss.com

Ace, The Daisy,
March 10, 1973

Lydia Criss—*Sealed with a Kiss*/www.lydiacriss.com

Lydia Criss—*Sealed with a Kiss*/www.lydiacriss.com

Lydia Criss photographed the band in flashy attire prior to their taking the stage opening for the Brats at a loft party on Bleecker Street in New York's Greenwich Village. Note the homemade KISS T-shirt Paul is wearing, made by Peter Criss's mother, along with a pair of sparkly blue pants Paul crafted himself using his mother's sewing machine, June 1, 1973

Paul and Ace in performance at Hotel Diplomat, New York City, July 13, 1973

KISS performs
a showcase for
Casablanca Records
staff, including
president Neil
Bogart. Blown
away by the show,
Bogart decides to
sign the band as
the first act on his
new label. LeTang's
Ballet Studio,
midtown Manhattan,
New York City,
September 1973

Paul and Gene recording
the first KISS album, Bell
Sound Studios, New York City,
November 1973

Eddie Solan/KISS Catalog Ltd.

Gene at the mic ready to lay
down a lead vocal during the
recording of the first KISS
album, Bell Sound Studios,
November 1973

Eddie Solan/KISS Catalog Ltd.

Ace tuning up during sessions
for the first KISS album, Bell
Sound Studios, November 1973

Eddie Solan/KISS Catalog Ltd.

First album outtake

Paul Stanley with bandit
makeup design, January 1974

KISS official record-signing photo op, backstage at Fillmore East, New York City, January 1974. *Left to right:* comanager Joyce Biawitz, Peter Criss, Paul Stanley, Neil Bogart, Gene Simmons, Ace Frehley, comanager Bill Aucoin

KISS, Casablanca Records launch party, Century Plaza Hotel, Century City, California, February 18, 1974

The demon incarnate, Casablanca Records launch party, Century Plaza Hotel, Century City, California, February 18, 1974

Ace hitting a high note,
Casablanca Records launch
party, Century Plaza Hotel,
Century City, California,
February 18, 1974

Wedged onto a bill with opening acts Les Variations and Flying Saucer and headliner Quicksilver Messenger Service, KISS performs to two thousand fans at Chicago's Aragon Ballroom, April 19, 1974

Photo session, New York City, January 1974

Photo session, New York City, January 1974

KISS Catalog Ltd.

Photo session, New York City, January 1974

KISS Catalog Ltd.

Promotional
poster for the
first KISS album

KISS Catalog Ltd.

Fire-breathing, NYC style,
March 1975

David Tan/Shinko Music Archives

they were all in his little cubicle in full gear and makeup. KISS made an impression because that's what the DJs on the air talked about off and on all day.

KEITH "KJ" JAMES (DJ, CHED-AM, EDMONTON): CHED was the dominant top-40 radio station in the province of Alberta, not just Edmonton. We were an anomaly—we had close to 50 percent of the radio audience. Back then we had such great relationships with all the label reps so we put [KISS] on the air as a favor because no one knew who [they were] at that time. Lou Blair, their label rep, brought Gene and Paul into the studio for the interview. They were obviously green but you could tell they were really excited to be on the radio.

PAUL STANLEY: Doing interviews was staggering. The idea that people wanted to talk to us was kind of mind-blowing. All of a sudden we were enough of a curiosity that people wanted to talk to us.

KEITH "KJ" JAMES: After we were done with the interview I had them record some radio IDs for my show saying things like, "You're listening to the Super 630 CHED." They were playing around with it and Gene was having a tough time doing it and was continuously making mistakes. He went off track and started goofing around doing different voices, like one as Paul McCartney, and also did one in a Spanish voice. This went on for fifteen minutes. All the while Paul was watching Gene do his thing. Then I said, "Okay, Paul, now you get in there and do a liner." Paul got in there and in one take nailed it. He just turned it on. He did the liner like he was screaming to an audience onstage. They gave me a copy of the album and I played two songs on my show, "Firehouse" and "Cold Gin," and it got good audience reaction. I also talked up their concert that night.

GENE SIMMONS: During the interview I said, "Listen, all you girls come on over and meet us, we're staying at the Holiday Inn." The promoter had set us up with a room, a kind of chicken coop with all these girls. I remember walking in and was struck by one of the girls who had green and yellow hair. I still don't remember her name. I walked over, grabbed her, and we spent that night together. That was my first groupie. I thought it was the most romantic thing you could do, wake up with this girl whose name you never bothered to learn. That's true romance.

MICHAEL WHITE: Only forty-six tickets sold for that first show, at about five bucks a head. So I had my forty-six people—I probably comped another thirty—and there's probably sixty Chinese students as well. There were no chairs set up. In those days people sat in the front or stood around. I didn't have a chance to see the band do a sound check because I was doing all kinds of other things like finding four hundred pounds of dry ice [*laughs*].

MIKE McGURL (KI *SS* **TOUR MANAGER):** The band literally played in a school cafeteria [*laughs*].

PETER "MOO *S***E" ORECKINTO:** We didn't have a stage so we started gathering all these cafeteria tables and put them together with gaffer's tape to build a stage. We needed a flat and strong surface so we put down plywood over the tables to dissipate the weight, otherwise if we put the LVM [levitating drum machine] on the table it would have went straight through it. We shook up soda and spread it out all over the floor to make it sticky so it wouldn't be slippery—it's an old theater trick to prevent people from tripping and breakin' their ass onstage.

GENE *S***IMMON** *S***:** With our platform heels we could slip and trip and that would be disastrous.

MICHAEL WHITE: The Dinwoodie Lounge only had a ten-foot ceiling and they weren't able to use the KISS sign that night because there was no room. We also couldn't use the scaffolding so they put the PA system on tables.

GENE *S***IMMON** *S***:** Because it was so small and the ceiling was so low, I couldn't spit fire. All we could do was assault the audience with our show.

MICHAEL WHITE: A group named Barbarossa opened both shows. They were a trio plus a vocalist. Barbarossa was a cover band that did obscure songs like "Dancing Madly Backwards" by Captain Beyond and "Grantchester Meadows" by Pink Floyd.

I'm backstage and I didn't know which room the support act was in and which room KISS was in. So I went looking for my support act and a sign on one of the doors said "Do Not Enter" and I figured, what the hell, I'm the promoter, I can enter any place that I want. I opened up the dressing room and there were candles all over the room, a blazing dagger in the middle of the table, and the four members of KISS all tricked out. They were having a little get-together and it seemed like a rite or ritual. I'd just smoked a fat one. Gene Simmons and the rest of the band looked up at me and I said [*meekly*], "Sorry," and shut the door as fast as I fucking could [*laughs*].

When KISS came onstage they opened with "Deuce" and they were loud. I'd never seen anything with as much attitude, makeup, and outrageousness. The Chinese kids were frightened. They stood up and started running into each other. They didn't know what to do. Nobody knew who this band was. They'd never heard their music. About halfway through the show I discovered where the forklift was. Peter Criss was doing a drum solo and his drums started going up and up right through the false ceiling. Tiles came down. I was told I could never book that lounge again because the forklift damaged the ceiling. There were complaints by the Chinese students the following day, and the newspapers ignored [the concert].

The next day the band played the gymnasium at the Southern Alberta Institute of Technology [SAIT]. It held eight hundred people and only 161 people showed up for that show.

MICHAEL HUBLER (VICE PRESIDENT, SAIT STUDENT ASSOCIATION): KISS was just starting out and they had a small road crew. Me and a few others in the student association pitched in and helped bring in their equipment.

MICHAEL WHITE: I'm inside the venue day of show and see all this scaffolding and figure they want to put the PA on it so we move the scaffolding on either side of the stage before the crew gets there. Wrong! My stage manager, Peter [Sookie], and I had to disassemble the scaffolding and put it behind the stage. Then I was handed

four-foot KISS letters, *K-I-S-S*. They weighed about eighty pounds apiece. I was wearing platform boots and had to climb the scaffolding in those and hang each individual letter.

MICHAEL HUBLER: It looked kind of amateurish because one or two of the letters didn't hang properly and were lopsided [*laughs*].

SUSAN HARP (CONCERT ATTENDEE): I was going out with Jim Irwin, the bass player in a band called Barbarossa, the group that opened for KISS in Calgary at the SAIT gymnasium. My sister Lisa, her friend Terry Farran, Julie Morrish, and I went to the concert because my boyfriend was playing in the band. We didn't have any clue about the headlining act. There weren't many people at this rinky-dink gymnasium and most, if not all, were there to see Barbarossa. It was really informal. Everyone sat on the floor and then all of a sudden these guys came out onstage in full makeup and costumes.

DAVE BELL (LEAD SINGER, BARBAROSSA): The crowd was like, "Holy shit, what planet are these guys from, and what are they *wearing*?" No one had a clue who they were. I remember their Warner Brothers rep standing by the side of the stage trying to gauge the crowd and see how the band was gonna go over.

SUSAN HARP: It was like they were performing a concert for ten thousand people and here there were only a hundred of us [*laughs*].

FRANK SHUFLETOSKI (PHOTOGRAPHER): Being that this was a concert held in a college gymnasium where the campus basketball and volleyball teams played, the acoustics were not optimal. There was a lot of reverb bouncing off the walls.

DAVE BELL: It was a wall of noise. They were so loud.

MICHAEL WHITE: This time the band got to use all of their equipment. They fired it up and I couldn't hear anything until about 3 a.m. the next morning. It was that loud.

FRANK SHUFLETOSKI: The initial reaction from the crowd was pretty quiet. The audience didn't know what to make of it.

SUSAN HARP: KISS was shocking and bizarre, but by the time the band was done they'd won over the entire crowd.

MICHAEL WHITE: So it's about two weeks later, I turn on the TV and I'm watching Dick Clark's *In Concert*, and there's KISS. The band had a remarkable support system from day one. I still cannot believe the weight this band had as early as they did in their career. I had Neil Bogart, the president of their record company, calling me, and you had planes being rented for small gigs at five hundred bucks a night.

FRANK WEIPERT (CANADIAN STUDENT CONCERT PROMOTER): I promoted KISS's third date on their Canadian tour [February 8, 1974]. The show was put on by the University of Manitoba's student union. At the time I was in charge of programming, which was the equivalent to the student concert promoter on campus. Leslie Monchuck, one of ATI's agents, was a big supporter of KISS. She called me up and said, "We've got this band and we want to see if we can make them fly anywhere else besides their hometown of New York City." The band had to fly everything by air to Canada,

Paul and Ace at the Southern Alberta Institute of Technology, February 6, 1974 Photo by Frank Shufletoski

including the drum levitation machine. I met them at the airport in Winnipeg and had to find a twenty-four-foot truck for their equipment.

We put on a student cultural festival called "The Festival of Life and Learning," which was quite big in Winnipeg and on campus. It ran for five days and there were many concerts. I wanted to do something different for the festival because a lot of the acts were safe, traditional folksingers and jazz and rock acts. I'd never heard KISS's music before and remember [that] they brought the first vinyl copies of their debut album with them, along with some original rhinestone KISS shirts.

The concert was slated to be held in the Tache Hall Auditorium. It was a beautiful hall but unfortunately it was three stories up, so all their gear had to be carried by hand, including the levitation machine, all of this in the middle of winter. February in Winnipeg, it had to be about 20 or 30 degrees below zero.

The show was free and it was packed. I put on an act before them called Mood Jga Jga. They were a fairly tame, influential Canadian jazz/rock outfit; one of their members was in the Guess Who. I decided we were gonna have KISS as the secret concert of the whole festival. We didn't advertise their appearance because there was no reason to advertise a band that had no history or market value. For me the excitement was doing something completely brand new and out of the box.

We'd flown the curtain behind the opening act to shield KISS's drum riser, the KISS sign, and stack of Marshall amps from public view. The curtain went up and KISS came on and everybody in the audience looked in absolute amazement. There was no apathy. Half of them were horrified—there were some beer cans that went flying to the stage—and the other half were like, "This is the most amazing thing I've ever seen." I was shocked that no fights broke out in the audience.

The stage was the size of a postage stamp, maybe sixteen feet deep and about twenty feet wide. It was so small that there was hardly room for the crew to stand on the side of the stage.

Halfway into the set the first real mishap happened during "Firehouse." The stage was at a slight angle and in the darkness when Gene was blowing fire, the container of kerosene suddenly went flying and all the kerosene leaked right across the stage. It was scary. The crew was on their hands and knees cleaning up the stage so the whole building didn't go up in flames.

So the show's over and the crew starts breaking down the set and they're getting ready to pull down KISS's sign. The piping on the stage was normally used to hang curtains or theater props but not designed to hold that particular size and weight of the sign. So the crew started lowering the sign very slowly and about six inches off the ground the pole snapped and the sign fell. The sign wasn't damaged but if that happened during showtime I might be telling you a completely different story.

The student newspaper, *The Manitoban*, ran a negative review of that show and they skewered me. They said that KISS was either gonna be the biggest thing on the planet or disappear into oblivion. They questioned my artistic judgment putting KISS on the bill. But I'm happy to say history proves me right on this one.

A publicist's job is to build public interest by corraling as much media coverage as possible and then feed it to the hungry promotion machine. When representing an outrageous new band who came on like kabuki alien gunslingers from outer space, getting the media to see past their freaky image was not easy.

BOB MERLIS: As a publicist, I thought KISS would be a tough sell because they were very gimmicky. I was a big Alice Cooper fan so I understood the combination of music and theatrics, but Alice Cooper had great songwriting and delivery. I felt KISS was a lot of flash and I wasn't able to dig into the songs at the time. One of the biggest challenges that I faced was getting the media to look past the makeup and get into the music. The media perceived KISS as a gimmick and a joke and not something they could take seriously.

Being the publicity manager at Warner's offices in New York, our initial reaction to KISS was very hopeful. The people at Warners were not aghast, appalled, or put off by the notion of KISS. They didn't say, "Oh my God, what are we gonna do with a band that wear makeup?" I mean, c'mon, we already had Alice Cooper on the label, we knew how to work this. And for me, I was familiar with KISS, as I'd already seen them perform at the Hotel Diplomat back in '73; I was managing the Planets and they opened for them.

Publicity-wise the most notable thing we did was take the band to the Georgette Klinger salon in New York City—which is one of these high-end places for society ladies—to get a facial. We had KISS get facials and did a photo session with them with towels on their faces, which was a way to preserve their mystique. That was a fun stunt and the media picked up on those images.

PAUL STANLEY: The first photo layout we ever got was in *Mandate* magazine. We didn't know what that magazine was. "What's *Mandate*? Is it a political magazine?" Nope. It was exactly what it sounded like, it was *man date*. It was a [pornographic] gay magazine. That was our first photo shoot for a magazine.

GENE SIMMONS: People would quote bad reviews to us. I remember one of our first reviews tore us to shreds and said we were just a bunch of loud noise. But in the way they described us and our show, it made us look like we were important. The review called us "four wild men from Borneo." I had to turn that negative review into a positive. [*Imitating mock stage announcer*] "Tonight, live onstage, the four wild men from Borneo!" Who the hell wouldn't want to see four wild men from Borneo? That sounds great to me. I'm going! [*laughs*].

KEN BARNES (MUSIC WRITER, PHONOGRAPH RECORD MAGAZINE): There was major resistance to KISS in the press. What you had were two groups coming out of New York in the early seventies, the New York Dolls, and then KISS came a bit later. Both of them wore makeup. KISS had a kabuki image and the Dolls' image was more sexually ambiguous. The Dolls were absolute press favorites starting in New York. As soon as they got out to the West Coast everybody loved them. I can't think of another band that had a higher ratio of press coverage to record sales. Once KISS started making inroads and becoming successful and the Dolls were not, despite all their great press, I think music writers took out their resentment and disappointment that the

Dolls didn't make it on KISS. KISS projected a lot of charisma to fans but it didn't translate to music writers, so that was another factor in the hostility and reluctance of writers to cover KISS favorably. Once KISS became successful with *Alive!* I think there was a certain arrogance that they projected and maybe an air of being too calculating in the way that they put everything together and that put off the press. The press really has never liked that sort of thing. They like their bands to be organic and spontaneous.

With Warner Brothers decidedly lukewarm about their new act, Casablanca president Neil Bogart resorted to unconventional measures to convince his industry colleagues that KISS was special.

LARRY HARRIS: Neil was like a kid in a candy store with KISS. We were on the ground floor of helping to make their stage show more exciting, and they were listening to us at that point. They kind of had no choice [*laughs*]. We'd take them to magic shops and hire people to help them with their stage show. Neil loved going to the magic shops because Neil was an entertainer before he was a music executive. He was a singer and dancer and put out a single called "Bobby" in the early '60s under the name Bobby Scott, which was a top-40 hit. At the magic shop Neil picked up some flash paper, which is thin paper that goes up in a flash of flame when near any kind of heat source. You can hold it in your hand as it . . . burn[s] but it won't hurt you because the flash doesn't last long enough. Neil would take out this flash paper in the middle of a meeting and say, "KISS is magic!" He smoked cigarettes back then so he'd touch a cigarette to the flash paper and there'd be a short burst of flame. It was highly effective and quite unusual.

17

ON THE RADIO

When KISS first stormed onto the music scene in early 1974, pop radio was cranking out slick chart-topping hits by the likes of the Jackson 5 ("Dancing Machine"), Terry Jacks ("Seasons in the Sun"), Redbone ("Come and Get Your Love"), John Denver ("Sunshine on My Shoulders"), Elton John ("Bennie and the Jets"), and novelty songs like "The Streak" by Ray Stevens. Barbra Streisand's easy-listening ballad "The Way We Were" was Billboard's top-charting song of 1974. It was clear that radio wasn't ready for a band of hard rock heathens like KISS. Songs about hookers ("Black Diamond"), anal sex ("Nothin' to Lose"), and alcohol ("Cold Gin") were unlikely to garner airtime. Even in their hometown, KISS was having a hard time getting any airplay.

BUCK REINGOLD: Top 40 in New York was top-20 radio. They only played twenty songs. There were two hundred records coming out a week and they only played twenty records, so it made it very tough to get a new band like KISS played on the radio.

In 1974, WNEW-FM was the top-rated rock radio station in New York City, blasting out hits by the Beatles, the Rolling Stones, and the Who alongside up-and-comers like Aerosmith and Ted Nugent. Popular nighttime DJ Alison Steele, who called herself "the Nightbird" on air, was a bit of an iconoclast—and an early supporter of KISS. She was the first to play the band on the radio.

DENNIS ELSAS: I was very friendly with Larry [Harris] and Neil [Bogart]. WNEW had a great relationship with Buddah—they had more FM-style records—and that relationship extended to Casablanca. WNEW played more new rock-and-roll music than anyone did at that time. As music director of WNEW, I heard everything first and I wasn't afraid of adding records that were well-produced rock-and-roll records. One of the great things about being music director and also being on the air—I was on the air every Saturday and Sunday afternoon—if I heard something new that week that I liked I could play it that weekend. I think Neil said, "If it's in the grooves, it's in the grooves" and for my ears, songs like "Nothin' to Lose" and "Strutter" were wonderful records.

BUCK REINGOLD: My wife and I were very close with Alison Steele and her boyfriend, who was an assistant district attorney. When KISS's first album came out, I called Alison and asked her to put it on the air for me. She listened to it and said, "What's gonna happen with it?" I said, "We're starting our new company and I'm calling all my friends to see if we can get some airplay on it. It's the only banana we have." And she played it.

PAUL STANLEY: The first time I heard us on the radio was a real big deal. We were told what time Alison Steele was gonna play us on WNEW. I was home eating with my parents waiting for us to come on. To sit by your radio and hear yourself on it was mind-blowing.

GENE SIMMONS: I was in bed under the covers with my then girlfriend in the basement of her parents' home when I first heard us on the radio. Alison Steele played "Cold Gin" and for a split second

I thought she put on Slade's new album by accident because "Cold Gin" sounded like that. Then I said, "Wait a minute, that's me!" To hear the band on the radio was dreamlike. It was magical.

ANNEMARIE HUGHES: I cried when I heard them for the first time on the radio. My mother thought I was nuts but I felt so proud and was bursting with pride. I was there from the very beginning and now they were taking off.

RIK FOX: For me, it was exciting to hear KISS for the first time on the radio, especially on a personal level, knowing you were part of watching a seed start to grow into a flower. When I told my peers in high school about this great new band they gave me all kinds of ridicule. They'd angrily say, "They're called KISS and they wear makeup? What are they, a bunch of fags?" By the time '74 hit and KISS were starting to get played on the radio, those same high school peers who ridiculed me for liking KISS said, "You were right, you were behind this band all the way. We should have listened to you."

DENNIS ELSAS: A lot of progressive rock stations dismissed KISS as a joke because they were not in the mainstream or considered alternative or underground. Their records were two or three minutes long, there were no drum solos, and there were no extended versions of songs until years later in 1979 with "I Was Made for Loving You." KISS had nothing in common with the traditional FM rockers like Nazareth or Foghat who got the FM stamp of approval. KISS weren't considered underground, FM hip, or cool. They were just another rock and roll band; the gimmick was the makeup and the outrageous stage show. In many ways radio was still trying to figure out what was next. We knew Elton was big, and Bowie. I don't think anyone was ready to embrace a band wearing makeup.

Scoring KISS airplay on a prized radio station like WNEW-FM was a rare victory for the radio promotion staff at Casablanca. Across the nation, radio programmers remained intractably resistant to this new band.

JOE SMITH: Trying to get KISS accepted for their music was a big challenge. Getting a disc jockey in Kansas City or St. Louis to play a KISS record was tough. What they looked like or the crazy things they did onstage didn't come into the equation. Video wasn't a factor back then so airplay was based solely on the music.

BUCK REINGOLD: I went on the road with that first KISS album and single and couldn't get anybody to play it. I used every means to get a record played, from drugs to money to women, and none of it worked. It was murder trying to get them played on radio. Their brand of hard rock music just wasn't radio friendly. It wasn't in the grooves. How did I go from being a fabulous promoter with number-one records at Buddah to being a bad promoter in the period of one year? How did that happen? That happened because KISS's music wasn't geared toward AM radio. Their songs weren't top 40. This was music meant to be played on FM.

The first time I went on the road with KISS I went to Memphis, and George Klein, who got Elvis Presley started, ran a big radio station there. KISS was playing a club in Memphis [Lafayette's Music Hall] and I invited him down to see them. He said, "No, I don't want to see them." I told him, "You've gotta come down, you owe me." So he came down to the show and the band was about forty-five minutes late. George was getting really pissed at me and was begging to leave. I told him he had to stay. He said, "Buck, I love ya, but it's my only night out and I've got other business to attend to." So I had to handcuff him to the bar so he couldn't get away. I said to him, "My job was to get you here to see them. Do you see them? Do you hear them?" And he said yes. So I unlocked the handcuffs and he stood on the side of the bar and watched them. When they were done he said, "I'm glad I stayed; it was a great show," but he still never played their record on the radio [*laughs*].

Another time I was in Bowling Green, North Carolina, and the program director at one of the rock stations refused to play KISS. I needed to get a certain number of secondary radio stations to play the record so I could convince the major stations that the record was

Ace tearing up the fretboard at the Foothills Arena in Calgary, May 20, 1974 Terry Munro

a hit. That station in Bowling Green was a key secondary station that I needed to get on board and start playing KISS. I found out that the program director had an old Volkswagen Beetle with a sun roof. So I called the Hershey chocolate company and they gave me a contact for their distributor in the South. The next day they delivered two big seventy-five-pound boxes of Hershey's kisses to my hotel room.

I went back to the radio station the next morning and the program director, who was also the morning DJ, was still on the air. I poured all two boxes of Hershey's kisses through his sun roof onto his driver's seat. That's 150 pounds of chocolate kisses! When he came out for lunch he opened up the door of his car and all the Hershey's kisses spilled out onto the street. Many of them had partially melted in the heat and were all sticky and gooey—and he started laughing hysterically. I walked over to him and he said, "What do you want me to do with all these fucking kisses?" I said [*sternly*], "Play the record and run a radio contest giving away Hershey's kisses." Needless to say he added the KISS record to his rotation and that helped us gain a little bit of traction with the major markets. That was a small victory, but it was really an uphill battle getting KISS played on the radio at the beginning of their career.

BILL AUCOIN: The truth of the matter was Warner Brothers hated KISS and thought the group was a disaster. They sent a memo around Warner's not to work the record. Because Neil knew so many people at Warner's someone slipped him the memo. He went in there with guns blazing and said, "How can you go against me? We just started a new label and this is my first act. I can't work this way." They admitted to him that they sent the memo and begrudgingly stayed on board.

STAN CORNYN: KISS was hardly Casablanca's first act at Warner Brothers. They had many others—even a lot of R&B—which didn't go anywhere. So when we experienced KISS at the intro concert, it felt to us like Bogart had found an act that fitted him well. Flash and fresh. We were delighted. All of that differs, however, from running a business. There, you cannot endlessly promote records that are going nowhere. KISS's first release didn't take off, despite our promotion men's enthusiasm for it. And every week, more singles to get behind. Each release has a clock ticking. When KISS's first release didn't sell, sorry, but . . . We gave it plenty of attention and if, eventually, it fell off the concentration list [the "memo"], eventually that happens to every record.

PAT VEGAS (BASSIST, REDBONE): The first time we played with KISS was in Valley Forge, Pennsylvania, at a theater in the round with a revolving stage [March 22, 1974]. It was a sold-out show and we were pretty hot then with "Come and Get Your Love," which was a top-5 hit at the time. We were in the dressing room and KISS came in without their makeup and introduced themselves and we had some laughs. I didn't tell 'em to break a leg, I told them to "wound a knee," which is Native American humor. Before the show, a couple of us sat in the audience and watched them play. They had these two red fire engine lights atop their amps that spun around real fast. They were kicking ass and the audience liked them a lot. We'd toured with Alice Cooper previously so we were familiar with a theatrical act like that, but KISS took it much further. We didn't think their makeup was weird because we wore Native American makeup on our faces. I thought, "Shit, these guys must be half Native American like us" [*laughs*].

PAUL STANLEY: We had camaraderie with the other bands we played with, but it ended once we went onstage. We loved you until we strapped on our guitars, and then we were there to destroy you.

Photo session, 1974. Waring Abbott/KISS Catalog Ltd.

18

KISSIN' TIME

Two months after its release, KISS's debut album was underperforming with radio airplay and sales were modest at best. WSHE, a Fort Lauderdale radio station, engineered a unique publicity stunt to promote the band: a kissing contest. Recognizing the event's potential, Nashville DJ Scott Shannon upped the ante and suggested that the band record a cover of Bobby Rydell's late fifties pop hit, "Kissin' Time."

SCOTT SHANNON (PROGRAM DIRECTOR/ON-AIR PERSONALITY, WMAK-AM, NASHVILLE): I remember seeing KISS live in early '74 at Muther's Music Emporium in Nashville. They were phenomenal performers but I worked for a pure pop radio station so it was pretty hard to imagine us playing loud headbanging music on a top-40 radio station. What I felt was missing from the songs on the first KISS album was music with a beat: it was just very frenetic music and not conducive for AM radio. I had a great working relationship with Casablanca, especially with Neil Bogart and Larry Harris. I remember telling Neil Bogart over the phone that the band needed a top-40 hit. I said, "Why don't you do something that these older programmers are familiar with? As a novelty, why don't you have them do 'Kissin' Time'?" I thought they could give that song a real rock-and-roll beat and make it accessible to top-40 stations.

Neil Bogart loved the idea and bullied the band into covering the song, which was rush-released as a single and also included on new pressings of their album.

KENNY KERNER: At the outset of the project Neil told us, "I've never had a credible rock band on Buddah or Kama Sutra Records and I want one on Casablanca." He wanted to make sure this album would be accepted by Warner Brothers so they'd get behind it and promote the hell out of it. They weren't gonna promote teeny-bopper singles. That's one of the reasons he signed KISS: he saw a band that would appeal to a real rock-and-roll audience. Nobody would be able to say this was bubblegum. So that's what we gave him, a real rock-and-roll band. Neil never mentioned that he was looking for hit singles. There was a big fight when Neil pushed the band to record "Kissin' Time."

LARRY HARRIS: KISS hated the idea and didn't want to do it. Neil threatened to drop them from the label if they didn't do it. So they buckled.

KENNY KERNER: They were disgusted, but what choice did they have? They had to go along with it. So we had to go into the studio months after the album was released to record it.

In 1959, Philadelphia teen idol Bobby Rydell landed a top-15 hit with his debut single, "Kissin' Time." Forcing KISS to record this peppy pop hit of yesteryear seemed like anything but a good idea.

PAUL STANLEY: "Kissin' Time" was one of the Neil Bogart ruses. He told us that it was just being recorded for a commercial and that it'll never come out as a single. We were perfectly capable at that point of writing our own material, and to have to record a Bobby Rydell song was unnecessary.

GENE SIMMONS: Musically, we changed it a bit; Paul came up with the chordal patterns. We recorded it really quickly—in two hours.

KENNY KERNER: We literally had the Bobby Rydell single, played it in the studio, and shouted out new lyrics. We'd play it and [*singing*] "We're kissin' in . . ." and someone would yell out "Detroit!" or "Philadelphia!" That's how the new version of "Kissin' Time" was written [*laughs*]. We never could have recorded it exactly like Rydell's version. It was too lightweight.

GENE SIMMONS: Neil told us it was going to be used for a radio promotion only and promised us it wasn't going to appear on the record. But he tricked us and included it on later pressings of the album.

LARRY HARRIS: In those days you thought if you mention their city in a song, that station is gonna have to play the song. "Kissin' Time" wasn't a hit but it did get them a lot of extra airplay on radio.

SCOTT SHANNON: As I recall we gave it limited play in Nashville. Their version of "Kissin' Time" wasn't exactly what I had in mind. I envisioned something that was poppier.

MARK PARENTEAU: I was a fan of the Philadelphia label Cameo-Parkway, the same label that released Bobby Rydell's "Kissin' Time." So I was already a fan of the song and thought it was a good idea for KISS to release their version as a single. The band was so deficient in having anything that was chartable that something recognizable like "Kissin' Time" would work for them. I remember playing it and the reaction was pretty good. The kids could latch onto it, it was a hummable song. It got good turntable play at a time when they needed to have something a little bit more identifiable.

With the hype machine now in overdrive, Neil Bogart used the publicity tricks he learned at Buddah to devise a massive promotional campaign, which was dubbed "The Great KISS-Off."

LARRY HARRIS: WSHE in Miami held a kissing contest. I didn't know they were doing it until I got a call from Eddie Pugh, our Warner Brothers regional promotion man out of Florida. He called me at home and told me it was a big success. I called Neil that night and told him about it. The next day Neil came in and said, "Let's spread the kissing contest around the country."

STAN CORNYN: That promo spread across American radio.

BOBBI COWAN: Neil got thirteen cities involved and each radio station held their own kissing contest.

LARRY HARRIS: We tied it in with top-40 radio who weren't giving KISS much airplay. We had local kissing contests in cities around the country. Whoever won in a specific market was flown to Schaumburg, Illinois, for the finals.

BOBBI COWAN: This was all part of what Neil did. He recognized that he needed to create a buzz about the band and that happened after this contest. KISS were involved—they judged the contest. It was one of many events that Neil came up with out of that amazing brain of his. Nobody could come up with promotions like he could.

JOYCE BOGART-TRABULUS: What KISS did onstage was akin to what Neil did in promotion.

Thirteen kissing contests were held nationwide. The winners of the Florida competition appeared with the band on The Mike Douglas Show. *An excerpt from Casablanca Records' press release details this promotional masterstroke:*

> This is one of the largest promotions in the history of radio. . . . We are trying to get Howard Cosell to cover our finals for ABC *Wide World of Sports*. . . . Tying in with the KISS promotion is the release this week of a new single by KISS especially recorded for the contests. . . . Each participating station in "The Great KISS-Off" will be given 250 KISS T-shirts [and] 500 posters promoting the station

and the contest. . . . The winners will be flown May 31 to Los Angeles to see and meet KISS as they perform at the Long Beach Auditorium. From there they will depart on an eight-day cruise to Acapulco to recuperate.

JIM MANFRE (ASSISTANT MANAGER, DISC RECORDS, SCHAUMBURG, ILLINOIS): I was the assistant manager of Disc Records at the Woodfield Mall in Schaumburg, Illinois, which was the largest mall in the world at the time. This was before the Mall of America was built.

BUCK REINGOLD: Bus companies marketed trips to the mall. People from two or three hours away would come in and have outings at the mall. Their parking lot was filled every day with hundreds of buses.

JIM MANFRE: "The Great KISS-Off" kissing contest was a national promotion set up by Warner Brothers Records, who were trying to make a big impression with their new label and newest signing. KISS was totally unknown at the time.

The label sent us hundreds of KISS posters, which we plastered everywhere in advance of the event. The local Warner Brothers promotion reps, Roy Chivari and Mike Sheid, convinced the mall to put on the event and found a furniture store to loan love seats for the contestants. The mall set up twelve love seats in the main court where couples would be locked in a continuous kiss around the clock until the last couple remained. The winning couple [Vinnie Toro and Louise Heath] went on for something like 116 hours straight!

The couples were given a five-minute break at the top of the hour for bathroom breaks and food. Other than that they had to keep their lips connected. I remember a couple telling me they could eat shrimp while they were kissing as they could stuff it into their mouths without disconnecting their lips. Unfortunately, they said, it smelled really bad [*laughs*].

GARY STROMBERG: Somewhere in the midst of the event a woman came storming into the KISS-Off and almost attacked her husband,

A happy couple in action at "The Great KISS-Off," Woodfield Mall,
Schaumburg, Illinois, June 8, 1974 Courtesy of Jim Manfre

who was in the contest with another woman. She saw him lip-locked
with another woman on the Chicago news—we got news crews
covering this because it was such a quirky event. She came down there
and this guy was so embarrassed. How stupid can you be? [*laughs*]

PAUL STANLEY: We show up for the event in all our gear and traipse
down through the mall to this store where they're holding "The
Great KISS-Off" finals. We're walking around thinking we own the
place. "Aren't we amazing, aren't we the shit? This is all for us." I
walked over to this couple and they had to keep their lips locked.
They looked over with their eyes to the side and through pursed lips
said, "Who are you?" [*laughs*]

JIM MANFRE: The kissing contest was in full force on Saturday and
the mall was bustling with thousands of shoppers. KISS was scheduled
to do an in-store autograph session that afternoon. I remember the

Ace, Paul, and Peter at "The Great KISS-Off" in-store event, Woodfield Mall, Schaumburg, Illinois, June 8, 1974 Courtesy of Jim Manfre

WEA (Warner-Elektra-Atlantic) people came through the store first followed by Neil Bogart, the president of Casablanca Records. They were very impressed, as we had tons of KISS albums positioned all over the front of the store. Then we were told KISS had arrived and brought them into the main court where we had Larry Lujack, a local radio personality with WCFL, on the microphone talking about the St. Jude Children's Hospital charity and announcing the band. When they walked out into the mall there were clearly some shoppers that didn't know what was going on and the looks they gave the group were priceless. There were well over a thousand shoppers watching from all around the main court on its three levels of balconies.

GENE ßIMMONß: We were on the bottom floor and these photographers wanted to take photos. Neil Bogart understood that without a big crowd it wouldn't look like a good photo so he started throwing dollar bills down from the balcony and caused a frenzy among the crowd with this money raining down. And just like that, the photographers had a good photo.

JIM MANFRE: At the same time, the DJ asked people to contribute money for the local charity, St. Jude's Hospital. We collected over $6,000 for the charity and in the process brought a lot of attention to KISS.

GENE ßIMMONß: St. Jude's Hospital was a charity overseen by the actor Danny Thomas. Jan Murray, the famous comedian, was on hand and accepted the check on behalf of the charity.

LARRY HARRIß: During the Great KISS-Off final, Neil, Buck [Reingold], and I were calling all the radio stations that had contestants and giving them hourly status reports on how their contestants were doing. Some national TV news outlets picked it up as well.

JIM MANFRE: There was an announcement that KISS would be signing copies of their new album in our store, and within minutes the store was packed. We sold several hundred albums, another hundred or so eight-tracks and cassettes, which was great for a new band. "The Great KISS-Off" was a huge success. The band was in the mall for less than three hours and they were exposed to thousands of people and made hundreds of new fans that day, all wanting to get close to an up-and-coming act at the very beginning of their incredible rise.

NANCY ßAIN: It was a marketing ploy to get KISS exposed on top-40 radio. If they were gonna get anywhere Neil wanted them to cross over and the kissing contest was his way of opening the doors.

Making it in the music business is a one-in-a-million crapshoot. And when your debut signing wears kabuki makeup, gleaming black leather, and seven-inch heels, you're facing roadblocks bigger than the Great Wall of China. The promotion team at Casablanca Records had a wide river to cross. Launching a carefully orchestrated campaign aimed at retail is critical to an act's chances at success. Casablanca worked hard to cultivate relationships with record distributors—the folks who provide product to record stores. And they wrangled optimal placement for KISS's album at record shops nationwide.

ERIC PAULSON (VICE PRESIDENT AND GENERAL MANAGER, PICKWICK INTERNATIONAL DISTRIBUTION): Retail outlets like Camelot, Warehouse, Peaches, and Tower Records were buying a lot of records from us but they didn't really display it; they just put it in the bins. What Neil Bogart was pushing for was to get KISS's product on an endcap so people could see the cover. We pushed hard to make it happen. When you walked into a record store and saw a long line of record bins from A to Z, at the front of the rack is the endcap, which displays the highlighted albums. Neil believed, and rightfully so, if kids would see the cover of KISS's first album they would buy it irrespective of what it sounded like. He believed if he would get that record in the hands of enough kids word would spread and with radio's help he'd turn them into a supergroup. The label also spent a lot of money on in-store presentations and advertising.

SAM RICCARDO (PROMOTIONS MANAGER, RECORD MUSEUM, PHILADELPHIA): While working at Record Museum and later at Listening Booth, the independent record distributors provided quite an assortment of promo material—KISS album flats, posters, cardboard stand-up displays, and die-cut mobiles. From day one the displays were really effective and stirred interest and curiosity about KISS. I remember a lot of customers coming up asking who this crazy-looking band was. Many of those same people left the store with the first KISS album under their arm without ever having heard it, so it worked.

Display contests were routinely done at East Coast record chains like Record Museum, Listening Booth, Sam Goody's, and Wall-to-Wall Sound to enhance sales and draw attention to new artists. The distributors also ran contests within record chains for the best KISS display, and employees would send in photos of their displays and vie for prizes. I won a lot of display contests and one of the prizes was I got to meet the band before a show in Philadelphia.

ERIC PAULSON: The creative retailers made sure the consumers were included as well. A retailer would put a huge KISS display in their store and invite customers to dress up as KISS and have their picture taken with the display. All of this helped generate awareness—and ultimately, sales—for this new act.

GENE SIMMONS: I remember going into a store in downtown Manhattan and buying a copy of our first album. That was a big thrill because this is where I bought Led Zeppelin records and now here I am buying a record by my group.

A strikingly visual band, KISS was ready-made for television. But the television landscape of 1974—a long seven years before the official launch of MTV in August 1981—presented limited opportunities for them. Somehow, the band managed to land high-profile appearances on several TV shows, including Dick Clark's In Concert, The Mike Douglas Show, *and* The Midnight Special. *This was the first encounter with the self-proclaimed "heavy metal masters" for many unsuspecting TV viewers in Middle America.*

JOYCE BOGART-TRABULUS: Neil knew Dick Clark going back to the sixties when he was part of a Dick Clark "Caravan of Stars" tour.

Gene, Paul, and Peter in their American TV debut on Dick Clark's *In Concert*, Aquarius Theater, Hollywood, February 21, 1974 Neil Zlozower/www.atlasicons.com

While at Buddah, Neil put out the double album *20 Years of Rock N' Roll* with Dick Clark. Dick made a lot of money off that album and he and Neil became friends. So when it came time to try and get KISS on *In Concert*, Neil said, "Dick, KISS is gonna be a big group, put 'em on." And he did.

PAUL STANLEY: Dick is an icon and somebody who I was thrilled and humbled to meet because I grew up watching *American Bandstand*. Dick was gracious enough to put us on *In Concert*, which was huge for us. It was filmed at the Aquarius Theater on Sunset Boulevard in Hollywood. It was a revolving stage. At that point in our career we were unknown to just about anybody. When that stage revolved and people saw us, there were a lot of slack jaws.

DICK CLARK: When KISS first appeared on *In Concert*, their appearance was unforgettable. I knew at the time we were either going to be making a huge impression upon the audience or participating in a total fiasco—fortunately, the reaction was positive, and the rest is history.

NEIL ZLOZOWER (PHOTOGRAPHER): The first time I ever heard of KISS I was at a TV taping for the show *In Concert*. I was down there shooting whoever else was on the show. A girl came up to me and said, "I'm with Bill Aucoin management, we have a new band called KISS and I'm wondering if you'd like to shoot them." So I said to myself [*sarcastically*], "Oh KISS, that's cute, they must be an easy-listening band like Bread, mellow doctor's office/dentist's office music." See, I was a hardcore rock-and-roll guy and liked bands like Deep Purple. But I thought, what the hell, I'll shoot them, what have I got to lose? Next thing I know this band comes out with these monstrous boots, the stage clothes, the makeup. I'm watching them

KISS performs in their TV debut, Dick Clark's *In Concert*, Aquarius Theater, Hollywood, February 21, 1974 Neil Zlozower/www.atlasicons.com

and go, "Oh my God, is this a fucking joke?" There's Gene sticking his tongue out and Paul on his knees playing his guitar. I thought it was ridiculous and felt this band would be laughed out of the music industry in two weeks. Unbeknownst to me, they went on to become one of the biggest bands in rock-and-roll history. Shows you what I know [*laughs*].

GENE SIMMONS: Dick came backstage after we played, and we were nobody. He shook each one of our hands and said, "Hello Gene, hello Paul, hello Ace, and hello Peter." It was shocking that he would take the time to be so gracious. He said, "If there's anything I can do for you, please tell me. We're proud to have you on our show." It taught us a big lesson in humility in the rock-and-roll world. We made sure that we were gracious with any new band that played with us and we learned that from Dick Clark.

PAUL STANLEY: I remember the night our appearance aired on TV. We were playing the Sunshine In in Asbury Park [New Jersey]. After the show we drove back quickly to the motel we were staying at and all huddled in a room to watch *In Concert*. It was amazing to see ourselves on TV for the first time.

GENE SIMMONS: Back in those days there weren't many outlets for bands to get on television. So we took what we could get and tried to get on everything, whether it was *In Concert* or *The Mike Douglas Show*. In the days before MTV and VH1, rock and roll hardly existed on television. There was Dick Clark's *American Bandstand* and one or two late-night rock shows like *In Concert* and *Midnight Special*, but that's it. Television was the answer. Bill Aucoin and Joyce Biawitz came from television so they saw television as a friend, not an enemy. At that time the only friend to rock bands was Ed Sullivan, who had thirty million people tune in every Sunday. If you appeared on that show, whether you were the Beatles or the Supremes or the Rolling Stones, you were launched. But we came out after *The Ed Sullivan Show* went off the air. We looked at any opportunity. As long as they didn't try to stop us from being who we were it was okay.

Long before the *Oprah* or *Ellen* TV shows, *The Mike Douglas Show* was the afternoon variety show that set the tone. It was a combination of Johnny Carson, interviews, and musical performances, and occasionally it featured rock bands. Once John Lennon and Yoko Ono cohosted an entire week, it became a cool thing to appear on that show. In '74 it was the game-changer. Bill told us, "Look, we can't get into houses with radio. *Rolling Stone* won't put us in their magazine. How are we gonna reach people? I'll tell you how we're gonna do it: we're gonna crawl into people's homes with our appearance on *The Mike Douglas Show*, when people least expect it." And that was a brilliant idea. So we're backstage putting our makeup on and getting ready to appear on the show and Bill asked us, "Okay, who's gonna go out there and talk with Mike?"

PAUL STANLEY: I just thought it was gonna be a disaster and I chickened out. So Gene went out and truly had nothing to say. It was a funny moment seeing him out there trying to talk in a weird voice telling Mike Douglas that he was "evil incarnate" and Totie Fields making a comment about him being Jewish underneath the makeup, saying, "You can't hide the hook" [*laughs*].

GENE SIMMONS: I didn't know that the comedians Robert Klein and Totie Fields were both out there and I was gonna get roasted. But I took my lumps. They wanted to prerecord us but we insisted on playing live. It was a chance to show Middle America our stuff. It was great exposure for us because a few million people got to see a new band they had never heard before.

19

BLACK-LEATHER BARBARIANS

In the early days—*before stretch limousines and private 747 clippers transported KISS around the world in grand style—the band toured on a shoestring budget. These were the days of cheap meals, cheap motels, cheap women, little sleep, and even less money. In 1974, KISS traveled from Asbury Park, New Jersey, to Anchorage, Alaska, in a beat-up station wagon, bringing their rock-and-roll circus from city to city in a never-ending quest to build an audience. The band truly paid their dues, united in the stubborn belief that superstardom was lurking right around the corner.*

SEAN DELANEY: On the first tour we had two vehicles, a station wagon and a twenty-two-foot Hertz rental truck. We had two roadies driving that, and I was with the band in the station wagon. In the beginning of the tour everything was fine. We're singing a song—"Ninety-Nine Bottles of Beer on the Wall"—and as the tour went on, the happiness sort of dropped because you're in a station wagon and you're driving six, seven hundred miles a day. You're tired, you're sick, you're getting paid nothing. People have never seen you,

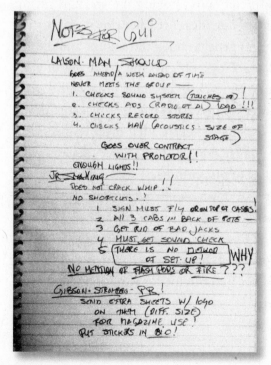

ABOVE: Gene Simmons's handwritten 1974 tour ledger KISS Catalog Ltd.

LEFT: Gene Simmons's handwritten instructions to manager Bill Aucoin for the 1974 tour KISS Catalog Ltd.

so when you first get up on stage the audience are throwing bottles and booing. So the tension is really heavy between the band. They would do things to me like they'd all sit in the backseat and take little pieces of cotton and stick them on top of my head. I'd be driving and I wouldn't even know. . . . I'd end up with a Marie Antoinette thing and driving to some redneck gas station, "Hey bud, fill it up." And they'd look at me and [the band would] all laugh and hide in the back. So the tension got worse and worse.

GENE SIMMONS: Sean was at the wheel and we were going through the hills of Tennessee. We'd all recently seen *Deliverance* with these cross-eyed hillbillies that either wanna saw you in half or fuck you up the ass.

SEAN DELANEY: We were down South and for these guys from New York we're in "hillbilly land." We wound up in a real nice development with a house and 8 acres of land, but to them it had to be hillbillies. I missed a turn and Ace starts poking me and telling me, "Remember where you're driving" and Peter starts poking me and I'm sitting there and all of the sudden I get an idea. I reached down and turned the ignition off, tapped the gas pedal to flood the engine, and the car goes *roomp, roomp,* . . . I said, "Guys, oh my God, we're out of gas." They were scared to death! Here they are, four guys with tinted black hair and skulls all over, some casual daytime makeup, down in the South, and they were panic-stricken. I tell them to get in the back of the station wagon and lay down. Then I cover them up with a blanket. So here's four sets of platform heels sticking straight up, and a blanket. I get out and sit down and drink two or three beers. Twenty minutes later, I walk back over to the car and they're still lying under this blanket and I started to laugh hysterically.

GENE SIMMONS: Peter flipped out, he was scared to death.

SEAN DELANEY: He would not speak to me for two solid weeks. Not a word. It's nice to get even.

KISS's early tours in 1974 proved to be a grand adventure for the four bright-eyed aspiring rock stars from New York City, testing their limits of endurance and revealing an exciting new world of possibilities.

PAUL STANLEY: Touring in the early days was both grueling and great. I think we were getting paid $60 a week, but we felt like we were living the dream. We were a rock band in a rented station wagon [*laughs*], but it was really exciting. We felt we were on a mission and were on the road to glory. We were a gang of people on a crusade who believed in something and were willing to do anything to promote it. There was a tremendous camaraderie in the band in spite of our differences, and the people around us shared that passion.

GENE SIMMONS: Those early years of KISS were far from glamorous. We rode in a station wagon hundreds of miles every day. We would take turns driving and sleeping in the back. We stopped and peed on

KISS at the Commodore Ballroom, Vancouver, British Columbia, January 9, 1975 Kim Barnatt

the side of long stretches of highway when we couldn't find a town anywhere near. We ate burgers at roadside taverns. We ate beans and franks because we couldn't afford better food. We were young and we were innocent. Ace and Peter would take turns mooning cars that went by or whipping out their cocks, doing anything to get a rise out of people. We were caught up in this idea where everybody you knew in school was getting up in the morning and working nine to five, getting married, and having kids, and here we were living on the road, just being rock-and-roll gypsies.

PAUL STANLEY: The trips were really long and somebody was always sick. We'd room two to a room and with all the girls around, the minimum that was in a room was three. It was cozy. There wasn't a lot of sleeping. Peter and I roomed together most of the time in the early days and we enjoyed each other's company. We had a lot of fun. But underlying any positive feelings that Peter had towards me was some very obvious resentment. He said that I didn't pay my dues and that he had worked really hard and struggled for years and I didn't. My only comeback was [*laughing*], "Well, you were waiting for me."

GENE SIMMONS: Throughout 1974 we were making $750 a night as an opening act and that had to pay for gas, the road crew, and hotels. The next year that went up to $1,500. We'd only have thirty minutes as an opening band and you'd have to go out there and bang it out and try and make each song memorable.

Money and fame weren't yet in the cards for the band, but during those early tours KISS did manage to enjoy one of the perks of being rock stars in training—women.

PAUL STANLEY: Other than the music, the biggest memories are the women. Just rampant sex. That's the time it was. We got the keys to the candy store. It was wild, having grown up a shy, pudgy kid who wasn't the most socially adept to suddenly find himself going from the one chasing to the one being chased. Honestly, I made sure I didn't run too quickly [*laughs*]. If rock and roll embodied anything it was total freedom, and the reason we wrote about that kind of stuff is because we were living it. I have to put it in perspective. As much as one might consider it debauchery and wild, abundant, random sex, I don't want anyone to negate the innocence of it. The women were fun. We were all celebrating this counterculture of rock and roll. A lot of it had to do with a subculture of women who loved rock and roll and part of loving rock and roll was giving yourself to it. I remember very clearly being with more than one woman who would tell me what band was coming through next week, and I'd say, "Say hi to so-and-so." There was no deception about it and nothing anybody was ashamed of.

Cameron Crowe's film *Almost Famous* was pretty much right on the money. It was very much a different time. Most of the women on tour—as odd as it might sound to say—were just nice girls. They were fun and not much different than me. There was nothing sordid about it. Sure, were there encounters with multiple women at the same time? Yeah, but I have to say that didn't change that feeling that it was fun and there was an innocence to it. It's very hard to explain if you weren't there.

WARREN DEWEY: One night while working on the band's first album I remember Gene telling me a story about how he came to New York as a kid with an Israeli accent. He told me something about being mugged, which he felt had changed his attitude and made him more of a cynic. I think he was studying to be a rabbi. Once I took Gene to my apartment on West Eighty-seventh Street. He always wore these boots with giant heels and I remember him clunking around on the wooden floors. Gene had a bad cold and my girlfriend made soup for him and gave him some vitamin C and a bunch of oranges. On the way back to the studio he asked me to let him know if we ever broke up. Even then he was kind of a hound [*laughs*].

ERIC WEINSTEIN: Back then with KISS it wasn't "sex, drugs, and rock and roll." They weren't druggies so it was more "sex and rock and roll." They had their pick of women every night. It was so extreme.

They always had tons of groupies. Because money was tight in those days they'd share rooms. We were at a Holiday Inn somewhere in Ohio and Paul and Gene were sharing a room and I remember the girls lined up outside the door all the way down the hallway, just fucking them left and right.

GENE SIMMONS: By the end of our first tour, there were so many girls that Sean Delaney was policing our hotel rooms to make sure we got enough rest. He'd literally break down the door of our rooms and physically remove girls that were in the room with us, apologizing all the time, saying, "We have a show tomorrow and you have to get rest!" I was aware if I lived in that town I'd have to take a girl out ten times, promise to be faithful, and maybe we'd be intimate. Here you could wake up with any number of girls whose names you'd never bothered to learn. I'd have sister acts, mother-daughter acts. Anything you could imagine. I remember this beautiful girl who was pregnant, and her sister came to my room for an autograph and within a half an hour we all wound up in the shower doing all kinds of things. Nothing was off limits. All the rules had changed.

One night we went to a club and Paul and I were looking at this girl and we were trying to figure out who was gonna go up to her. So I walk up to her and bring her to the table and she's very sexy. Here she was in this little Catholic girl outfit with pigtails, looking very cute. Slowly I'm looking at this girl and she's making it very clear that she's available. Paul kind of nudges me and goes, "That's a guy." Then she takes out her wallet and shows what she looked like as a Navy corpsman. She'd just gone through a sex change but hadn't as yet cut off the appendage [*laughs*]. Paul's roadie was drunk out of his mind and he's complaining to us, "You guys get all the chicks and I don't get anything." I told him, "Well, tonight's your lucky night" [*laughs*]. This poor guy took this girl back to the hotel and who knows what the hell happened. And to this day we've never told him that she was a guy [*laughs*].

Once the Polaroid camera was invented I started taking photos of the girls I was with. It became a ritual. The next day the guys in the band would say, "What ya got? How many girls did you get?" Every day I'd take out the book and show them the photos. I must have taken thousands of photos. There were so many girls, I'd write their name and the name of the city on the back. I've got to say that none of the girls were treated badly. They were treated very well and respectfully. The girls were shocked that I didn't smoke, drink, or get high. In Florida somebody broke into our room and stole some Rolex watches and one of my books of Polaroids. But that's the only one they got.

While KISS were sowing their wild oats on the road, the band's hard-working road crew were focused on less salacious pursuits, like making it to the next gig in time, which remained a daily challenge. On their way to a gig in the Midwest, several hungry crew members pulled into a cheap roadside dive to inhale a quick lunch. A surprise awaited them inside. . . .

PETER "MOOSE" ORECKINTO: One time while traveling to a gig we wound up in Kokomo, Indiana. We were driving north and we're tired and starving so we pulled into this Pioneer Chicken. It was me, J.R. Smalling, Mick Campise, Rick Munroe, and Paul Chavarria.

J.R. SMALLING (KISS STAGE MANAGER): I'm wearing a Superman T-shirt, Mick has got his rooster haircut with the feathered earring, and Moose is wearing a T-shirt and a black leather KISS jacket with rhinestones.

PETER "MOOSE" ORECKINTO: There's a little guy in front of us who's built like a fireplug. He's got this .357 hanging out of his back pocket and wearing this white jacket with a sewn-in cloth disc on his back. Across the top in an arc it said "United Klansmen of America" and at the bottom it said "Ku Klux Klan."

J.R. SMALLING: We walk in and Mick freezes. The place is packed. Every head in the place turns to us and it goes deadly quiet. Here we are in the restaurant and everyone is wearing muddy denim jeans and jackets. It was obvious they had come from a cross burning the night before and they look at us like we're from Mars.

PETER "MOOSE" ORECKINTO: We turn around and look and there were about forty or fifty people—kids and adults—all wearing the same jacket. Uh oh. So it was a good old Klan meeting at the Pioneer Chicken.

J.R. SMALLING: Some guys walk by us and turn around so they make sure we can see the twelve-inch-wide patch on the back of their jackets of a guy in a white sheet on a white horse. He's reining the horse up on two legs with one hand and he's got a javelin under the other one. Mick says, "What are we gonna do now?" [*laughs*]. And I said, "We're gonna tough this shit out."

PETER "MOOSE" ORECKINTO: They're staring at us and if looks could kill, we'd all be dead. I remember turning to Mick, "If they fuck with us we're gonna have to grab one and kill 'em." J.R. was a big African American guy and they didn't like seeing him there, either. We were tough. We all carried buck knives. We were on the road. We're moving trucks, we're crossing the country, we're sleeping in the front of the vehicle. We just didn't want to be fucked with. I can still see all these hog-looking faces with nasty looks on them.

J.R. SMALLING: This is where Moose and I got the expression "back to back." We stood in line back to back. We wouldn't take our eyes off of anybody in that place [*laughs*]. Thankfully, nobody came up to us and tried to do anything. We're standing there looking as tough as we were. We get up to the front of the line and this little girl, maybe sixteen or seventeen, said [*imitating Southern accent*], "Hi, sir, can I help you?" I told her what I wanted and she said, "Will that be to stay or to go?" [*laughs*]. And I said, "To go . . . and fast" [*laughs*]. We drove the rest of the way looking in the rearview mirror thinking they were gonna follow us. They didn't follow us, but when we got to where we were going we found bullet holes in the back of the truck.

PETER "MOOSE" ORECKINTO: Now that's what they call a close call.

J.R. SMALLING: Sometime later we passed through Peru, Indiana, the winter home of some circus or the other. The local sentiments were evident there as well. I remember seeing a bunch of fifty-gallon drums that were used as trash bins and all of them had "KKK" spray-painted on the side. Someone took a picture of me pissing into the can. I'd love to find a copy of that photo.

MICHAEL DES BARRES (LEAD VOCALIST, SILVERHEAD): We played with KISS a few times. The first was early in their career at a show in New York City [Academy of Music, January 26, 1974]. Johnny Thunders [of the New York Dolls] came backstage and gave us angel dust for the first time. Silverhead had just come to America and he got us thoroughly stoned. While not the extraordinary colossal magnificence it is today, KISS's stage show then was brilliantly homegrown. That was what was so intriguing about them before they had all the huge pyrotechnics and special effects. It was KISS, but a sort of modified KISS [*laughs*], minimized into a munchkin KISS. We were so loaded and thought, "Now we've got to follow this band with fire and drum risers going up to the ceiling!"

Silverhead came from a completely different place than KISS. British rock stars are a hybrid of Edwardian dandyism and Robert Johnson. We were smoking hashish, quoting Arthur Rimbaud, in love with Brian Jones, in the grand tradition of Oscar Wilde playing a slide guitar. It was very different from the Japanese anime approach that KISS had. We were really oppositional. We came from that decadent seventies cocaine scene, and KISS—and particularly Gene—were coming from an extraordinarily interesting place. I could see that he was completely and utterly committed to this demonic character that he created. He is truly a great kabuki-style actor. I've told him this many times. The characters that they created are living, breathing iconic characters. I always described Gene's character as a lonely monster. If you really look at him up on the stage he's a lonely carnal beast that moves slowly and dribbles blood.

In terms of their music, Gene is a real Anglophile and studied bands like Slade. He was a student of what was popular and what he could absorb and give back, like every artist does. The combination of Paul's purism with the groundbreaking rock-and-roll bands like Humble Pie, the Small Faces, and Rod Stewart, all of whom he adored, and Gene's more pop glam sensibilities, that's how the frisson was created that created KISS. I thought their music was fantastic but the interesting thing was no hipster community would admit to it. What they were doing was the complete antithesis to that Warhol loft mentality. We were stumbling around Warhol's loft while they were putting on their platform boots.

MICK BOX (GUITARIST, URIAH HEEP): We worked with KISS when they supported us and we supported them. When they supported us they asked if they could use explosions and, of course, we were using them ourselves at the time. Little did we know that when they went on they'd set off enough explosions to start a small war [*laughs*]. So when *we* came out with our fireworks, they paled in significance [*laughs*]. There was never any doubt that KISS were gonna be big provided they could come up with the songs. And of course, they did. When you strip away the makeup and costumes you've gotta have some good records, and they did.

We had loads of laughs with them on the road. I remember one time we were staying at one of those hotels with those interior domes with the swimming pool and Jacuzzis. One night we got a bit crazy and Peter Criss filled up the whole swimming pool and Jacuzzi with bubble bath [*laughs*]. There were bubbles everywhere, you couldn't find your way out the door [*laughs*].

J.R. Smalling, KISS's trusty stage manager from 1974 to 1976 KISS Catalog Ltd.

KISS was not alone in their journey toward world domination. Also along for the ride was the small and fiercely dedicated road crew that included Mike McGurl, J.R. Smalling, Peter "Moose" Oreckinto, Mick Campise, Paul Chavarria, and Rick Munroe.

PAUL STANLEY: We were a gang. We were roving barbarians and everybody who was there had a function and was a necessary member of the team.

MICK CAMPISE (KISS ROADIE): Everybody in the road crew wore black leather jackets and mirror sunglasses. We had a presence.

GENE SIMMONS: Our road crew guys looked the part. They were huge. These were big guys named "Moose" and "Junior."

PAUL CHAVARRIA: Our leader was J.R. Smalling. We called him the "Black Oak" because he was so big. He could take on anybody and do anything he had to do.

J.R. /MALLING: I'm six-foot-three but I think the minimum platforms that we all wore were four inches, so I was six-foot-seven in the boots. When we rolled in it was intended that people knew the crew was there and to give a little hint of the swagger, strength, and confidence of what was gonna come later in that evening. I think the road crew's swagger came as much from the necessity to have that kind of aura as because we're fuckin' New Yorkers [*laughs*] and we're not used to getting shoved around. Moose and I never shoved anybody around that didn't deserve it. But isn't it funny that no one can say we abused them? They can only say how professional we were. I used to tell the crew, "You can say whatever you want to anybody as long as you say it with a smile."

GENE /IMMON/: They were physically imposing and proud. They often had to fight other road crews to get us sound checks and to make sure the power wasn't pulled on us.

MICK CAMPI/E: We viewed ourselves as the band's protectors. We took care of the band as if they were our family. It was all for one, one for all.

PAUL CHAVARRIA: The road crew would kill for KISS. We would die for those guys. We would dive in front of them if people got in their way. We would attack somebody if anybody tried to pick a fight with the boys. We were their security.

PAUL /TANLEY: They were totally about KISS and believed in the band and they backed it up.

MICK CAMPI/E: Moose and J.R. used their size to intimidate anyone wanting to mess with the band, whether it was a headlining act or their road crew. We made a statement: "Don't fuck with KISS or the crew or we'll clean your clock."

PETER "MOO/E" ORECKINTO: There were a number of times, especially in the Deep South, where the band had some close calls.

People would taunt KISS saying, "Are you a queer? We're gonna kick your ass!" We would always quietly and diplomatically get in there and protect the band and say, "Look, boys, we don't want to get into any trouble." The last thing we wanted to do was expend our energy on a fight and get hurt.

I remember once after a show somewhere back in '74, there were lots of people milling around—groupies, stagehands, and the road crew. We were busy packing up and trying to get out as quickly as possible. J.R. and I noticed a kid walking away with Ace's '57 Les Paul. No case, he just took the guitar. Me and J.R. followed him out into the parking lot and we said, "Do you know we could pound you into the earth? Give us the fuckin' guitar back, you stupid little asshole." He was really pissed we caught him.

MIKE McGURL: Everybody—the road crew and KISS—was really tight-knit. We were with each other 24/7. We were an extended family. We took care of each other and had each other's back. That first year we lived on the road and were touring all the time. We had very little time off. The band hadn't gotten that big taste of success so everything was new to them.

ERIC WEINSTEIN: To be a KISS roadie you couldn't do it half-assed; you had to give your life to the cause and bust your ass 24/7.

J.R. SMALLING: It wasn't just a paycheck for us: we really believed in KISS. It was a mission. We did whatever it took to get things done. We took great pride at being able to put that show on every night. It was always "we"—*we* rocked that show, *we* fuckin' killed them with that show. That's how we felt with KISS. The show was as important as the music or even more important and for a musical act that was unheard of.

GENE SIMMONS: KISS was very lucky to get a road crew that was very loyal and actually believed in the band as a sort of crusade. They would stand on the side of the stage and get off on how the crowd was responding. In those days people hadn't seen anything like us; they hadn't witnessed anything like a band like KISS.

PAUL CHAVARRIA: Every guy on the road crew that worked for KISS in those days was a perfectionist. We wanted everything to be right.

ERIC WEINSTEIN: KISS took their show really seriously and they'd get really mad if things went wrong, like if the drum riser didn't work on cue. You knew they were serious and in order to work for them you had to be just as serious. You wanted to be there for their success; you wanted to be there when they got a gold record.

PETER "MOOSE" ORECKINTO: Being a part of KISS's original road crew was ultimately rewarding, but in truth, everything was a struggle. It was hard, dirty, dangerous work. KISS was an upstart band that nobody had ever heard of. We were so focused on our boys becoming big that we pushed the limits, even to the extent of killing ourselves to make it happen.

PAUL CHAVARRIA: Back in those days there was a lot of negativity around about KISS and their lack of talent. We looked at them completely differently. These guys were some of the hardest working, ass-busting rock and rollers out there. As time went on people started seeing that KISS was a very talented band that had it. The crew caught on to that really early and that made us even more committed to the cause of helping them make it.

PAUL STANLEY: The original road crew really believed in the band in a way that they were willing to lay themselves down for us. They were willing to do whatever was necessary to get the show up and to make sure the band got a fair deal in terms of time onstage, and if that meant—and I'm not advocating this—pulling a knife on somebody, they did it. If it meant bullying or intimidating people, they did it.

J.R. SMALLING: One night at the Ambassador Theater in St. Louis, KISS was onstage. Our cases were lined up against the back wall and all set to pack up and get out of there as quickly as possible. We used these huge Ampeg bass cases that were about five feet tall. We could tell that Argent's production manager, this Indian guy who grew up in London named Solomon, was getting ready

The Demon, Academy of Music, New York City, March 23, 1974
Bill Green/www.billsacademyofmusic.com

to cut the band's set short and turn the lights on. So I made my
way over to him, shoved him into one of the amp cases, and locked
the fuckin' case [*laughs*] until the band was off the fuckin' stage.
The band's playing and he's banging away inside of the case and
no one could hear him [*laughs*] until the band came offstage. After,
one of Argent's crew lets him out of the case. We're standing on
this big proscenium stage and this guy said something to me like,

TOP LEFT: **Paul at the Academy of Music, New York City, January 26, 1974** Bill Green/
www.billsacademyofmusic.com TOP RIGHT AND ABOVE: **Peter and Ace at the Academy of Music,
January 26, 1974** Len DeLessio/www.delessio.com

Gene at the Foothills Arena, Calgary, Alberta, May 20, 1974 Terry Munro

"You think you're pretty smart. What would you do if I put a knife to your throat?" So he puts a knife to my throat, and I took the knife and turned it on him [*laughs*] and he was holding the knife to his own throat [*laughs*]. That definitely settled the argument, and Argent never messed with us again.

ROD ARGENT (KEYBOARDIST, ARGENT): I had no idea that went on. We certainly would never have stopped KISS from doing an encore. That was roadies throwing their weight around. I'm really sorry that happened because I hate it when things like that happen to us.

RUSS BALLARD (GUITARIST, ARGENT): The first time we played with KISS was at the Academy of Music in New York [March 23, 1974]. I remember walking into the theater from the back and seeing this big KISS sign, the lights, and a big drum rostrum. We

knew nothing about KISS and had no idea that they wore makeup.
ROD ARGENT: They came onstage and I felt like a dwarf next to them.
They had the highest heels I'd ever seen [*laughs*] and looked like giants
when they walked past us onstage. I thought, "Wow, what is going on?"
[*laughs*]. I'd never seen anything like this before. We'd never heard of
KISS at that time but I was impressed with their performance. They
were doing theatrical rock and roll to the extreme.

RUSS BALLARD: We watched their show that night and thought it
was hilarious. They were great musically and they were the only
people doing it. We played with them quite a few times throughout
'74, and as the years progressed the show became more refined
and exciting. If you're a heavy band in a market of very heavy
bands it's hard to break through. But if you're in a market of one,

New York Dolls/KISS tour poster, Flint, Michigan, June 12, 1974 Courtesy of Brad Estra

which they were with the makeup and stage show, they had the market cornered. KISS was like the American version of Slade. They crafted music that was made for arenas. Ironically, in later years KISS covered a few of my songs. Ace Frehley had a big hit with "New York Groove," KISS had a hit with "God Gave Rock and Roll to You," and Peter Criss recorded two of my songs on one of his solo albums: "Some Kinda' Hurricane" and "Let Me Rock You."

BOB "NITEBOB" CZAYKOWSKI: The first time KISS opened for the Dolls was in Flint, Michigan [June 12, 1974]. Jerry Nolan, the drummer for the Dolls, and Peter Criss had been friends growing up. When the Dolls came to sound-check, Jerry looked at the gigantic drum set that Peter was using in KISS and decided to write all over the drum heads stuff like "fuck you" and "you're a jerk," just screwing around with him. He thought it was funny, but Peter didn't think it was funny. He was really furious and told his roadie that he had to change all the drum heads because he couldn't play a show with that stuff written on them.

After we played the Allen Theater in Cleveland with the Dolls and KISS [June 14, 1974], the festivities moved back to the Holiday Inn. There was a massive amount of rock-and-roll-style seventies partying going on. Back at the hotel there was some shenanigans when the Dolls threw a fire extinguisher out the window and it caused a big mess. The tour manager for the Dolls went, "We're gonna get in a lot of shit for this!" Someone said, "How are they gonna know who did it?" And he said, "Because our fire extinguisher is missing." So someone said, "Let's take the fire extinguisher on KISS's floor and maybe they'll blame KISS." This was more street goofing around kind of style; they were trying to keep their asses out of the fire. The next day I remember the tour manager for KISS was arguing at the hotel front desk that his people had nothing to do with this.

Another time we were playing Baton Rouge [June 16, 1974] and three bands were on the bill—KISS, the New York Dolls, and Blue Öyster Cult. I remember watching KISS from the side of the stage with David Johansen and seeing the fire, smoke, and dry ice. I remember David going, "This is going into some kind of extreme weird theater." He felt it wasn't about the music as much as the theater. The Dolls didn't do anything like that. We hardly ever used a backdrop. There were no special effects. It was just five guys with guitars, drums, and amps. But I have to say, the Dolls had faith in what they were doing. Nowadays you'd never let a band open up and use all those special effects, but they let KISS go wild.

PETER "MOOƧE" ORECKINTO: In late December '74 we were playing the Michigan Palace. Someone threw up ten bullets on the stage with all our names on them—the band and the road crew. I saw a bullet that said "Moose" and said, "Yeah, right," and I put it in my pocket. Maybe it was the mob's way of saying, "You sleep with the fishes, here's a bullet with your name on it." We took it as someone may be gunning for us or someone was sending us a message. The next night we played in Canada and the only way you can head north into Canada is through the Detroit tunnel. We get to the other side and customs took our bullets away from us. They opened them up and saw that they were live and confiscated them.

Fiercely devoted and loyal, KISS's road crew would routinely place themselves in harm's way, all for the love of rock and roll. Tragically, while en route to a KISS show, a member of the band's road crew lost his life in a car crash.

ABOVE: Live at Academy
of Music, New York
City, January 26,
1974 Bill Green/www.
billsacademyofmusic.com

LEFT: Live at Academy
of Music, January 26,
1974 Len DeLessio/www.
delessio.com

GENE SIMMONS: J. B. Fields, one of our truck drivers, God bless him, was driving during a very bad snowstorm across a bridge with our equipment. There was a woman driving towards him that was gonna crash. To save her life, he drove off the bridge and he was killed. It was very tragic. He was a good guy with family and kids. He made the ultimate sacrifice.

From Anchorage, Alaska, to Tokyo, Japan, KISS has played thousands of shows over nearly four decades. But an early show in the band's career remains a gig both band and crew will never forget.

MIKE McGURL: We were somewhere in Indiana and were supposed to fly to Billings, Montana, the next day. It was in the middle of winter and we went to the airport and all the flights were canceled because of horrendous weather. I called Bill Aucoin and told him, "All the flights are canceled, we're not gonna get out of here on a commercial airliner. Do you want me to try and charter a small plane?" Bill agreed and said, "Yeah, if you can talk the band into it." I worked out a deal with a guy who had a six- or eight-seat twin-engine Cessna. He told me he could get us to Billings. By this time it's getting into early evening and it was snowing like crazy. I had to tell the band we were gonna get on this plane and fly to Billings. We went over to this hangar and they see the plane on the tarmac and they all freaked, especially Gene, who hated to fly. He kept mumbling, "Buddy Holly, Buddy Holly." [*On February 3, 1959, a plane crash in Clear Lake, Iowa, claimed the lives of rock-and-roll stars Buddy Holly, Ritchie Valens, and the Big Bopper.*] We had to get on the plane and take the flight. The band was freaking out and didn't say a word the whole flight. It was a real white-knuckle flight, with the band gripping the armrests, numbed with fear. That flight was like a roller-coaster ride. The plane was dropping all over the place. It was just really bad. They were scared to death.

We got to Billings and it was bitter cold, probably 20 below zero. We arrived at the venue and the crowd was there but there was no road crew and no equipment. I panicked. There were three or four thousand people and an empty stage. No one knew where the road crew was. I told the crowd, "The road crew's on their way, as soon as they get here we're gonna rush to get the stage put together." The venue had provided a sound system so we were able to play music, and the audience just sat there quiet and peaceful. The road crew finally showed up around ten or ten thirty. We had a whole bunch of volunteers from the audience and we humped that gear onto the stage in about five minutes. They did a quick setup and the show went off and it was great. That was definitely a night to remember.

MIKE QUATRO (MICHAEL QUATRO JAM BAND): We played with KISS early on in their career [April 4, 1974] and shared a common vision for theatricality. We were starting to do a very costume-driven pyrotechnics show ourselves. I changed costumes three times during the show. For the opening number, "In the Court of the Crimson King," I wore a purple crimson king's robe with a hood and a plastic mask, which was made to look like a Frankenstein monster with glitter. We were using flash pots as well. But when I saw KISS I said, "These guys are taking it to the next level." I remember speaking with the guys in the dressing room and agreeing that we're not just here to play music, it's show business. It's about entertaining audiences. And KISS understood that better than anybody.

SUZI QUATRO (RECORDING ARTIST): I headlined Michigan Palace for two shows in 1974 [April 12 and 13] and KISS was my opening act. It was my first time back since I'd had recording success with my English band, so it was local girl comes home and that was pretty cool. I watched their set and thought they were an unusual act—they dressed pretty funny. The best thing they had going for them was their image. The crowd treated them more like a curiosity as it was still pretty early in their career and not many people knew who they were. I get a kick out of thinking that KISS opened for me early in their career. I brought that up to Gene Simmons many years later when I did his TV show *Rock School*. I said to him, "First of all, I'll have to teach you how to play bass guitar [*laughs*], and second, don't ever forget you supported me" [*laughs*]. He knew I was a serious bass player so he took it all tongue-in-cheek.

KIM SIMMONDS (GUITARIST, SAVOY BROWN): A lot of bands wanted to get onto Savoy Brown tours because we were doing good business across the country, from Alaska to Florida. We were skeptical at first about having KISS on the bill because of the nature of a band that wore outrageous costumes and makeup, but they were a breath of fresh air, a fun band in the era of serious musicians. They were breaking all the rules. I vividly recall standing in the crowd watching them perform for the first time. There's a lot of competition and jealousy in music and you need to sort your feelings out. None of those feelings came into play in regard to KISS. Instead of not liking them because they were the polar opposites of what I was trying to do in music, as soon as you saw them you had to like them. The crowds felt the same way too. A lot of opening acts don't have the nerve to put on a big show but KISS had no problems saying, "This is who we are, this is what we do." They were good guys and were fans of Savoy Brown from the old days. KISS went a different route than us. We were somewhat snobby serious musicians and they were the polar opposites but we got on very well.

COLIN PATTENDEN (BASSIST, MANFRED MANN'S EARTH BAND): KISS opened quite a few shows for Manfred Mann's Earth Band in '74 and I watched a lot of their shows. They were the surprise underdog. Unlike the headliner, who had to deliver each night, the opening act had a lot less pressure on them. There was no expectation for the opening band, and KISS blew everybody apart. They had balls to go up onstage and do it their own way without compromise.

KATHI McDONALD (RECORDING ARTIST, CAPITOL RECORDS): I played two shows with KISS in 1974 [April 17 and 18] at the Lafayette Music Room in Memphis, Tennessee. Their look was scary, but in an exciting way. I'd never seen anything like it; it was original and untouchable. They went up and rocked the house. At the time I was promoting my album *Insane Asylum* on Capitol Records. It was ballsy rock and roll so my music was cut from the same cloth as KISS. The band asked me to join them onstage so I went up and sang with them during an encore. I was wearing a long black velvet spaghetti-strapped dress trimmed in black boa feathers and I fit right in with them.

A May 1974 tour of Canada was beset with problems reminiscent of the struggles surrounding the band's previous visit to the Great White North.

FRANK WEIPERT: I co-promoted a show with Savoy Brown, Manfred Mann's Earth Band, and KISS in May of '74 in Edmonton at the Kinsmen Field House and it turned out to be a total train wreck. KISS's PA system was coming in from the same company who did the sound and lighting the night before in Winnipeg. It was a sixteen-hour drive from Winnipeg to Edmonton and the company assured us they'd make the date on time. I arrived in mid-afternoon at the venue and the PA system still hadn't arrived, although the entire stage set was in place. We were told the truck with the PA was

Gene at the Foothills Arena, Calgary, Alberta, May 20, 1974 Terry Munro

running late and would be there at 6 p.m. Given that our doors were set to open at seven and our start time was at eight o'clock with KISS we were really cutting it close. When the PA arrived the gear went up in absolute record time.

The show starts and not even halfway into KISS's first song the mike starts clipping and the vocals fall out. The PA kept going out through the set. The sound problems were absolutely staggering; everything seemed to go wrong. As the set wore on speakers were blowing left and right. The band was definitely aware of it but rolled on. On that level they were absolute troupers. The sound problems continued all night. By the time Savoy Brown was done the sound was reduced to something you'd hear out of a transistor radio [*laughs*].

It was clear that something had overloaded the PA on the electrical side, and it was decimated. Their PA was in ruins. You're talking about a hundred-thousand-dollar system going up in smoke. I said to the guy in charge of the PA, "Talk to me. What happened?" He said he didn't know. I looked behind the stage and noticed a distribution panel and asked him, "Didn't you run all your power through that panel?" And he said, "No, when we got here, we asked a couple of the house techs and they told us the power was pretty good in this house so we didn't bother hooking up the distribution panel." I told him I figured out every time that the air conditioning went on and every

The Cat Man, Orpheum Theatre, Boston, May 11, 1975 Leo Gozbekian/www.leog.biz

time there was a power surge going into the building it was going directly into your gear. He looked at me and went, "Oh my God, I've basically smoked my own PA!" A distribution panel is the same thing as your power bar at home. You plug it into the wall and you have a surge protector to protect your computer. Imagine that on a scale multiplied about a thousand times. It was a sound nightmare. At the beginning of the evening you had a fully working PA and by the end of the night the only equipment left that could produce a sound besides the band's equipment were a few minor speakers pointed out into a seven-thousand-seat hall.

Right from the start KISS were storm troopers. They knew exactly what to do onstage. I worked with Alice Cooper at the same time. Offstage Alice was a very quiet, mild-mannered guy, but when he gets onstage he ceases to be Vincent Furnier and he becomes Alice Cooper. I would lay that same thing on KISS. The minute they went onstage they're KISS: they're larger than life. It didn't matter if their set was powered by one little fifty-watt amp, they'd still destroy the audience.

Gene and Ace, Aragon Ballroom, Chicago, April 19, 1974 David Slania

20

HAVE ROAD, WILL TRAVEL

A punishing schedule of one-nighters meant driving all night to the next gig, leaving the road crew little time for more than a few hours of sleep. Wired on multiple cups of coffee—and occasionally something stronger, like "white crosses," a mild amphetamine—the road crew was always racing against the clock to mount KISS's increasingly elaborate stage show, which had become a Broadway production on steroids. It was now a spectacular sensory and aural assault of towering fireballs, ear-shattering bombs, ghostly dry ice, sophisticated lighting, and dazzling special effects like fire-breathing, blood-spitting, exploding drumsticks, a levitating drum riser, and a confetti storm.

MIKE McGURL: Right from the beginning it was a big show. It wasn't a normal rock-and-roll show where you rolled in your amps and your drum riser and that was it. The energy behind mounting a big production like this was extraordinary.

JAY "HOT SAM" BARTH: In the early days it was an adventure just to keep things running. It was a combination of duct tape, sweat, and determination. With a grueling schedule and an environment of spit, blood, smoke, fire, and bombs, we all had our work cut out for us.

J.R. /MALLING: We were in constant motion. Where it stopped for other acts setting up the typical stage gear—amps, guitars, and drum set—our jobs were just starting. There was always something that had to be purchased, whether it was eyeliner, makeup, lipstick, or flash powder.

RICK MUNROE: Peter's levitating drum riser was always breaking and needed daily maintenance. That levitating drum machine was originally developed for [TV personality] Steve Allen to levitate his piano, but it couldn't hold the weight of a real piano. We had the same issue with the levitating drum machine barely [being] able to hold the weight with Peter on top of it. It was always at the breaking point.

ERIC WEIN/TEIN: The drum riser was basically two pieces of plywood on top of a forklift with a curtain around the front of it. Peter used to fuckin' beat the shit out of his drums and you'd think, "Oh my God, this guy's gonna fall and the whole thing's gonna collapse."

RICK MUNROE: There were times we had crew guys pushing it along to keep it going or when it got stuck [*laughs*].

J.R. /MALLING: From the LVM [levitating drum machine] to the dry ice, none of the special effects we used were built for being on the road two hundred days a year. They were magicians' props and illusions built for use in Vegas and TV. Just keeping our special effects equipment working from the abuse of constant touring was a real challenge.

MIKE McGURL: It was a real challenge to put the show up each day, but we had a very dedicated crew. The load-in was normally at five or six in the morning and sound check was usually by five. Just getting the gear into the venues was brutal. The crew worked really hard.

PETER "MOO/E" ORECKINTO: We were the first ones to lead the parade with open fire and open explosions. You'd have to demonstrate those fire and explosive effects to the fire marshal in each town. They wanted to ensure the explosives weren't too powerful and they were

TOP: **Gene and Paul fine-tuning their makeup**
ABOVE: **Sharing a private joke** Photos by Norman Seeff/www.normanseeff.com

The roar of the greasepaint Chuck Boyd/www.chuckboydgalleries.com

concerned with the height of the flames. We were prepared with fire extinguishers positioned at different parts of the stage at all times. It was a public safety issue. You've got thousands of people in the audience and if anything went wrong, with all our explosives and fire the whole place could go up like a tinderbox.

PAUL /TANLEY: Considering the type of show we were doing in small clubs and theaters, we were very lucky to have gotten away as unscathed as we did.

MIKE McGURL: It would take the whole day to construct the stage, lighting, and sound gear. Even during sound check they were adjusting lights, laying cables, wiring sound, and testing the special effects up until the showtime.

While the road crew was addressing any outstanding technical issues and gearing up for the start of the show, the four members of KISS were ensconced in their dressing room, undergoing their transformation into larger-than-life rock-and-roll superheroes.

GENE SIMMONS: The roar of the crowd and the smell of the greasepaint is very apropos of KISS, and no other band can say that. You start putting on the makeup and the outfits and the whole thing becomes ritualistic. What you wear and how you dress definitely has something to do with how you feel. And it's no different than commandos and Indians wearing war paint. They put on war paint because the fiercer they looked, the fiercer they felt. The ritual

Mirror star, Orpheum Theatre, Boston, May 11, 1975 Ron Pownall/RockRollPhoto.com

LEFT: Ace practicing licks before the show
RIGHT: **The inner sanctum** Photos by Chuck Boyd/ www.chuckboydgalleries.com

itself is very empowering and the same goes for me. You literally go through a change. I took to the makeup like my second skin. By the time I'm done putting on my makeup and costume I feel stronger and much more powerful.

PAUL STANLEY: Putting on the makeup and costumes is a transformation in a sense but it's also more an amplification and magnification of an aspect of my personality. It's not all of who I am but it's part of who I am and it's brought to the forefront. It's a ritual in the sense of bringing that part of me out.

GENE SIMMONS: In the dressing room before the show we would play music and talk. In the early days there was a real camaraderie. Ace would tell jokes and the next day he'd say, "Tell me that joke

ABOVE, LEFT: Paul with his cherished Gibson Firebird guitar, Orpheum Theatre, Boston, May 11, 1975

ABOVE, RIGHT: The lord of the wasteland, Orpheum Theatre, Boston, May 11, 1975

LEFT: Space Ace, Orpheum Theatre, Boston, May 11, 1975
Photos by Ron Pownall/
RockRollPhoto.com

The God of Thunder Chuck Boyd/www.chuckboydgalleries.com

about the clown who went to outer space," and I'd say, "Ace, you're the one who told *me* that joke" [*laughs*].

PETER CRISS: I used to put eggs in Gene's boots and when he'd go put them on he'd look at me and say, "You sonofabitch, Peter!" We would make fun of each other, which was so healthy.

GENE SIMMONS: The only times there were ever hands raised in the band was when Ace and Peter went at each other once in Chicago. Then they apologized to each other and fell into this kind of drunken stupor, crying, "I love you" the way drunks do. While we were putting on the makeup and outfits you didn't need to get yourselves too psyched up because you could hear the audience from inside the dressing room screaming.

PETER CRISS: Then the last five minutes before we went on, no one was allowed in the dressing room because that was our time for meditating. We'd all grab each other's hands and say, "Let's kick ass!"

MIKE McGURL: And when the show was over, the crew had to tear it down and start all over again. The crew would have to break down the gear, load it into the trucks, and head to the next gig. They'd be lucky if they were on their way by two or three o'clock in the morning. Hopefully they'd only have a few hundred miles to travel to the next gig, but if it was longer it caused major problems. The crew was perpetually exhausted.

RICK MUNROE: To be a roadie for KISS you had to be like MacGyver and be able to fix whatever came your way. It's safe to say we used a lot of bailing wire and duct tape to keep the show going [*laughs*].

Getting ready for showtime, Orpheum Theatre, Boston, May 11, 1975
Ron Pownall/RockRollPhoto.com

JAY "HOT SAM" BARTH: One night in San Antonio the power supply for the main sound system mixing console blew up. This was about forty minutes before show time. This is one thing we had no spares for. Since it runs on 12 volts, I thought of car batteries. I borrowed the batteries out of the band's two limousines [*Authors' Note: Although KISS had yet to achieve stardom, limos were a luxury occasionally afforded touring bands*] and hooked them up with C-clamps and vise grips. Thankfully, it made it through the show. However, the band was pissed because they couldn't go straight to the hotel after the show. Gene's exact quote was, "What the fuck do you mean Hot Sam has the batteries?" [*laughs*].

Whether you were crushed against the front-row barriers or observing the show from nosebleed seats, the KISS sign was visible, fire-branding the band's incandescent logo into the psyche of all in attendance. It also came with its own share of headaches for the crew.

RICK MUNROE: It was a big challenge getting that four-foot KISS sign up every day. It was a high-maintenance KISS sign with four big plywood letters. One time I even had to split the letters [*laughs*] because there was no room to put it up. I had *K-I* on one side of the stage and *S-S* on the other [*laughs*].

From the opening machine gun chords that kick off "Deuce" to the dramatic set closer replete with levitating drum kit and explosive flash pots, a KISS concert was much more than your typical rock-and-roll show: it was theater of the mind and body, an orgy of sound, fury, and dazzling visuals. Whether they played a club, theater, or coliseum, before KISS hit the stage the crowd was treated to a grand introduction foretelling the scorching rock-and-roll excess in store for them.

MICK CAMPISE: Throughout the band's first tour in '74, Sean Delaney was in charge of the stage announcements. Shows would routinely begin with him loudly bellowing into the mic, "Put your two lips together and give a warm welcome for KISS!"

J.R. SMALLING: I thought that intro was really weak and that they needed a stronger one. There was a Toyota commercial which said, "You asked for it, you got it—Toyota." I thought that would work great for the intro so I modified it to, "You wanted the best and you got it, the hottest band in the land . . . KISS!" I was the guy that wrote it and said it at least five hundred times in concert over two-and-a-half years. I wasn't nervous doing it. It was power. I'm the first voice that people are hearing from this band that they'd waited months or years to see.

For both band and audience, a KISS show was a communal, unabashed celebration of the joys of loud rock-and-roll music.

BUCK REINGOLD: KISS was the loudest band on the street. When you went to a KISS show and you sat in the audience, you not only saw them but you felt them. It was a physical experience as well as one of sound and visuals.

PETER "MOOSE" ORECKINTO: This was spectacle. This wasn't just another rock-and-roll show. That's what people were looking for. Right from the beginning KISS was never booed off the stage, they were cheered off the stage. The crowd enjoyed the dynamics of the show; they were enthralled and mesmerized. From the drum riser to the fog machines, flash pots to the confetti to Gene spitting a huge fireball out of his mouth, audiences didn't know what was coming next.

PETER CRISS: All rock audiences want two things: they want to rock and roll and they want to get up and sweat. That's what we give them. We'll give an audience anything they want. If they want one encore we'll give it to them. If they want two encores we'll really give it to them. You can walk through one of our concerts and find anything you want: people covered with glitter, Hell's

Angels, rednecks, guys with dresses. We look out of our dressing room door and half of the people waiting for us are six-foot chicks with whips.

In February 1974, during KISS's short Canadian tour, one of the band's shows was held in a most peculiar venue: a school cafeteria. Returning to Canada a few months later, the band were once again confronted with performing at an unusual, less-than-rock-and-roll setting.

FRANK WEIPERT: I co-promoted three KISS shows in May of '74 in Winnipeg, Edmonton, and Lethbridge, all just a few months since they played their first shows in Canada. Savoy Brown and Manfred Mann's Earth Band co-headlined and KISS was the opening act. People that had seen them a few months before showed up to cheer them on and KISS were very well received. So we get to Lethbridge, Alberta, and arrive at the Exhibition Hall only to find that it was used for one thing and that was exhibiting livestock. It was a barn, basically.

MIKE McGURL: Boy, was that a weird venue [*laughs*]. It smelled like a cattle barn; the awful smell of manure was in the air. It was like a stable for cows and horses, with dirt floors and sawdust.

FRANK WEIPERT: About a thousand kids showed up and the band played well. But it was a strange gig. Lethbridge, Alberta, is the closest you'd come to a Texas small town. We got back to the hotel and the next morning the band and I were sitting in the coffee shop of the Holiday Inn. We were planning to fly up to Calgary on a small commuter airline. All of a sudden the local police, the Royal Canadian Mounted Police, are in the hotel. The hotel had called the police about a disturbance from one of the bands. And the culprit wasn't KISS but Savoy Brown, who decided to do a number like the Who and toss the TV out into the swimming pool. We were guilty by association, being in the same hotel as the two other bands. Everyone was put up against the wall and questioned by the police. The local airline bans us and refuses to take our passage up to Calgary, which was a forty-five-minute flight. We found ourselves having to scramble that morning to get rental cars to escape out of Lethbridge alive. Thank you, Savoy Brown [*laughs*].

MIKE McGURL: Once we played an outdoor show at a drive-in theater in Alaska [June 2, 1974]. It was held at night but it felt like the daytime because during the summer in Alaska it never got dark. Savoy Brown was the headliner and Kim Simmonds, the guitar player for Savoy Brown, was drunk out of his mind to the point where he was totally incoherent and couldn't function.

KIM SIMMONDS: I was drunk as a skunk and having trouble standing. I was under a lot of strain at the time because of my heavy workload so this was a rare occurrence for me to be that intoxicated onstage. I could barely manage to stand upright and kept falling down. The guys in KISS were on the side of the stage and kept coming out to push me back up [*laughs*].

PETER "MOOSE" ORECKINTO: My most embarrassing moment working for KISS was at a gig the band did at Eielson Air Force Base in [Fairbanks,] Alaska [June 4, 1974]. We set up the stage and watched these young air force personnel come in dressed in coats and ties and their ladies wearing formal dresses. They wanted to slow dance with their dates, and here comes this band that looked like fuckin' lunatics in full makeup and costumes. In one way it was the funniest thing I'd ever seen but I also felt bad for the band and the crowd.

PAUL CHAVARRIA: It was a lovers' crowd and here we came to rock out and the two didn't mesh. You had Gene's tongue hanging out all over the place, blood all over the stage, and flames, and that didn't bode well for romance.

PETER "MOOSE" ORECKINTO: The crowd was cordial but I think they wanted to listen to some slow mellow music so they could dance and get romantic with their dates. And KISS's music was anything but mellow or romantic [*laughs*]. And adding to the surreal nature of that day, at that time of year in Alaska it was light twenty-two hours a day, which was very strange.

MIKE McGURL: We were playing one show and Gene was sick and had laryngitis so he couldn't sing. Backstage we were trying to figure out how to handle the set without Gene singing. I had to go out and explain to the crowd that the show was delayed. Man, they started throwing stuff at me, rolls of toilet paper. Paul had to sing all of the songs and it really strained his voice dramatically. By the end of the set Paul's voice was shot but he came through and pulled it off.

PETER "MOO/E" ORECKINTO: KISS was playing the Agora in Columbus, Ohio, and we could hear the rumble and roar of this big storm coming. All of a sudden it hit and immediately the power went out during the band's performance. The whole place went dark. One thing you don't want is a bunch of rowdy and angry rock-and-roll fans in a room with the lights off and no emergency lighting or lit exits. The band had to stay on the stage in the darkness with the loud din of the crowd. You'd hear people yelling at them: "Hey, what the fuck?" "Turn the power back on!" "I wanna hear 'Strutter!'" "'Black Diamond!'" The show was delayed for some time until the power finally came back on. Man, that was a close call.

DAN McCAFFERTY (LEAD VOCALI/T, NAZARETH): We did a bunch of shows with KISS and Blue Öyster Cult in the early days. I ran into them backstage on that first show and they were in full garb and getting ready to go on. They looked seven feet tall compared to me 'cause I'm a short-arse Scotsman [*laughs*]. We watched their show and thought they were great, as did the audience. KISS took rock shows to the max with the fire and explosions, almost like, "How daft can we really be?" I thought, "These guys are gonna be really huge or they're gonna implode." We came back to America the next year and KISS were headlining arenas. After our last date with Blue Öyster Cult and KISS, there was a party back at the hotel. And I remember these long-haired guys in T-shirts and jeans came up to me and said, "Hey man, thanks for the tour, good luck to you." After they left I pulled someone aside and said, "Who was that?" and they said, "Oh, those are the boys in KISS." I'd never seen them without their makeup so I had no idea who these guys were [*laughs*].

SPENCER KIRKPATRICK (GUITAR, HYDRA): We played with KISS on around eight to ten gigs in '74 and '75 in support of our *Land of Money* album on Capricorn Records. There's always been that schism between the North and South going back to the Civil War. KISS were the first folks who were nice to us on the road that hailed from up North. We played a gig with KISS and Quicksilver Messenger Service in South Bend, Indiana [December 29, 1974], at a really old theater [Morris Civic Auditorium]. It was a hoot there. I'm sure they never had any pyrotechnics there before. So when KISS's explosive flash pots went off, it caused a real big stir because big pieces of plaster started to fall down from the ceiling. That caught the ire of the fire marshal, who was also getting real concerned because their balls of flames were going up to the ceiling.

KISS and Hydra shared a love for loud music. We weren't like most of the Southern bands; we were more into the British end of things. That's why KISS seemed to appreciate what we did. I remember watching their sound check at the Aragon Ballroom in Chicago [November 8, 1974]—we were playing that night with KISS and UFO—and they were just standing in place without their makeup going through their set and it was impressive. It gave me much more appreciation for them. I was never one for gymnastics onstage so when I saw the guys knock it out onstage without any effects, I realized they were a great band on a music level, too. We also played with KISS at Beggars Banquet in Louisville, Kentucky. It was a small rock club with really low ceilings so they had to lessen the flash pot charges. If they hadn't they would have burned the whole place down! Rock and roll has always been a little bit reckless and KISS embodied the whole lifestyle. Every time we played with them there was never a single face in the crowd that showed anything other than awe, amazement, and enjoyment. KISS took it to the next level, had a game plan, and really capitalized on it.

A far cry from the sophisticated, state-of-the-art, elaborate staging used on the band's tours in the late seventies, the group's early stage show operated on a shoestring and experienced its share of technical mishaps.

MIKE McGURL: The drum levitating platform was always problematic. It looked great from the audience but it never worked right. It was just a nightmare. His drum kit never went up smoothly and there were times it even got stuck with Peter halfway up. That didn't make Peter happy and that wasn't the effect the band was going for.

MICK CAMPISE: When we saw there was a problem a bunch of us ran behind the drum kit and we would grab hold of a forklift and pull it backwards towards us so the front end of the drum kit wouldn't tip over. This almost became a nightly occurrence because that damn chain-link contraption wouldn't work right.

MARK "ZERO" STINNER (KISS'S SPECIAL EFFECTS DIRECTOR): Before Gene blew fire, I'd give him half of a cup of kerosene which he'd hold in his mouth, and then I'd hand him the stiletto, and its handle was soaked with cotton and lighter fluid. He'd light the torch with the candelabra and would walk out into the center of the stage and breathe fire. I was crouched in a running back position with a wet towel around my neck just in case his hair caught fire, which it did several times. Then he'd stab the stiletto into this piece of foam and come offstage. I'd hand him a cup of Scope mouthwash and he'd rinse his mouth out and resume the show. We always kept a bottle of ipecac syrup around just in case because if he accidentally swallowed some kerosene he could die. So the ipecac syrup was always on hand because it would make him throw up.

PAUL CHAVARRIA: We were doing a show in Norman, Oklahoma, and that night Gene accidentally set me on fire. Gene came over, took the liquid from me, and I gave him the torch. That night was bad. He goes and blows the fire and the flames just went all over him, his face and his hair. I went flying out and threw this wet towel over him to put the fire out and he still had a whole bunch of liquid in his mouth and he spewed the rest of the stuff and it hit my jeans. His torch was still lit and my jeans burst into flames immediately. I'm putting him out and now I'm on fire [*laughs*].

There are these safety commercials that say, "When you're on fire, roll." When it's happening to you, you don't think about that, you're standing on a stage and you're burning. I put him out and I take off running and jump off the stage. These two firemen were standing on the side of the stage. One of them tackles me to the ground and the other fireman uses a fire extinguisher to put me out. I run back to my side of the stage and Gene comes back at the end of the song and I go, "Are you okay?" And he goes, "No thanks to you, you asshole! Where the hell were you?" He didn't recall that I had put him out. I was always aware we could have a bad night and he could burst into flames [*laughs*]. We were lucky because he was good at it. It was always up to me to make sure every door was closed and there was no ventilation that could blow and cause the flame to go back at him. He'd go back and forth and see which way the wind was blowing and pick up on that.

PETER "MOOSE" ORECKINTO: Nobody in the rock-and-roll arena was using fire and explosives as part of their stage show. We were the first. The use of pyrotechnics was a big selling point to the kids who came to see the band. The power and energy of their music combined with all the pyro made it an eye-popping spectacle. Word got around through the fans, "You've gotta see this band—you won't believe what they do onstage." Paul always said, "We put on a show to give the audience their money's worth." With the fire and flash pots, it was like bringing off-Broadway theater to the rock stage.

MIKE McGURL: Fire was a big part of the KISS show [but] balls of flame were rolling up to the ceiling, which was a real big problem. We had these metal canisters positioned around the stage and they had a little cup on top of it. In that cup was sterno from camping stores. They were all hooked together with a compressor. Inside the canisters was this powder called lycopodium powder. It was used by magicians for creating special effects and was a rather inert powder. If it was just sitting in a bowl and if you'd toss a match into it, it wouldn't burn. But when you pumped compressed air through it and it shot up past this cup of burning sterno it created this fireball. The higher the air pressure, the bigger the ball and the higher it went.

Every place we came to play the fire marshal would be waiting for us. He'd say, "I have to see this special effect." We'd set it up for him and turn the air pressure down real low so it would create a fireball maybe a half a foot, eight or ten inches in diameter. It would go up about three or four feet [and then] it would dissipate. Well, when the show came around [*laughing*] we'd crank that sucker up and we'd have a fireball that was two or three feet in diameter and it would roll right up to the ceiling and dissipate across the ceiling. I was always amazed we never burned anything down. There were times a fire marshal caught on to what we were doing and then I'd have to sit and negotiate with him—"How much is it gonna cost us to get this special effect happening?" And I'd have to slip him a few hundred dollars.

MARK "ZERO" STINNER: Once KISS was playing in Chicago and the fire marshal wouldn't let us use the fire, explosions, and bombs. That night there was nothing we could do about the fire, but the soundman and I had a trick up our sleeves and we started working on sounds on a Moog synthesizer. During the show I was out at the soundboard and when it came time for the explosions I just hit those keys to simulate the bombs and explosions [*laughs*]. But they were just sound effects [*laughs*].

GENE SIMMONS: In terms of our stage show, we reacted intrinsically to what we thought was cool. We went back to all the stuff we react to, Fourth of July fireworks shows and things exploding. We wanted to go where no band had gone before. We realized you were paying as much for a concert ticket, which only lasted an hour or two, as you would for a record album, which you could play over and over again for years. A concert was over with the snap of a finger. So what are the memories you take from it? We thought visuals should be a big element and we were constantly brainstorming about what we could do in the show. We tried to pick themes that made sense lyrically and thematically, like the fire-spitting in "Firehouse." We came up with visual bits and tried to figure out what songs made sense to use them in. We didn't want people dancing at our shows. There's nothing to dance to at a KISS concert. Just shut the fuck up and look at the stage. We're literally risking our lives up there: the least you can do is watch what we do.

RICK MUNROE: Their stage show was choreographed and well planned out. Gene made it very clear to me that they wanted each song to be a series of vignettes: Act One, Act Two, and Act Three, just like a theater show.

MIKE McGURL: There were all sorts of lighting and effects cues that had to be hit at particular points in songs, from the dry ice to the flash pots to the flames.

PAUL STANLEY: From one night to the next, the flash pots, which are the explosives in front of the stage, could virtually blow a hole in the stage and the next night could sound like a pop gun.

MARK "ZERO" STINNER: Everything had to be choreographed and precise because when that wall of flames went off they would've caught fire if they were standing in the wrong place.

PETER "MOOSE" ORECKINTO: Even something as innocuous as the confetti was carefully thought out. Towards the end of KISS's set we used two confetti cannons to fire out a shit-storm of confetti onto the band and the crowd as a celebratory effect. We bought optically safe confetti, which meant the confetti didn't have sharp edges. This would protect fans from getting their corneas scratched from the confetti and thus the band from getting sued.

PAUL CHAVARRIA: There are so many people in music that went to universities and schools to learn about how to stage a show. With us, we basically learned everything at one of the greatest universities in the world. It was called KISS U. You went there and you learned everything about rock theater. You could learn about sound, lighting, staging, logistics.

RICHARD ROBINSON (WRITER, ROCK SCENE): Gene knew me because we had friends in common. I'd produced the Flamin' Groovies' *Teenage Head* album on Buddah Records and knew Neil Bogart. Back in the seventies Gene came to see me rehearse my magic and illusion show in my loft and gave me a great piece of advice. He said, "You should set the stage on fire first to get the audience's attention" [*laughs*]. That pretty much sums up KISS's approach to their entire career. And I must say it's an excellent way to get attention and worked out very well for them.

Life on the road with a traveling rock-and-roll band is anything but predictable. There's always an unexpected obstacle to derail the day's plans. And at one KISS gig in Hammond, Indiana, in October 1974, the shit literally hit the fan(s).

PETER "MOOSE" ORECKINTO: We were doing a gig at the Parthenon Theater. The show's going well and we came up to the last song of the set, which was "Black Diamond." The song climaxed with multiple loud flash pots. Little did we know that a family of pigeons was living up in the rafters. When the concussions went off it was so powerful that dust, bird shit, and feathers rained down on the unsuspecting audience. Everybody was wondering what this new special effect was. I laughed my ass off. It literally scared the shit out of the pigeons [*laughs*].

JOYCE BOGART-TRABULUS: The group was playing the Midwest, opening for Rory Gallagher, an Irish blues guitarist they should not have been playing with, but we could not get them on other tours. The club was enormous. It must have held three thousand kids, and Neil had invited every DJ, promotion man, and distributor in the Midwest. The group was introduced as, "From New York . . . KISS!" The crowd booed (they don't like New York there) and started throwing things at them. But by the second song the joint was rocking and the crowd was going nuts. They blew everybody away. They loved this group and all the Casablanca people were beaming at the reaction. They ended the set and the crowd thundered their need for an encore. The place is rocking off its foundation and the band's not coming out. A few minutes went by and nothing happened. Neil and I were getting nervous. A few more minutes and the crowd is on the verge of taking the place apart. I'm at the back of the club with Neil and he looks at me and screams over the din, "Where the hell is your group?" I fight my way through the beer-swilling rowdy crowd to the backstage area and find the back doors open to the cold outside and Peter on the ground with the road manager trying to revive him.

J.R. SMALLING: The ceiling was so low that the drum riser couldn't elevate to its full height. The ventilation was terrible and the flash pots went off at the end so the place is thick with smoke. The drum riser goes up and Peter's head is literally in this blue haze of chemical smoke.

JOYCE BOGART-TRABULUS: When the drum riser rose during "Black Diamond," all the smoke from the flash pots went to the top of the room, causing Peter to pass out and fall in a dead faint backwards ten feet down only to end up in the arms of a very alert and very strong road manager.

J.R. SMALLING: I saw it coming and caught him just in time.

JOYCE BOGART-TRABULUS: Eventually they went out and played an encore. That's commitment [*laughs*].

RANDY GIRARD (DRUMMER, JOE): Joe opened for KISS on December 22, 1974, in London, Ontario. We had just finished setting up our equipment onstage when two of KISS's roadies who were venue scouts walked in and told us, "Put your PA system back in your truck; you're gonna use our PA system." During the sound check I remember sitting behind my drum kit and hitting my bass drum. It sounded like thunder coming out of the PA system. After our set, our bass player, Brian Danter, said, "C'mon, Randy, let's go down and meet the guys in the group." I was already a fan of KISS and had a copy of their first album. We went into the dressing room and I thought they'd say hello and then kick us out. But Gene Simmons made us feel so at home. He was such a humble guy, as were the rest of the band. I'll never forget Peter Criss telling me, "You did a great job on the drums," which he didn't have to say, so that meant a lot to me. A friend of ours followed us in the dressing room and captured some of that meeting on Super 8 film. In the footage we're shaking hands with the band and getting autographs. I still have the photo they signed for me. Gene was also showing us his new bass guitar that he'd just received and was telling us how he was looking forward to using it that night. We were a small-town group that got to see how a professional group like KISS operated. The one memory I will always keep from that special meeting with KISS is how they treated us . . . like we were good friends.

Evansville Coliseum, Evansville, Indiana, December 31, 1974. The Cleveland-based power pop outfit Raspberries, best known for the hits "Go All the Way," "I Wanna Be with You," "Let's Pretend," and "Tonight," were the opening act.

ERIC CARMEN (LEAD VOCALIST/GUITARIST, RASPBERRIES): Raspberries opened for KISS on December 31, 1974, in Evansville, Illinois. Boy, was that a strange bill. It was originally supposed to be KISS headlining with Iggy Pop opening. The tickets had been sold for weeks with that bill. A week before the show, the mayor of Evansville said he didn't want Iggy Pop playing there because he was afraid he'd cut himself with glass and dive off the stage into the crowd and they'd be responsible. Suddenly Iggy was off the bill and somehow we were offered the slot and our management took the gig.

So we're sitting in the dressing room and the door opened at some point and in walked all four guys in KISS. They looked seven feet tall and were head to toe in the full KISS regalia: makeup, platform boots, black leather, and chains [*laughs*]. It was the most amazing thing I'd ever seen. I was always a fan of concept in rock and roll. And I'd never seen anything like this. This was very impressive.

The crowd was expecting to see Iggy Pop and we walked out there and they were booing and throwing things at us. Our drummer, Michael McBride, got hit in the head with a penny. Our guitar player, Wally Bryson, gave the audience a piece of his mind and went up to the microphone and said, "Fuck you!" But eventually we got them to calm down and made it through without getting killed [*laughs*] and maybe even won a few people over.

I remember going out to the side of the stage to watch KISS perform. They were eight times louder than anybody I'd ever heard. It was just ear-shattering. I remember one of their roadies poured kerosene and Scope mouthwash into a large Dixie cup. I looked at that and wondered, "What the heck could that be for? Kerosene and Scope? Within a couple of minutes, Gene came over to the side of the stage, took a big slug from this Dixie cup, grabbed a two-and-a-half-foot torch, and breathed fire. I was like, "Oh my God, these guys are unbelievable!" I'm for giving it your all in rock and roll [*laughs*] but I was thinking to myself, "If this is what you've got to do to make it in rock and roll, then I quit" [*laughs*]. I didn't fault KISS for what they were doing. I was actually kind of jealous that four guys had that kind of commitment to what they were doing that they were willing to do just about anything. I watched their entire show and they were really, really good at what they did. And there was good music to back up the theatrics. Paul was a great frontman and Gene was absolutely frightening up there.

After the show was over, I remember talking to Gene and Paul in the hallway. They were both very friendly. Paul said, "We used to play songs like yours with three-part Beatle harmonies, and then this happened" [*laughs*]. I was happy to learn afterwards that Paul had come to see the Raspberries at Carnegie Hall in 1973 and very flattered when he showed up backstage to see us in LA for our reunion show in 2005.

JIM FOX (DRUMMER, JAMES GANG): James Gang played a few shows with KISS in '74 and '75. I knew nothing about KISS in advance and remember watching their show for the first time and I was completely stunned. Rex Reed, a famous New York music and movie critic, once wrote a review of an album that I liked very much and said, "It was like finding a stunned bat in your living room." And that's exactly how I felt when I first saw KISS [*laughs*]. I remember all of us watching KISS and having a collective feeling of "huh?" [*laughs*].

James Gang were probably one of the most anti-theatrical bands ever. I don't think we ever had a backdrop, let alone a show. It wasn't part of what we thought or what we did. We just went out there and played the best we could. So with KISS we just could not understand what we were seeing. James Gang did a sixty-date tour with Alice Cooper, so we weren't strangers to theatrical rock, but KISS took it a step further. It was like nothing we'd ever experienced before. It took a while to get a handle on what they were doing—we played a few more shows with them—and then it clicked in and I enjoyed it. Above everything, we thought KISS was a home run. We all saw the potential of this combination of music and visual entertainment.

MARTIN TURNER (LEAD VOCALIST/BASSIST, WISHBONE ASH): We were doing a gig with KISS in San Diego [January 19, 1975] and we were right at the end of an American tour. It had been a six-week schlep and everyone was fed up and wanting to go home. All of our gear was falling apart at the seams. We had busted amplifiers with blown speakers. We were just limping through the end of the tour. We'd heard of KISS. There was a big buzz about them and they were supporting us. I can say very, very few bands upstaged Wishbone Ash. We always played good shows. But on that particular occasion they were absolutely brilliant—they were flying. They came on with all the war paint and stacked heels and they did a great set. They were very dynamic and highly theatrical. It reminded me of Arthur Brown, David Bowie, Mott the Hoople, and Alice Cooper as well. You could tell KISS was destined to be very successful. Needless to say, we were not happy at all to have to follow them that night [*laughs*].

ANDY POWELL (GUITARIST/VOCALIST, WISHBONE ASH): We had everybody opening for us: Aerosmith, Bruce Springsteen, ZZ Top, Bob Seger, and KISS. They had a plan and knew what they were doing. It was a concerted attack. Our crowd didn't quite know what to make of them. You could tell a new kind of theatrics was coming into rock and roll. Our show compared to theirs was fairly orthodox. It was all about the guitars, and they delivered something much more than guitars. It was about theater, it was about rock-and-roll circus. KISS went over very well but they couldn't fail to make an impact because what they were doing was so different. The biggest band we'd opened for was the Who and they were about as close as you got to spectacle. KISS took it onto another level. It was the beginning of arena rock.

ALAN GRATZER (DRUMMER, REO SPEEDWAGON): We were playing some sort of mini-festival with KISS and Ace Frehley came out of his dressing room with a drink in his hand—this was before they played. He had no makeup on and it struck me how many pockmarks were on his face, which might be why they wore so much makeup [*laughs*]. He was walking sideways and obviously had quite a bit to drink and I was like, "Wow, he's doing this *before* going onstage?" [*laughs*]. We tried to save the drinking for after the show [*laughs*] but here he was staggering and barely made it down the steps. But KISS was still able to pull off the show that night. Loudness covers up a lot. It's amazing what a little volume can do, which we'd rely on once in a while ourselves.

We were opening for them at some indoor arena and I remember standing below Gene Simmons on the side of the stage but looking straight up. It looked like great theater. Here was a guy with blood pouring out of the side of his mouth singing, and his tongue was lurching in and out. It was very impressive. They were a great act that was fun to watch. They were so unique and different. I stood there just mesmerized watching him.

NEAL DOUGHTY (KEYBOARDIST, REO SPEEDWAGON): I do remember one thing about KISS: at the time we played with them, I thought they were ridiculous and could not believe people liked them so much. It took years before I realized what a genius idea they had.

Today KISS is championed by many for their astute business acumen, but as the band readily admits, their reputation as shrewd marketing geniuses is overstated.

RIK FOX: I went to see KISS play at the Sunshine In, a little dive in Asbury Park, New Jersey [June 17, 1974]. There was a photo of KISS that appeared in *Circus* magazine where they're standing around a bus sign. I painted that, detail for detail, on the back of my denim jacket surrounded by flames along with the KISS logo and wore it for the first time to that show. When I walked through the crowd I got stopped by fans every few feet that were impressed by it. After the show, Gene grabbed me by my shoulders and shoved me into Bill Aucoin's face and goes, "Look at this guy's jacket. Do you see the potential of what this can be?" He thought it would be a great way to market the band. Bill said, "Maybe you should come up and visit us at our office." I went up to their office and they were tapping me for ideas because we were the kids supporting the group so my opinion was valuable to them.

21

ROCK BOTTOM

Keeping an elaborate and exceedingly expensive show like KISS out on the road was a less-than-profitable proposition for the band, its label, and its management.

PETER "MOOSE" ORECKINTO: It got so bad that we had to use our own money to fill up the fuel tank. Because we had to get from each gig in lightning speed, I remember getting two speeding tickets from the state of Tennessee and the band didn't have the money to pay for them. The state police called my parents in New York and they had to cough up the money. [The band] didn't have the money to pay for storage either, so I had to store all of the band's equipment in my parent's garage in the Marble Hill section of Manhattan. Everything from the KISS sign to Marshall stacks to Gene's SVT bass cabinets to the LVM to the special effects case was in my parents' garage [*laughs*]. That's how strapped for cash they were.

MICK CAMPISE: Sometime in 1974, KISS was in San Francisco playing the Winterland. That tour was financed by Bill Aucoin's American Express card because the label had no money. At that time, the road crew was getting paid $100 a week and the band was getting paid $50 a week. But because of all the money problems we hadn't been paid for a while. The road crew was upset and threatening to quit if they didn't get paid. They were also holding the gear as ransom. Moose said to me, "You tell those motherfuckers by the time they get to Tulsa if they haven't paid us we're gonna throw the equipment off a cliff." Gene, Ace, and J.R. Smalling flew to LA for business so that left, me, Peter, and Paul stranded at the hotel in San Francisco unable to leave because Bill's credit card was overmaxed.

RICK MUNROE: We were staying at an upscale hotel called the Miyako Hotel. Mike McGurl came in and said, "Hey, I didn't get any money from anybody so we're stuck in San Francisco until we get some money in." So they moved us from the Miyako to a cheaper place.

PAUL STANLEY: They put us up in this dive which was ironically called the Vagabond Inn [*laughs*].

MIKE McGURL: It was a real dump. It reminded me of a run-down homeless shelter.

MICK CAMPISE: They wouldn't let us leave until the bill was paid. Between me, Peter, and Paul we had less than $2 to our names. I had the majority of the money and chose to feed the three of us instead of just me. We made a pact. I told them, "I believe in you guys and I'm gonna stick with you. If the other road crew members want to quit, that's up to them." Peter and Paul said, "Stick with us, Mick, we'll take care of you." So anyhow we walked across the street to this little convenience store and bought a loaf of bread and peanut butter and lived off of that for three days until Bill's credit card cleared. That's how bad it got financially on the road with KISS in the early days. And if you're wondering, eventually the road crew got paid and the gear was saved.

PAUL STANLEY: Sure there were tough times, but it was still fun and magical. We weren't gonna die. It wasn't killing us. We had no fear for our lives. To me it was the kind of stuff you look back on. If you have real faith and belief in your ability to succeed you just look at that as part of your book full of memories.

Money—or rather, the lack thereof—continued to be a major concern in KISS's early days, and the band was willing to do almost anything to make a buck.

PAUL STANLEY: Everybody was scrounging to try and find a way to supplement the meager money that we were making with anything that could be thrown our way. Early in our career, KISS recorded a commercial for a music tape and record store chain in Ohio called Mr. T's. It was an opportunity to make some quick cash and do a commercial for a radio campaign. It was a song called "Mr. T." [*Reciting the song's lyrics*] "Mr. T, Mr. T, he gave me music. Mr. T, Mr. T, he gave me love. . . ." I can't remember the rest of it [*laughs*]. The problem was they were looking for a typical-sounding rock band [*laughs*] and they didn't think we fit the bill, so we didn't get the gig.

GENE SIMMONS: Later during the mid-seventies, Paul and I sang on an AMC truck commercial.

PAUL STANLEY: [*Reciting lyrics*] "Buyer protection and economy, the hot cars from AMC."

GENE SIMMONS: Howard Marks had a radio jingle company and he had no relationship with KISS in those days except he shared office space with our manager, Bill Aucoin.

PAUL STANLEY: Unlike the Mr. T commercial, the AMC truck ad was accepted and aired on the radio. I would hear it on the radio. I'd be driving in my car sometimes and go, "Why is my ear suddenly tuned to the radio?" And I'd go, "Oh my God, that's me" [*laughs*]. It sounded like the Marines singing—very, very masculine, boisterous, jubilant, and sure about these hot cars on AMC. That was a buyout. We did it, got a couple of bucks, and it was over.

GENE SIMMONS: We loved the process. We loved the recording studio. Not as much as playing live, but it was a lot of fun. It was larger than life to do commercials. It was like you're not only in a band but you're wanted by AMC trucks. We want you. We want your voices. It was a validation. We didn't think about what was cool and what wasn't cool.

KISS was determined to succeed and, in 1974, took to the road with a vengeance. As an opening act in a medium-size hall or as headliners in clubs and small theaters, the band's arresting image, stage show, and primal powered musical muscle helped them win over audiences across America. But these victories paled next to the grim reality of their finances. Despite a steady slate of gigs, their records weren't selling, and the expense of their lavish theatrical stage presentation was bankrupting them. Then there was some good news: Atlanta contracted KISS fever. The band performed ten concerts at Alex Cooley's Electric Ballroom—the most shows they had ever played in one year at a single venue.

ALEX COOLEY: KISS played at Alex Cooley's Electric Ballroom many times in 1974. The Electric Ballroom was an old big-band ballroom that was attached to a fading hotel called the Georgian Terrace. It's located directly across the street from the Fox Theater, the venue where Lynyrd Skynyrd recorded their live album *One More from the Road*. The Electric Ballroom held about two thousand people and we put on shows by everyone from Bruce Springsteen to Billy Joel to KISS. KISS was already starting to do good business or I wouldn't have kept bringing them back. They were almost like our house band in '74 [*laughs*]. Atlanta audiences took to KISS very early and they became one of Atlanta's favorite bands. They caused extreme excitement during their shows here. People ate it up and everybody was on their feet through the whole set. KISS were one of the hottest bands in Atlanta at the time.

KISS's exhausting tour schedule would have felled lesser bands. The group's first casualty of the unrelenting parade of one-nighters was Paul.

PAUL STANLEY: We were flying to Atlanta, which was a great place to play, but I wasn't feeling great on the plane. By the time we got to the hotel I was literally laying in the hallway I was just so deathly ill. The first show got cancelled but then I played the second show.

MICK CAMPISE: The band plays their full set and did three encores and they still wouldn't let us off the stage. Then they decided to start the set over and play "Deuce" again and that's when Paul collapsed. We ran and dragged him off the stage.

ALEX COOLEY: I remember being in my office and getting a call from KISS's road manager who said, "Paul's very ill, you need to get down here right away." So I drove down to their hotel, which was not a very good hotel—it was located directly across from the Greyhound bus station—and I went up to his room. He was deathly pale and obviously very, very sick. I took him to my private doctor who took care of him.

PAUL STANLEY: I couldn't swallow and my throat had these huge white patches on it. Alex Cooley came in with a doctor and he shot me up with Ritalin. Ritalin can raise the dead in large doses and I got up and said, "I'm not doing the show. Ten minutes ago I was deathly ill and now I'm walking around, this just doesn't seem right." When you're so sick that the doctors don't know what's wrong with you it's kind of scary. I flew back to New York and was literally bedridden. Every few days I'd get driven to a doctor who would take blood to make sure all my organs were working. He said it was viral and they had no idea what it was. I'd get out of bed to walk to the bathroom and the rest of the time I was sleeping and this went on for weeks. That was the sickest I'd ever been. And then it all just cleared up.

BILL AUCOIN: Paul always had a problem with weight; he was always a little chubby. He got sick for days in Atlanta and lost all this weight. I'll never forget speaking to him on the phone and he said, "Boy, do I look good." So he got well and thought he looked so terrific that there was no way he'd be chubby again. He finally saw in himself what he wanted to be.

Handling the pyrotechnics in KISS's huge theatrical show was dangerous for the road crew. Before the band's December 30, 1974, show at the National Guard Armory in Springfield, Illinois, Peter "Moose" Oreckinto was the victim of a pyrotechnic effect gone awry.

MIKE McGURL: A company [Kim-Lon] in New York that was doing our special effects came up with this idea for a drumstick that shot flames. They were hollow metal tubes that had a battery in them and a heating coil.

PETER "MOOSE" ORECKINTO: The back piece had a nipple on the very end with a hole, and in that hole was an Estes engine igniter. It's basically a little baby spark plug that hobbyists use for gas-powered planes. On top of this pipe there was a battery holder which held two double-A batteries. At the very top of the battery holder there was a push-button switch.

Peter "Moose" Oreckinto, KISS roadie, theatrical pyrotechnics and sound mixer 1973–1976
Courtesy of Peter Oreckinto.

MIKE McGURL: Moose was in charge of loading them up and stuffing flash paper down the tubes and setting them [beside] the drums. This paper didn't burn if you set a match to it, but if you held it in your hand and crushed it and opened your hand real fast it would burst into flames. It was a magician's trick.

PETER "MOOSE" ORECKINTO: At the end of "Black Diamond" Peter would drop his drumsticks and pick up these other drumsticks, aim them out over the audience, push the button, and it would shoot out a blue ball of flame twenty, twenty-five feet over the crowd. Peter always aimed high so it didn't hit the audience. The flame would dissipate to nothing so it was a neat little effect.

MIKE QUATRO: I'm playing our set and all of a sudden I heard this big loud bang and went, "What the fuck was that?" I think the audience thought it was part of our act but it wasn't. After our set I found out about the tragic accident that happened to one of their roadies.

PETER "MOOSE" ORECKINTO: I was loading them up backstage and I'm preparing the sticks. I put in one battery and heard a click. I start putting in the next battery and it clicked and *kaboom*! It blew up in my hand.

MIKE McGURL: Moose screamed and started running towards us. He said, "It exploded, I'm bleeding, I'm bleeding!"

PETER "MOOSE" ORECKINTO: That thing shouldn't have exploded but it did. It wasn't my fault. It wasn't double-loaded and I didn't use any powder. But when you play with fire you're eventually going to get burned. It happens to everybody.

PAUL STANLEY: I remember seeing Moose with all this blood pouring out of his hand and a horrified look on his face.

MIKE McGURL: Sean Delaney grabbed a wet towel and wrapped it around his hand.

PETER "MOOSE" ORECKINTO: In addition to my left hand being severely damaged, I also had a hole in my stomach and a hole underneath my chin.

J.R. SMALLING: I ran backstage and asked, "Has anyone called 911?" and someone said, "Yeah." We couldn't wait any longer because blood was gushing from Moose's hand like a fountain, so we had a runner who worked for the promoter drive Moose to the hospital.

PETER "MOOSE" ORECKINTO: On the way to the hospital the guy driving the car stopped at every red light. Remember, this was New Year's Eve weekend in downtown Springfield, Illinois, and it was dead quiet and nobody was on the road. I was incredulous and started screaming, "What the fuck are you doing? Don't stop at any red light, I'll pay for the fuckin' ticket if we get one, just get me to the hospital!" So we finally get to the hospital and I go crashing through the emergency doors holding my hand. I was in surgery for hours and they thought I was gonna lose my hand so it was touch and go. I had to sign a document in front of two Illinois state troopers that number one, nobody put me up to it, and number two, if they needed to, the doctor was allowed to amputate my hand. I told the doctor, "Whatever you do, don't cut my hand off, just sew it back together." I woke up the next day and I still had the hand.

J.R. SMALLING: The ER doctor that admitted him said that if his nickname was "Slim" instead of "Moose" he probably would have lost his hand.

PETER "MOOSE" ORECKINTO: They kept me on watch because had it become infected they would have had to cut my hand off. I still have pain in my left hand and thumb which reminds me every day of that fucking accident.

PAUL CHAVARRIA: What hurt the most was to see your brother get hurt like he did. That scared the shit out of us. Moose's tragic accident made everybody realize that we weren't invincible. It gave us a harsh reality check. We were messing around with explosives and we could really hurt ourselves. What we're doing here is really dangerous business.

Britain's glam rock scene had exploded in the early seventies in a glittery collision of style, spectacle, and deliciously commercial songs. One of glam rock's most popular acts was Slade, an unruly rock-and-roll gang of cartoonish misfits renowned for their wild theatrics, colorful costumes, and boot-stomping anthems. Between 1971 and 1975, "Slade-mania" reigned in the UK. The band charted fourteen times with hits like their signature fist-pumping anthems "Cum on Feel the Noize" and "Mama Weer All Crazee Now." Their sound, image, and stage presentation were a major influence on KISS, who opened shows for the band on a slate of U.S. dates in 1975.

MICK CAMPISE: Both the road crew and KISS couldn't wait for the shows they did with Slade. They were a huge influence on KISS and everyone was excited to have them share the bill with us. KISS showed them a tremendous amount of respect. The road crew and Peter and Ace tried to drink with Slade at the Holiday Inn, but those British Welsh guys drank us under the table—except for Ace, who held his own quite well [*laughs*]. There are only three bands I can recall that both KISS and the road crew watched from the side of the stage, and that was Slade, Montrose, and the Raspberries.

PAUL STANLEY: Slade was awesome. In many ways Slade was the English counterpart to us. Slade wrote these great anthems. Live, they were simple, but boy did they put their boot up your ass. Noddy [Holder] is a great singer. The whole band looked like some sort of cartoon come to life. They were like a steamroller. It was similar to where we were coming from. They had great songs, and live they were just great.

GENE SIMMONS: My girlfriend at the time had Slade records [*Slade Alive!* and *Slayed?*] in her basement and I put them on and I was floored. The stuff just floored me with its simplicity and guitars. They were a big influence on me, but not until I saw them.

NODDY HOLDER (LEAD VOCALIST/GUITARIST, SLADE): I knew KISS was very influenced by Slade. It was a great compliment for a band like KISS to mention us as an influence. They took everything that was good about Slade and took it to the farthest extreme. Like Slade, KISS did anthem songs but in an American way.

JIM LEA (BASSIST, SLADE): They called one of their albums *Alive!* I thought, "Bloody hell, they're nicking our album title" [*laughs*] because a few years earlier we'd released an album called *Slade Alive!* But a guy who used to look after us in America said, "Don't worry about it, those guys are crazy about you, it's an homage, take it as a compliment" [*laughs*]. Also, with "Rock and Roll All Nite" Gene said they wanted to write a song like Slade's "Mama Weer All Crazee Now."

GENE SIMMONS: The philosophy of their song "Mama Weer All Crazee Now" influenced the writing of "Rock and Roll All Nite"; the part, "You drive us wild, we'll drive you crazy" is the same.

PAUL STANLEY: My mirror Iceman guitar was actually not a unique or original idea. Noddy had a top hat with these huge circle mirrors on it. So when they hit Noddy's top hat these beams of light came out of his head. And it was such a cool idea that that's where the idea for the mirrored guitar came from.

JIM LEA: I'd never heard of KISS before. We first played with them in Chattanooga, Tennessee [September 10, 1975]. So we went on and played and came off. I was standing at the side of the stage watching them and ran back into the dressing room and told the band, "Has anybody been out to see this lot?" [*laughs*]. Don [Powell, Slade's drummer] came out and stood next to me. I thought KISS was half funny and half scary, not the whole band, just Gene. I didn't know what to make of KISS at all. There was a little band in England called Light Fantastic who had a bass player that dressed up like Dracula, and he'd jump off the balcony and knock himself out [*laughs*]. We just thought Gene was like that guy. They'd finished the main part of their show and Gene walked toward us. He must have been ten feet tall with those massive boots, dog collar with the spikes, and the hair sticking up on top in that samurai style, plus he's got all this blood spilling down his face. Don was saying [*in a frightened voice*], "Bloody hell, he's coming at us, what are we gonna do? Oh my God, should we go?" [*laughs*]. And I said [*in a frightened voice*], "No, no, we don't want to seem like we're frightened of him, just bloody well stand there" [*laughs*]. He came and stood next to us and looked down at me and said, "Hey, how's Roy Wood [leader of popular sixties British band the Move]?" [*laughs*].

The next night we were playing in Knoxville. I went backstage and there's a guy with long frizzy hair, T-shirt, and jeans sitting on a flight case. I walked past him and he said, "Hey, Jim Lea!" I was pretty shy and didn't like being singled out. He starts talking to me about our album *Slade in Flame* and said, "The drummer in our band is crazy about your album. His wife plays 'How Does It Feel' all the time, and I think that's a great song, too." I said, "Are you playing tonight?" And he said, "Yeah." And I said, "What's your band?" And he said, "KISS." And I said, "What do you do?" And he said, "I'm the bass player" [*laughs*]. I wouldn't have recognized him for all the tea in China [*laughs*]. Gene said, "We modeled ourselves on Slade because you were four different personalities and that's what we wanted to be." He told me it was an honor to have us on the bill. They did a very American comic book version of it. Gene said that Slade were the first band that showed an audience how to riot. KISS grasped what was going on so they said, "Okay, we'll have their idea and we'll just Americanize it." And that's what they did. Where we might have had a confetti machine, they just made everything James Bond. To this day I hold great affection for the band. It's almost like if the guitarist left I could put the makeup on and just join the band and nobody would know the difference [*laughs*]. Back in the seventies KISS took a bad rap as being a joke as musicians but I thought they were good players and a really good rock band. Paul was really good as a frontman. He was like a Marc Bolan [frontman for T. Rex], and I really liked Ace's guitar playing as well.

DAVE HILL (GUITARIST, SLADE): In the mid-seventies we toured the States with everyone from ZZ Top, Aerosmith, and KISS. We had a lot of fun with KISS on the road. Slade may have been a big influence on KISS, but they really made it their own. KISS are very much like Slade in being professional and very committed to what they do without compromise. It wasn't tough opening for KISS. I think we went over well. We were a good support band for them because we were an exciting band. We're always been pretty down-to-earth working-class guys with good families that worked hard to get somewhere. And KISS is the same in that regard. Their show was very powerful and theatrical. If you look at them they're like blown-up versions of what went before. If they were gonna wear platform boots they were gonna have the biggest. They saw an idea and made it bigger than it was before. The salesmanship of not only just having the right product but the right way to sell it as well is what Slade had got and KISS as well.

DON POWELL (DRUMMER, SLADE): We had great times touring with KISS. I was totally blown away watching them perform; the whole stage set was fantastic. We were touring with them when *Alive!* was released. They showed us great respect and it was a great bill. Gene Simmons said to us, "You're the best warm-up band we've ever had" because we got the crowd up and running before they came on and tore the place apart.

Once we were playing with KISS and something happened with their monitor or PA system and they had to use ours. But they were used to a much bigger setup than what we had. During the show, Gene Simmons kept running across the stage to our monitor guy named Johnny Jones, screaming at him, "Turn the fucking monitors up!" Here's Gene with all the blood dripping down his face and our monitor guy having this huge argument. I was standing on the side of the stage watching it and it was such a funny sight. Our monitor engineer was a third the size of Gene Simmons and here he was pointing and shouting at him telling him to shut up [*laughs*]. There was nothing Johnny could do; our system was much more limited than what KISS was used to.

DAVE HILL: We'd hang out with the band after shows. I remember speaking to Gene Simmons and I'm very small and when I'm looking up at Gene it's like looking at the Empire State Building. He told me about when he and Paul came to see Slade play at the Academy of Music in New York. I was wearing these huge platform boots and I was strutting down the walkway and fell backwards with my guitar [*laughs*]. I was lying on the floor and couldn't properly get up because I was wearing the platforms so I stuck my feet in the air acting like it was part of a trick. Gene told me how much he loved it. I think he thought it was part of the act [*laughs*].

RONNIE MONTROSE (LEAD GUITARIST, MONTROSE): I'd seen and heard things about KISS before playing shows with them. There'd been a few reviews saying the best things that are happening in the early seventies are Montrose, Aerosmith, and KISS. The first time we played together was in Salem, Virginia [June 20, 1975]. I remember one of their roadies came back and said, "Aw, c'mon man, you've gotta go back and meet the band." So I walked into the dressing room and there's Gene putting on his makeup. Paul was very shy around me, trying to explain and rationalize KISS's success. He said, "A year ago we were playing clubs and now it's come to this." They had a unique idea to put makeup on and do a big show rather than do straight-up hardcore rock like Montrose and Aerosmith. But his justification was that they were headlining big arenas and coliseums. But he was very, very shy about it. I said, "No, you're doing good, it's cool."

I'd never seen them play so I stayed and watched their show. It hit me so strong. There were some theatrical rock shows like Alice Cooper and the Crazy World of Arthur Brown, but nothing like KISS. It was like Mardi Gras meets Ringling Brothers meets comic book heroes. It was a powerful, powerful show. Montrose ended up doing quite a few shows with them. Years later, Eric Singer [current drummr of KISS] invited me to see KISS in Concord [California]. He said, "You've got to go out there and get in your seat before the show." So I get to my seat and right before they went on they played "Bad Motor Scooter" by Montrose. And that wasn't done just because I was there. Eric told me, "They play that every night." I was really honored. That's amazing to me and a real nice tribute.

JOHN O'DANIEL (LEAD VOCALIST, POINT BLANK): At this point in time KISS was very secretive about their identities and no one saw them without their makeup. After one of the shows we played with KISS, me and some of the other members of the band were sitting in a restaurant ordering breakfast. A gentleman to the right of us in a suit said, "You guys sounded really good last night, I enjoyed your show." We said thanks and at the same time we were trying to figure out what a guy in a three-piece suit was doing at a KISS/Point Blank show. That guy turned out to be Gene Simmons. He was dressed in a business suit and looked like he was selling insurance [*laughs*]. He invited us over and we talked for about fifteen to twenty minutes. Point Blank was the direct opposite of KISS. We're from Texas and we do things a little different here. We wore blue jeans, boots, and hats and had no production at all when we performed onstage. Gene said, "Our bands are totally opposite. People pay to see KISS and they pay to hear Point Blank." I think that was his way of saying to us, "You may be an opening act but we know you're here."

Their crowd gave us a bit of a go. You walk onstage and the first three rows are filled with people looking back at you all painted up. The people in those rows were flipping us the bird and yelling profanities. As we walked offstage, the bass player and I both turned around and flipped off the crowd and told them to screw themselves. I went backstage and destroyed the bathroom. I was irate! A day or two later, one of the KISS roadies came into our dressing room and said, "Hey man, that happens to anybody who plays with us. It doesn't matter who opens for us, our fans are our fans and they're gonna do that." What was funny is they had eighteen semi trucks and we had a van [*laughs*]. Nine of us and all our gear packed into this van, following them around the country.

RUSTY BURNS (LEAD GUITARIST, POINT BLANK): After one of the shows we played with KISS somewhere in California we were having a big party in my room, which was located across the hall from Gene's room. We're in the room drinking and all of a sudden we hear all this commotion. I opened the door and looked out and saw thirty-five or forty girls all lined up down the hallway. A couple of them got into a fight over who was gonna be with Gene that night [*laughs*]. So we were out there trying to calm these girls down. Then the door opens and the next girl who was standing in line goes into Gene's room and the one who was already in there went flying out of the room. He had a pretty good revolving door of the most beautiful women I've ever seen in my life. After a while he came out into the hallway and said, "Okay girls, I'm kind of done, but here, let me introduce you to my friends in Point Blank" [*laughs*]. And he started sending girls over to our room [*laughs*]. We started bowing to the guy because it was a really wonderful gesture for a guy of his stature to be giving us his girls when in actuality he was getting the gum out of his hair, if you know what I mean [*laughs*].

JOYCE BOGART-TRABULUS: Neil [Bogart] and Larry Harris and I flew into St. Louis for a festival concert that KSHE, a radio station, was sponsoring. [The band] were playing to an enormous crowd of over forty thousand people. KISS had never played during the day outside in the sun and bright lights—they'd never played an outdoor concert before. As the day got hotter the makeup melted and the wind and sun obliterated the special fire effects and even made them dangerous to the band and the rest of us on the stage. But the worst thing was the way the stage was constructed. It seemed to be just boards over risers that were not tied down well, and every time the group jumped—about every sixty seconds—the amps behind them would start to fall down. Neil, Larry Harris, and I spent the whole concert holding up the amps. We couldn't hear for weeks.

PETER CRISS: We were doing this big show at this big hall and Paul said, "Hey, let's have some fun. Let's get out of the car in drag." And we did it. Paul went out with a bodyguard to a J.C. Penney's and he bought all the women's outfits [*laughs*]. He was very good at it, by the way. He picked out matching outfits with hats, wigs, and dresses and bras and nylons and high heels and matching bags, earrings [*laughs*]. It was the whole fucking nine yards. We did it to surprise Bill [Aucoin] and to freak out the press. Here we pulled in and the doors opened and Gene put his long leg out first with a high heel like a chick [*laughs*] and it was great, they were

Rock and roll in the great outdoors, KSHE festival, St. Louis, March 31, 1974
Bill Parsons

blown. I forgot about all that. That was actually very cool. Then we all started coming out shaking our asses and we all had tissue paper padded in our bras. It was a wonderful idea of Paul's.

MARSHALL CRENSHAW (GUITARIST, ASTIGAFA): I was in a Michigan band called Astigafa, which stood for "a splendid time is guaranteed for all." My first experience playing in an arena was opening for KISS in the mid-seventies [June 18, 1975]. We were into the Grateful Dead's psychedelic stuff when they had two drummers and we were also into the Allman Brothers. Astigafa did a lot of jamming, stretching out the songs, did ambitious arrangements with lots of harmonies. We had a manager, and I swear to God, his name was Paul Stanley. He was from Oak Park, Michigan. He kept us busy as a bar band playing in Ohio and Michigan. At some point Paul wanted to get into concert promotion. The first show he handled was this KISS concert.

PAUL STANLEY: The poster for that show said "Paul Stanley Presents" and it had a big picture of me playing a Flying V—and Gene was absolutely livid, and he thought that somehow I had something to do with it.

MARSHALL CRENSHAW: Our manager told us, "Guys, I have this great gig for you as an opening act for KISS." I was the only guy in the band that didn't want to do it because I thought the audience would hate our guts and want to kill us. I really thought we'd be humiliated. But when we played the show there were so few people there inside the arena that we didn't get a bad reaction—or particularly a good one, either. But we came out of it unscathed and nobody threw anything at us, which I feared.

There was a great thing that happened that day that really made an impression on me. We were backstage hanging around and one of the guys from KISS—I later found out it was Paul Stanley—was cruising around the arena on roller skates and playing a Gibson Melody Maker. He came into our dressing room and was completely friendly and sweet to us, talking to us about gear. I just thought, "Man, this is great." All I'd ever heard about were horror stories of opening acts getting shit on by the headliners, but Paul was real gracious and I thought that was very cool.

MORGAN FISHER (KEYBOARDIST, MOTT THE HOOPLE): During Mott's winter 1975 U.S. tour we shared the bill with KISS on several occasions. The band were very professional and committed to playing a great show every night, but were also fun to be around, so we hung out when we could. I got on particularly well with Gene, and during the few days we had off at Christmas both he and I found ourselves in New York. In fact, he invited me over to his apartment on Christmas Day, and being far from home and having nothing else to do, I went on over. Now everything from those days is remembered through a hazy glow of alcohol so I will tell it as best I can.

I was a little surprised that no one but Gene was there, having expected a party or at least some kind of celebration. He cordially waved me into his compact apartment, and I started drinking. About every five minutes he'd pick up the phone and tried to call a girl, so he—and maybe me, too—could have some company. I think he may even have had a little black book. Well, it was Christmas night, so either no one answered or they were busy at some other celebration.

After an hour or two of trying—kudos to him for persistence—he sighed and said, "Let's get outta here" and suggested we head down to a nearby all-night cinema. As we trudged through the freezing snow—at least warmed a little by the alcohol—I asked Gene what was showing. "I dunno," he said, "but it's usually something good."

Well, we were both utterly happy to see that tonight's show was a "Christmas fun night"—a collection of Bugs Bunny and related cartoons plus documentaries about the guys who made those wacky flicks. We had a hilarious time watching one classic cartoon after another, and were also intrigued and delighted to see and learn about the team who made them. Frankly, they seemed like a jazz-loving bunch of potheads—which kind of makes sense if you think about it.

I guess it was probably still dark as we stumbled out of the cinema several hours later, shook hands, said, "See you later," and headed to the welcome warmth of our respective beds. I guess that was the last time I ever saw Gene. It was good to have hung out with him and the band. We admired the hard work they put into their shows and had some laughs seeing the guys fooling around without their makeup on. Gene was still able to put the fear of God into girls by driving them wild with his long, lurid tongue hanging out.

DENNIS DEYOUNG (LEAD VOCALIST/KEYBOARDIST, STYX): It feels like we did a lot of shows with KISS. I thought they were a very tight hard rock band. I'm a melody guy and I always thought their thing was about the live spectacle more than the records. They are, in my opinion, the exception to all rules. I've always believed that the song is king above everything. And with KISS they have defied that. The thing that still remains for KISS is the image and the live show, what they represented as a concept to an audience. That's not to say a song like "Rock and Roll All Nite" is not worthy of consideration, but it's secondary to their personas.

I watched KISS play a couple of times and thought, "Holy shit." We had played shows with Alice Cooper where Alice was theatrical in a Halloween-come-to-life way; KISS was theatrical in a more adolescent, comic book manner. KISS never feared us. And believe me, we played with a lot of bands as a support act who feared us because we deserved to be headliners and they knew it. But KISS never cared because they were so confident in their connection with their audience. We could go out and blow the house down and they knew they'd come on afterwards and blow the whole house *up*.

22

DIRTY BUSINESS AND DIVORCE WITH A BUNNY

Those in the concert business are no strangers to greed and corruption; they witness everything from scams to skimming. In the concert industry there are predators of all shapes and sizes waiting to pounce on unsuspecting prey. Despite modest record sales, KISS slowly began to gain a foothold on the concert circuit; by the end of 1974 they'd moved from opening act to headliner, performing in small theaters and medium-size venues. Their heightened profile on the touring circuit led to encounters with promoters who liked to help themselves to an extra slice of the profits.

MIKE McGURL: There was a real sleazeball promoter we worked with down South. By 1975, KISS was a headliner and receiving a 60/40 split of the concert sales, 60 percent going to KISS, 40 percent to the promoter. You had to have a bonded ticket agent print the tickets. You'd get a manifest from the ticket agent saying he printed this many tickets starting from this number and ending at this number.

This was done to prevent the promoter from ripping bands off and printing tickets themselves.

What this promoter did was after they ran out of the printed tickets he'd start selling tickets off a roll of tickets like the ones that said "Admit One" which you'd get at a movie theater. He'd sell three or four hundred extra tickets that way and not report it. One of the crew came to me and said, "I was out at one of the gates and I saw a couple people handing the ticket-taker something that looked like a movie ticket." I went outside and stood by one of the ticket-takers and sure enough I saw a couple of people coming in with those tickets. I got the road crew together and stationed them at the different ticket entrances and had them count how many people came in with those type of tickets. I confronted [the promoter] so he couldn't do it anymore. I caught him red-handed, and he said, "I was just trying to make some money here, you can't blame me for that." And I said, "Yeah, I can" [*laughs*]. From that point on every date KISS did for him I put someone in the road crew in the ticket office until showtime to ensure he wasn't skimming off the top.

The brass at Casablanca were upset by the modest sales of KISS's debut album, blaming them on Warner Brothers' half-hearted promotional efforts. Ultimately, Neil Bogart chose to sever ties with the label and establish Casablanca Records as an independent entity.

BOB MERLIS: Casablanca was our distributed label and I felt we treated the label the same as our Warner and Reprise labels. Maybe on a higher level they weren't as much a priority to the company. But there was no conspiracy within Warner Brothers to derail KISS—from a business point of view it would be stupid to be at war with yourself. However, I think there was some skepticism at Warner Brothers about Casablanca—maybe not at the top where the deal was made, but many people in the field were unsure about it because the label was antithetical to the Warner Brothers approach. It was big,

big hype, very promotion-oriented, get it on the radio right away. The fact that without a hit album the "Kissin' Time" promotion ["The Great KISS-Off"] took place and stations all over the country participated speaks volumes. Even without significant airplay for a record they could get a radio promotion. The ex-Buddah people, now working for Casablanca, were masters at manipulating radio. Buddah was a very singles-oriented company with all that bubblegum music, yet Neil aligned himself with Warner Brothers, a company that was perceived not to even care about singles. It was the home of the important album.

JOE SMITH: There was a big difference in philosophies between the two labels. Warner Brothers had prestigious artists like Van Dyke Parks, Tom Waits, and Randy Newman. Their presence on our roster helped attract other artists. And here was Casablanca, a label that wasn't concerned with building careers or developing artists. That wasn't their mentality.

BOB MERLIS: The Casablanca philosophy was "whatever it takes to get a hit single maybe we'll sell some albums." Warner Brothers was very artist-development oriented. Their philosophy was "we'll work on this album and it'll lay the base for the next album." They wanted the bands to tour and have people pick up on them organically, whereas Buddah was hard sell, twist arms, whatever it takes to get it on the radio and sell a lot of 45s and hope you sell some albums thereafter.

STAN CORNYN: Neil's mania about making *this* record a hit overwhelmed any sense of "at what cost?" Sure, take chances. But don't sink the boat over one single. Or one act. Eventually, radio decides, and then the public decides. Being successful takes more than hype. A record company that hopes to last for many years to come behaves differently from a one-nighter at the craps tables in Vegas.

BOB MERLIS: The first KISS album didn't do that well. We only worked KISS for one album.

NANCY SAIN: The problem from Casablanca's point of view was

[that] Warner Brothers was our lifeline. They controlled sales, they controlled retail, and they controlled how much product was put out there. Neil had a very aggressive personality. He was really good at his job. When you're an entrepreneur you don't just sit around and wait for a record to be a hit, you make things happen. Warner Brothers was in the business of "Let's put it out and see what happens." Warner Brothers had their priority records and it wasn't any of the Casablanca releases. It became obvious we were in the wrong place.

JEFF FRANKLIN: Warner's didn't understand Neil. Neil couldn't work within the system because Neil had only worked with independent record distributors.

STAN CORNYN: It seemed like Neil and staffers like Buck Reingold were always at our office "waiting to see you." Casablanca guys had daily dreams to push on Warner Brothers and they pushed with élan.

BOB MERLIS: I'd heard that Casablanca was just driving the home office insane. Neil wanted more money spent on advertising, marketing, and tour support. It just didn't seem to be enough for Neil. Nothing was enough for Neil.

STAN CORNYN: Casablanca was not a success, and it seemed to drive Bogart bats. In 1974, album after album came out, and nothing hit. Remember the Bob Crewe Generation? Neither singles nor albums did anything more than slip below the top-200 charts in *Billboard*. That got to Neil's gut. When your gut's aching, one thing people will do is find something to blame besides themselves. Bogart came to believe that Warner Brothers' home and field promotion staffs were not focusing on Casablanca's releases. That's partly true, but those staffs focused on what records were getting radio play.

Neil overspent Warner Brothers' investment money. And hits had not followed. He was in the hole. He went to Mo [Ostin] and asked for more. Mo decided to lend him more—about $750,000, I believe. But it was beyond the current contract between them, so it was a loan to be repaid, not just a write-off. I suspect the deal ended because both Mo and Neil were ready. From Neil's viewpoint, he felt that Warner Brothers was not behind his work.

BUCK REINGOLD: I went into Neil's office and told him, "If we stay another year with Warner Brothers we're gonna go down the drain." He said, "What do you mean?" I said, "I paid somebody off on the Warner Brothers staff to tape the weekly promotion conference call to find out what they were saying."

STAN CORNYN: When he heard a tape of our weekly "promo hotline" community call to all promo personnel across the country, Neil heard our promotion head, Gary Davis, casually mention that Warner Brothers' label releases deserved staff concentration more than any one-shot release. Bad wording, Gary. Neil heard only that Warner Brothers' priority was being placed on their own acts, and Casablanca releases were being pushed less by our field forces. Perhaps there was some truth to that, though many distributed, "not our own label" acts got lots of promotion and hits from Warner Brothers.

JOYCE BOGART-TRABULUS: Neil went nuts. He wasn't gonna let them promote their acts and let KISS die. He couldn't work within that corporate structure. He worked in a more hands-on way, working as an independent one on one with sales and promotion in every city with each distributor, with each radio station.

STAN CORNYN: Mo looked into what had happened and knew it was wrong. Neil stormed up to see Mo. He wanted out of the deal. Mo didn't have to agree to that but—with the proviso that Neil would repay that $750,000 loan—a divorce was agreed to. And Bogart did repay the $750,000. Casablanca and Warner Brothers Records had only been married about one year. Or, as it's put in Hollywood, a quickie.

JOYCE BOGART-TRABULUS: To this day when Mo Ostin sees me he says, "He paid back every dime. I never expected him to be able to do it but he paid me back every penny." But that's not surprising because Neil was a man of his word.

PAUL STANLEY: We were naive and not really aware sometimes of the impact of certain moves. Clearly at that point for us it didn't take a rocket scientist to know a small label that just lost its funding and clout was in trouble. The appeal of a small label is that you can get boutique treatment but you have the clout of a larger entity. It was obvious all of a sudden that we were on a boat without a sail. We were in trouble.

JEFF FRANKLIN: I knew a guy named Lou Horowitz at the First Los Angeles Bank, who was the banker for Casablanca. They were a small bank so they could only loan X amount of dollars. But here's how we got around that. We had Casablanca Records, we had Casablanca Tapes, and we had Casablanca Chocolate City Records. So we were getting credit lines for these different companies. Initially we got advances from independent distributors to get Neil back into the independent record business. We went to these guys and said, "We're getting out of Warner Brothers and going independent; we need advances against what we sell you." The indie distributors wanted Neil back—they made money with him and loved him—so we got large advances and that gave us money to run the label after we got out of the Warner's deal.

STAN CORNYN: A new day for Casablanca dawned. A deluxe set of offices on Sunset Boulevard, and every employee at the new Casablanca got a leased Mercedes in his or her deal.

It continued to be difficult to sell KISS to radio; Casablanca needed ingenious strategies to garner airplay. The band, label, and management made a concerted effort to break the band in Detroit. The city would become the first to embrace KISS in a big way—but it was anything but easy.

MARK PARENTEAU: Larry [Harris] and I had done lots of different projects together, from their Buddah/Kama Sutra days to Casablanca. Larry and I had a great rapport. He had great energy and was great fun. It was the days of music directors and disc jockeys being spoiled rotten. He would fly us here and there and we'd get whatever we wanted. There were grand amounts of what was actually payola, but it

Independence day: "Casablanca Is Now Independent" press ad Courtesy of Mark Cicchini

was more like "gift-ola." Casablanca was really good at coming up with gifts. I remember getting the rhinestone-encrusted black logo KISS T-shirt. It was very important for Larry to break KISS in Detroit. If KISS couldn't make it in Detroit, they weren't gonna make it.

JAAN UHELSZKI (MUSIC WRITER, CREEM): The reason why Detroit is the heavy metal capital of the world is because we were all factory kids. Everybody's parents worked for one of the Ford Motor companies or Chrysler or GM. We respond to hard, heavy music.

MARK PARENTEAU: Detroit was gritty, it was loud. This was still the heyday of General Motors, Ford, and Chrysler. The automotive industry hadn't been hit yet by Japan so it was all about big, oversized American cars. Everybody had a job. The reality was these kids who grew up in the suburbs worked in those loud, gritty factories. The city was ugly on the outside and those factories that they worked in were loud and dirty and I think the music had to reflect that. The music had to be loud, flashy, and over the top to break the drone of everyday life in Detroit.

PAUL STANLEY: Detroit has such a fertile history of great rock and roll, from Mitch Ryder to Bob Seger, the MC5, Ted Nugent, and early Alice Cooper. You go to Flint, Michigan, and you've got Grand Funk Railroad.

BOB SEGER: Pop acts don't do as well in Detroit as serious rock acts do. I always considered KISS a serious rock band. They were trying to rock the house and I think Detroit connected with that wild rock-and-roll spirit that KISS has.

MARK PARENTEAU: Look at all the acts that came out of Detroit. Everything had to have that wild, show business craziness to it. And that's because life was so boring. If you were working the line making cars and riveting on bumpers and you had a little radio on your workbench, the music had to overcome that volume level in the factory. James Taylor and Carly Simon didn't make it. It had to be loud, hot, and flashy and take you out of that horrible world. The reality of working in those factories was so bleak that it was important they could listen to what was coming out of the radio and imagine being that rock star. Ultimately, KISS's music transcended that reality and took them to a fantasy place.

ROBERT DUNCAN: Detroit never cared what the rest of the country thought about their music. It's one of the cities that have a distinct local culture, the way New Orleans, New York, San Francisco, and LA do. With *Creem*, Detroit had its own rock magazine which was not averse to thumbing its nose at critical opinion or popular taste. Detroit fans are not afraid of things that are loud and quote-unquote "dumb." And KISS fit right into that.

JAAN UHELSZKI: We're a no-frills town. We're a tough town and we need entertainment. We want it big, we want it loud, we want it over the top, and we don't want to think.

CHAD SMITH (DRUMMER, RED HOT CHILI PEPPERS): People would go to clubs and arenas still wearing their work clothes and they're ready to let loose. If you don't bring it they're gonna let you know. And if you do they'll really embrace you and love you. And KISS brought it times ten [*laughs*]. People want to be entertained and forget about putting the bolts on the cars. They just want to let loose and have a good time, and KISS is the greatest band for that.

SUZI QUATRO: Detroit likes their rock and roll served up with the gas on full, so a band like KISS was a natural for my town. They were very energetic and powerful. You can't do anything halfway in Detroit. As long as you're steaming ahead, Detroit gets you.

GENE SIMMONS: KISS's career was made in the heartland, not on the coasts. People in the Midwest didn't react to styles or fashion. [Detroit] was a city of hard-working people and the sound of the city was LOUD. To this day there are people around the world that think KISS is a Detroit band.

PAUL STANLEY: Why did Detroit embrace us? I'm not sure, but it was a love affair from the very beginning. From the days of the Michigan Palace, which hosted some of our earliest shows, we were embraced. It was very special. I can remember being a headlining act in Detroit when we were still an opening act in other places.

MARK PARENTEAU: I'd been a radio guy my whole life and had been trained in hearing hit songs. I had an acute awareness of the charts and what was a hit. By the time Larry came to me with KISS he'd come to me previously with acts like Stories, and I'd heard their song "Brother Louie" and said, "That's a hit, Larry, that's gonna be huge," and it turned out to be a number-one record. He also came to me with "Pusherman" by Curtis Mayfield, and I went, "That's perfect for Detroit." I felt I knew what was right for the audience.

LARRY HARRIS: I walked into WABX, the big progressive rock station in Detroit. Mark Parenteau, the music director, was on the air. I went into the studio with the first KISS album and Mark said, "No, they're wearing makeup. I don't wanna play them."

MARK PARENTEAU: I'd already seen them at the Casablanca launch in Los Angeles and I loved everything about it except for their music. I remember putting the needle on the first KISS album and I just didn't hear anything that was exciting and would work for my audience. "Strutter" was boring. "Cold Gin"—boring.

LARRY HARRIS: He told me there was this band he loved called Aerosmith who'd put out a new album and he'd rather play Aerosmith than KISS. We proceeded to do a couple of lines of cocaine on the KISS album [cover]; it was all black so the cocaine worked really well on it.

MARK PARENTEAU: He was really putting the press on—"I need you to play this and make this happen in Detroit!" As much as I liked Larry, my first job was to do right by my audience. Credibility was everything. I didn't want to jam it down my audience's throat if it wasn't gonna work.

LARRY HARRIS: I came up with an idea. "I'll pay for the radio station to put on a concert and you can have any bands on the bill, but KISS has to be one of them."

MARK PARENTEAU: Larry and I made this gentleman's agreement. He said, "If your audience freaks out about KISS and has them on their feet, you need to start playing them on the radio in top rotation." I agreed and the bet was on.

We sold tickets for 99 cents, which was the frequency of the radio station. It was a benefit concert for Belle Island, which was the island between Detroit and Canada. It was like Central Park: it had a zoo, fountains, and walking areas. It was a beautiful area with a great view of Canada. We used to have WABX smoke-in days where in the spring we'd invite all the hippie masses to come smoke pot [*laughs*]. So our effort would be to clean up Belle Island.

LARRY HARRIS: The show was held at the Michigan Palace [April

Backstage at the Michigan Palace, April 7, 1974. Aerosmith was the headlining act.
Left to right: Peter Criss, Paul Stanley, Ace Frehley, Casablanca Records senior vice president/
managing director Larry Harris, WABX-FM music director and DJ Mark Parenteau, and Gene Simmons
Courtesy of Mark Parenteau Archive Collection of Rock Radio

7, 1974] and on the bill was Aerosmith, KISS, Bob Seger, and Ted Nugent.

MARK PARENTEAU: I remember going to see KISS rehearse in the afternoon. Gene was breathing fire and his hair got burnt and he was very pissed about that. That night I remember there being some enmity between KISS and Aerosmith stemming from a recent show they did together [on March 24, 1974, in Owings Mills, Maryland]. KISS came in with so many effects and space they needed that it caused battles.

JOYCE BOGART-TRABULUS: We needed space for the guys to run around onstage. We had effects, flash pots, a drum riser. As an opening act you didn't get a lot of space. It's the headliner who got all the space and they controlled the stage.

PAUL STANLEY: It wasn't a rivalry from our end as much as we wanted a fair shake. We wanted to do our show. They may have seen that as rivalry because we wanted our due.

JOYCE BOGART-TRABULUS: With Aerosmith's road manager, I did a bait and switch thing where I engaged him in a discussion and kept distracting him. While I was doing that the crew was moving the backline and creating more room for our show [*laughs*].

JOE PERRY (GUITARIST, AEROSMITH): KISS opened for us and they had so much production and it made us adjust. I remember the drum riser breaking a lot. It would stop and start. At that point they were still trying to do their show on a shoestring.

MIKE McGURL: Audiences just went berserk over KISS. I think it's just a natural thing that a headlining act didn't want to be usurped by the up-and-comer, so that was part of the tension between Aerosmith and KISS.

JOE PERRY: There were some weapons pulled at that Michigan Palace show. The vibes between the road crew wasn't too good. They were at each other's throats. Aerosmith weren't huge in '74; we were battling to build an audience. There was no MTV or Internet—it was all about playing live and making an impression on an audience. KISS was in the same place as us. We always checked out the opening band to see what you were up against. We were both on the way up so I always looked at it as us having a friendly competition with them. When I went out to see KISS play, the audience was going crazy and they didn't [even] have a big show back then. That first record was straight-ahead rock and roll, nothing fancy. I thought they were a little hokey but the audience was going nuts. I watched them for a while and then went back into the dressing room and was shaking my head in frustration, saying, "What the hell's going on? Is that what people want? Are we gonna have to dress up in tutus and put on Halloween costumes to make it?"

LARRY HARRIS: Because the promoter Steve Glantz didn't have much experience, it took a long time between sets to get the equipment ready for the next band. KISS went onstage and the audience was already drained from the Seger and Nugent sets and the long setup between bands.

MARK PARENTEAU: Michigan Palace was packed. Larry and I were standing on the floor and he said, "By the third song, if the crowd doesn't absolutely love KISS then you're off the hook and you don't have to play them on the radio." So the band comes on and plays a couple of songs. The crowd didn't know the songs so they were just absorbing the band in makeup and its theatrics. KISS goes into the third song, "Firehouse," and at the end of the song Gene spit fire and the entire place erupted. The kids went nuts. It was so Detroit—the smell of burning rubber was always in the air. From that moment forward they never sat down.

LARRY HARRIS: Mark yelled at me over all the noise and said, "You win."

MARK PARENTEAU: The next day we started playing "Strutter" and all these other KISS songs and the city loved it. They had to have the Motor City and it worked. The buzz was on about KISS.

LARRY HARRIS: After KISS was done, a lot of the audience started to leave; they were just exhausted. Steven Tyler [Aerosmith's frontman] was backstage screaming at his record label, "How could you let this happen?" It also reinforced the fact that it was really hard to follow KISS onstage even if you were Aerosmith. But eventually because of that we had to have them start headlining their shows and focused on cities who'd give us radio support.

TOM HAMILTON (BASSIST, AEROSMITH): My first KISS memory took place before there was a KISS. We were down in New York City playing at Max's Kansas City doing a showcase to get a deal. We were staying at the Ramada Inn up the street on Eighth Avenue and feeling unbelievable about what was going on in our lives. We had a big party and a girl we knew brought a friend, this guy with a high crackly voice and an easy laugh. When he said something funny his voice would go up in a high register. The party really got going and everyone got really wasted. Finally, at the end of the night that same guy wandered into my room and passed out. And that was Ace. I had to get some of our crew guys to get him out of my room 'cause I wanted to go to bed [*laughs*].

Flash forward a year or two later and Aerosmith were headlining a gig in [Owings Mills,] Maryland, at Painters Mill Music Fair, a theater-in-the-round, and KISS was the opening act. We'd heard about this band called KISS and we thought it was a silly name. We're doing a sound check in the late afternoon and these four guys came walking up and introduced themselves as KISS. I looked at Ace and said to myself, "Oh my God, I know him! Who the hell is that guy?" Then I realized he was the guy who passed out in my room at the Ramada Inn a year or two earlier [*laughs*].

Later on that night, the audience was in the venue, we were in the dressing room getting ready, and KISS was onstage. I remember somebody from the road crew rushing into the dressing room saying, "You guys better have a look at this." It was one of those ominous suggestions. I remember going out to the side of the stage and seeing Peter's drum riser at its full height, the red beacon lights were going, and there was tons of theatrical smoke all over the place. It was quite a sight. I thought, "Oh my God, this is so stupid," but I couldn't take my eyes off of it because the crowd was going nuts. So it wasn't something that I could totally dismiss. When we went on it was a terrible feeling. It felt like we were going on with our pants down. I'm pretty sure we got a great reaction that night but we felt like, "Boy, did they ever pull the rug right out from under us." The impact of what KISS were doing was undeniable even though I felt it was kind of corny. We had a rivalry from then on.

From there we played with them in Detroit and I remember hearing that there had been a confrontation involving knives between the two crews. We were headlining again and KISS was opening and they needed a lot more stage space than most opening acts. Of course, we didn't want their gear interfering with our gear, so that caused problems between the road crews. Back in those days I had an exaggerated competitive attitude to a band like KISS. Part of that was me being really proud of our band. To be fair, I had a grudging respect for them. Back in the early seventies, being deemed commercial was not cool, but KISS didn't care about being commercial. They concentrated on the smiles on the faces of the kids that came to see them. They were about fun and putting on a spectacle, which they'd mastered. We felt it was important to blow them off the stage. The audience was there to see us but I don't think it was possible to see their show back in those days and not be entertained by them. Nobody was doing what they were doing. They executed a theatrical show better than someone like Alice Cooper. Over the years we've crossed paths with KISS and did a tour with them back in 2003 so we know them much better now and get along really well.

JOE PERRY: I always respected KISS and their whole commitment to putting on a show. They were different and new and I could see they were gonna be big. They knew what they were doing and they were banging on all cylinders. Before we did dates with them I remember hearing their album for the first time at [Boston DJ] Maxanne Sartori's apartment—her boyfriend at the time was Billy Squier. Maxanne played me the record and I really liked it, especially "Strutter." It was good, solid rock and roll.

23

ROAD WARS

KISS *continued to deliver an explosive show that married spectacular theatrics and heavy metal thunder throughout the tours of 1974. But the band was plagued by headliners insecure about following these rowdy young upstarts onstage.*

ERIC WEINSTEIN: When you're an opening act you don't get a lot of respect. The headliner and road crew is always trying to fuck with you. They don't want to give you a big part of the stage. They don't wanna give you lights or full sound. They don't want to give you anything.

MIKE McGURL: KISS's show was technically advanced for groups back then. Bands were intimidated by the sheer magnitude of what we were doing. Even though KISS was an opening act, they put on literally explosive shows. What happened is KISS blew everybody off the stage, and this caused major problems.

RICHIE WISE: They had a lot of trouble as an opening act because their show was so much better and louder. They were blowing people away in places like Detroit and Cleveland, where they were big on hard rock. The headlining acts often placed restrictions on

ABOVE: Turning it up to 10. Take notice of the unique stage city backdrop. Stanley Theatre, Pittsburgh, April 15, 1975

LEFT: Paul at the Stanley Theatre, Pittsburgh, April 15, 1975
Photos by Len DeLessio/www. delessio.com

TOP: Gene at the Stanley Theatre, Pittsburgh, April 15, 1975
ABOVE: This was one of the shows where the KISS sign could not be hung
above the stage and instead found its home onstage. Stanley Theatre, Pittsburgh,
April 15, 1975 Photos by Len DeLessio/www.delessio.com

A close call, Stanley Theatre, Pittsburgh, April 15, 1975 Len DeLessio/www.delessio.com

the band in terms of their staging: they weren't gonna allow them to use their full PA system, or they weren't gonna allow Gene to spit fire or blood.

MIKE McGURL: They'd say, "You've got forty minutes, not a second over, or the lights and sound will go off," and if we went over, they'd do it. For the most part we pretty much did that. There were instances when audiences went absolutely nuts and wanted encores. I'd have to sit and negotiate with a tour manager and tell them the crowd was gonna go berserk if you don't let them back onstage. Usually they'd let the band come back on for an encore or two. There were some bands that were adamant about no encores.

PAUL STANLEY: No matter when we go on, when we hit the stage it's our gig and we're going to give it everything we've got. A lot of the big groups don't care for the opening act to have that attitude. When we play with another group and we're not headlining, they want us to play crippled. They always do these numbers on us like saying, "You can't use the backlights" or "You can't have a sound check." Steppenwolf wouldn't let us use our own lights or flash pots so we refused to play the gig. We went back there [to St. Louis] and sold out an eleven-thousand-seat hall on our own. You can't suppress what people want.

MIKE McGURL: I remember coming to fisticuffs with the tour manager for Blue Öyster Cult because he killed the sound and lights. Man, we went at it backstage. I had him up against the wall and was trying to cave his head in with a wrench. I was livid. But he finally gave in and let us do an encore. The word spread fast that this band was just showing everybody up. After that tour all of those bands that KISS once opened for were now opening shows for them. Man, talk about a role reversal. That's called sweet revenge.

PETER "MOOSE" ORECKINTO: We always tried to make friends with other road crews by loaning them a tool like a drill if they were amenable. Sometimes they were like, "Oh fuck off, Yank." But they could always use a drill to fix something like a latch on an anvil case.

MICK CAMPISE: KISS was playing with Golden Earring, who were from Holland, and they pulled the plug on us when KISS's set ran a minute or two over. Never mind the fact that the kids were going crazy and didn't want them to leave the stage. We confronted them and they acted like they didn't understand us.

In 1973, Southern rock boogie merchants Black Oak Arkansas scored their biggest hit with their bawdy cover of LaVern Baker's fifties smash, "Jim Dandy." The following year, in late November 1974, KISS opened a slate of dates for the band in the South, and their explosive stage show drew the ire of the raunchy rebel rockers.

PAUL CHAVARRIA: Black Oak Arkansas came at us with a Southern attitude of how they do things. They didn't like the way the band looked or their music and were ready to rumble with us all the time.

JIM DANDY (LEAD VOCALIST, BLACK OAK ARKANSAS): Black Oak never was blown offstage by anybody and that includes KISS. We didn't need makeup. The first gig we did with KISS was in Atlanta and they burned down our backdrop, and I think it was on purpose [*laughs*].

GENE SIMMONS: We didn't do it on purpose. Is he crazy? We didn't want to set the stage on fire and kill people. Black Oak had this theatrical curtain behind them. I spit fire but that night it was ten feet high and it accidentally caught their curtain on fire. The fire department had to come out and put it out. We got thrown off the tour and our booking agent is ripping his hair out going, "I can't keep these guys on tour."

JIM DANDY: You gotta take your hat off for KISS. They put their heart and soul into it. They were a one-of-a-kind act and their determination was admirable. To put on that makeup and gear night after night takes sacrifice. You get out of it what you put into it and they never gave up, gave in, or gave out. You gotta give 'em credit for what they did, and they're still doing it to this day.

Black Sabbath were the inventors of heavy metal. Classic metal songs like "Paranoid," "War Pigs," and "Iron Man" pioneered a brutal, primordial sound that blended pummeling riffs with dark, twisted imagery. The original metal masters would cross paths with the fledgling upstarts for gigs in Boston, Baltimore, Syracuse, New York, and Providence, Rhode Island. The pairing of KISS and Black Sabbath—like their previous pairing with Black Oak Arkansas—resulted in quite a bit of enmity.

PETER "MOOSE" ORECKINTO: KISS opened a show for Black Sabbath, who were being very British, very pushy and nasty, telling us, "You can't do this and you can't do that."

RICK MUNROE: I remember a showdown in Providence, Rhode Island [August 8, 1975]. Black Sabbath set their stage up and didn't leave enough room for our drum riser or room for the band to stand in front of it. They had room to back up their gear but they didn't want to. Bill [Aucoin] came to us and said, "They won't back up for us so we're not gonna play. Just take the equipment and put it in the truck—let's get out of here." So we put all the gear into the truck and as I was putting the padlock on the back of the truck, Bill came out, gave everyone a $50 bill, and said, "Here, put it back up again: they flinched." So we put the equipment back up and played the gig.

J.R. SMALLING: KISS didn't have a problem with Sabbath; Sabbath had a problem with KISS. Each night they had only fifteen feet of stage space and half a dozen lights. Sabbath did everything that could be done to diminish their vibe.

PETER "MOOSE" ORECKINTO: Sean Delaney marched up to the ticket window and was told that everybody was asking them about KISS. So he goes back to Black Sabbath's road manager and he's furious. He's got that intense Charlie Manson look in his eyes and says, "Look, 90 percent of the people coming to the ticket window are asking about KISS, not Black Sabbath. So we *will* use our special effects and we *will* have a sound check." They were about to come to blows with us. Needless to say, we got to do a sound check and use all our special effects that night [*laughs*].

GENE SIMMONS: Geezer [Butler], the bass player in Sabbath, was off on the side of the stage and we were about to go on. I wanted to go up to him and say hello because I liked his bass playing. I smacked him on his shoulder and said kiddingly, "Hey, Geezer, we're gonna fuck you up tonight."

J.R. SMALLING: A half an hour after KISS left the stage, Black Sabbath's crowd is still chanting, "KISS! KISS! KISS!" They threw us off the tour. Ozzy was man enough to come backstage and shake everybody's hand and say, "Man, any time the headline act can't hold their crowd that opening act must be a motherfucker. You guys are great."

GEEZER BUTLER (BASSIST, BLACK SABBATH): I used to enjoy watching the support bands back then, bands like Alice Cooper and

Yes who were unique in their own way, but nothing prepared me for KISS. Sure, Arthur Brown had used fire onstage before, but only as a crown of flame, and Alice Cooper had used makeup and stage props. But KISS was like nothing I'd seen before, with their space-age clothes, kabuki/horror–style makeup, and their bloody loud bangs. I had never seen eight-foot flames onstage before, not to mention anyone spitting fake blood and eating fire while playing bass. They completely blew me away. I think they were the hardest act we've ever had to follow.

GENE SIMMONS: Years later, Ozzy told me, "That's when I knew I had to leave the band, because anybody who gets spooked by the opening band doesn't have the heart of a lion."

GEEZER BUTLER: We saw them at the hotel the next day. Gene Simmons told me he was an admirer of my bass playing and I told him I loved their act. Then he showed me a few X-rated Polaroids of their previous night's post-gig activities and we chatted for a while.

Whereas bands like Black Sabbath and Black Oak Arkansas were intimidated by KISS's ferocity, established Midwest rock icons Bob Seger and Ted Nugent enjoyed sharing the stage with the rising hard rock sensations.

BOB SEGER: We played a lot of shows with KISS and they were really good to us. I really liked Ace, Gene, Paul, and Peter as people. They were very nice to us and gave us as much room as we needed onstage and also made sure we got a sound check every night. And that wasn't typical back then. Some acts we opened for, like Jethro Tull, didn't make things easy on us [*laughs*]. The big thing I remember from when we opened for them is during our set we'd hear the audience going, "KISS! KISS! KISS!" [*laughs*], especially in Philadelphia. It was deafening. I had to say to the band, "Just keep playing, guys, there's not much we can do about it" [*laughs*]. But occasionally they'd settle down and listen to us.

Playing with KISS gave us an opportunity to play in front of a lot more people, too. It's always good to get on a big stage and get used to the reverberations of a big arena. You don't get that in a club. I'd often watch KISS play [from] the side of the stage and I learned real quick not to stand too close to the pyro [*laughs*]. I also learned when all the explosions came in so I didn't lose my hearing [*laughs*]—I knew when to put my hands over my ears [*laughs*]. I was really impressed with KISS's live show and liked songs like "Rock and Roll All Nite." They had the genuine rock spirit. I'd played with Alice Cooper before that, so their big theatrical presentation with the fire and pyro and Gene's tongue didn't faze me. It was just another way of getting their act across. All the kabuki stuff aside, they were a rock band. They were just like us and I thought they played really well. The biggest thing I learned from playing shows with them was to be gracious to the opening act. I can't say enough how generous and gracious they were. They didn't need to be that way, and they were. We were nobodies back then, pre–"Night Moves," and it was really nice of them to do it.

TED NUGENT: Paul and Gene put together KISS because they wanted to be rock gods. That's why the whole outrageous showmanship, fireballs, and the vaudevillian, over-the-top insanity was created around the KISS imagery. I, on the other hand, could give a rat's ass about rock stardom. I just wanted to make music that drove people berserk, even though I ended up putting on an outrageous show because the music drove me crazy. I think we were real kindred spirits in that they were driven by the same musical translation that Elvis and the Stones and the Beatles delivered from the black artists of America. People like Howlin' Wolf, Muddy Waters, Bo Diddley, Chuck Berry, James Brown, and Sam & Dave. That inescapable primal scream music is really the guts of KISS music.

What I remember most about those early days playing shows with KISS is being enthralled by the bombardment of fascinating imagery and outrageousness with the flames and insane costumes. That primal musicality manifested itself in giant blood tongues and

Blowin' fire, and minds, Stanley Theatre, Pittsburgh, April 15, 1975
Len DeLessio/www.delessio.com

flames out of the mouth. With the energy and touring schedules, the preparation for their show, the gregariousness of backstage, and the velocity of night-after-night concerts, playing shows with KISS was overtly intoxicating. I saw that KISS loved the same music that I loved. They loved the defiant, uninhibited nature of their stage presentation and my stage presentation. I think the guys in KISS and I connected more on those defiant levels of, "Oh, I can't let a bomb go off onstage? Well, watch me—I'll let off twenty. My guitar's too loud? Well, let me bring in eight more Marshall stacks, motherfucker" [*laughs*].

The first time I saw KISS play was when we shared a bill at the Tower Theater in Philadelphia [May 3, 1975]. I was well aware of KISS, but to actually see the illegal fireworks and to actually see the height of their platform boots was mind-boggling [*laughs*]. I can't even adequately describe the over-the-top nature of it all. I fucking loved it. I wasn't out-of-the-box and pushing the envelope, I had blown up the box and set the envelope on fire. To see somebody else do it in their own way was so inspiring. I thought I was the baddest motherfucker in the world but when I saw the insanity level that these guys pumped into their show I went, "Oh yeah? Well, watch this." I was challenged by that and there's nothing more important than that. I knew I couldn't settle for what I think is intense and outrageous because these guys are showing me a whole new level of intense and outrageous and I better turn up the fuckin' heat.

Even in its infancy, KISS's stage show was a sonic and visual blitzkrieg of the senses that often left unsuspecting audiences stunned and wondering what they'd just witnessed. Yet even a stage show that rivaled a three-ring circus wasn't going to convert all the nonbelievers who viewed KISS as a bad rock-and-roll punch line.

PAUL /TANLEY: I remember playing at the Agora in Cleveland and walking out onstage seeing some cute girl in the front row laughing and elbowing her boyfriend. All you can think is "Watch *this.*" And like everybody else, the smirk was wiped off her face very quickly. We lived for the challenge of winning over audiences one fan at a time.

In the spring of 1974, KISS's fanbase in Detroit was painfully thin. Recognizing the importance of breaking into this critical Midwest market, the band played countless shows in the region and steadily built a solid following. And two years later, KISS would unleash the anthem "Detroit Rock City," a sonic monument to the fanatical devotion of their fans in the Motor City.

MARK PARENTEAU: The second or third time KISS came to Detroit, Larry [Harris] was sitting in my studio the day of their show, which was sold out. Our phone was ringing off the hook from listeners complaining they couldn't see them. So I ad libbed over the radio and said to the listeners, "Why don't you dress up like KISS, put on the makeup—they'll think you're in the band and let you right in the backstage door." It was just a throwaway line. I got to the show that night and Larry went, "Look!" and there were all these guys dressed up like KISS. Larry and I were amazed. I was totally blown away by that. It was the first time we'd ever seen anything like this. At that time, how many bands were there where you can dress up like the band? Suddenly dressing up like KISS had become a big thing and today has grown into a phenomenon.

MIKE McGURL: From the first day I started working with KISS I knew they were gonna be huge; it was just a matter of time. I never worked for a band before where I saw that kind of delirium coming from an audience. I could see the obsessive way the audience reacted to them. It was the first time I had ever seen audience members dressed as members of the band. I'd walk through the audience and I would see Gene, I would see Paul, or Ace or Peter. And not just one or two—lots of them. I thought, "Wow, something's happening here."

And the buzz wasn't limited to Detroit. By the end of 1974, it was beginning to spread like wildfire throughout the country.

ERIC BLOOM: We played some shows with KISS in '74 and '75. We headlined over them for some shows and then they started to catch fire.

BUCK DHARMA: We had a thirteen-foot box truck with all our equipment in it and I remember being impressed that KISS had a semi truck and ten-guy crew [*laughs*]. We've never worked with another act before or since that were mounting such a huge production as an opening act. I was definitely impressed by their show and probably a little jealous because KISS looked like a surefire success because it was so audacious and over the top. I liked some of their tunes. They never presented themselves as a cutting-edge group either song- or playing-wise but they played well enough and rocked hard enough to sell millions of records. It wasn't just the makeup that sold them; you had to like the music too.

ERIC BLOOM: They took off very fast. We'd later wind up opening for them at Nassau Coliseum in Long Island [December 31, 1975].

BUCK DHARMA: We never felt like we were in competition with them; they were doing something entirely different. KISS was in a genre unto themselves. With the KISS juggernaut you just got out of the way.

The band's nonstop touring was starting to pay off.

GENE SIMMONS: It was Halloween '74 and in downtown Manhattan there was a parade with gay people dressed up in costumes. I remember watching the parade and all of a sudden seeing people walking in the parade wearing our makeup and costumes, and I went numb. I was dumbstruck. You didn't see someone dressed up like a member of Manfred Mann or Argent in a parade. That really hit me. It was big. It was at that moment that I felt something was really starting to happen with KISS. We were on the verge of a breakthrough.

ERIC BLOOM: At one point we were both recording at the Record Plant: KISS was in one studio and Blue Öyster Cult the other. We were in different studios on different floors. Some guy got into the building with a bass that he wanted to sell. He made this handmade mahogany bass with wood inlays and was really proud of it. He came in to see Joe Bouchard, our original bass player, and wanted to see if he wanted to buy it from him. Joe passed and I said that maybe Gene might be interested. I walked the guy up to KISS's studio and introduced him to Gene. He told him he had a bass and that he might like it. Gene put it on and said, "How does it look on me?" And this guy was busy trying to explain the merits of the bass and its two-octave fretboard. Gene said, "Octave, schmoctave—how does it *look* on me?" [*laughs*]. He took a roll of money out of his pocket and bought it.

24

THE "DARTBOARD TOUR"

No guts, no glory: KISS was driven to succeed at all costs. That tireless mission to make it exacted a tremendous physical toll on their road crew, particularly during the group's three tours of America in 1974.

PETER "MOOSE" ORECKINTO: Every day was an adventure. The road crew jokingly referred to KISS's first three tours of '74 as the "Dartboard Tour." Take a dart, throw it at the map of the United States, and that was your next gig. That's how random it was and how brutal the travel was from gig to gig.

J.R. SMALLING: Our philosophy was to connect the dots [*laughs*]. You put a map in front of a booking agent and you tell him to go for it: "We're from New York and we want to play everywhere between here and LA and back again."

PETER "MOOSE" ORECKINTO: The routing never made sense. Wherever management could get a gig for five thousand bucks, the band was there. Sometimes that required driving like a fucking maniac upwards of nine hundred to one thousand miles in one day to get to the next gig and there'd be no time for sleep.

MIKE McGURL: The routing was totally illogical. When you book a major tour you want to ensure that the cities are no farther away than 250 miles because you have to move a great deal of equipment day to day. To try to get ATI to grasp our logistics was almost impossible. They were just trying to book the band as many places as possible. That routing was brutal on the crew.

PAUL STANLEY: I can remember after a gig, we'd get into a station wagon, drive seventeen hours, get out of the car, go into a dressing room in a club, get made up, and go out onstage. There was no rhyme or reason or logic to the routing except it was a gig.

GENE SIMMONS: The routing was insane. You had to have at least five shows a week in order to pay everybody's salaries, gas, lodgings, and food. We played as often as we could. We often played six, seven days a week.

PAUL STANLEY: We needed to make money so whether it meant driving from Ohio to a gig the next day all the way down in Florida, you did it. And your next show might be in New York. None of it mattered. You just put your head down and went along with it.

PETER "MOOSE" ORECKINTO: We played every ice skating rink, every ratty club, high school, or theater that would have us. It didn't matter what the gig paid or how far we had to travel to get there.

J.R. SMALLING: The exhaustion factor was ridiculous. That first year we did over two hundred one-nighters and also recorded two albums. We had a feeling like it was us against the world.

PETER "MOOSE" ORECKINTO: It was rock and roll commando-style. We were spreading the gospel of KISS, one town at a time.

GENE SIMMONS: In the early days we'd play with anybody at any time. Looking back we played with everyone from John Sebastian, Albert Hammond, Fleetwood Mac, and Dr. John. We played with Billy Preston, who tried to pick me up one night. There was even going to be a KISS/Queen tour in late '74, but it never happened.

PAUL STANLEY: We would play with anyone whether you were a folk, blues, country, R&B, or rock act. We went onstage with the idea that we would destroy anyone. The variety of people we had to play with had more to do with ATI than us. There was a time when shows back then were much more eclectic. The beauty of the Fillmore East was you literally had Led Zeppelin playing with the Woody Herman Orchestra. You had bills with diversity to them and interesting blends of music. I certainly wasn't opposed to playing with all kinds of acts. Rory Gallagher was a bit of a stretch.

GENE SIMMONS: We were making $85 a week per man and we were deeply in debt but all we knew was we were having the time of our lives.

PETER "MOOSE" ORECKINTO: Here's an example of three days in the life of a KISS roadie over a four-day period in the early days. We'd play a show in St. Louis and then have to drive all night, nine hundred miles, to do a gig in West Palm Beach [Florida]. We'd get there about six o'clock and Blue Öyster Cult wouldn't allow us onstage so we got bumped off the bill. We get a few hours sleep and then drive to Toronto for a show. From there the next day we'd have to drive down to play the Aragon Ballroom in Chicago. It was insane.

LARRY HARRIS: Smart routing was out of the question. They'd have to jump from one area of the country to another the next day. It cost us a lot of money to do that but it worked.

MIKE McGURL: To this day I could never seem to figure out why we always seemed to get booked across Canada in the wintertime and across the Deep South in the summer. It ticked me off—that just didn't make any damn sense. Why couldn't they just flip those around? Playing shows across Canada in the winter, you can't even imagine how brutally cold it was and playing the Deep South in the summer was way too hot.

DOUG BANKER (CONCERT PROMOTER, DOUG BANKER PRODUCTIONS): Back in '74, I booked a KISS date into the Thunder Chicken club in Comstock Park, Michigan, for something like $750 or $1,000. I remember the show well. Some of the bouncers were rednecks and thought the band was weird (or at least the way they dressed) and I ended up hiring security to make sure none of the bouncers beat them up [*laughs*]. I was totally impressed with the band's show at Thunder Chicken and the fact they went all out—full show, costumes, the flames, the blood. The show was intense. Even though they weren't well known yet they acted like they were. KISS didn't work their way into being a wild band with a great show, they started out that way. I remember getting a kick out of the fact that even way back then no one was allowed to take any pictures of them without their makeup on. It seemed silly at the time because not a lot of people even knew who they were yet. But they were way ahead of their time, and as it turned out, they knew exactly what they were doing. They had a do-or-die, conquer-the-world-or-bust attitude and approach to their music, show, and career. They were visionaries, and their history now speaks for itself.

Riding high on the excitement of their first national tour, in August of 1974 KISS descended upon Los Angeles to begin work on their second album, with producers Kenny Kerner and Richie Wise at the helm. They hunkered down in Village Recorders in Santa Monica, California, the historic studio housed inside an old Masonic Temple that was home to such acts as the Rolling Stones, Fleetwood Mac, Bob Dylan, Neil Young, and Steely Dan. Boasting a heavier and more metallic sound than their debut record, Hotter Than Hell *was issued in October 1974 and sold moderately well. A batch of songs from the album became mainstays in the band's live show for years to come: "Let Me Go, Rock 'n' Roll," "Parasite," "Got to Choose," "Watchin' You," and the title track.*

KENNY KERNER: Richie and I had moved to LA so we wanted the band to record their second album here. We knew the second album had to show development, and it does from a recording perspective.

It sounds more like an album than a raw presentation of the band live. The band didn't like it out in LA. They didn't drive, which makes it difficult to get around [*laughs*]. Paul's guitar was stolen on the first day of recording.

RICHIE WISE: I wanted to make a harder, more forceful record. I thought the guitars on the first album weren't distorted enough. After seeing KISS live I wanted to make a record that was more live-sounding. There were some good songs on *Hotter Than Hell* but a better recording would have served it better.

KENNY KERNER: The material wasn't as strong on *Hotter Than Hell*. It's the old story: you have all your life to write your songs for your first album and six months to come up with the songs for the second album. It took a little bit longer to record than the first album, but it wasn't a Fleetwood Mac album [*laughs*]. It was recorded live, but we did a lot more overdubs and vocals. So it sounds a little more finished and polished. Neil gave us zero input on the album. He kept his distance. He may have shown up after dinner and said, "Hi guys, how's it going? Can I hear something?"

GENE SIMMONS: We saved up some songs from the last record that we hadn't recorded, things like "Watchin' You" and "Let Me Go, Rock 'n' Roll," and we also wrote some songs on the spot. I brought in "Goin' Blind," a song I wrote with Stephen Coronel in the Wicked Lester days.

ACE FREHLEY: *Hotter Than Hell* was a harder album to record than our first record because we had toured so extensively and then all of a sudden the record company wanted us to put out another album. You don't have ten songs you've been rehearsing for a year. That was a tougher record to do but it was fun and it was different. Working in LA was fun. It was the first time we were out there.

PAUL STANLEY: It was our first extended trip to Los Angeles. We were living the rock-and-roll lifestyle of an up-and-coming band at the Ramada on Sunset Boulevard in Hollywood. We lived there while we recorded the album.

MIKE McGURL: That was an absolutely crazy time. Some of the band and crew were jumping off the roof into the swimming pool from two stories high. It got out of hand.

PAUL /TANLEY: We had a grand old time and were living large. It was a real eye-opening period coming out to Los Angeles and the amount of women was staggering. We were within walking distance of the Rainbow. The Rainbow became my version of a church or synagogue. I was there every night 'cause it was full of women whose only criteria for going back to the hotel with you was that you were in a band, and that suited me fine.

Hotter Than Hell was the first album where we couldn't rely on material that we had written in high school. Although there were some leftover songs on the album from our club days, it really came down to writing a new batch of songs, which was daunting. There was a lot of pressure on Gene and myself because we had years to sift through all our material to come up with what we felt was the best material for the first album. For the second album it was instant rock. We only had a couple of months to write the songs. We were recording the album at Village Recorders in Santa Monica and wanted to make a sonically more accurate record of who we were, but unfortunately that got lost in the mix. It's not a great-sounding album, but the material is really good. In hindsight, not only did we want to make the record heavier but we were also trying to make the writing a little heavier to compensate for what we felt was missing from the first album.

RICHIE WI/E: During a session the band pulled a prank on Paul and used gaffer tape to tape his hands together. I remember cutting off the tape with a razor blade in the studio and cutting him on the wrist. I felt really bad because it affected his guitar playing for a while. I remember that because it was traumatic in the same way the record turned out to be.

PAUL /TANLEY: We were spending our days in the studio working

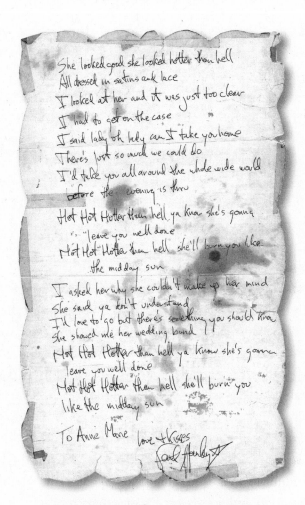

**Paul Stanley's handwritten lyrics for "Hotter Than Hell,"
circa 1974** Courtesy of AnneMarie Hughes

on an album that we hoped would remedy the sonic deficiencies we found in the first album. We were never as rock-and-rolly or good-timey as we sounded on that album. We were much heavier live. So we tried to capture sonically how we sounded live. Unfortunately, the people that we were working with were probably not the right people to be doing it with.

RICHIE WISE: I take full responsibility for the failure of that album, bad sound decisions, and bad creative decisions. I was very disappointed in the record. Between the mixing and not knowing what the studios sounded like—the speakers in the control room didn't accurately replicate the sound—in the attempt to go left, we went right. The sound of the record was always iffy. I remember mastering the record forever in an attempt to make it sound better. I wanted to make it louder and more forceful and to have a better sonic presence. The mastering made it even worse. Looking back, the first album had a lot of smiles and laughter but the second album didn't cut it—it wasn't cohesive and it failed to jell. The first album had a vibe that the second album didn't have. That album felt forced in every way.

GENE SIMMONS: During the recording of *Hotter Than Hell* was the first time we realized we had two troubled guys in the band— Peter and Ace. Before they became chemically and booze addicted, before they got deep into it, the dark side of Ace and Peter came out. The demands, the entitlement, the irresponsibility, not showing up on time and being self-destructive and being confrontational to the guys in your own band who helped make all of this possible. During *Hotter Than Hell*, Peter confronted Paul and I and said, "If I don't have a song to sing on this record I'm leaving the band" so Paul gave him the song "Mainline" to sing. We initially liked that arrogant bravado and appreciated a guy that stood up for himself, but threatening to leave the band was out of line. And he did it again while we were recording Ace's song, "Strange Ways." Peter did a seven-minute drum solo on that song and it was horrible. It was the worst thing we ever heard. He threatened to leave the band again if we cut the solo but we did it anyway.

PAUL STANLEY: Peter threatened to quit the band a few times in those early days. It wasn't a sword he should have waved about lightly. But we never thought about getting rid of him. The chemistry in the band is a big part of what made us. There's nothing wrong with volatility in a relationship. That can sometimes bring out the best and we were no exception to that. It was the diversity, the differences, and the friction that propelled the band. We were out there promoting the cause and that made for the bond between us.

GENE SIMMONS: Ace veered off into the dark side on that record. The night before the *Hotter Than Hell* album shoot Ace got into a bad car accident.

MIKE McGURL: We had a couple of rent-a-cars. I had one and the road crew had one. I'm in my hotel room one night and there's a knock on the door and it's Ace. Ace called everybody "Curly." [*Imitating Ace's voice*] "Hey, Curly, can I borrow the keys to the rent-a-car? I wanna take a ride up into the hills." I said, "Okay, Ace, leave the keys at the front desk, don't come knocking on my door."

ACE FREHLEY: Something pissed me off. I got drunk one night and I kept driving around the Hollywood Hills. I kept going around the same block faster and faster [*laughs*] until I lost control and hit a telephone pole. I think I was just testing destiny. I got out of the car and I had cut my head and there's blood running all down my face.

MIKE McGURL: So about three or four hours later I'm sound asleep and I hear [*imitates the noise of someone pounding on a door*]. I open the door and Ace is standing there and his whole face is full of blood. I'm going, "What the fuck?" And he said, "Hey Curly, I had a little accident."

ACE FREHLEY: I go, "I wrecked a car." One of many [*laughs*].

MIKE McGURL: I get the road crew and we find an emergency clinic, get Ace all stitched up. Afterwards I said, "Ace, where's the car?" And he goes, "I don't know, I think it's up on Mulholland Drive somewhere, I don't remember. I ran it off the road." I said, "How did you get back to the hotel." He said, "I walked down Sunset Boulevard" [*laughs*]. He walked down Sunset Boulevard bleeding profusely and no one stopped him to say, "What's wrong?" [*laughs*]. The next day I got the crew together and went looking for the car. He had rolled it over a hill and it went down about fifty, sixty feet and it ran up against a big rock. That was the only thing keeping it from going all the way down the cliff. I don't know how he survived it—the car was totally destroyed. It was a brand-new Monte Carlo and it was in my name. I had to call Avis and tell them where their car was [*laughs*].

GENE SIMMONS: He could have been killed. We were just happy he was okay but he smashed up one side of his face so badly that he had to have stitches.

ACE FREHLEY: For one photo session we did for the *Hotter Than Hell* album, this doctor told me I couldn't put makeup on it. I could only put makeup on half of my face so all the shots were profiles [*laughs*].

GENE SIMMONS: He did the entire photo session for the front cover with only one side of his makeup on. The art department had to create the other side of his face.

Hotter Than Hell album cover shoot, Raleigh Studios, Hollywood, August 1974. As a result of a car accident in the Hollywood Hills the previous night that required facial stitches, Ace's makeup was applied to only half of his face. Norman Seeff/www.normanseeff.com

Hotter Than Hell album cover shoot, Raleigh Studios, Hollywood, August 1974
Norman Seeff/www.normanseeff.com

NORMAN SEEFF (PHOTOGRAPHER, *HOTTER THAN HELL* ALBUM COVER): The *Hotter Than Hell* photo shoot was done at the Raleigh stages in Hollywood. The front and back cover were shot on the same day. I had gone to Japan with my film crews and we published my book *Hot Shots* there. As part of my Japanese trip I was photographing and filming top Japanese groups. I also wanted to meet Japanese artists in different arenas. It was a whole ensemble of young Japanese art directors, photographers, and producers. One of the people they introduced me to was Tadanori Yokoo, a profoundly exciting Japanese artist. He was a guy who was pushing the envelope in Japan when Japan was still very conservative. Yokoo wasn't a copyist; he took his imagery out of traditional Japanese art. I was very excited by what he was doing. He was a combination of Timothy Leary, Andy Warhol, and Picasso.

KISS had enormous ability to work almost symbolically and graphically. They used their bodies in a very mannerist graphic way. I felt Yokoo's work and the kind of painted facial imagery of KISS would really work together beautifully. As we went further, I thought, "Why not put the title in Japanese as well?" I called in a brilliant designer, John Van Hamersveld, to do the design. He was the only guy that I felt could take it and pull it off and at the same time add his own individuality to it. And he just nailed it.

JOHN VAN HAMERSVELD (VISUAL ARTIST, *HOTTER THAN HELL*): In that period, I'd designed album covers for the Rolling Stones (*Exile on Main Street*), the Grateful Dead (*Skeletons from the Closet*), Bob Dylan (*Pat Garrett & Billy the Kid*), and Steve Miller (*The Joker*). The Norman Seeff photography studio was just down the street from Casablanca Records, on the Sunset Strip. Norman had been selling photos to Neil Bogart for artists like Donna Summer and Johnny Carson. Norman was *the* rock entertainment photographer at the time and everyone wanted his style of photograph. He called me at the Chapman Park Studio Building in LA where I was packaging album covers at that time. He explained he needed me to pull the package together for the band and Casablanca Records real quickly.

So a messenger from Norman's office arrived with the contact sheets and I focused on Gene Simmons as a Japanese robot figure. I immediately thought of the archetypal Japanese pop artist Tadanori Yokoo and his famous posters like Koshimaki-Osen [Japanese theater group] done in 1966 to 1968. I went to Japantown in LA that afternoon to look for ideas. One was to get a symbolic image that the Japanese would know. I got a translation of the chikara symbol, which means "power," from one of the printers called Toyo Printing in Little Tokyo.

I created all the parts and pieces wrapped around the photograph. The silver disk as a solid background gave the image strength, separating the photograph as a vignette. The thumb with the green fingernail on the cover was a drawing I did of my own thumb. I come from the psychedelic sixties. Every once in a while I was able to bring it into context somewhere, so I used psychedelic layering on the front and back. As for the back cover, for the image in the center, I combined the band's makeup to create a symbolic facsimile logotype to represent KISS. I created a drawing in black line, and made a color Xerox of it with gouache watercolor painted with speckles on the paper and surrounded the image with the Seeff photographs. Incorporating the color and layering with Norman's photos on the back cover was again a nod to my psychedelic consciousness. The

KISS posed with the brain trust, comanagers Joyce Biawitz and Bill Aucoin and Casablanca Records president Neil Bogart at the *Hotter Than Hell* album cover shoot, Raleigh Studios, Hollywood, August 1974 Norman Seeff/www.normanseeff.com

package looks Japanese. The success of the packaging is in the combination of photography, art direction, and good graphic design.

NEIL BOGART: It's nice for a band, other than a Japanese group, to put out an album with Japanese liner notes. If for nothing else, it gives our fantastic fans in the Orient something different, as well as being aesthetically pleasing. All the photos on our second LP, titled *Hotter Than Hell*, were from a party we had which was something right out of *Satyricon*, even featuring naked women in bird heads.

PAUL STANLEY: *Hotter Than Hell* was an amazing cover that really captured the band. It was the first thing I saw that truly reached beyond the American album covers typical of the time, which I thought were so boring. I was a huge fan of British albums and album art, and the cover of *Hotter Than Hell* really smacked more to me of [Cream's] *Disraeli Gears* as opposed to Marshall Tucker. The Japanese writing was wild and came out of nowhere. The essence of that cover was so far-reaching it really blew me away.

NORMAN SEEFF: The album's title dictated the party shot, the *Satyricon* fantasy concept for the back cover. We created a party atmosphere. The whole Casablanca crew was there.

JOYCE BOGART-TRABULUS: Neil and his whole family were there, including his mother and father, and we were all in costume [*laughs*]. Neil was wearing a turban and makeup and I was wearing animal skin [*laughs*].

NORMAN SEEFF: I hired actors and wardrobe people who went to Western Costume in Hollywood and went through everything, "Wow, an animal head!" or "Here's something with feathers." They brought back stuff that they thought could work, a kind of *Fantasia* imagery for the group.

PAUL STANLEY: Norman was well known for creating an atmosphere in his work. It was an environment that filled a soundstage and seemed like the perfect opportunity to get loose and do something that was very akin to the band. It was like walking into a Fellini film. It was pretty crazy. There were beds hanging from the ceiling and

Hotter Than Hell back cover photo shoot, Raleigh Studios, Hollywood, August 1974
Norman Seeff/www.normanseeff.com

silver-painted half-naked women with bird heads and guys in tights or swim suits.

NORMAN SEEFF: Everyone had a freedom to self-express. As bacchanalian as those photos look, frankly, it was just like a theatrical production. It was seriously creatively focused work. I think the beauty of it was creating a space for pure, spontaneous creative expression without boundaries. The way I shoot, nothing is ever posed. I'm not a photographer in the sense that I'm trying to achieve an image. It's more about creating an experience and just being a documentarian. Unfortunately, that session wasn't filmed; I started filming my sessions in 1975.

It's "Cold Gin" time again . . . Witness a heavily inebriated Paul Stanley at the *Hotter Than Hell* back cover photo shoot, Raleigh Studios, Hollywood, August 1974
Norman Seeff/www.normanseeff.com

KISS had this unique capacity to work with each other in terms of body language. They walked in and explored space, almost like dancers. KISS was doing a rock-and-roll ballet for the shoot where each of the individuals was playing a part. It was incredibly exciting. Once they realized it was an open space for exploration they just picked up and ran with it. The process of getting imagery out of them was effortless. They came in and they delivered.

PAUL STANLEY: Things did get a little out of hand, for me especially. The thought was, let's get loose and be part of what's going on. I started drinking to loosen up and it got a little too loose.

GENE SIMMONS: That session was one of the few times that I've seen Paul drunk. He was blitzed. The only thing that was missing was Rod Serling going [*imitating Rod Serling's voice*], "Witness Paul Stanley—entering the Twilight Zone."

PAUL STANLEY: I was so drunk that they had to lock me in a station wagon to keep me from hurting myself, and it took me a long time to figure out how to get out of the car [*laughs*].

GENE SIMMONS: After that photo shoot we were brought back to the Ramada Inn on Sunset Boulevard and for some strange reason I dove right into the swimming pool in my full outfit. That was a big mistake because the next day it shrank [*laughs*].

25

HIGH TIMES, HARD TIMES

Neil Bogart thought and dreamed big. It didn't matter that Casablanca was hemorrhaging money as a result of KISS's substantial touring expenditures and tepid record sales. Outfitting his promo team with a fleet of luxury cars and launching extravagant promotions, Bogart was living the high life, and he gleefully presented the image of a label flush with cash to the industry at large. Bogart was a gambler at heart, and he had rolled the dice by signing a band like KISS. His attraction to one-of-a-kind acts defined the ethos of Casablanca Records, and by the time the KISS machine was in high gear, the label had amassed an impressively eclectic and stylistically diverse roster of artists.

DON WASLEY (VICE PRESIDENT OF ARTIST DEVELOPMENT, CASABLANCA RECORDS): What Casablanca did was sign all the misfits, rejects, and left-of-center acts and brought them straight to the forefront, not the least of which was KISS.

JOYCE BOGART-TRABULUS: Neil was one of a kind, and he liked groups that were one of a kind. Think of all the acts on the label.

GARY MAJOR (MUSIC DIRECTOR, WKLO, LOUISVILLE, KENTUCKY):
They had an unusual roster of artists like KISS, Donna Summer, the Village People, Parliament, and the all-girl band Fanny.

PATTI QUATRO (LEAD GUITARIST, FANNY): Fanny signed to Casablanca in 1974. No one at any other label wanted to take a chance on signing an all-girl rock band, but Neil Bogart did. It was hard to get executives to see the big picture when they had such a small screen. They acted like we had a body that wouldn't quit and a brain that couldn't start. It was their vision or no vision. Neil was the opposite. He had huge vision. Neil and the people that worked at Casablanca were much more open-minded and that was reflected by the kind of acts he signed to the label, people like KISS, Donna Summer, Angel, and Saturday-morning TV stars the Hudson Brothers.

MARC NATHAN (REGIONAL PROMOTION DIRECTOR, CASABLANCA RECORDS): The commonality with all of these artists was that Casablanca was not a major label and it wasn't coming from a real cookie-cutter perspective. You had a label like Elektra which always delivered these heritage AOR [album-oriented rock] acts and you had Warner Brothers that had a lot of California acts. Casablanca was a haven for the renegades that might have been discarded by major labels, and KISS was leading the charge. Could you imagine another label making a priority out of a record with a group that wore crazy kabuki makeup?

DON WASLEY: Before I accepted the position at Casablanca I was really reluctant to do it because I was a music guy and I didn't get KISS. Once I accepted the job the first thing they had me do was fly to Salt Lake City to see KISS perform. That's when I jumped into the pool. This was not a band I was enamored with at all. Once I saw them I got it. If the music started to lag, every five minutes there'd be something that would galvanize you to the stage. It was Barnum and Bailey. It was literally the greatest show on earth. I saw this KISS infrastructure and how it worked and it blew me away how well-oiled the machine was. Sometimes they'd get into makeup before they went to a venue and they'd leave the venue with their makeup on and go back to the hotel. That's called a "runner." It was like one of those "Elvis has left the building" kind of things. There were still bombs going off onstage and they were gone [*laughs*].

GARY MAJOR: From a promotional standpoint they put their money where their mouth was. When a record company is trying to establish an artist they pull out all the stops and Casablanca was relentless in their quest to make KISS successful.

JOE SMITH: When I signed Casablanca I told Neil, "You've got to keep your costs under control. We're taking a major shot with you and we don't have millions to pour into your label." And Neil said, "Absolutely. I promise we'll keep the spending down" [*laughs*]. Well, it didn't work out that way. Neil was a big spender. He couldn't help himself. I remember going over to the Casablanca office one day and looked into the parking lot. I went upstairs and screamed, "It looks like Stuttgart [Germany] out there! There's only Mercedes and BMWs outside, when are we supposed to be saving money here?" We were spending a ton of money on Casablanca, way more than we were spending on our big artists like James Taylor, Van Morrison, and Neil Young.

JOYCE BOGART-TRABULUS: There was a gong in the office of one of the promotion guys that worked there and every time he would get a record added to radio by KISS or another act he'd ring the gong and everyone in the entire office knew we'd gotten another radio station to play KISS. There was an enormous amount of enthusiasm running through the office.

LARRY HARRIS: Casablanca was a true seventies record label. It was all of the things people associate with the music business in the seventies: the drugs, the sex. There was sex going on in the office during business hours. There was drug-taking going in the office, too. You could smell marijuana in the halls. There were heavier drugs too, like cocaine and our drug of choice, Quaaludes.

PAUL STANLEY: What I didn't like and didn't find myself wanting to be a part of was the incredible amount of drugs. If you didn't see the drugs you saw the effect. People were out of their mind. To me people didn't seem to be doing their jobs. Most people seemed to be crazy, wild, and unfocused. Look, it was an excessive time. It was the time of Studio 54 and incredible excess and sex, drugs, and rock and roll.

MARC NATHAN: It was a party atmosphere. It was young and energetic. People were all pulling for the cause and there was a lot of debauchery going on. There was a drug culture at all the labels. But with Casablanca being a little more free-wheeling and independent it was magnified. Casablanca lived up to its reputation all the time. I don't think you could walk down the halls of Columbia or Atlantic Records and see some of the things you might have seen at Casablanca; Neil was very much into the exhibition aspect of it. It would not surprise you to see a monkey walking down the hall delivering records to the executives. There was crazy stuff going on, but people worked hard at the label. If someone from Casablanca was representing the label at a radio station, at a concert, at an in-store, we were known to carry the party into our work atmosphere.

JOYCE BOGART-TRABULUS: Behind the mystique of Casablanca being a party label, there was a lot of hard work, too. You can't make a band like KISS happen unless you're working on it all of the time.

BUCK REINGOLD: Neil was the first person in the office and the last to leave. I loved working for him. I was his pitbull. I was his protector. And when he had a problem, I got it done. We broke our ass for him. Neil was one of the most innovative, hard-working, and hard-playing men. When he believed in something he'd go balls out on it and with KISS he gave it 100 percent.

JOYCE BOGART-TRABULUS: The people that worked for Neil were extremely devoted. Neil believed in everybody on his staff working as a team. If you were a secretary or mailroom guy and you had an idea, you came to him with it. And he listened. If it was good, he used it. When you talk to people today that worked at Casablanca, they remember it as being a slice of Camelot. It was fun, it was challenging, it was the most perfect place to work.

GENE SIMMONS: If we were on another label, the chances are we would have never gotten out of the gate to run the race, and that's because we were intrinsically a live band. New bands in those days needed singles and we didn't write singles and we weren't cutesy and your sister and your mom were scared of us. Casablanca didn't care. They believed.

And while the party never stopped, by the end of 1974 Casablanca was on shaky financial ground and Neil Bogart's dream of a successful record label was turning into a nightmare.

LARRY HARRIS: After the Warner Brothers deal went south, we were in dire straits.

GENE SIMMONS: Casablanca wasn't paying royalties on time because they didn't have money. Neil, bless him, kept borrowing money from all sorts of people just to stay afloat.

LARRY HARRIS: It got so precarious that Neil, who was a big gambler, had to go to Vegas once to get a line of credit. It was ten grand, which in those days was forty or fifty grand. He came back home with that money to take care of payroll and expenses.

KISS were starting to gain a foothold on the concert circuit as a result of their spectacular live show and grueling touring schedule, but sales of their two studio albums, KISS and Hotter Than Hell, *were below par, which didn't help the cash-strapped label.*

LARRY HARRIS: Even though KISS hadn't sold a ton of records, Casablanca believed they'd eventually break. When they performed in front of an audience, [the audience would] go crazy. The first album sold 100,000 on Warner Brothers, which wasn't terrible. The next two albums [*Hotter Than Hell* and *Dressed to Kill*] did a little bit

The album that almost bankrupted Casablanca Records, *Here's Johnny: Magic Moments from the Tonight Show* Ken Sharp Collection

better; they were still selling upwards of 150,000, which in those days was not bad. So we felt that the strength of their live show would eventually catapult them to a breakthrough.

Compounding the label's financial crisis was the misguided release of the double LP Here's Johnny: Magic Moments from the Tonight Show *in November '74, less than a month after* Hotter Than Hell *hit stores. The album featured the likes of Groucho Marx, Jack Benny, Lucille Ball, Judy Garland, Richard Nixon, Ike and Tina Turner, Lenny Bruce, Sammy Davis Jr., Aretha Franklin, and the Smothers Brothers. Because* The Tonight Show *with Johnny Carson was such an inveterate cultural institution, Bogart believed that a collection of its highlights would be a home run and infuse the rapidly dwindling Casablanca coffers with cash. He was wrong.*

NANCY SAIN: Johnny Carson was number one on television and Neil thought this album was a good idea, but I don't think anyone else at the label thought that way.

JOYCE BOGART-TRABULUS: Neil went to the independent and foreign distributors and said, "I'm going independent again and I need advances."

ERIC PAULSON: Amos and Danny Heilicher from Pickwick International advanced him a half a million dollars to get him through that stretch. People like Milt Salstone from M. S. Distributors in Chicago also helped provide some cash flow.

JOYCE BOGART-TRABULUS: He was positioning a record he could ship and sell a lot of copies and what Neil gave them for the advances was *Magic Moments from the Tonight Show*.

BUCK REINGOLD: We shipped three million dollars worth of albums and we got paid by the distributors in ninety days for those records.

NANCY SAIN: The album comprised the audio from *The Tonight Show*—comedy sketches, monologues, and interviews. The unspoken agreement was that Johnny would talk about the album on *The Tonight Show* and show the album cover. He did that a few times and then NBC objected and he was told he couldn't do it anymore. Once we found out that our main source of promotion was gone we were devastated because we knew the record was dead in the water. All the records were pressed—it was a very expensive record to press because it was a double album—and our distributors were sitting on them. The record came out and it was a bomb. Casablanca lost a ton of money.

LARRY HARRIS: But there's a silver lining to the story. Because everybody thought it was gonna be a big album we were able to get advances from all these independent record distributors around the country.

BUCK REINGOLD: If we didn't have that piece-of-shit album we never would have survived.

JOYCE BOGART-TRABULUS: It gave Neil the cash flow to help finance KISS and his other acts.

LARRY HARRIS: Without the Johnny Carson album the label wouldn't have been able to raise the money needed to stay in business. Depending on what size market they were in, we'd get $50,000 from one distributor, another $25,000 from another, as advances against future sales. So we'd supply them with Johnny Carson albums, KISS albums, T. Rex albums, and they'd in turn sell them to the record stores. We'd get money up front for the product we gave them which they assumed was gonna sell. We really shipped 750,000 units of the Johnny Carson album. But because of the way the record business was built in those days, for every ten albums you'd buy, you'd get two albums free. So instead of giving you a discount on the invoice, you got the product as a discount. So selling 750,000 albums plus giving two free copies with every ten copies, you're over a million. The joke in the industry was we shipped 750,000 and took back a million albums, which happens to be true. So we actually lost money on the Carson album but we didn't take back the albums quickly. We kept doing a new advertising campaign so we didn't have to return the albums and give that money back right away. So the Carson album kept us in business long enough to keep paying KISS's road tour expenses and keep the label alive. Even though the Carson album was not a success retail-wise, it was a success in keeping the doors open long enough for us to have a hit.

Today's bands customarily release an album every few years; KISS's recording output in the seventies was downright herculean by contrast. In 1974 alone, the group released not one but two studio albums, KISS *and* Hotter Than Hell.

LARRY HARRIS: Their contract called for an album every six months. Neil believed you had to have a constant product flow because that kept your name alive. You didn't want to wait two years between albums. Plus we also needed it for cash flow. Every new KISS album sold a hundred thousand copies up front, so we were able to get the cash and keep the label going.

PAUL $TANLEY: It was a challenge because there was a goal, and that was to have mass success. When an album didn't succeed we went back into the studio and made another one. It's just that simple.

GENE $IMMON$: From my perspective, that forced productivity wasn't a struggle for the band. We weren't aware of it being a strain on us having to come up with so much material and record so many albums in a short period of time. We just felt lucky to be given a chance to do what we were doing.

Photo shoot, Beacon Theatre, New York City, March 21, 1975

Performing before a sold-out crowd of 9,500 fans, KISS takes Long Beach by storm, Long Beach Auditorium, Long Beach, California, January 17, 1975

Bloodletting

Opening for Suzi Quatro and Blue Öyster Cult, KISS revs it up in the
Motor City, Michigan Palace, Detroit, April 13, 1974

Gotham warriors of rock, Kiel Auditorium, St. Louis, November 7, 1974

Hotter Than Hell back cover
photo shoot, Raleigh Studios,
Hollywood, August 1974

Bottoms up! Ace getting in
the mood, *Hotter Than Hell*
back cover photo shoot,
Raleigh Studios, Hollywood,
August 1974

Dressed to Kill album cover outtake, Twenty-third Street and Eighth Avenue,
New York City, October 26, 1974

KISS Catalog Ltd.

**Beacon Theatre, New York City,
March 21, 1975**

Bob Gruen/ www.bobgruen.com

**Subterranean subway terrors, *Creem* magazine
shoot, October 26, 1974**

Orpheum Theatre, Boston, May 11, 1975

Ron Pownall/www.RockRollPhoto.com

Ron Pownall/www.RockRollPhoto.com

**KISS serves as the middle act on a bill, sandwiched
between opening act Journey and headliner
Hunter-Ronson, Orpheum Theatre, Boston, May 11, 1975**

Backstage at Capitol Theatre, Passaic, New Jersey, October 4, 1975

KISS takes part in a horror-rific photo shoot. Pictured with the band is model Megan McCracken, replete with "Bride of Frankenstein" seared lighting bolts in her hair, Hempstead, New York, August 23, 1975

In one of the shows recorded for the band's *Alive!* album, KISS pulverizes Detroit Rock
City, Cobo Hall, Detroit, May 16, 1975

KISS video shoot for "Rock and Roll All Nite" and "C'mon & Love Me,"
Michigan Palace, Detroit, May 15, 1975

Photo shoot, Michigan Palace, Detroit, May 15, 1975

Scorching Michigan Palace, Detroit, May 15, 1975

Alternate *Alive!* front cover image, Michigan Palace, Detroit, May 15, 1975

Chip Dayton

Uncropped front cover for first KISS tour book

Wall of sound

Ace gearing up for the band's pivotal headlining appearance at
Detroit's Cobo Hall, May 16, 1975

Confetti storm, Providence Civic Center, Providence, Rhode Island,
December 29, 1975

Providence Civic Center, Providence, Rhode Island, December 29, 1975

Heavy metal masters, New York City, March 1975

26

HEAVY METAL MASTERS

In between writing songs and recording sessions, the band lived on the road, opening for the likes of Aerosmith, Argent, and Savoy Brown. Their mission was simple: to blow the minds—and ears—of unsuspecting audiences nationwide. Thanks to the unyielding support of their loyal fan base, Rush—like KISS—have enjoyed decades of success as a touring and recording act. In 1974 and 1975, Rush opened fifty-two shows for KISS, and the bands forged a strong friendship and a playful camaraderie.

PAUL STANLEY: I remember the first time Rush played with us and John Rutsey was still their drummer. They started with "Finding My Way," and this cool song starts and Geddy [Lee] lets out this yelp. We were like, "Yeah baby, this band's got the goods." In the beginning they were much more Zeppelin meets Humble Pie. Once Neil [Peart] joined, the band's sound really moved in a progressive rock direction.

GENE SIMMONS: We liked the band right away because they sounded like a Canadian Zeppelin. In those days they were trying to be Led Zeppelin and they did it pretty convincingly.

MICK CAMPISE: KISS and Rush were a great bill. Rush played with KISS on many shows in '74 and '75. We got along with them great. KISS hit it off with Rush better than any band. They grew up on the rock-and-roll circuit together.

ALEX LIFESON (GUITARIST, RUSH): We were both coming up at the same time and were both unknown bands basically and we really slogged it out together. We played a lot of shows and played a lot of consecutive nights. We drove like crazy. We did every gig we could at primarily small venues. There was a carnival aspect to our shows with them in the sense that we were all carnies on one big show.

GEDDY LEE (BASSIST/LEAD VOCALIST, RUSH): We did a lot of shows together. We met them when we opened a show for them in Canada—I think it was London, Ontario. It was one of our first gigs playing outside of the bar circuit. They were really nice to us and very friendly. When we went on tour in '74 and were scrounging for shows, KISS had a good memory of their experience with us and brought us out as their opening act. We played fairly small theaters all over America, which varied in size from a thousand capacity to a couple of thousand seats.

ALEX LIFESON: I think I watched every show. What they did for their audience, the amount of effort and preparation that they put into their shows, was impressive. They always gave 1,000 percent for every show. We respected them for that and we learned a lot from that, too. We were quite young and we were learning from other bands how to treat other musicians that were on your shows.

HOWARD UNGERLEIDER (RUSH TOUR MANAGER): Before we did shows with KISS we did about seventy shows opening for Aerosmith, and they treated us really awful. We never got a sound check. We weren't allowed to put our gear onstage until the doors opened. The PA system was turned down and limited so we could barely be heard in many of the places we played. KISS wasn't anything like that.

GEDDY LEE: KISS treated us really well and made sure we got a sound check. We worked with a lot of different bands and not all of them were accommodating in terms of giving us a sound check or stage restrictions. I think that came out of insecurity. KISS didn't feel like that. They gave us a fair shake as often as they could. When you had a show as powerful as theirs, they had confidence that whatever came in front of them they could handle.

HOWARD UNGERLEIDER: They were a breath of fresh air. They weren't threatened by Rush. A lot of other acts we played with were really freaked out by Rush because they were going down huge as an opening act. KISS didn't care if Rush got an encore or got the kids going. Gene appreciated it because it got the crowd even more pumped up for KISS.

GENE SIMMONS: I remember playing a show at Winterland in San Francisco [June 1, 1975], and the promoter, the Bill Graham organization, managed the Tubes. They insisted the bill be KISS, the Tubes, and Rush opening the show. When Rush got into their dressing room there was no food or drinks. Geddy came up to me and told us they were really hungry. So I immediately went to Bill Graham and told him in no uncertain terms, "Put some cold drinks in their dressing room and feed the band!" and they got fed. The guys in Rush came over and thanked us. Personally, we got along really well. We were always looking after them. It wasn't about ego. We had a very good relationship with them. We didn't play the heavies of being the headline act and telling them what they could or could not do. Back at the hotel when the chicks were there we'd invite them into the parties.

GEDDY LEE: We were very green, and KISS was a little ahead of us on the circuit building a following. The fact that we were so green and nervous and the fact they treated us so well made such an impression on us. Their road crew was so professional and such good people.

PETER "MOOSE" ORECKINTO: Rush were cool guys—fun, smart. They weren't punks and didn't have a mean bone in their body. We loved being around them. We'd help them load their gear and they'd help us load our gear. No fuckin' road crew does that.

MICK CAMPISE: Rush thought enough of the original KISS road crew that they thanked some of us on the back of their *Caress of Steel* album. They used our CB handles—at the time CB radios were really big; when you were on tour your truck had to have a CB radio, which enabled you to keep in contact with your crew. My CB handle was the Texas Heartbreaker, Moose was the Beast from the East, and Paul Chavarria was Chatterbox.

GEDDY LEE: We were both still trying to make a name for ourselves and we felt like comrades in arms. We learned a lot about putting on a show and the sense of professionalism they had back then. They worked really hard. You can say what you want about their music, that's a matter of personal taste. But there was no denying that they were one of the hardest-working bands out there and they made sure they gave people their money's worth, and we respected that a lot.

ALEX LIFESON: The key thing we learned from playing with KISS is always give 100 percent in a live show. Be the best you can be and give it your all every single night. We also learned from them the importance of visuals as well, which is part of being an entertainer.

GEDDY LEE: A lot of the groups we admired growing up were British progressive bands who always gave you something extra, something more than you expected in a live show, and KISS was that kind of a band. For us to see how their crew operated and watch them put on this big show night after night was an important learning experience. It was a great introduction to America for us to be as new and green as we were and to have a band that treated us so well and showed us a level of professionalism to put on the best show.

SKIP GILDERSLEEVE (RUSH ROADIE): Rush were influenced by the spectacle aspect of KISS's show. As soon as they could afford it they started using projection and all that. I feel a lion's share of that was from seeing what KISS was doing, where you have to give the kids more than just standing there and playing. In many ways KISS and

KISS and Rush backstage celebrating Ace Frehley's birthday, Mosque Theater,
Richmond, Virginia, April 27, 1975 Courtesy of Geddy Lee

Rush broke in the same way. In the beginning, they both built their
success on playing live because their records weren't selling as well.
GENE SIMMONS: They also learned politics from us. Meet the
promoter, meet the program director, collect phone numbers, send
people cards. They learned the importance of building a relationship
with the industry. We'd fly with the guys in Rush on the same
plane and Geddy and Alex would see me writing postcards to radio
program directors saying, "Thanks a lot and here's my address."
They found that peculiar. They said, "Do you know this guy?" And
I said, "I've never met him before but we're gonna be coming back
into town." And it was an *aha* moment. They understood that this
was a way to build goodwill in the music industry.

PAUL STANLEY: There are good guys in bands and there are great guys. Rush were great guys, fun to be around, no pretense. We seemed to share a sense of humor. Our backgrounds were similar. We shared a great bond with the whole band.

ALEX LIFESON: We hung out a lot. We'd go out to eat and hang out with each other. Gene and I used to correspond through the mail and I still have a few of those letters. There was a very heartfelt connection between both bands even though musically we were moving in two completely different directions. Their vision was looking at rock and

Gene Simmons, Rush's Geddy Lee, and Paul Stanley at the last show on the KISS/Rush tour, Civic Arena, San Diego, June 7, 1975 Terry Bert/www.terrybertimages.ifp3.com

roll as entertainment whereas we were looking to make *the* album and write *the* song. But despite all of those differences there was a real sense of unity in what we were doing and how we were doing it together. If there's affection towards us from their camp there's certainly lots of it from ours.

GEDDY LEE: During our last show with KISS in San Diego [June 7, 1975], KISS came out onstage in full makeup during the last song of our set and hit us with cream pies [*laughs*]. Their road crew joined in too.

ALEX LIFESON: We weren't expecting it. They had all their forces intact.

TERRANCE BERT (MUSIC PHOTOGRAPHER): Gene and Paul were rolling black marbles across the floor during Rush's set and the guys from Rush were trying really hard to avoid stepping on them and falling down. Soon things really got out of control.

MICK CAMPISE: Gene grabbed a cream pie and smashed Geddy in the face, taking him by surprise, just like the comedian Soupy Sales. Then the fight was on. We pelted Rush with cream pies, string cheese, and silly string.

ALEX LIFESON: We were covered in cream. Our instruments were covered in cream. It was a real mess [*laughs*].

GEDDY LEE: I was slipping all over the stage [*laughs*].

TERRANCE BERT: They really leveled Geddy especially. He was a real mess, caked with pies and shaving cream. I took some photos that night of the hijinks, including a great one of Geddy, who is covered head to toe and laughing hysterically while Gene and Paul are holding him up to keep him from falling down.

MARK "ZERO" STINNER: Poor Neil [Peart]. I was crouched behind him and before he knew it I slammed the pies in his face. His drums were covered with whipped cream and sounded like they were wet noodles.

ALEX LIFESON: I had to take my guitar apart afterwards to get all the crap out of the pickups.

Pie fight! Civic Arena, San Diego, June 7, 1975
Terry Bert/www.terrybertimages.ifp3.com

MICK CAMPISE: Then it was Rush's turn to get even.

HOWARD UNGERLEIDER: After KISS ambushed Rush, in between the set changes I put limburger cheese in all their fans. So when they put their fans on during their performance it just smelled awful [*laughs*]. It got really stinky [*laughs*].

PAUL STANLEY: We were very staunchly against the whole idea of having the audience bear the brunt of an inside joke but we really liked the guys in Rush.

MICK CAMPISE: Rush came out during KISS's set dressed in war paint like Indians, headbands, feathers, and started flinging pies at the band.

PAUL STANLEY: Geddy was wearing an Indian headdress and shooting rubber arrows at us trying to sabotage our show. We did things to each other that we never allowed other bands to do.

ALEX LIFESON: We got them back that same night but ours was just a little battle and theirs was like a war. They really annihilated us.

MICK CAMPISE: The stage was a real mess but it was a great way to end the tour.

HOWARD UNGERLEIDER: That night we had a wild end-of-tour party at a hotel called Little America Westgate. Three of the members of KISS—Peter, Paul, and Ace—Geddy, Alex, and Neil from Rush, myself, and a bunch of other people were in this room and things were getting a little bit out of control. We were drinking quite a bit. Alex from Rush was doing this routine as this character called "the Bag."

ALEX LIFESON: "The Bag" was a character that would come out in Gene and Ace's room after a show when they had a little bit of a crowd and we'd had a couple of drinks. "The Bag" was a character that took over the whole energy of the room [*laughs*]. I'd wear a paper laundry bag over my head that I drew a face on, and I wore it over a particularly gross costume which was just sweatpants with my arms tucked in the legs coming out the knees.

GEDDY LEE: Peter had a character which he used to bring out called "Monsieur Louie" [*laughs*]. He'd put on an ascot and draw a pencil-thin mustache on his face and speak in a French accent. We'd get tanked up either backstage or in our hotel rooms and goof off. Alex and Peter would do comedic riffing off of each other.

GENE SIMMONS: Alex would sit on Peter's lap and they'd do a puppet act and everyone around them would start laughing hysterically.

HOWARD UNGERLEIDER: Toward the end of the night, Peter, who was now a little bit out of his mind, picked up this large plant in a clay jar and went to the window and heaved it out. No one knew that below the balcony where we were standing was actually a glass roof atrium over the lobby [*laughs*]. And this plant crashed through this glass roof into the lobby, and luckily nobody was hurt.

GEDDY LEE: If memory serves me, it wasn't Peter but it was "Monsieur Louie" who threw the potted plant out the window [*laughs*].

Not your typical rock star, Gene Simmons freely admits he's never imbibed alcohol or taken drugs. But on one occasion, while on tour in the Motor City, he accidentally got an up-close-and-personal slice of the "high" life.

SKIP GILDERSLEEVE: We had a party for KISS after one of their shows with Rush at the Michigan Palace in the balcony lobby [December 20, 1974, Peter Criss's twenty-ninth birthday]. The caterers were hippies from the old Grande Ballroom days, a famous venue that hosted shows by the likes of the Who and Cream.

GENE SIMMONS: While everyone's smoking and drinking, this good-looking girl walks by and someone's nudging me, going, "Look at her tits!" and I'm going, "No, no, no, look at those brownies."

JAAN UHELSZKI: I was at the party and talking to Gene and Paul. Gene has a notorious sweet tooth and was hovering over a plate of brownies. I said to him, "I wouldn't eat those, they're hash brownies." He said, "How would you know that?" And I said, "I live here, I know these people." And he goes, "No, I'm gonna have one."

GENE SIMMONS: And they were massive. They were as big as your fist.

JAAN UHELSZKI: I remember him eating a big fat one, like a two-by-two-inch brownie [*laughs*].

GENE SIMMONS: I wound up eating six of them.

PAUL STANLEY: I remember Gene saying to me, "My head is so small and my arms are so long [*laughs*]. And I said, "You know what, enjoy it."

GENE SIMMONS: It felt like my head shrank to the size of a peanut, like when you let the air out of a balloon. I became paranoid and thought everybody was looking at me. I remember screaming into Jaan's ear thinking she couldn't hear me because my head was really small and that also meant my vocal chords, too. I said, "Let's get out of here, they're laughing at me."

RICK MUNROE: After the party a bunch of us decided to go out to White Castle to get something to eat and Gene said, "Can I come with you?" He was a sight to behold in the real world. He had really long hair, he was wearing high-heel boots, and had on a tarantula belt buckle. I knew the brownies were loaded and that the crew had eaten some but I didn't know Gene had eaten them [*laughs*]. So we walk into this White Castle and we're looking around for a seat.

GENE SIMMONS: I was really thirsty and I remember screaming, "Get me a glass of cold milk!" I was very self-conscious and thought everybody was looking at me because I had a little pinhead. But in reality they were all looking at me because I was screaming.

RICK MUNROE: I said, "Did you eat some of those brownies?" And he said, "Yeah, I did," and then I realized what was going on, he was starting to get high. It was just the paranoia of being stoned. And then he told me, "I feel so stupid." He didn't know why he was feeling stupid and why he was feeling numb [*laughs*]. We laughed and said, "If you ate those brownies you're stoned." That didn't make him happy. But we ate and he was shoving burgers into his face. We made him understand that it wasn't like he was trippin'. He was just a little numb [*laughs*].

GENE SIMMONS: I'd never been high before. After we ate, we went back to the hotel and Jaan helped walk me to my room. My arms were swinging like that old "Keep on Truckin'" ad and it seemed they got huge the farther away they got and the closer my arms got to me the smaller they appeared. And my shoes seemed enormous, like the size of a monster truck. It was a really strange feeling. I remember finally getting to my room and I took out the key and it looked like a sledgehammer, but somehow I managed to get inside.

JAAN UHELSZKI: That was the first and only time he ever got high—so his sweet tooth took him down.

New York stand-up comedian Kenny Kramer (the inspiration for the Seinfeld character Cosmo Kramer) was the unlikely opening act for KISS on December 23, 1974, at the Paramount Theater in Wilkes-Barre, Pennsylvania. It would prove to be the gig of a lifetime—but for all the wrong reasons.

KENNY KRAMER (COMEDIAN): I was working with an agency called ATI who also handled KISS as well. They were sending me out on gigs all over the place. Rock-and-roll audiences weren't really used to a comic as an opening act. When I opened for KISS they were still playing small venues. There was supposed to be two shows that night, and KISS were hours late. I went on at eight o'clock, did my act, and came off. More time passes and now it's nine o'clock, nine thirty, and the audience is really getting restless. They're going crazy and screaming, "KISS! KISS! KISS!" and stomping their feet. The promoter is starting to get worried because KISS is nowhere in sight, so he says to me, "Kenny, go out there and calm them down" [*laughs*].

So I went out and the crowd wasn't happy. They knew as long as I was out there it was delaying KISS getting on the stage. I tried to hold a talent contest, and brought people up from the audience to tell their favorite joke. That worked okay for the first ten or fifteen minutes but when they realized KISS might not even play it started to get ugly. They were screaming and booing and throwing paper and

shit at me. I said, "If you're gonna throw something, throw money."
All of a sudden I started getting pelted with quarters and half dollars
and it really hurt. There must have been a hundred bucks onstage by
the time I got off. With a second show scheduled, there was already
an audience gathering outside in the dead of winter and the first
show hadn't even started yet with KISS. Finally KISS showed up at
around ten or eleven o'clock and still had to put on their makeup and
costumes. The band finally went on close to midnight, did the show,
and the audience went crazy. They saved the day but the second
show was canceled.

*KISS's fans were as over the top in their enthusiasm for the band as
KISS was over the top onstage. And sometimes that over-the-top enthusiasm
got quite personal—and a bit out of hand.*

MIKE McGURL: The fans could get out of control. We were staying
on the fourteenth floor at a Holiday Inn in Jacksonville, Florida. It
was one of those circular towers. I'm sitting in my hotel room after
the show and doing my expense report. It was about two or three in
the morning and I had a whole bunch of money on the table that I
was counting because back in those days everybody paid you in cash.
The hotel had a balcony that overlooked the bay and I had the doors
open and a breeze was blowing in. All of a sudden I hear grunting
and movement outside and I go, "What the fuck?" I stand up and go
toward the balcony and all of a sudden this girl walks into my room.
She was fifteen or sixteen. I'm starting to panic because I'm sitting
there with forty or fifty thousand dollars on the coffee table. I'm like,
"Who the hell are you?" And she goes, "Is this Gene's room?" [*laughs*].
And I went, "No, it's not Gene's room." She knew the band were
staying on the fourteenth floor and had climbed up the outside of the
building from the sixth or seventh floor where she had a room [*laughs*].

27

BEHIND THE CURTAIN

*L*ife on the road is far from glamorous. Beyond the brutal travel schedule, the excruciating boredom of being imprisoned in a hotel room—albeit with a comfortable bed and room service—grows old pretty quickly. And a rock star who's bored can be a dangerous thing.

ACE FREHLEY: I was sitting in my room at the Edgewater Hotel in Seattle with one of our road crew, John Harte. In the gift shop they sell these hooks, shrimp you can put on them, and fishing line. You can fish out your window. So I called up John Harte and said, "Do you want to watch the ball game together? Bring up a six-pack of beer." So he said, "All right, Curly." Right before he came I put three shrimp on this triple hook and threw it out about fifty feet. It was a one-hundred-foot line. I didn't want to hold it so I tied it on the chandelier above us where we were sitting. If the chandelier moved, we knew we had a bite. So me and John are having a beer and watching the ball game and the chandelier moved a little. I said, "Is that an earthquake or a bite?" [*laughs*]. And he goes, "I think you're getting a bite." Then it fucking moved dramatically. So I quickly unhooked it and wrapped it around my hand three or four times and all of a sudden I was tugging on this fucking thing and it was beating me. So I said, "John, I can't handle this," and he grabbed it out of my hand. And John couldn't bring it in. Then we looked out the window and we saw what looked like a fucking great white [*laughs*]. That thing must have been twelve, fifteen feet long. So we just let it go. There was no way we would be able to pull it up. Those fucking things weigh a ton. I thought I was gonna catch a twelve-inch fish and I end up catching a fucking great white [*laughs*].

DON WASLEY: Sometimes after a show, in the hotel Ace and Peter would get together and literally have kind of a seventies version of *American Idol*. These groupies would line up and come in and sing and dance. Who knows what the lucky winner of the evening won? [*laughs*]. Ace would be enjoying a glass of champagne, laughing hysterically through the whole thing while these nervous girls would sing in the hotel room.

BUCK DHARMA: After one show with KISS there was a big party in a high-rise Hilton hotel in Jacksonville, Florida, and things started getting out of hand. Pieces of furniture started going out the sliding doors on the balcony and landing five flights down into the pool, which had to be drained. They gallantly picked up a major part of the tab for that stunt.

MIKE McGURL: Ace drank a lot. He was a big beer drinker. Heineken was all he ever drank. Ace was always out of control, even when he was straight [*laughs*]. He believed he was a space alien. You'd watch Ace walk down a hallway and he'd swerve from one wall to the other. You'd think he was smashed but he wasn't, he was perfectly straight. You'd go up to him, "Ace, what's wrong with you? You can't walk a straight line." Then he'd say, "I can't get used to the gravity on this planet, Curly" and then laugh hysterically. There were many times Ace was bombed and he'd still play brilliantly. He could be totally out of it. But once he got on that stage with a guitar in his hands he was brilliant. He never had a bad show as far as I can remember.

PAUL /TANLEY: Ace had a well-documented problem early on with alcohol and it became more of a worry for us. There was a time where Ace managed to do shows sober and then get wasted after the show. Ultimately, the line got crossed and then it became a real problem. Same in the studio. The idea of having to work quickly to get a solo done before he would get wasted was not the optimal way to work. That escalated over time. The more famous we became the worse it got. When the race started Ace came out of the gate quickly but his pace didn't stay. By '75, there was a sense that his free spirit didn't necessarily include the discipline to apply himself to his craft. At one point I remember being a little dissatisfied with Ace, and probably his personality, and his lack of dedication and perseverance, was overshadowing my opinion of his playing and his ability to progress. But there's no arguing that he was a great player. I remember being in my room at the Hyatt on Sunset in LA and I heard somebody playing terrific guitar, someone playing with the feel and point of view of all the music that I loved. I remember very clearly thinking to myself, "That's the kind of guitar player we should have." I literally looked over the balcony and it was Ace.

Bill Aucoin had issued a dictate: no photos of the band without their makeup. Despite tight security measures, a press photographer or enterprising fan would occasionally capture a member of the band au naturel.

JOYCE BOGART-TRABULU/: Bill was really adamant about the band not being photographed without makeup. It was a way to build mystique around the band.

PAUL /TANLEY: That was Bill's idea, and it was brilliant. With the way we looked without makeup we couldn't compete with our iconic makeup images. We couldn't compete, we could only dilute it.

GENE /IMMON/: He said, "I don't want you guys to ever be seen without your makeup." Bill was so enamored and blown away by how far we were able to take the concept by itself that he kept talking in movie terms. The old movie stars like Marilyn Monroe and Marlene Dietrich insisted in their contracts that they could never be seen without their makeup or hair fully done. Movie stars had glamour. The ones who survived the test of time and became iconic were stars who kept their image consistent.

FRITZ POSTLETHWAITE (KISS'S ONSTAGE AUDIO ENGINEER): Unlike other famous people, they couldn't show their faces. This was a unique situation. There is not another star I can think of that could not be seen in public. Whether we were having lunch in a corner restaurant in New York or trying to get into a movie theater, we had to be on constant alert, like the Secret Service. In airports, truck stops, hotel lobbies, we were all on the lookout for photographers.

MIKE McGURL: There were some close calls with people taking photos of the band without makeup. But for the most part if someone grabbed a photo of a band member without makeup the security guys would politely say, "We can't allow photos of the band," and they'd literally take the camera from them, rip out the film, and give them ten, fifteen, twenty bucks.

DON WASLEY: We'd do radio interviews and they'd cover up their faces so no one could take a picture of them without makeup. It gave them this mystique that no other act had. There were a lot of close calls. I can't tell you how many times I saw bodyguards rip cameras out of people's hands or pull film out of cameras.

PAUL STANLEY: One of our guys went to jail over it and we had to bail him out for taking film out of someone's camera. I also think that the press played along with it. In some ways the press realized they got more mileage out of us not being seen than bursting the bubble.

RICK STUART (KISS'S DIRECTOR OF SECURITY): The first time photos of the band without makeup were ever published was in Gothenburg, Sweden. The band did a press conference there without makeup and no photographers were present. The next day I got up pretty early and there was a newspaper under my door. I couldn't understand what it said but there were photos of the band without makeup on the front cover of the newspaper. Obviously, someone shot them with a James Bond–type of spy camera, and although the photos weren't that clear, that kept us on high alert. It was always a challenge to keep them from being photographed without makeup.

SAM RICCARDO (PROMOTIONS MANAGER, RECORD MUSEUM): I went to see KISS at Convention Hall in Wildwood, New Jersey [July 23, 1975], one of the shows they recorded for *Alive!* I made sure to show up early so I could get up front for the show. I heard a roadie saying Gene was out front. Then I saw this big gangly guy with long reddish-brown hair sitting by himself on the Jersey boardwalk, drinking a Coke and checking out the ladies. I was freaking out and knew that it had to be Gene. So I grabbed my little Bell & Howell movie camera and starting shooting. Somehow he saw me and started walking toward me. I thought I was gonna have an exclusive for *KISSer* [the first KISS fanzine]—a member of KISS without makeup—and now I didn't know what was gonna happen. I could have run away but something made me stay. Gene came over and was very polite; first thing he said was "How much was the film?" I said, "Five bucks." He pulled a $5 bill out of his wallet—which I still have to this day—and said, "Inside you can take all the film you want but don't try that again," and he took the film and walked away. So I didn't have an exclusive for *KISSer* but I'd met a member of KISS and that was good enough for me.

MICK BOX: In those days you used to fly everywhere. When we arrived at airports the buzz of media trying to get pictures of the band without makeup was incredible. They'd put on masks or scarves to try to shield their faces. What a great publicity stunt that was because it created such a buzz.

DAVE LUCAS: Back in 1974 they'd be escorted backstage and we weren't allowed to go in the dressing room. From the concert promoters to the fans, their road crew was very protective of their identity and protected the band from interacting with anyone, which was a way to keep the mystique going at all levels.

JAY "HOT SAM" BARTH: Ace liked the anonymity it afforded him. I remember him telling me, "When I get home, I can walk around and nobody bothers me because I'm not wearing makeup. I can get on the subway with a six-pack and nobody knows who the fuck I am" [*laughs*].

JAAN UHELSZKI: I was on the road with KISS and some kid came up to the band and singled out Gene and said, "You're Gene?" KISS was never photographed at the time without their makeup. Gene said, "How do you know?" And he goes, "I just had a feeling." Gene really wanted to know how he knew so he quizzed him in a really sweet way. It really touched my heart because during the time they'd say, "We're nothing without our fans," and they really meant it. So the kid said, "I've got something for you" and pulls out this little live chameleon that they used to sell in dime stores. You could see in his eyes that Gene was really touched by the gift and he took it back to the hotel and was petting the little chameleon all the way. That is not a euphemism.

DON WASLEY: We were in New Orleans and the band and I went to a big media dinner. We started hearing stories from some of the radio guys that this renowned Mafia don owned the restaurant. The son of this Mafia kingpin asked if he could get a picture taken with the band without makeup and they said no. Then this Mafia kingpin comes over and says, "Jeez, you told my son you wouldn't take a picture with him. I'd really appreciate it if you let him take a picture with you." Everyone was like [*laughing nervously*], "Bring him over!" I think it was the first picture taken of the band without makeup with a fan. Let's just say, it was an offer they couldn't refuse.

POWER PLAY

By November 1974, KISS had gained a reputation as one of the hottest new acts on the concert circuit. But in the midst of the band's Hotter Than Hell *tour, they were rocked by the news that their label was having yet another financial emergency and needed another album pronto to infuse the coffers. At the same time, a major power play was unfolding between the group, producers Kenny Kerner and Richie Wise, and Casablanca Records.*

LARRY HARRIS: We hadn't paid KISS any royalties since day one. Aucoin was putting a lot of money on his American Express card to finance a tour, and the credit card company was chasing him around the country to get paid. The label was in hock putting them on the road. We felt we'd spent plenty of money on them. We thought, "The hell with royalties, we don't have the money to pay them. Let's just try to make them bigger and bigger." But it got to the point where the band felt they were selling enough albums that they should be receiving some kind of royalties.

JEFF FRANKLIN: KISS was so far in the red there was nothing to get. There was so much money spent on them, where did they expect royalties to come from? We poured a ton of money into the label and KISS. Neil had mortgaged his house and I was in it for a half a million, million dollars. Our cards were on the table. Neil would call me and say, "Do you have a hundred grand?" I said, "For what?" He said, "They need it." I said, "I haven't got it but I'll get it for you in a week."

RICHIE WISE: The band were working so hard and making it happen on the concert side, which they didn't think had anything to do with the record company. And they felt the label was dropping the ball on the record side. From my perspective, Casablanca didn't know how to break a rock band like Warner Brothers or Atlantic [did].

JEFF FRANKLIN: Without Casablanca or ATI, KISS wouldn't have made it, and that's not ego. I've done a ton of record deals and represented a lot of superstars. No record company would have believed in them like us. Everyone else thought KISS was absolutely absurd. CBS thought it was absurd, RCA thought it was absurd. They felt KISS wasn't music, it was the circus. I don't believe any record company would have done what Neil did.

NEIL BOGART: Sure it was tough to try to establish our company and break a new group at the same time. But we believed in KISS, so we just crossed our fingers and hoped the money would hold out.

KENNY KERNER: Bill Aucoin and Joyce Biawitz were managing KISS, and at the same time she was comanaging KISS she was dating Neil Bogart, which presented an immediate major conflict. Gearing up for the next KISS album, the band were still being produced by Kerner and Wise and we were all on good terms. Everyone was dissatisfied with how Casablanca was promoting the albums so Bill secretly put out some feelers and met with various labels. One of the major labels [Atlantic Records] made a serious offer. We had a meeting at my apartment—the four guys were there, Bill, Joyce, and Richie and I. Bill discussed what was going on and said we could leave the label and take this offer on the table. He said this new label really believed in the potential of the band.

Nobody was happy with how things were going and they were open to the possibility of going with another label. So we broke up the meeting and Joyce went straight to Neil and told him about this meeting and that the band was thinking of leaving his label. So Neil fired Richie and I from doing the next KISS album. *Dressed to Kill* was produced by Neil Bogart for the simple reason that he wanted to win back the group. He wanted to pull them away from Bill Aucoin and pull them away from Kerner and Wise. It was easy to pull them away from us because we worked on a contract from album to album.

PAUL STANLEY: I don't believe it had to do with politics between him and Bill. He wasn't trying to take the band away from us and we would never go.

LARRY HARRIS: From my perspective, Neil chose to produce *Dressed to Kill* so he could save money and not have to pay a producer forty or fifty grand.

JOYCE BOGART-TRABULUS: Of course he wanted to save money. Neil had sunk so much money into the band from day one and they hadn't delivered any hits. He was taking matters into his own hands. There was definitely friction over Neil producing *Dressed to Kill*. But Neil knew what would work on radio and what an audience would like. He wanted to get them on the radio. He was like, "Let me get in there and make some hits!"

With little time to prepare new material—their last studio album had been released just a few months prior—in January 1975 KISS found themselves back in the Big Apple, holed up in Electric Lady Studios to record their third studio album, Dressed to Kill, *with Casablanca Records president Neil Bogart in the producer's chair.*

PAUL STANLEY: We were out on the *Hotter Than Hell* tour and playing the Santa Monica Civic Auditorium with Jo Jo Gunne.

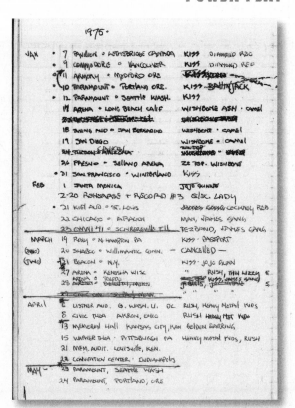

Gene Simmons's handwritten 1975 tour ledger Courtesy of Mark Anthony

Neil came backstage and said, "The album's tanked, I'm pulling the plug on the tour, and you need to go back to New York. We need another album." Our albums had a tendency to run their course very quickly. They'd sell and then they'd sputter out. We gulped and said, "How can we do another album when we don't have any songs?" We were short of material. In the beginning we were releasing albums every six months. Back then it wasn't uncommon for bands to do two albums a year. We certainly saw that as the plan until we succeeded. It was always with the goal in mind that if that album didn't succeed, how about this one?

We were nowhere near ready to do an album so it was write as you go. We wrote the songs for *Dressed to Kill* in the studio. Gene and I would write them in the morning and then Ace and Peter would show up and we'd say, "Today's song is called 'Rock and Roll

Orpheum Theatre, Boston, May 11, 1975 Ron Pownall/RockRollPhoto.com

All Nite,'" or "Today's song is called 'Room Service.'" Many of the songs on that album were pretty much created on the spot.

GENE SIMMONS: We weren't selling records. We were barely getting by. I didn't get a chance to do much writing because we were constantly touring. Some of the songs that wound up on it were leftovers—"She" and "Love Her All I Can" went back to the Wicked Lester days. I was the one who pushed us to record the two Wicked Lester songs. I felt they were good songs and belonged on a KISS record because they were based on riffs.

Throughout the seventies, when discussing their pre-KISS band
Wicked Lester in interviews, Gene and Paul would refrain from
revealing the name of the group, fearful that Epic Records would
realize what they had in their vaults and release it to earn a quick
buck. And it almost happened.

RON JOHNSEN: At some point after KISS became widely known,
someone at CBS recognized that they had some early recordings
done by Paul and Gene that were never released. I was called one
day by CBS. They told me they wanted to put out the Wicked Lester
album and wanted to see if I would remix them to make them more
contemporary sounding than they were originally. This was in
1977. All the tapes that were mastered at Electric Lady were sent
to the label and I went back in and remixed them. Casablanca got
word that Epic was working on these tapes. Everybody freaked
out—the band, their label, and their management. KISS certainly
didn't want this record to come out at that time in their career.
The sound of that record was much poppier than the hard rock
they were doing, and it lacked a strong direction. It's like having
a model that's doing real well and all of a sudden somebody
releases some pornographic photos of her. So somewhere along
the line Neil Bogart made arrangements with Epic, bought the
masters, and killed its release.

GENE SIMMONS: *Dressed to Kill* was certainly the record where we
flew by the seat of our pants. On the first two records we basically
reproduced what we did live. Neil Bogart had come down and taken a
personal interest in the band. He was probably our biggest supporter.
He told us he wanted to produce the record. He said, "Look, I have
a point of view of what you should be doing and I have to be there

KISS with Casablanca Records president and *Dressed to Kill* producer Neil Bogart inside Electric Lady Studios, New York City, 1975 Bob Gruen/www.bobgruen.com

to make sure you're gonna do it." We convinced Neil that we should do it together because we were a little afraid that Neil would take us down to what he did best, which was disco.

PAUL STANLEY: Neil made a strong suggestion bordering on insistence that he would produce the album. He wanted to make the album quickly and do it for less money. Neil's function was to try and stop us from doing too many takes [*laughs*]. He really wanted to move things along. I remember being in the studio with him and literally we'd do a take and he'd go, "That's fine, that's good enough." And I'd be like, "I'm not so sure, I think we should do it again." Now whether he was right or wrong I can't say but he wanted to produce the album. I don't really know what he contributed because the songs were what they were and the instrumentation is pretty simple. Perhaps he kept us from getting too involved in the minutiae.

GENE SIMMONS: In terms of producing, Neil was more of a cheerleader. He talked about concept all the time, not sonically or the arrangements, so he was helpful in that way. Not musically but conceptually. But what he did know was that he wanted to capture more of what he saw live than what our records became in the studio. And again, we didn't take a lot of time with sounds. Everything just went down fast.

PAUL STANLEY: I remember us trying to make an album that had a little more texture to it. So we mixed acoustic guitars into the tracks to give the guitars more definition. BTO [Bachman-Turner Overdrive] had some songs which had very chimey-sounding guitars ringing through so we decided to use that approach on "Anything for My Baby" and "C'mon and Love Me." For that album, Ace was using an amp inside a cardboard box [to achieve a very punchy sound] and he'd taken a Sharpie and drew designs on it and it said "amp" on it [*laughs*].

A lot of people love *Dressed to Kill* and pick it as their favorite KISS album. I always thought that sonically what we were about always eluded us. I was always desperately trying to get the sound that I heard in my head onto a record and I didn't know how to do it. We didn't have the ability in technique and technology and the people we were working with were not up to the task. That album lacked the sonics that would make it world class. Funnily enough that's probably part of what makes it KISS: the distinction it had was that [*laughing*] it didn't sound like a lot of other bands.

Sessions concluded in late February, and the album was rushed into release on March 19, 1975. It peaked at #32 on the Billboard *charts. Most notably, the album included the band's quintessential party anthem, "Rock and Roll All Nite."*

RICK MUNROE: Neil said, "I need the sound of a crowd on this," so he called everybody who was there into the recording studio and had us clap and sing the chorus.

electric lady studios
52 west 8 street
new york city ny 10011
212 777-0150

CLIENT	Casablanca Records	DATE Feb.12,1975 Wednesday	INVOICE Nº 16629		
	1112 North Sherbourne Los Angeles, California	PROD. Neil Bogart	W.O. No. J6431		
		STUDIO	BOOKED	ACTUAL	
		B	AM 4:00 PM	4:00	A P
ARTIST	Kiss	TIME START			
P.O.#		ENG. DW GL	AM 12:30 PM		A P
		TIME STOP			

DESCRIPTION		UNIT PRICE	AMOUNT
8 1/2 Hours	16 Tk. Recordg	95.00	807.50
2 Reels	2" Tape	95.00	190.00
	8% Tax on tape		15.20
Song Titles: I Wanna Rock n Roll Room Service			
	RECEIVED F 9 19 1975 RECORDS		
		TOTAL	1012.70

ORIGINAL

Electric Lady Studios recording paperwork for *Dressed to Kill* album, February 12, 1975 Ken Sharp Collection

PAUL STANLEY: We brought all our friends into the studio to sing backgrounds on it—friends, girlfriends, sisters, brothers—anybody.

EDDIE SOLAN: The band wanted to create a party atmosphere on the song so they roped in a bunch of people to sing on it. So me, Lydia Criss, Neil Bogart, and some roadies sang on the choruses.

JOYCE BOGART-TRABULUS: Neil and I sang and clapped on it along with Neil's kids—Tim, Jill, and Brad.

MIKE McGURL: We were called in not so much to sing but to provide drunken hooting and hollering [*laughs*]. They wanted something in the background that sounded like people were having a good time.

RICK MUNROE: After we were done I remember Neil said, "That's still not enough people," so he layered and layered it until it sounded like a big crowd.

PAUL CHAVARRIA: All of us in the road crew wore leather jackets. On that song, they put microphones up to our leather jackets and recorded the sound of our zippers going up and down—[*imitates sound*] "zip, zip, zip"—and that's on the chorus [*laughs*].

DRESSED TO KILL: A VISIT TO THE STUDIO

BINKY PHILIPS: One day I got a call from my old high school buddy, Paul Stanley. "Hey, Binky, ya wanna come down to a session at Electric Lady?" Paul was in and out of town all the time, constantly on the road, but I heard from him two or three times a month, always filling me in on the latest triumph or moments of road craziness. Around Thanksgiving he'd told me that he'd be in town for a while recording the next LP but that he might be too crazed to see me before their next foray into the wilds of America. So this invite was unexpected.

"Wow, cool, Paul. I've never been in Electric Lady and I'd love to hear what you've got so far."

"Oh, fuck, we're still recording. But I want you to see this. Come down tomorrow afternoon. I think Ace'll be doing some solos."

The next day was a very gloomy, overcast day but I was psyched. I'd passed Electric Lady on Eighth Street over a hundred times over the years. It was always a little thrill just to walk by, and here I was about to attend a KISS session there. I rang the bell, spoke into the intercom, and was buzzed in. Jimi Hendrix had only been dead a few years, and for me the vibe in the joint was still heavy.

I don't recall which room KISS was recording in, but I'm certain it was the smallest and cheapest. My band, the Planets, had already done a few demos for labels and we'd been in nicer, bigger rooms. The recording/mixing console took up almost half the control room. The ceiling was really low—maybe not even eight feet. Claustrophobic! The place was a mess: empty food containers, half-empty food containers, magazines, scattered packs of guitar strings—junk everywhere. It was obvious the band was living in this room eighteen to twenty hours a day. It was like a dorm room stuffed with equipment and four very individual, headstrong hooligans. Given that this room, like all of the studios at Electric Lady, was underground, I felt I'd entered some odd music dungeon. It didn't smell bad—maybe old French fries—but the air was seriously stale and getting staler.

Peter was lounging and kibitzing from the far end of the console, Gene was sitting next to the engineer, very intense, Paul was running back and forth between the control room and studio, talking over guitar parts and tone with Ace, who was wearing headphones with a Les Paul strapped on and plugged into a Marshall half-stack.

All four KISS-ers gave me a big silly hello. The name "Binky" lends itself to dopey rhymes, and by now, I was well known amongst the others, not just [as] Paul's pal.

The general vibe was crackling. Here were four guys who'd gotten so lucky; they were recording their *third* album. Their notoriety had not yet translated into dollars—Paul had filled me in on their almost shockingly bad financial situation—so there was a slight air of grim determination along with dazzled happiness that they were "living the dream." Gene and Paul were drug-free but it was like they had both snorted crystal meth. They were just churning with "let's do this" energy and focus in this tiny space.

It was very obvious that Neil Bogart was not really producing this record: the band was. For almost the entire forty-five minutes I was there, Neil was on the phone, having some kind of conference-call meeting about another Casablanca artist while all four members of KISS and the two engineers were just zooming along without any input from

Mr. Bogart beyond, "Sounds good!" He'd sunk a ton of money into KISS so maybe he was just there to make sure the boys worked.

Anyway, whatever happened, the band was in the enviable position of having no one telling them what to do, but that also meant no one else to blame if this third album faltered, at least amongst themselves.

It was clear to me within minutes I was a mere fly on the wall. I have a feeling Paul had invited me down with the intention of letting me hear some rough mixes of the almost-finished tracks. But reality had intruded and they were still doing Ace's solos and would be for several hours. "Sorry, Binky."

I seem to recall they were working on Paul's "Love Her All I Can," a truly fun track that Paul cheerfully admitted he'd swiped from "Open My Eyes" by Todd Rundgren's Nazz. And I only heard it in ten- to twenty-second chunks while the engineer was tweaking the EQ or something. But it sounded live-in-the-studio hot and more urgent than anything on their first two albums. And the chords in the hook were twisted and original.

If you've ever been involved in a recording, you know it can be exhilarating work capped by proud accomplishment. But you also know that if you're just hanging out it can get pretty damn tedious pretty damn fast.

Food arrived just as Ace was gonna crank out a take. Dang! Everything stopped, and as everyone in the room started tearing off lids and wrappers, I said my "Wow, sounds great" and "See ya"s and split, frankly happy to get some fresh air and natural light.

To this day, *Dressed to Kill*, the one album the band produced themselves, with some of their career-best songwriting, has a warm place in my heart, and I suspect it does with the band, too.

Luck, timing, and fate all play a role in the trajectory of a rock-and-roll band, and sometimes a happy accident results in unexpected brilliance. Case in point: the circumstances behind the cover of the band's third studio album, Dressed to Kill.

JAAN UHELSZKI: I remember going up to Gene after one of their shows at the Michigan Palace and telling him I had a great idea for a story. I said, "I'd like to do a comic strip on KISS," and he agreed that it was a good idea. They weren't my first high-concept story for *Creem*. I did a BTO diet guide for *Creem* [*laughs*], but the fact that they went along with one of my wacky ideas just thrilled me.

BOB GRUEN: I was working for *Creem* and they came up with the idea of a KISS photo novella, which was a comic book–type story in photographs. In the story, KISS starts off as mild-mannered reporters in their secret identity wearing suits and ties. They're in the subway station reading the newspaper getting ready to go to work and they read that there's going to be a concert by John Cleveland, which was *Creem*'s play on an artist like John Denver but subtly disguised. *Creem* had that kind of sense of humor. KISS was outraged that mediocrity was so widespread and they decide they had to save the world with rock and roll. They went into a phone booth, pulled off their clothes, and emerged as KISS. They went around town putting up posters for this phony concert by John Cleveland, and when all the people show up KISS comes out and saves the world with rock and roll. For this great service that they've done they receive an award and get medals pinned on them, and then they have an orgy. That was a staged photo taken backstage after one of their shows at the Capitol Theater in Passaic, New Jersey. I was watching the audience while they were playing to see where they were cheering the most. I told some girls, "I need some of you to be in a picture hugging and kissing the band," and I promised I could take them backstage. So I brought four or five girls backstage. The girl with Peter was Lydia, his wife at the time, and the girl with Gene was his girlfriend of several years.

Beacon Theatre, New York City, March 21, 1975 Courtesy of Brad Estra

While we were together shooting, I had KISS stop for some group photos on the sidewalk at the southwest corner of Twenty-third Street and Eighth Avenue dressed in the suits. They liked the picture so much that they decided to call the album *Dressed to Kill* and use that image on the cover. I think it's a great image. It strikes people as very unusual and funny. It's very rare to see KISS wearing anything but their costumes, so this humanized them in a way. On the album cover you can see Gene wearing my ex-wife's clogs [*laughs*], and the band also used some of my ties, including the yellow one Gene's wearing. They also borrowed one of my suits as well. They were recording the album at Electric Lady and I went down there for another session. We did a bunch of pictures with them in the recording studio wearing the suits as if that was their normal day-to-day look.

JAY FERGUSON (KEYBOARDS, JO JO GUNNE): The first time we played with KISS was at the Santa Monica Civic [February 1, 1975]; we headlined and they opened. We played a few shows with KISS. On the face of it it's a funny pairing because it's so West Coast and East Coast. The core band of Jo Jo Gunne was total West Coast Topanga Canyon surf-vibe band doing a Little Feat look at Americana and then we got a little more hard rock and mainstream when we played shows with KISS. We weren't really prepared for what was gonna happen. I liked KISS's sense of style as [I was] a kabuki fan, but opening acts are fairly modest and they're working their way up. We were backstage in our dressing room and heard this thunderous thumping going on. Someone from the road crew ran into the dressing room and said, "You won't believe what they're doing to the stage. They're blowing off fireworks and confetti." KISS just destroyed the stage and did their full-blown act. At that time I was playing an open-top grand piano à la Elton John, and it was just full of all the remnants from KISS's explosions. It was a funny crowd. They'd come to see us and couldn't get their heads around KISS quite yet. They were definitely battered. Not long after that show we played with KISS again at the Beacon Theatre in New York [March 21, 1975], but this time they were headlining and we were opening. It was a turf thing: that was more their territory and the West Coast was more our territory. It's a great testament to the changing fortunes in rock and roll. They were just on a swing on

Dressed to thrill, New York City, April 1975
David Tan/Shinko Music Archives

their unstoppable rise. I saw them play that night. We'd played with Alice Cooper and seen some gothic rock theatrics, but this was taken to the extreme. But I was entertained. I thought these guys weren't writing anything special song-wise, but I've got to give it to them for putting this together. They were catching the zeitgeist with their material and taking off.

RON DELSENER (CONCERT PROMOTER, RON DELSENER PRESENTS): I first booked KISS at the Beacon Theatre [March 21,

1975], and I didn't want to do it. I was pretty hot at the time—I was doing shows all over the place. KISS wanted to step up in terms of being a headliner. They'd never headlined a big show in New York City until they played the Beacon. I was staying at the Beverly Hills Hotel and laying out by the pool and Larry Harris came to me and said, "You gotta do this band." I said, "Well, I've heard about them but it's not my kind of music and their whole look is a cartoon." Larry said, "Listen, I'm telling you, you're gonna do great." I didn't want to book them but he guaranteed me that the show would sell out and I wasn't gonna lose money. So we put the band on at the Beacon, and it sold out.

GENE SIMMONS: Ron Delsener didn't want to promote us. So we rented out the Beacon Theatre and hired Delsener to promote it. We should have played a much larger venue like Madison Square Garden.

RON DELSENER: I'd never seen anything like them. I booked the Crazy World of Arthur Brown in the late sixties and he wore a helmet and set his hair on fire and climbed up the scaffolding towers in Central Park, but KISS took it to another level. They blew me away with their explosions and costumes. It was American theater, and there was a real audience for it. From there I booked them at Madison Square Garden and all the big arenas. That experience with KISS helped me in the sense that I don't listen to hearsay and now I make sure I see every act myself before I make a decision to book them.

JOHN SCHER (CONCERT PROMOTER, METROPOLITAN TALENT): Alice Cooper and KISS were the forerunners of theatrical shock rock. Early on, Alice was bigger than KISS but he wasn't able to sustain the hits like KISS did. It was pretty obvious from the very beginning. Not only were they great live but nobody was doing what they were doing. There wasn't a lot of development time with KISS

Gene Simmons celebrating after the Beacon Theatre show with Neil Bogart, New York City,
March 21, 1975 Len DeLessio/www.delessio.com

from opening act to headliner—maybe a year, year and a half. That's much quicker than how things happened for other bands and I think it's because of their uniqueness. They gave the fans all they could ask for. When they first started out, the whole concept of arena rock was in its infancy. Big acts played theaters. KISS were one of the bands to help pioneer arena rock.

29

MEDIA BATTLES

KISS *emerged long before the advent of MTV and social media, at a time when there were few media opportunities for a band that wore kabuki makeup and outlandish costumes. Back in 1975, Carol Ross, vice president of the music division of the high-powered public relations firm Rogers & Cowan, was enlisted to oversee publicity for KISS. Her job was anything but easy.*

CAROL ROSS: KISS was the first client I brought into Rogers & Cowan, one of the major international public relations agencies. During a creative staff meeting, I showed pictures of KISS and everyone went into shock. In my eyes, KISS took what David Bowie was doing to another level. I explained to the staff that this was not a gimmick— this was an imaginative concept. I had to lay out a campaign to get the press interested in KISS because at that point no one had taken them seriously. In the early days, when I'd call press to see if they might be interested in doing a story or interview on KISS, I would have to hold the phone away because they'd be laughing hysterically. "KISS? Are you kidding me?" They thought KISS was big joke. That really upset me and made me ever more determined. I said to myself, "I'm gonna show these guys because one day they'll all be calling begging me for an interview with the band and I'm gonna be choosy" [*laughs*]. And mark my words, it happened. Revenge is sweet. But at the time I kept banging up against closed doors. I went back to Bill Aucoin and said that we have to educate the media to what KISS is all about. I figured that I had to take all the negativity from the media and make it positive. To make KISS more attractive to press, I had them embellish on the background of their characters: the monster, the spaceman, the lover, and the cat. They needed to go deeper about how they came up with the concept. I helped them build a backstory and that helped develop a little depth. KISS were press-savvy from the beginning. That's the beauty of the band. They were so ready.

PAUL STANLEY: It doesn't hurt to be fairly bright and articulate. Early on I realized that part of the complaints that a lot of performers and celebrities have with the press is they print exactly what you say, and what you say isn't always exactly what you mean. So you need to make sure you say what you mean. I never saw the press as a problem. I saw what you give them as crucial, plus I knew how to ruffle feathers and knew how to promote our cause.

CAROL ROSS: Gene was the one that the press gravitated to. He had the great charisma and he knew how to work the media. They each contributed their own personality to the angle of a story. Ace was very lighthearted and had a great sense of humor. Peter was a lot more serious and emotional. Paul could be both depending upon who he was talking to. Gene had all of it, the lightheartedness, the humor; he had depth, the intellect.

GENE SIMMONS: Every week I'd go out and buy *Cashbox*, *Record World*, and *Billboard* and I'd read the articles and learn things. You were seeing the Wizard behind the curtain, not just the magic of *The Wizard of Oz*, so you get a different perspective. It starts with sense of self. If you think you're just a bass player then that's what you are and you'll get the respect you demand. If you've got something to say, and a way to say it that's seductive, then people will naturally come to you. And if you're fearless about how you present yourself you'll get attention. But you better be careful what you wish for; you have to have the goods to back it up.

CAROL ROSS: KISS was a band who understood publicity, which helped make a difficult task a little easier. They really trusted me and we were able to create wonderful campaigns to generate publicity. We had to focus our energy on reaching the teenagers because the band was being torn apart by the critics. To their credit, the band understood it was going to be a hard climb. The lack of positive critical response hurt them a little bit but they understood where it was coming from and knew it was just a matter of time before it turned around. The band were so determined to make it and willing to do anything that needed to be done to make people aware of them. They told me, "Carol, we'll do anything. If you want us to lay down in the middle of Broadway, whatever it takes, we'll do it." So I said to them, "Okay, I'm gonna take you up on that." That was my other way to generate publicity. I always believed if you can't come in the front door you come in the back door. KISS was not a band that you do your normal PR routine. We had to find extreme ways of generating publicity for them.

A few close friends of mine within the press were nice enough to start doing little favors for me. I had given them breaks with other clients and sometimes in this business you have to do that. You say, "I'll arrange for you to speak to so and so but I want you to give some consideration to KISS." That's ultimately how we started to make the breakthrough. When things started to break for KISS, all of a sudden everyone was admitting they were a phenomenon. And everyone in the media wanted to take credit for breaking the band.

At that time everybody wanted to be on the cover of *Rolling Stone*. It was frustrating to me that I was never able to get KISS on the cover of *Rolling Stone* magazine. Jann Wenner [founder and publisher of *Rolling Stone*] hated the band. He always killed a KISS cover story. He said, "It's my magazine; I don't want them on the cover." Jann Wenner felt if he put KISS on the cover of *Rolling Stone*, [the magazine's] credibility would go down the tube. I disagreed and felt, "How can you deny what the world had accepted and embraced?" When we'd pitch *Rolling Stone*, [the editors] were very cautious: "Sorry, Carol, it can't happen at this time." The band were disappointed, but after a while it became a joke. They'd say, "Okay, we must really be doing something right because *Rolling Stone* ignores us." With the kind of press rejection they had at the beginning of their career, they became very thick-skinned.

JAAN UHELSZKI: *Rolling Stone* turned their nose up at KISS because then—and now—they're really very snobbish about what they cover. KISS was head-banging, get-yer-ya-ya's-out. It was low art. If *Rolling Stone* was going to cover low art, they were going to do it in an intellectual way. Paul Stanley was fond of saying that "we *are* our fans," because KISS identified with their fans. There was no separation between them. They could have easily been out there watching some band. In Paul's case, it would have been Led Zeppelin. We were exactly the same at *Creem*, so we were the perfect fit for KISS.

LEONARD HAZE (DRUMMER, YESTERDAY & TODAY): Gene was hanging in our dressing room before a show we were playing that night at the Santa Monica Civic with KISS and Jo Jo Gunne, who were headlining [February 1, 1975]. Gene was telling us about his plans for the band and he was always thinking six years ahead. Then Paul stuck his head in the dressing room and said, "Anybody wanna play football?" Joe Alves, our guitar player, and I said, "Sure, we'll play." So we played a game. It was Joe and I and some of our road crew against Paul Stanley and some of KISS's road crew. I remember that Paul was wearing these really huge platforms with big heels and Joe said, "Are you really gonna play in those boots?" and Paul responded nonchalantly, "Yeah, why not?" And he did, and he burned me for a touchdown in those heels" [*laughs*].

While garnering press coverage for KISS was challenging, getting KISS on the radio was even harder.

LARRY HARRIS: As an example of how bad it got to get KISS played on the radio, I once took a Cleveland music director to a KISS show and handcuffed him to a chair so he couldn't leave and had to watch the band's show. That's how I was able to get him to add the record to their playlist [*laughs*]. When I worked as the progressive FM promotion guy at Neil's label, Buddah, he taught me that it wasn't up to me to choose or pick the artists, it was up to me to get them played. It could have been three midgets with a camel and I would have gotten them played on the radio. KISS was a group I had to get played. It didn't matter what I thought of them; that was my job. We ignored those at radio who refused to play KISS and concentrated on keeping the band on the road all the time. We got them as many gigs as possible.

NANCY SAIN: It was a major challenge. Neil's attitude was that this was like guerilla warfare. There were no excuses. Our job was to do what it took to get KISS's music on the radio. A lot of the radio guys just got worn down [*laughs*]. Buck Reingold was vice president of promotion and also Neil's brother-in-law. They were married to twin sisters. He was a very aggressive guy and he was in charge of the major radio stations. Casablanca had people wired all over the country calling radio stations requesting to hear KISS. I'd take my top-40 people out to dinner and then to a KISS concert. They'd complain, "No, no, no—I hate them." And I said, "But your audience doesn't." So I'd drag them into the venue and we'd stand in the back because they'd want to be able to leave as soon as I let them [*laughs*]. I pointed to the crowd of mainly eighteen-to-thirty-four[-year-old] men and said, "There's your audience. And that specific demographic equals advertising dollars."

LARRY HARRIS: We had some close friends in radio at WNEW in

New York so they were never resistant to anything we did and played KISS at the beginning. I had trouble in Boston; initially we could get only one DJ to play KISS. In those days DJs could play what they wanted to. I was able to convince radio in Detroit and St. Louis to support us but overall it was an uphill battle. There was a lot of resistance to KISS at radio because of their makeup. I was constantly hearing, "We can't play a band that looks like that."

GENE SIMMONS: They were saying that we didn't have hooks in our songs and we weren't writing love songs. They also said our songs had too much guitar in them and the lyrics were too sexually suggestive for us to play on the radio. When you listened to the radio back then, it was girls' music sung by guys. Some of the stuff that was popular back then was Bread and the Carpenters, and we, of course, had nothing in common with that kind of music.

PAUL STANLEY: We were babes in the woods, as green as the grass in summer. We had no idea what constituted success or what the politics behind the scenes were. We accepted whatever we were told and didn't have any basis to question it. I remember the concern was always getting out there and playing live so that we could build a following.

GARY MAJOR: Most of the general managers of the radio stations were in their forties or fifties and KISS were not up their alley. They saw the album cover and their outrageous image and went, "Oh my God!" I think that's one of the reasons radio was resistant to playing the band. Many of them also felt their sound was too raw and hard to be played in optimal drive times. We [WKLO, Louisville] didn't have a problem with them and played their music as far back as the first single, "Nothin' to Lose." I felt it was only a matter of time until they hit it big. When you don't march to the same beat as everybody else, then you have to be able to stand up for what you believe in and that's what KISS did.

PAUL STANLEY: Radio wasn't embracing us but the people *were*, in enormous quantities. It became a pattern that the establishment would turn a blind eye and that the general population was championing us. Regardless of what album sales were, the numbers at concerts kept increasing markedly and I could sense the build happening.

NEIL BOGART: To build an artist you have to build a following. If they become fans they become record buyers.

RICK MUNROE: I clearly remember KISS opening for ZZ Top and you'd look out into the audience and see half of the crowd wearing cowboy hats and half in KISS makeup. It was a strange sight. Here we were the opening act and we had almost the same number of people wanting to see us as wanted to see ZZ Top. That made me think, "Wow, this is really starting to happen!"

70

ROCKIN' IN THE U.S.A.

From the very beginning, KISS's rousing hard rock sound and larger-than-life stage show had been built for arenas. From their first major gig at New York's Academy of Music on December 31, 1973, KISS had moved from opening act to headliner in record time. In late March 1975, by the time the boys hit the road for Dressed to Kill, their fan base was growing exponentially. KISS were smart and hungry to succeed. Blitzing audiences across America, they built their following at the grassroots level, playing major cities and secondary markets that many other bands ignored—places like Johnstown, Pennsylvania; Kenosha, Wisconsin; and Missoula, Montana.

PAUL STANLEY: Major cities got to see major talent . . . [but] most of the country was ignored by most bands. I've always believed you don't choose where you're born. That's not a stigma that you should get punished for. We basically went everywhere. We were grass roots. We were blue-collar.

GENE SIMMONS: You couldn't just play major cities; you had to play all the in-between towns. There were towns we played that I'd never heard of before, like Ypsilanti, Michigan. It didn't matter if it was a little town in Arkansas or a major city like Los Angeles, New York, or Boston—you had to get yourself out there in front of the people and make your mark.

PETER "MOOSE" ORECKINTO: We'd play clubs, ice skating rinks, cafeterias, small theaters—anyplace that would have us, we'd be there. You couldn't be choosy. And if that meant we had to play a bunch of off-the-map towns, we'd do it. For a lot of the fans that couldn't afford to get to the major cities we'd bring the show to them. That's where you go and play a club and impress five hundred kids and a high percentage are gonna go out and buy your record and tell their friends about the band. It was an exponential progression on a grassroots level and was a crucial element toward building their popularity. None of the big acts of the time like the Rolling Stones, the Who, David Bowie, or [Led] Zeppelin played the small cities. KISS built their popularity one small city at a time.

JULES BELKIN (CONCERT PROMOTER, BELKIN PRODUCTIONS): Belkin Productions handled the Midwest region—Ohio, Michigan, Iowa, western Pennsylvania. We started promoting KISS shows in the spring of 1975 and you could tell they were really starting to happen. Most of the dates we promoted with KISS that year did extremely well. We started promoting the band in secondary markets like Akron [Ohio], Erie [Pennsylvania], and Dayton [Ohio], playing smaller theaters. We also booked them into larger cities like Cleveland as well. We were building them throughout the year playing these secondary cities. The band attracted a younger blue-collar audience and the shows sold great. There was such a tremendous buzz about KISS. To give you an example of how quickly they accelerated into larger venues, in '75 we had them in Cleveland at a three-thousand-seat hall and it only took six or seven months for them to graduate into the larger halls. By January of '76 they were playing at the Coliseum in

Orpheum Theatre, Boston, May 11, 1975 Ron Pownall/RockRollPhoto.com

Cleveland, which held twenty thousand people. That same month KISS also played much larger facilities in Dayton and Erie. This shift marked their real breakthrough into the rock-and-roll big leagues.

On October 9, 1975, in one of the most surreal press events ever orchestrated, KISS descended upon the unsuspecting small town of Cadillac, Michigan, for "KISS Day." More than thirty-five years later, residents of the small town are still talking about the band's historic visit to Cadillac High.

JIM NEFF (ASSISTANT HIGH SCHOOL FOOTBALL COACH, CADILLAC VIKINGS, CADILLAC HIGH SCHOOL): There's a common phrase in football: "Keep it simple, stupid." The initials for that ironically are K-I-S-S. Our '73 team won nine games and was undefeated. In '74 we lost our first two ball games and thought the kids were playing really tight.

DAVE BRINES (HEAD HIGH SCHOOL FOOTBALL COACH, CADILLAC VIKINGS, CADILLAC HIGH SCHOOL): The kids were down and the coaches were down. We had a staff meeting and I said, "The kids aren't having any fun. We need to do something."

JIM NEFF: I told our head coach, Dave Brines, who was an old marine, "Maybe if we play some music in the locker room it'll loosen the kids up. The kids aren't having any fun." He jumped right on it and agreed. He said, "You're the music guy so you select the band." I'd heard KISS already and owned the first two albums, *KISS* and *Hotter Than Hell*. I figured KISS would be perfect. They were a new group and not too many people knew about them at that time. I told Dave that KISS was crazy and wore makeup and that we could have a lot of fun with it.

DAVE LAURENT (TRI-CAPTAIN, CADILLAC VIKINGS, CADILLAC HIGH SCHOOL): On this Monday we gathered and it was a typical meeting reviewing the previous game, watching film, discussing opportunities and our plans for the new opponent. What wasn't typical was the defensive discussion. Coach Neff told us we were going to have some fun on defense and change our calls. He handed out a couple of pages and walked us through our new KISS defensive scheme. As I recall, he told us about the group, showed us their first album, and gave descriptions of the names he was assigning to our defensive positions and what their roles would be. The new defense was our rallying cry for the rest of the season and everybody bought into Coach Neff's idea.

JIM NEFF: Before practices and games we started playing KISS music in the locker room. I checked out one of the old record players from the school library, a turntable with one speaker, and cranked KISS's music. The kids really liked it. Football teams are supposed to have their game faces on and be totally serious, and that just loosened the kids up.

HARRY HAGSTROM (OFFENSIVE AND DEFENSIVE TACKLE, CADILLAC VIKINGS, CADILLAC HIGH SCHOOL): Jim [Neff] was real rock and roll but our head coach was kind of an old-school tough guy. So it was out of character for him to go along with allowing KISS music to be played in the locker room, but I give him a lot of credit for going along with that.

DAVE BRINES: When we started playing the music the whole atmosphere changed. The next ball game we won pretty handily.

DAVE LAURENT: We all became part of the KISS Army and KISS became a very relevant part of the rest of our season. After losing two games we were down and [Jim Neff] used his creativeness to come up with a very special way to get us back up to a higher level of performance and success. He made it fun for us and took a chance with an idea that was out there, and it worked. It worked so well that it moved us to be a team in the truest sense of the word but more importantly brought everyone and every group in the Cadillac community together.

HARRY HAGSTROM: We really rallied around KISS's music and the energy from the music brought everybody together as a team.

DAVE LAURENT: We finished the year 7–2, winning the last seven games of the year, giving up an average of only seven points per game in the KISS Defense.

JIM NEFF: Halfway through the season, after we'd won a few games in a row, I turned the cover over of KISS's first album and there was an address for KISS's management, which was Rock Steady at the time. So I sent a letter telling them what our team had done. In the back of your mind when you're twenty-something years old, you think, "Maybe I'll get lucky enough and they'll send me a poster."

A few weeks later I'm sitting at home in my La-Z-Boy chair one evening and the phone rings and it's Gene Simmons and Paul Stanley. They were backstage at a concert and about to go on and they wanted to know what was going on. They gave me a phone number and said, "Give us a call every time you win a game because we want to know what is happening." So I did. For the next year after every game I called their office and usually spoke with Alan Miller, who worked for KISS's management, and I'd give them the final score.

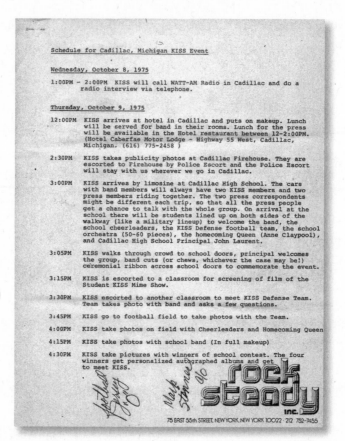

Rock Steady schedule for KISS's Cadillac High School event in Michigan, October 1975
Courtesy of Jim Neff

I found out KISS was playing Cobo Hall in Detroit [May 16, 1975]. The local promoter was a guy named Steve Glantz. I called him and asked if we could bring some kids down from our team, and they gave us ten tickets. Dave Brines and I took two cars and we took eight players and saw them perform at Cobo Hall. That's the first time our kids had any contact with the band. They'd never seen them before.

Then I find out that KISS was gonna play at Western Michigan University at the Herbert Read Field House in Kalamazoo, Michigan, which was located 120 miles south of Cadillac. I sent another letter to Alan Miller at KISS's management and said, "KISS is gonna be in

Kalamazoo. It looks like they're gonna have a few days off between that show and their next show. Do you think there's a chance that KISS would come up for our homecoming and appear at the pep rally and sign some autographs?" He said, "Yeah, there's a chance they can do that, let me see if we can arrange that." Then my wheels started to turn. If we had some amps and instruments ready to go, maybe they'd do a song at the pep rally? So I proposed that to Alan Miller and he said, "The band really wouldn't want to use someone else's gear, but what would be the possibility for bringing the whole show there?" So that's when the whole thing started to become this huge event.

CAROL ROSS: Once the band got wind of this event they were up for it. That was the beauty of KISS: they were up for everything. As for the support of Casablanca, if we needed Neil's participation in a promotion he was there 100 percent. We never had to convince him. We never had to sell him on anything when it came to KISS.

JOHN LAURENT (PRINCIPAL, CADILLAC HIGH SCHOOL): When Coach Neff approached me to bring KISS to Cadillac, I said okay. I didn't know who KISS was at the time. Then I went to Bill Smith, our school superintendent, and told him we might be able to get KISS to Cadillac and he shrugged his shoulders like I did when I was first told about it. He didn't know who the hell they were but he said okay, too.

DAVE LAURENT: My dad didn't know how the conservative population of Cadillac would react.

JOHN LAURENT: As soon as word got out that KISS was coming in for our homecoming I received many telephone calls from angry parents condemning them, saying, "How could you bring these kinds of people into Cadillac?"

DAVE LAURENT: The community was excited but the local pastors and ministers and others were very vocal about questioning why he would let this happen.

DAVE BRINES: The Association of Ministers denounced it. They thought a band that wore makeup were possibly devil worshippers.

JOHN LAURENT: I got a letter from the president of the local pastors and it said, "How could you bring this demonic group into town?" I wrote them back a letter and said, "How could you people of the cloth condemn people without even knowing them?"

DAVE LAURENT: Needless to say my dad, who was the school principal, stood by his decision. Making a decision to support Coach Neff with the KISS visit was very out of the norm for him, but I really believe he saw it as a great way to bring the community together. Boy, was he right.

JOHN LAURENT: KISS's visit to Cadillac turned out to be the most positive event that the town has ever had in its history.

JIM NEFF: We planned to hold the concert in the senior high school gym, which could squeeze two to three thousand people. We had to deal with all the things you'd need to do to pull off a concert in this little teeny town. Things like how do we handle tickets? How do we handle security? But thankfully, everything came together.

We kept everything a secret. No one knew KISS was coming until right before the show. If the word got out beforehand, what would happen if five to ten thousand people showed up? We'd be in deep trouble. No one could grasp the concept of how big the band was. The principal had a son on the football team and he'd been down to Cobo Hall with us to see the band so the principal was behind it and had an idea about the band. But there was no way to describe to people like the mayor, police chief, and the fire chief the magnitude of the band or what was going to happen. But they went along with it because they didn't know any better.

Everything just seemed to fall into place. I thought, "Wouldn't it be a great idea if all the students were in KISS makeup?" We got in touch with Carol Ross and she arranged to get us the makeup we needed. We had teachers volunteer to put it on everybody's face. We used the cafeteria as a base for people to put on KISS makeup. If you

TOP: Ace surrounded by an army of female Aces, Cadillac High School football field, Cadillac, Michigan, October 9, 1975 Fin Costello/KISS Catalog Ltd./www.fincostello.com
ABOVE: The Bat Lizard leads the charge, Cadillac High School, October 9, 1975
Fin Costello/KISS Catalog Ltd./www.fincostello.com

look at the photos taken at the concert, everybody's in full makeup, which was surreal.

CAROL ROSS: I hired Waring Abbott to be the main photographer and tell the story in pictures. Now that I opened up this door we set up a press junket and I made sure every magazine from *Rock Scene* to *Reader's Digest* was represented.

HARRY HAGSTROM: When they told us that KISS was coming to Cadillac it brought the whole school together. Back in those days there was division between jocks and freaks, and KISS brought everybody together. The whole town united around a common theme: KISS.

BILL BARNETT (WIDE RECEIVER, CADILLAC VIKINGS, CADILLAC HIGH SCHOOL): The whole school went out and met them in the parking lot when they arrived. Here comes this big black limousine, and we'd never seen a limousine in our town. Gene Simmons was the first one out of the sunroof. He stood on top of the roof and the entire high school went crazy. It was like a scene from another planet.

JIM NEFF: On the day of the concert the band walked through the school, took pictures with the KISS Defense and the students. They also made it out to the football field and took photos with the football team, cheerleaders, and school band.

BILL BARNETT: It was a real mob scene. It was almost like KISS were giant magnets wielding this power, pulling all these kids towards them.

HARRY HAGSTROM: Ace Frehley jumped up in my arms and I carried him all the way to the band room. That's where all the cheerleaders, coaches, and players got to interact with the band and ask them questions. They weren't that much older than we were and everyone got along great.

CAROL ROSS: We visited the fire department and did a photo session with the band on the fire truck and with all the firemen. Waring Abbott took some fabulous photos of young kids in KISS makeup.

Gene and Paul meet a new generation of KISS fans, Cadillac High School, October 9, 1975
Fin Costello/www.fincostello.com

GENE SIMMONS: We were sitting in the stands in the high school gym for a presentation with the rest of the students. For some reason I made my way to the front and sat down on the floor with these little kids who were all wearing KISS makeup. I remember having an argument with this three-year-old kid over something who was very lucid about his point of view. The kids and the grown-ups started gathering around and I found myself relating to him as a grown-up, and this was a three-year-old! He followed a few rules of marketing, which was the message, the consistency of the message, and the logic behind the message. This kid could have been a thirty-six-year-old man [*laughs*].

RICK MUNROE: The crew members weren't really looking forward to setting up in a high school gym, but the excitement of the town and school was very contagious. We put a plan together that let us take it easy with the load-in; we knew how much this meant to everyone and we were going to do our best to make the appearance and concert a success for all involved.

JIM NEFF: Later that day when I saw all the semi trucks hauling in the equipment for the show, that's when the magnitude of the event really hit me. Funnily enough, the only thing we couldn't get in was the KISS sign because it was too big. A couple of crew guys were getting ready to saw a post out of the center doorway and I had to stop that. So one of the art students put together a posterboard sign that said "KISS." It looked like big lips. That's what you see in old pictures behind the drum kit.

RICK MUNROE: It wasn't that the KISS sign was too big or awkward to set up; we just thought this hand-drawn poster of KISS done by one of the high school students at Cadillac was cool and it would be a great idea to display it rather than our sign—not to mention we were all tired from our road schedule. We, the crew, had spent the night before in a hotel after the [Kalamazoo] show and drove to Cadillac the morning of the show. While at the hotel, Zero, one of our crew members, went missing. He was my roommate at the time and he left our room to get ice and never came back. This girl I was with whom we'd met at the show went looking for him several times that night, but—no luck. The next morning I went looking for him and could not find him nor had anyone seen him. We were all at the bus ready to leave. We waited for him, but we needed to go: Cadillac was waiting for us. So we left without him. He was our pyro guy and we were just going to have to limit the pyro and all pitch in to get it done. As we were setting up Zero showed up, barefoot, in shorts, no shirt, the clothes he was wearing when he left the room the night before. He told us when he woke up he was behind the ice machine at the hotel [*laughs*].

MARK "ZERO" STINNER: Doing a show in a high school gym was challenging. My twenty-foot fireball, which would go about fifteen feet in diameter, had to be cut way down for that show, otherwise we would have set the whole place on fire.

JIM NEFF: I remember there was a concern that we didn't have enough power needed for KISS's show. We went down to the transformer room, and the guy had two battery cable jumpers, and he hands me some rubber gloves and said, "Okay, I'm gonna clamp onto this power grid, and if I guess right we're good, and if I guess wrong I'm gonna die, so pull me off—you've got the gloves on" [*laughs*].

HARRY HAGSTROM: Before their show that night in our high school gym, the band came to our homecoming pep rally, which was one of the coolest things that happened during their visit. Gene blew fire at the bonfire and everyone went crazy! That still sticks in my mind thirty-five years later as being one of the most indelible memories of their visit.

DAVID NEFF (DRUMMER, DOUBLE YELLOW LINE): My brother Jim, who put on the event, was able to arrange for my band to open the show. Looking out into the crowd and seeing a sea of people

KISS poses with local opening act Double Yellow Line, Cadillac High School, Cadillac, Michigan, October 9, 1975. *Left to right:* Peter Criss, John Cook, David Neff, Paul Stanley, Dennis Niec, and Gene Simmons. *Cadillac News*

Flaming Youth . . . Cadillac High School crowd gets ready for the KISS show,
Cadillac High School gym, Cadillac, Michigan, October 9, 1975 *Cadillac News*

with KISS faces was surreal. We were KISS fans so it was a thrill
to open for them. Before we went on we were able to get a photo
with the band. We did a short thirty-minute set, mainly covers of
songs by Paul McCartney, Uriah Heep, and Bad Company, and we
were able to get the crowd fired up. Our performance was taped
on a reel-to-reel machine and we were planning to tape KISS's
show as well, but their roadies came by to make sure we took the
machine away. Had we been able to tape KISS's set, that would
be a valuable bootleg today. It was quite a thing to see KISS
bring the whole show into a high school gymnasium. When they
came on, the crowd was taken aback because they weren't used to
experiencing a show of that magnitude, that much staging and
production, lights, PA. It was a lot more than they'd anticipated,
but they loved it.

JOHN LAURENT: My son David was backstage with Gene Simmons trying to get him to swap his shirt for a Cadillac Vikings sweatshirt, and he did [*laughs*]. I went back there because I'd heard that during their concerts Gene Simmons spits blood. I told him, "Gene, I understand you spit blood during the concert. Gene, I don't want any blood." And he said, "You don't want the blood?" And I said, "No, I don't want the blood; I've had enough telephone calls" [*laughs*]. He said, "You sure?" And I said, "Yeah, I'm sure." So he said, "Okay, you don't get any blood, but we'll give you a hell of a concert."

JIM NEFF: It was incredibly loud—I'm talking standing-under-a-jet-engine, make-your-ears-ring-for-the-next-decade, slam-you-into-the-back-wall loud. Some people described the experience as trying to tread water in a hurricane; it was just wave upon wave of relentless sound. The gym had windows along the upper levels

KISS rocks out in the Cadillac High School gym. The KISS sign was replaced by a homemade sign drawn by an enterprising Cadillac High School student. *Cadillac News*

and we opened those windows, and there are stories about people who sat in their backyards a mile and a half to two miles away and listened to the concert.

DAVE LAURENT: The concert was an unbelievable experience. No words can describe how loud it was or how cool it was to see every single person in the crowd, kids and parents alike, with their faces painted.

PAUL STANLEY: Looking out into the audience and seeing everyone in makeup was surreal. The beauty of it was that it was multigenerational and crossed all age boundaries—you had children, teenagers, parents, principals, town officials. It was so across-the-board that it was pretty stunning. Interestingly enough, we evolved into more of that as time went on. Today that's part of what I take the most pride in. We're multigenerational and tribal as opposed to most bands, which are age-specific and have a very clear demographic. At most rock concerts, if you see your little brother there you don't want to be there. We're not confined to those restrictions. At a KISS concert it's thumbs up to your neighbor, your little brother, and your grandfather because you're all part of this giant secret society. It's interesting that Cadillac in some way foretold the future.

HARRY HAGSTROM: I was wearing makeup, as were about 75 percent of the audience except for the moms and dads and a few young kids. They asked the band not to play "Cold Gin" because of the reference to alcohol and Gene didn't spit blood. Maybe it was also done because there were a decent number of grade school kids there too.

BILL BARNETT: After hearing all the negative buzz about KISS from pastors and local churches, many of the parents took their kids to the show 'cause they wanted to be there in case things got too wild. But that never happened. By the end of the concert, KISS had won over the parents, too. They shared the same euphoria as their kids did over seeing this amazing band.

JIM NEFF: The concert came off without a hitch and everyone had a blast. The next morning there was a monthly civic breakfast already scheduled with all the town officials and bigwigs in attendance. All of the officials on the dais wore KISS makeup, which was just crazy. We said, "Why don't we have KISS there?" And the mayor agreed and said, "We can give them a key to the city."

PAUL STANLEY: To see everyone on the city board in KISS makeup was so terrific. To see people embracing a school's victories on that scale was just amazing. It was just magic.

JOHN LAURENT: When I spoke at the press conference I said, "I've been trying to unite Cadillac High School ever since I've been principal, and KISS did it in one day."

"KEY TO THE CITY" ACCEPTANCE SPEECH
CADILLAC, MICHIGAN, OCTOBER 10, 1975
PRESS CONFERENCE EXCERPT

PAUL STANLEY: I just want to say on behalf of KISS, after getting the key to the city I hope you never change the locks.

WILLIAM SMITH (CADILLAC SCHOOLS SUPERINTENDENT): On behalf of the Cadillac school district and all of the student body, I express our appreciation to all of the performers and the workers for an excellent presentation. I would assure you this, there are a great many people in the community of Cadillac today who have a little different attitude and impression of the young people who were here last night and are here today. And we would say this to you: the lock will not be changed, and anytime you want to return we would be tickled to death to have you.

JIM NEFF: The band took part in our homecoming parade. We let the kids out early from school for the parade. There must have been a couple of thousand people that were there. Mitchell Street,

KISS takes part in a special parade. Gene and Paul throw out Hershey kisses to the crowd lining the streets, Cadillac, Michigan, October 10, 1975 *Cadillac News*

the main thoroughfare, was renamed "KISS Boulevard" for the day. It was a small-town parade. There was a marching band and fire truck. We had KISS music being played. Each class did a float. Every float had some kind of a KISS-related theme. KISS followed on their own float, which was built on a big flatbed hay wagon and was being towed by a car. When the float went by with KISS on it everybody started running and following it; they were like pied pipers. When it got to the end of the parade, the whole student body and half the band were surrounding them. The town came alive.

HARRY HAGSTROM: Everybody was screaming and hollering, and the band was throwing chocolate candy kisses to the crowd.

JIM NEFF: It was total pandemonium and there were still KISS floats in the parade as late as 2009 [*laughs*].

GENE SIMMONS: It was very inspiring going down "KISS Boulevard" on that float. Seeing the whole town in makeup was like landing on planet KISS.

JIM NEFF: After the parade was over I assumed we were gonna head back to the school and the band would get in limos and leave town. We had the students out on the football field so they could all wave goodbye to KISS.

MILISSA CODDEN (CHEERLEADER, CADILLAC VIKINGS, CADILLAC HIGH SCHOOL): I'd spent some time with Gene the day before, hanging out with him and the rest of the band while they were taking part in all of our homecoming festivities. I thought he was gonna say goodbye and give me a hug. But Gene proceeded to scoop me up and said, "I could take you home with me." And then suddenly out of nowhere my dad appeared. He was there working as an on-duty police officer. He tapped Gene on the shoulder and said with a fatherly tone, "Over my dead body" [*laughs*].

JIM NEFF: The football field is situated next to Lake Cadillac. All of a sudden from out over the lake we hear this loud roar and see a helicopter. No one knew this was gonna happen; that was totally

Take-off! Cadillac High School football field, Cadillac, Michigan, October 10, 1975
Fin Costello/KISS Catalog Ltd.

KISS. The helicopter landed in the middle of the field and as the band moved toward it the fans started running after them.

PAUL STANLEY: It was unbelievable. We jumped into this helicopter, which had a sliding door because it was a military helicopter. It was like, "Now hold on!"

HARRY HAGSTROM: Once the helicopter lifted off to about 100 feet, KISS threw out these flyers that said, "Cadillac High—Kiss Loves You," and everybody scrambled to get them.

PAUL STANLEY: And then the helicopter banked to the side and we flew away from this amazing scene. It was just so surreal.

BILL BARNETT: It was big city meeting small city in America. It was culture shock but it all came together. We embraced them and they embraced us.

DAVE BRINES: Their visit to Cadillac High changed a lot of minds among the adults about rock and roll. Everybody had a good time and the results were all positive. It brought everyone together, young and old.

JOHN LAURENT: KISS's visit is still the talk of Cadillac today. I probably could have gotten fired over the thing, but it turned out to be a tremendous success [*laughs*].

BILL BARNETT: KISS's visit to Cadillac changed my life. They made me want to be a musician. I've played in bands for thirty years and, in fact, I'm in a rock-and-roll band at age fifty-two and today I'm also the mayor of Cadillac, Michigan.

JIM NEFF: As great an event as this turned out to be we lost money [*laughs*]. What did I know about budgeting for an event like this? [*laughs*]. We came up with a $3.50 ticket price for the concert in the school gym and hoped it could cover the band's expenses. We made $4,228 from proceeds for the concert and our total expenses were $10,024. When it was added up we lost almost $6,000. But KISS chipped in for the difference so we didn't lose any money. The band didn't make a cent, we didn't make a cent, but we made history in the process. This is their town; we love them and they love us.

FRITZ POSTLETHWAITE: Cadillac was the beginning of KISS thinking of themselves as successful. For me it was the beginning of my involvement with the band and the start of some close friendships that lasted for a good deal of time. I worked for a major touring sound company doing one-nighters and festivals with name acts. I was finishing up a long and exhausting Bee Gees tour of the U.S. and Canada when the owner of the sound company called me in the Montreal airport via pay phone. He asked me to troubleshoot a new band on his roster that was having sound problems. This always meant that they played too loud. Loud onstage monitors seemed to be my forte. I politely declined as I had not been home or out of a venue for a long time. He persisted, as he was in a desperate spot. The band was just beginning to break and he wanted to keep them as clients. It was KISS. There were only a few shows left on this leg of the tour and then they would be off. He made it difficult to refuse, so I agreed to try to sort out this band that I had never heard of.

After the first show I was appalled and excited. The costumes and production were ridiculous. Held together with duct tape and baling wire. Bowie and even Dylan wore makeup, but this was absurd. The music was so basic it seemed it was almost superfluous. But the crowd's enthusiasm and the effects were remarkable when the bombs went off at the beginning of what I later came to know as "Deuce." But I couldn't see myself working with what my rock snob attitude told me was a geek show. For a few dates I did sort out their onstage sound. Then came Cadillac. I thought I had gone through the looking glass. A town full of people with KISS makeup? The day before I had questioned whether they had more than a handful of fans and then I saw an entire community that looked like them.

CAROL ROSS: When we came back to New York, Waring and I sat on the floor in my office and went through hundreds of pictures and we made special packages of exclusive photos and story lines for each publication. No one got the same thing. All of these publications felt special and that's why we got such amazing coverage.

The Cadillac High event was the breakthrough for mainstream press. When we got *Reader's Digest* to do a story on KISS, when we got that mainstream media, that's where we first solidified their importance. It was amazing. I had gotten every magazine and newspaper to cover it. This event became international news. It was the breakthrough. It was a massive task and expensive for KISS, but the fact that we generated publicity not by pitching stories but by an event was how we had to present KISS in most instances. We used that event mentality later in the band's career when KISS took photos on top of the Empire State Building or pouring their blood into the printer's ink for the first Marvel KISS comic. These were events and they generated a huge amount of press.

FIN COSTELLO (PHOTOGRAPHER, *KISS ALIVE!*): I think that the band and management were well aware of the publicity value of this event. From my point of view as a photographer, it was a roller-coaster ride. You could have shot a million photographs and you still wouldn't have captured all that was happening. Everyone was wearing makeup, mothers were painting their babies' faces. I came from a background of photojournalism. I wanted to do what *Life* magazine was doing where you'd have a picture story. KISS was very cooperative and trusted me and let me do what I needed to do.

In those days, KISS understood American culture and they understood the potential of what they were doing. They rose to every occasion. They weren't playing stars. There's a great set of photos I took of the band in Cadillac when we had them up in the fire engine and Gene's chatting to this chubby little police lady. He was chatting away to her like she was his neighbor or sister. You had this bizarre situation where you're out in the boonies and you had this police lady chatting to this weird-looking man in this weird outfit with weird makeup on [*laughs*]; it was bizarre! As celebrity culture developed over the ensuing years, anybody who was successful became distanced from their audience very quickly. That wasn't happening then with KISS. They were just part of the crowd, chatting away to everyone. At that point, when KISS was in their ascendancy, they were excited, they were full of new ideas, and they were full of energy. And every day was a new experience for them climbing the ladder of success.

Original "KISS Loves You!" flyer Courtesy of Ross Koondel

31

CRITICAL MASS

T hen and now, KISS was the band the critics loved to hate. Back
in the seventies, prominent national rock magazines like Rolling
Stone and Crawdaddy regularly took potshots at the band,
denigrating KISS as talentless bozos or worse.

JOYCE BOGART-TRABULUS: KISS were dubbed "Hype of the Year"
in 1974 by *Rolling Stone*. They wanted that respect and credibility,
and that kind of stuff bothered them.

PAUL STANLEY: I think the negative press made us more staunchly
aware that we were the black sheep and that we were the outsiders.
And that's what rock and roll is supposed to be. So we didn't see
it as a negative; we kind of embraced being the black sheep. That
Rolling Stone wanted virtually nothing to do with us was so overt
that you couldn't help but realize their resistance was about more
than the music. It's people forgetting why they once loved music and
becoming everything that they detested.

GENE SIMMONS: We were befuddled by the critical reaction coming
from magazines like *Rolling Stone*. They were paying attention to

bands like the Grateful Dead, who we thought were garbage. It seemed anything that was uncool they liked.

ROBERT DUNCAN: Here's how I might pithily sum up the fear of the band among critics: KISS were the barbarians at the gate. When all of the KISS solo albums came out I got an assignment from Dave Marsh to review those for *Rolling Stone*. I wrote this long, funny, tongue-in-cheek review, and it was going to be my first lead review so I was pretty excited, but it never ran. Jann Wenner read it and killed it.

KISS was honest about doing what everybody else wanted to do. There's not a big band from the seventies that didn't have some hardcore agents and managers that were playing some real showbiz hardball and marketing themselves and carefully choosing where they performed and who photographed them. But KISS came out and said, "This is what we're doing." KISS's music and their lyrics were not self-consciously arty as other artists like Jackson Browne and Bruce Springsteen. Generally, artists were striving for a literary quality, to be considered seriously as poets. KISS weren't going for poetry; they were doing pretty simplistic, dumb music. Just celebrating the simple pleasures of a heavy beat and loud guitars. The critics were looking for something deeper. I was one of those critics who thought it was dumb and made fun of it a lot of the time. Some of that poetic rock stuff is still great and holds up, but when you look back today some of the so-called dumb stuff like KISS is more fun.

By contrast, Creem, *Detroit's irreverent rock magazine, embraced KISS; they were one of the group's few early supporters in the press.*

LARRY HARRIS: *Creem's* audience was young males for the most part. Anything that was very visual is the type of thing they'd want to get on the bandwagon and support. And KISS fit the bill perfectly. I made a deal with Barry and Connie Kramer, the publishers and owners of *Creem,* and provided them with KISS albums as an incentive for subscribers and that helped get them more subscribers so they owed us for that, which would translate to coverage. We'd also bring KISS to *Creem* to hang out and make friends with some of the writers, so we were actively working magazines like *Creem* and *Circus* like we did radio stations.

CAROL ROSS: We built such a good relationship with *Creem* and we provided much more access to KISS because of the support they showed the group. They paid attention to the fans and were smart enough to realize if they featured KISS enough times their circulation was going to skyrocket. Once the publications started seeing what was happening with the band they all jumped on the bandwagon, but to get them there was so tough. Early on I had to use favors to get them press by providing access to other big artists we represented like Paul McCartney & Wings and Billy Joel.

JAAN UHELSZKI: I actually inherited the KISS beat at *Creem* because no one else really wanted it. The readers of *Creem* and the people who created *Creem* weren't much different from the guys in KISS. We all came from normal, humble beginnings. I think we saw a reflection of who we were in what they were. Also, being the low man on the totem pole at that time, I would take any story just to be published. And this one just dropped in my lap because nobody else wanted it. I liked their spirit and that they weren't pretentious. This is also going to sound crazy but I liked that they were so nice, that they were really good to their fans and had this sense of wonder. They had the high concept but Bill Aucoin refined that high concept. He approached KISS like it was *Supermarket Sweep* [an ABC game show that followed shopping cart–wielding contestants frantically racing through a supermarket vying for prizes]. In the same way he created that great TV show, he made KISS a commodity and a unique experience that people could really get off on.

My favorite quote by Goethe sums them up for me: "There's nothing more powerful than an idea whose time has come." If there's a great idea or high concept and you can pull it off with the music, I'm there for the idea, which is probably a terrible confession to make for a music critic. With KISS, I saw the future. They came out in dire times and were such a reflection of the time—the oil crisis and Ford, GM, and Chrysler's loss of faith—and here was this band looking like superheroes saying, "We're not gonna give you our philosophy on how to fix it, we're just going to head-butt our way through it." There was something so primal, something so simplistic, something so right, and something so successful about the way they approached music.

Later in their career, KISS would be lauded for being extremely press savvy. But a visit to Creem's *offices in 1974 proved that the band still had a lot to learn.*

JAAN UHELSZKI: They first came into my life when their promotion man at Casablanca Records called and asked if we would do a *Creem* profile—the fake ad we used to have in the magazine based on the Dewar's Scotch ad. So without any hesitation, Larry Harris brought them to our office—a rather casual suite of offices in suburban Detroit, above a movie theater, to meet the staff of *Creem* and have a photo session with Charlie Auringer, *Creem's* art director. They walked in without their trademark makeup, looking like four rather normal rock types dressed in their street clothes. Very politely they asked if they could take over the girl's bathroom to suit up. The transformation was incredible. When they had their makeup on they became towering giants and they took up more psychic space than they did without the makeup on. It was pure bedlam, with the staff secretaries fighting to sit on Gene Simmons's lap and the dentists across the hall from us popping in to see what all the commotion was. And there was a lot of commotion; it was strange what havoc a few jars of clown makeup, red lipstick, and eyeliner could wreak. Charlie Auringer took some shots with them in full regalia and that was it. Or so we thought. They retired to the bathroom again, removed the makeup, and were about

TOP: Kiss and makeup, *Creem* magazine shoot, Birmingham, Michigan, June 1974
ABOVE: KISS tricked into posing without makeup Photos by Charlie Auringer/www.BackstageGallery.com

to pop back into their waiting cars, but Charlie convinced them to pose for a few pictures without their makeup.

PAUL STANLEY: Somebody said to us, "We just spoke to Bill and he said you should take some pictures without makeup." And what do we say? "Oh, okay." We were naive and we got duped. Afterwards we called Bill up and said, "We did the photo shoot and we did the pictures without makeup." He was just aghast and in total disbelief. "You did what?" We said, "Well, we were told you said we should do it." But that misstep really didn't come back to hurt us. The visual of KISS with makeup was so much more appealing than seeing us without makeup.

JAAN UHELSZKI: We liked them and they liked us. That was the beginning of our relationship with the band. After that, anything we asked their management for, they always complied. We gave them a lot of coverage when everybody else was treating them like a joke. To me it was a campy, bizarre, death-of-art, Warholian kind of thing. Why would we ruin their superhero kind of appeal by printing that photo of them without makeup? It never really entered our minds to do that. Okay, maybe it entered our minds, but we never had any intention of running that photo in *Creem*. At *Creem* we were really honorable; our word was our bond. But here's how one of those photos got out years later.

I was living in Beverly Hills with my sister and I was away for a week working on a story. She had a friend named Gary Lewis who used to be a photographer for Rona Barrett's gossip magazine. My photo albums were out and they were filled with all of the relics of my past, and that included Charlie's photo of KISS without makeup. When I got back into town that particular photo book with the picture of KISS was gone. He had stolen the book and sold the photo of KISS without their makeup to the *National Enquirer*, who printed it [in the January 30, 1979, issue]. *Creem* eventually published that photo in the early eighties [in the February 1981 issue], but that was long after that photo got out.

In pitching a piece on these rising stars to her editor at Creem, *Jaan Uhelszki used their accessibility to score a major press coup.*

JAAN UHELSZKI: Like me, Connie Kramer, the publisher's wife, saw KISS as a great idea, too. She'd read a piece in *Esquire* where the writer, Blair Sobel, had been an Ikette [a backing vocalist for the Ike & Tina Turner Revue]. She said, "You should definitely do this with KISS." Connie and I ruminated about dressing up like KISS. "How funny it would be if I dressed up like KISS and no one would know the difference," I said. "You know what, I'm going to see if they'll go for it." I called Larry Harris, their record promotion guy who initially introduced us to them, and I told him I wanted to perform with them and write a story from the perspective as one of KISS. It was a George Plimpton kind of thing—participatory journalism. I was surprised when he agreed. The only stipulation was I couldn't call them a glam band. As if they were!

After they agreed I had this sinking feeling—now I really had to go through with it. I'm not shy but I never had any desire or inclination to be a singer or a musician. For me, it was the thrill of the story. When the day finally arrived for me to do the story, I went down to KISS's sound check at Cobo Hall. Once I got there, I realized that the band had no idea that I was going to go onstage with them—their record company and management hadn't bothered to tell them. When I explained my intention to perform with them, they thought I was kidding. But they would do anything to further their career and they saw this as a good career move. They allowed me into their world because they saw the greater good. They were just so futuristic in their thinking of how to approach a career in a way that so few other bands were at that time.

Finally we got it all straightened out, and I went home and packed a bag with six-inch-high platform heels, a pair of dancer's tights, a leotard, and some rather Gothic-looking jewelry, and met the band at the airport the next morning. Much to my dismay, we took a small private plane with the band to Johnstown, Pennsylvania, where they were performing. It was incredibly bumpy and I spent the ride in a state of hysteria—but all that turbulence did manage to distract me. I hadn't even begun to worry about my performance at that point, although it was less than twelve hours away. Johnstown was a coal-mining city. There had been an awful flood there years and years ago, and the city was scarred by that. It had a rather dark, doomsday kind of vibe. But it didn't seem to bother the band; they were seasoned travelers by 1975, and the cities had begun to blur.

Once we were checked in, they began giving me advice about being onstage, like a frustrated flock of stage mothers. "Don't look at the audience," Ace advised as we had lunch. "Remember, wear your guitar really low; it's sexier that way," Paul reminded me, as if I knew. And on and on, until it was too much to remember and began making me more nervous instead of less. The oddest part of the entire experience was being made up. It was absolutely hilarious and strangely revealing to me. They had tacitly agreed that they didn't want just one of them making me up. I had to have a combination of each of their makeup insignias. I remember Paul hissing to Gene, "Don't make her up to look just like you." Ace didn't pull any punches, then or now, and blurted out, "God, Jaan, you don't know anything about makeup." This was the seventies and nobody really wore makeup. It was a more, how you say, natural time—except for KISS of course. As a reporter, the good part for me was that KISS weren't inhibited about having someone there observing them. This seemed like some logical extension of the joke of their very existence, taking it one step further.

By the time showtime came around I was almost paralyzed with fear. Their manager, Bill Aucoin, watched me like a hawk so I wouldn't bolt, calmly attempting to talk me down. When the crucial moment came—at the first strains of "Rock and Roll All Nite"—he actually pushed me onstage. "Get out there!" I think I just couldn't get over how absurd it all was. I remember thinking, "My God, I was dressed up like them," except I think I looked more like Catwoman. It was bizarre. I sang on the choruses of "Rock and Roll All Nite," and as a result learned an important lesson about rock stars. Once you're out there you totally understand what it's all about. There's a surge of power and adrenaline that's intoxicating. When you're out there in front of a screaming crowd, there is no fear. All I remember thinking is I didn't want it to stop.

I think that experience has impacted everything I've written afterwards because I know what it's like to live, if only for five minutes, on the other side. It was an amazing thing for me. I definitely have much more empathy and much more of an understanding of musicians and that thrill, and how hard it is to give up that surge of power you get every night. You understand what it is like to stand in front of people. It was not a huge crowd that I played in front of—probably about six thousand people. But I felt a sense of raw power. It was a galvanizing, out-of-body force, making me become much more than myself. Strangely enough, I was the only person to have played onstage with KISS. [*Authors' note: In December 2003, Aerosmith guitarist Joe Perry joined KISS onstage for a spirited version of "Strutter" at shows in Oklahoma City and Los Angeles.*] It started off as a joke. My story on KISS for *Creem*, "I Dreamed I Was Onstage with KISS in My Maidenform Bra," was published in 1975. In some ways it made my career, and it certainly helped theirs.

PAUL STANLEY: It was a fun moment. It was us having a good time with somebody who was a member of the inner circle. Jaan was a supporter and a chum. She was really fun and very bright and it seemed like a "why not?" situation.

GENE SIMMONS: We had a real fondness for *Creem* magazine. They were really early supporters. It was a real rock-and-roll magazine. They weren't afraid to say a band sucked, and we got some of it right between the teeth every once in a while. All of that is okay if they don't take themselves too seriously, as long as the critic doesn't say, "I am the tastemaker and what I say is most important." They'd poke fun at themselves.

Music writer Robert Duncan was one of the only other members of the press who regularly covered KISS for rock magazines like Creem, Circus, *and* Hit Parader.

ROBERT DUNCAN: The first time I ever saw KISS live was in San Francisco at the Winterland in [June] 1974; Savoy Brown and Manfred Mann were the headliners. *Creem* asked me if I'd go see KISS and do an article on them. Seeing them live I have to say I was skeptical. Perhaps I was too hung up on authenticity. They were so show business and I was coming from this (no doubt) false aesthetic that it has to be authentic and from the heart, and KISS was clearly putting on a show. I felt Alice Cooper was more dangerous and subversive. KISS didn't strike me as subversive; it struck me as show business. KISS was fun to write about. I'm a guy who likes to look at both sides of everything; as a writer that's what I like to do. They were both the rock apocalypse, the end of all things good in rock and roll, and then kind of the avatars of a more entertaining future. It was easy to write about both sides of the coin. So I made a very conscious effort to write critical articles about them. I wrote for a dozen rock magazines at the time. I'd write a laudatory article in *Gig* magazine and a highly critical article in *Creem*—all of it with tongue firmly in cheek.

The next day after their show at Winterland I interviewed the band at this modest hotel in San Francisco. I was talking to Gene, and Paul walked in late. He said, "Guess where I've been?" and pulled his shirt aside. He'd just come back from getting a rose tattoo on his shoulder from the famous tattoo artist Lyle Tuttle, who I also have a tattoo from.

Gene and Paul were very press savvy; Ace and Peter seemed a little bit passive. Gene and Paul were definitely running the show. I thought, "Wow, these guys have thought it through" to a degree that I'd never heard people think it through. It was almost like they were businessmen in rock garb. I thought this could work. Nobody else was really thinking this way. They were into marketing when it was anathema to the rock culture. They were willing to talk about it. In many ways KISS were more authentic than other bands. The Eagles could pretend to be an authentic American country rock band but in the meantime they were really all about hardcore Hollywood hustling. I think I was naive at the time, thinking, "Oh well, these guys are sleazy businessmen and everybody else is for real," but the truth is they were just more transparent about it.

While mainstream rock-and-roll magazines like Rolling Stone *and* Crawdaddy *dismissed KISS as a flash in the pan and unworthy of coverage,* Circus, *one of the era's most popular rock magazines, was another early supporter.*

GERALD ROTHBERG (PUBLISHER, *CIRCUS* MAGAZINE): I started *Circus* magazine in 1969 and we focused on a specific kind of rock-and-roll music, which was eventually termed arena rock or heavy metal. The base age for our readership at *Circus* was thirteen to nineteen. What set *Circus* apart from other magazines like *Rolling Stone* and *Crawdaddy* was we didn't take a standoffish attitude to rock acts. We were a fan of the artists. We covered KISS early in their career. The readers reacted positively to the band from day one. The more we covered KISS, the more the readers wanted. The more the *Circus* audience wanted, the more we did, so it became an event feeding on itself. I built a strong rapport with the band, their manager Bill Aucoin, and Casablanca. We worked very closely together. Unlike other magazines of the time like *Rolling Stone* and *Crawdaddy*, we didn't feel KISS was beneath our audience. I felt this was the kind of band our audience would like.

GENE ℐIMMONℐ: *Creem* and *Circus* were more closely aligned with what was actually going on in the street.

GERALD ROTHBERG: We never put KISS down the way *Rolling Stone* did. They were totally against KISS because of their lack of intellectualism. KISS's music was hard and heavy, the performances were theatrical, and their image was perfect for [our] magazine. We wanted to report on them. They provided access and were also open to doing promotions. During the band's seventies heyday, KISS was one of the biggest draws for the magazine.

Just as Casablanca's Larry Harris had finessed the band's coverage in Creem *magazine, his sleight of hand garnered KISS a massive amount of coverage in* Circus.

LARRY HARRIℐ: *Circus* had a poll in the back of their magazine for things like best band, best guitarist, best drummer, and best album. I took an idea from WMMS, a radio station in Cleveland, where they were able to win a contest in *Rolling Stone* for best radio station. They had their listeners and employees fill out this poll—and WMMS in Cleveland wasn't the biggest market in America, but wound up being voted the best radio station in America. I did the same thing with *Circus.* We bought hundreds and hundreds of copies of the magazine and we filled out the polls and picked Ace as the best guitar player, Peter as the best drummer, Gene as the best bass player, Paul as the best singer, KISS as the best band. We sent them in, and it worked. *Circus* didn't know we were stuffing the ballots. They judged the result of those polls and began covering the band more in the magazine. Perception is reality, so people began perceiving that KISS was the best band, and people perceived that was true. So they had to go check out their album because they wanted to hear who *Circus* picked as the best band. Funnily enough, when Neil [Bogart] was a singer he had a record up against Elvis Presley on a New York radio station and he had all his friends call in and he wound up beating Elvis Presley [*laughs*].

With each successive studio album, KISS sold more and more records. But it was their nonstop road work that cemented their status as a must-hear band. Across the nation, in blue-collar cities like Detroit, Cleveland, Boston, and Philadelphia, the group enlisted a fiercely devoted battalion of rock-and-roll soldiers known as the KISS Army—the brainchild of an ardent fan named Bill Starkey.

BILL STARKEY (FOUNDER, KISS ARMY): My father took me and my brother to see KISS in concert on a snowy Sunday on December 8, 1974, at Roberts Stadium in Evansville, Indiana. ZZ Top was the headliner. Hearing [KISS's] records was one thing, but seeing them live took it to another level. KISS blew me away. Three weeks later, on a dare from my father, my mother would take us to see them once more in Indianapolis, on December 28 at the Indianapolis Convention Center. By that time I was a lifer KISS fan.

Coming from my basement in Terre Haute, Indiana, equipped with all the evidence we felt we needed, me, my friend Jay, and my younger brother preached the gospel of KISS to anyone who would listen at school. We called ourselves the KISS Army because we felt a kinship with the band, who our local radio station routinely left off their playlist. We too were "left off" when it came to the usual school social functions. No, we weren't the most popular, the best-looking, or most athletic of kids. But we leveraged our passion and deep love of KISS to recruit others to our cause, which was simply to get KISS played on the radio.

Four months later, on April 22, 1975, KISS would headline at the Indianapolis Convention Center, and it was time for me to take Jay and any nonbelievers to their first KISS concert. The next day we joined ranks and proudly strolled through the halls of our high school to proclaim the greatness of KISS. We were met with, "If KISS is so great, then why aren't they on the radio?" This time the challenge was not thrown at my feet but at those recent converts in my high school who attended their first KISS concert. They would now be the ones making the phone calls to radio stations asking them to play KISS and wearing their homemade KISS T-shirts to the mall. The local radio station in Terre Haute, Indiana, WVTS-FM, knew who we were and enjoyed coming up with ways to frustrate us. Playing half a KISS song on the air or refusing to say it was a KISS track was all done deliberately so that we might go away and find something else to do.

Little by little the radio station gave in, and as a truce, the program director suggested that I continue to mail in my "threats" to his station. KISS was coming to our city and he wanted to read them on the air leading up to the show. The DJ still poked fun at us on the radio but that only made our ranks grow and our cause nobler. The KISS concert sold out, which was previously only something Elvis Presley could claim. Other bands that had generated years of airplay, compared to the relatively brief airplay KISS was receiving, never came close to filling our arena. The KISS Army would become the name by which all KISS fans would be recognized. Every band had fans, but who had an army?

Decades later I proudly recall how something that started in my parents' basement would be embraced worldwide by people of many backgrounds and in countries all over the world. Regardless of race, religion, language, culture, or age, people would unite for the same cause but on a larger scale. That became the KISS Army. People would identify with the plight of a bunch of kids who marched on a radio station because they felt it was the right thing to do. The experience I garnered from that crusade has ingrained in me a spirit to always question the status quo. To never be satisfied with something that you know could be changed for the better or made right. Lastly, to persevere and to keep moving forward regardless of the challenge. That's how my experience as being the commander in chief of the KISS Army has impacted my life and how I look at life.

CAROL ROSS: When the KISS Army formed, it became such a support system for the band that nothing else mattered. I was able to use the KISS Army as a press device, too. If I found a journalist who told me that they weren't interested in doing a story on KISS I'd bring up the KISS Army. I said, "How can you turn away when they have such a powerhouse of a fan base? How can you ignore that?" Then sometimes I'd get some of the fans in the KISS Army to talk to some of the press. So I utilized all the ammunition I could. With KISS we could never use the standard pitch to get an article. We always had to go beyond that. You'd have to set the stage and give [the press] everything, let them imagine it, and visualize a story. You had to make them feel the magnitude of what was happening with this band. Ironically, the more that KISS rebelled, the more fans they got.

BUCK REINGOLD: It's the old story: if your parents hate 'em they're gonna be a hit. It's the same way parents didn't like the way Elvis Presley gyrated onstage. Parents thought KISS was too loud and crazy with their makeup and costumes and they hated them. Any time one generation hates something, you have a better chance of the kids loving it.

PAUL STANLEY: The KISS Army typified what became historically consistent, which is the fans are vocal and very adamant about their support of the band. And it all started with the original KISS Army in Terre Haute, Indiana. The greatest armies on Earth are the volunteer armies because people are there because they want to be there, and the KISS Army is no different.

GENE SIMMONS: The KISS Army was created for the fans by the fans. It didn't have any structure. There was just a sense of nationhood that didn't begin in New York or LA but in Middle America. At the same time we started thinking about an anthem with "Rock and Roll All Nite"—a song that defined what we were doing—there was a groundswell happening among our fan base. There was a real sense of fandom and the fans felt connected not just to the band but with each other. And if you were brave enough to put the makeup on, you became a star, too. It continues to this day.

32

ON THE SKIDS

n 1975, *despite a gradual rise in KISS's fortunes, their record label was in dire straits and hemorrhaging money, threatening the band's lifeblood.*

NEIL BOGART: It was a year of total disaster, other than KISS. We couldn't exist within a major corporation. We were all used to working as independents, going through independent distribution. All of a sudden, we were part of a major company. We couldn't work within its framework. It wasn't that they were wrong or we were wrong; we just couldn't work that way. That was eight months of wasted time. And then there were the next four months of getting out and starting up again. Then the first major product of the label as an independent was a Johnny Carson album, which sold a lot of records but was a financial disaster. It took me another six months to raise enough money to pay off the debt before I could really start moving forward again. We were on very shaky footing. The dirt was up to my eyes already. In December 1974, after the Johnny Carson album, which was not successful—we lost almost enough money to close the company—some of the people here came to me and said, "Neil, we need a Christmas card. Whattaya wanna do?" And I said, "Oh, show a gold record and snow falling. I don't know." "But whattaya wanna say on it?" they asked. And I thought about it for a minute—how dark everything looked for the label, and I said, "In every desert, there is an oasis."

BILL AUCOIN: We didn't have any money. In fact, I couldn't afford rent. Fortunately, I lived in a house where the landlady was a creative person and so she understood. So she just let it slide for a while. My friends said I was nuts because I managed a group wearing makeup. They said, "You better take Bill out tonight, otherwise he is not going to eat." So they would take turns calling me and saying, "How about going out tonight?" That's how I ate.

JOYCE BOGART-TRABULUS: We were all strapped. We had no money. When I was working for KISS there were days I had to choose between taking the bus home or having a hot dog. It was tough to keep them on the road financially. I was always at ATI on a Friday sitting by Ira Blacker's desk waiting for hours for that week's check because we desperately needed the money [*laughs*]. Sometimes I'd have to call Neil and beg him for money for the band.

BILL AUCOIN: Money was really tight. I'll never forget Paul coming into the office and I think he wanted to borrow a little money but we were barely getting by.

PAUL STANLEY: I went up to Bill's office to ask for a raise. I was making $60 a week and wanted a $5 raise. I sat down with him and we started talking. While we were talking I saw that he had a hole in his sweater, which was taped from the inside.

BILL AUCOIN: Then I sat back and put my feet up on the desk and he saw that I had a hole in my shoe [*laughs*].

PAUL STANLEY: From the hole in Bill's sweater to the hole in his shoe, it was clear to me that this was not the right time to ask for more money [*laughs*]. I was thinking he was the big dog, and then I realized he's in the same boat we are. I remember people asking me back then, "How does it feel to be rich and famous?" And I said, "Well, I can tell you how it feels to be famous."

CAROL ROSS: They had no money. Bill was using his American Express credit card to finance the band's entire *Dressed to Kill* tour. He believed they'd eventually make it big but he was understandably worried about risking that much money. Bill put on a good front. His feeling was that he had to show complete confidence and not let down his guard.

BILL AUCOIN: We were pouring a lot of money into the band based on a true belief that KISS could do it. I mean, you always know inside whether it's there, it's just when it's going to break, when it's going to happen. The feeling was always there that it would happen in the end.

JOHNNY "BEE" BADANJEK (DRUMMER, THE ROCKETS): Jim McCarty and I were in Mitch Ryder & the Detroit Wheels and had hits like "Jenny Takes a Ride" and "Devil in the Blue Dress." In the late sixties we did a series of shows at the RKO Theater in New York for the famous DJ Murray the K, which had a lot of acts on the bill. It turns out that Gene Simmons was in the audience to see one of those shows. When the Rockets were playing shows with KISS, Gene told me, "After seeing Mitch Ryder & the Detroit Wheels I wanted to be in a rock-and-roll band." Of course, beyond us I'm sure there's others that equally inspired him as well.

JIM MCCARTY (GUITARIST, THE ROCKETS): The Rockets played tons of shows with KISS through the years [1974–1979].

JOHNNY "BEE" BADANJEK: Gene came into our dressing room and pulled me aside the first time the Rockets opened for them [October 19, 1974, in Toledo, Ohio]. We were out on the road promoting our first record. He said, "Here's the deal: every day, you want to get your picture in the paper and do every radio interview that you can do. You need to get your name out there every day." We were musicians' musicians. Jimmy [McCarty] has people like Eric Clapton, Jimmy Page, and Eddie Van Halen who really respect him as a great guitar player. When Paul and Gene had the Rockets out on tour with them, they knew they had to be on their toes and bring their A-game each night. Opening for KISS, if it's not your party, is tough. They sold out every show in all the old hockey arenas. The KISS crowds were just insane. We had to rock hard each night and give them a run for the money.

JIM McCARTY: Opening for KISS is not the most enviable position a band would want to be in, especially back in those days [*laughs*]. It was almost impossible. The crowd was not interested in anything you were playing; they just wanted to see KISS. There was a show we did with them in the Midwest somewhere and right in the middle of our first song I got smacked in the chest with something and it scared the hell out of me. I thought it was a roll of toilet paper but Bee swears it was a cheeseburger. So I look out and see the little son-of-a-bitch that threw it and he's about twelve or thirteen rows back and he's snickering to his buddies. So I stopped the band and went up to the microphone and said, "You know, you may not be interested in what we're playing but there's a few people in the crowd interested in hearing us. And if you want to step up here on the stage I'll shove this guitar up your fuckin' ass!" Then we started playing again and the crowd started going, "Yeah!" The cops came in and took the kid away and we continued with the set. We got a "yeah!" out of the crowd when I started cussin', so we did all right that night. I liked KISS. When you got past the gimmick they backed it up with some good solid rock-and-roll tunes.

JOHNNY "BEE" BADANJEK: Sometimes we'd hang out in Ace's room after shows. He had one of those original videocassette recorders, this big old clunky machine that looked like something from the moon. He had a whole bar set up. After one show we had a few drinks and sat around with him and watched the Rolling Stones movie *Cocksucker Blues*—we'd never seen that before. We'd also go out with KISS sometimes to play pool at a bar or hit a club in town.

After one show, we went to KISS's hotel and they were having a party in the banquet room—nice shag carpeting, plush hotel, tons of food and drinks. I don't know who started it, it might have been Gene or one of their crew guys, but it erupted into a huge food fight. I was sitting in the corner at a table with Peter Criss and I'd never spoken to him before. All of a sudden everything started flying—cake, grapes, stuff was hitting the walls. People were getting smeared with custard pies. Things really got out of hand. There were sixty, seventy people in the room and the place just erupted into chaos. The manager of the hotel came in and was screaming, "My room, my room!" Food was plastered all over the walls, shrimp cocktails dripping down. Out of this whole huge food fight Peter Criss and I were the only ones who didn't get hit with anything [*laughs*]. The manager kicked us out and I'm walking down the hallway with Peter and I said, "By the way, my name is Johnny, I never had a chance to thank you for having us on the tour" [*laughs*].

Despite the artistic merits of KISS's first three studio albums, capturing the raw and brutal kinetic power of their live shows remained frustratingly elusive. Enter producer Eddie Kramer.

EDDIE KRAMER: When it came to the live album Neil felt, "Shit, I better get Kramer to do this because he really understands how to record a heavy rock band." Neil called me and said, "I'd like you to consider working with KISS and doing a live record with them." I said, "Neil, that's very interesting, can I call you back?" I was really of two minds as to what to do because sitting on my desk was a demo for the first Boston album that [Boston founder] Tom Scholz had sent me. I remember listening to it and saying, "Shit, this thing is bloody good, what do I do now?" I remember picking up the phone and calling Tom and saying, "Listen, the demo you sent me is really incredible. Just put it out the way that it is; I can't really add anything to that." Then I picked up the phone and called Neil and said, "Okay, let's do it" [*laughs*]. The challenge for me was how do you capture a band like KISS who have fireworks and bombs going off and they're jumping up and down like maniacs? In a live situation, it's physically impossible for them to play in time and in tune, let alone to try to think about making a live record. So I thought this would be an enormous challenge.

By 1975, KISS was truly "hotter than hell" and selling out arenas across the country. With producer Eddie Kramer at the helm, KISS recorded shows in Cleveland, Ohio; Davenport, Iowa; Wildwood, New Jersey; and most crucially, the city that first put them on the map: Detroit.

PAUL *S*TANLEY: Before we started officially recording shows for *Alive!* we taped a few shows for reference. We recorded shows in four or five cities for a few reasons. Bands can often mistake energy for tempo. What we found was that the tempos on our songs when we played live were excessive. So we recorded some shows and listened back and had to tone it down because we were playing them too fast. With all the running around and jumping we were doing onstage, it was better having three or four shows to choose the best tracks to cull a live album from. *Alive!* was a sonic souvenir of our show.

EDDIE KRAMER: Detroit was an insane show. It was a big hall and sounded pretty damn good. The road had really hardened them and made them into a well-oiled machine.

Backstage at Cobo Hall, Detroit, May 16, 1975 Fin Costello/KISS Catalog Ltd.

MARK PARENTEAU: KISS recorded parts of *Alive!* at Cobo Hall, which was this big round arena located right on the Detroit River looking toward the bucolic area of Windsor, Ontario. Cobo Hall was the major arena in Detroit at the time. It held 12,500 people. If you could fill Cobo, you were happening. KISS filled Cobo many times; they sold out multiple nights there.

LEE NEAVES (KISS FAN PICTURED ON THE BACK COVER OF KISS ALIVE!): It was a great place to see a show and had great acoustics. There wasn't a bad seat in the house. Cobo Hall has a lot of history. All the major live albums were recorded there—KISS, Bob Seger [*Live Bullet*], J. Geils [*Blow Your Face Out*], Yes [*Yessongs*], the Doors [*Live in Detroit*], and Journey [*Captured*]. There's a reason all these top bands chose to record there. When you went to a Cobo Hall show it was like you were sitting with twelve thousand of your friends.

STEVE GLANTZ (CONCERT PROMOTER, STEVE GLANTZ PRODUCTIONS): I made up my own term for these guys. It's almost like Hitler-rock, because that audience—because of their beat, they're mesmerized by the music. I mean they have that audience hypnotized. They could say, "We're going out there and lifting up this building," and they'd

Preshow, Cobo Hall, Detroit, May 16, 1975 Mark Stockwell

just go lift it up. That's the kind of control they have. That's why their following is so strong and indestructible. That's why there's no question in my mind that they have something I've never seen any other group have.

EDDIE KRAMER: For the band's show in Wildwood, New Jersey, we were in this fifteen-hundred-seat place right on the boardwalk, and it was the middle of the afternoon and there was no scaffolding for the PA system. I said, "Where's the PA?" They sent out some of their roadies who stole scaffolding from a local building site, which was definitely a bad move, knowing the number of guys from that site that would kill them for that. Then when we were all ready to go, and the crowd was going absolutely bananas, Bill Aucoin was backstage and he was talking to the manager of the venue, who was a real gonif—a real crook. He told him, "The band's not gonna go onstage." And he said, "Whattaya mean?" Bill said, "Well, you haven't paid me. You have a choice. You can cancel the gig and you'll have a riot on your hands or you can pay me now." The guy had to pay him then and there [*laughs*].

With Casablanca perched on the precipice of financial ruin and record sales anemic in spite of the band's overwhelming popularity on the concert circuit, their next record had to be the home run that landed them in the rock-and-roll big leagues. Inside Electric Lady Studios, the pressure was on to deliver KISS's make-or-break album—and deliver it fast (and under budget) so the band could go back out on the road.

EDDIE KRAMER: When we got back to Electric Lady and started the laborious process of mixing it, Gene and I put together a list of all the shows and listed which songs were the best and what we were gonna use. It was absolute intensity to the nth degree to get it done. Paul and Gene came back into the studio and we had to remix

Live at Cobo Hall, Detroit, May 16, 1975, one of the shows taped for *KISS Alive!* Mark Stockwell

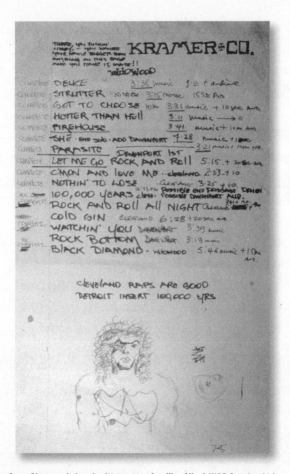

Gene Simmons's handwritten notes for *Kiss Alive!* KISS Catalog Ltd.

a portion of it because it wasn't strong enough, it wasn't big enough. I had to do a number of things to make it sound bigger by doubling up certain things, electronically manipulating things to make them sound bigger than they actually were.

PAUL STANLEY: Eddie Kramer was great at helping to create *Alive!* and I say "create" because the album was really an enhanced version of what took place. It was enhanced in a way to make you feel part of the event. It put you in the crowd. Live albums didn't do that. So the crowds were enhanced in a way that better replicated what it was like to be there. There was some controversy about that, but truth be told it's the most accurate-sounding live album of its time.

EDDIE KRAMER: The whole idea of the album was to make it sound larger than life. The challenge was (a) it was a double album, and (b) the performances were a little bit ragged. But the cool thing was I was able to utilize maybe six or seven tape machines running different loops of different kinds of applause. In a lot of cases the applause would be spotty and not in the right place, and we wanted to be able to build the applause to make it sound big. There was a huge difference in the sound of the audience in a small venue like the one we recorded in Wildwood compared to a larger venue like Cobo Hall in Detroit. We made forty, fifty, sixty tape loops of audience. We had tension rods keeping all the loops going. It was like a film mix.

NEAL TEEMAN: I worked as an assistant engineer for Eddie Kramer at Electric Lady Studios on *Alive!* For that album, the band was way behind schedule so Eddie booked both studios in Electric Lady. He was in one studio mixing and I was in the other doing minor overdubs with KISS, adding one line of a vocal or a guitar lick. It was a race to the finish to get it done quickly and under budget so the band could go back out on the road.

EDDIE KRAMER: It was also challenging because we had to overdub a lot of stuff. I don't care how great you are, there is no way you can do the kind of stuff that KISS does onstage and come off sounding in tune and in time. It's impossible. You knew the moment you heard the tapes that there were things that were not gonna sound good on record and you had to fix them. The boys were very cool about it. Paul's voice was plopped in a few times to make it sound good, the same with the rhythm guitars, and the same with Ace's guitars. Most of his solos we kept intact. Paul's raps were just culled from various performances and edited together. The drums were good, Peter Criss's vocals were good. We fixed what we had to fix and left what was great. You did it carefully and cautiously and made sure you grabbed the vibe and matched up the microphones and the sounds as best you

Electric Lady Studios paperwork for *KISS Alive!* overdub sessions, July 28, 1975 Ken Sharp Collection

can. You'd want to salvage a great performance which was marred by a few bad notes, and you'd fix them. You do what you do to make the record sound great. It enhanced their performances. I don't think that we were cheating. What we were doing was just fixing up a very, very tough live performance where the artists were not totally in control.

PAUL STANLEY: KISS has always been so visual and certainly in the beginning being theatrical had to have impact on the precision of what we were playing. When you're at a show, it's not just an aural experience but a visual one as well. When you are home you're focused on the sound alone, so we had to fix some mistakes—wrong chords, bum bass notes. We did whatever needed to be done to replicate . . . what you remember experiencing.

THE BIG PICTURE

B *y the mid-seventies, Irish-born photographer Fin Costello had earned a reputation as one of the hottest music photographers, capturing exciting images of rock royalty, including the Rolling Stones, Led Zeppelin, Bruce Springsteen, Pink Floyd, and Humble Pie. In May 1975, Costello was enlisted by KISS to shoot the cover of KISS Alive!, which is often cited as one of the quintessential rock album covers of all time.*

FIN COSTELLO: My career had taken off as a rock photographer in 1971. In 1973, there was a massive crash in Europe with the oil crisis so I decided to move from London to the States. Both Deep Purple and a company called AGI [Album Graphics Incorporated], who were in a brownstone building right next to New York's Museum of Modern Art, helped me with the immigration issues. I had a family and lived in Weston, Connecticut, and was working as a freelancer. One day I was down at Todd Rundgren's studio in New York City photographing the Brecker Brothers [a jazz duo consisting of brothers Randy and Michael, whose debut self-titled album was issued in 1975]. I went up to AGI's office and Peter Corriston, who became one of the leading designers of the time—he designed the covers for Led Zeppelin and the Rolling Stones—was working on the cover of *Dressed to Kill*. I'd come from England with the whole glam thing—Gary Glitter, Slade. I said, "This is ridiculous—who are these guys?" Peter said, "They're playing the Beacon Theatre tonight." I'd previously been at the Beacon Theatre photographing Little Feat, which was more my kind of music. It was a great place for photography so I said to Peter, "I'll come with you." He arranged some passes and I walked into the Beacon just as the band walked onstage. I had seen some theatrical stuff in my time but I'd never seen anything like this. Flash pots and explosions went off as they walked on. It was like Dante's Inferno. I had a fish-eye lens and thought if I could get down to shoot it'd be brilliant. So I got down to the front and it was an amazing sight, with kids climbing up onstage and hands everywhere. I didn't really listen to the music. It was just this thunderous beat. I remember the color more than anything else. I photographed the whole show and most of the pictures were included in their first tour program for *Alive!*

I remember calling [publisher] Gerry Rothberg at *Circus* and asking if he was interested in photos of KISS and he said no. Six months later it was a different story.

So I took the pictures into KISS's management office and set up a slide projector in Joyce's office and showed Bill and Joyce the pictures, and they were really impressed. I was really selling myself, and I had my Deep Purple *Made in Japan* and *Uriah Heep Live* album covers with me.

Bill said, "Hold on, can you come back later today and show it to the band?" So the band came in, I showed them the whole set of pictures, and they loved them. They hadn't seen anything like these images, as my approach was shooting close to my subject. A lot of photographers shot from a distance but I wanted to get right in there. In a lot of my pictures I'm shooting a foot away from the musicians.

I wanted to capture the immediacy and power and the only way to do that was to stick the camera right in their faces, and it worked. It made them so dramatic.

Then Bill asked me to work with the band again and said, "We can't afford to pay you but can you get money by shooting the band for various rock magazines?" They wanted me to promote the band, and I had all these connections with European and Japanese rock magazines. I was able to deliver the goods because every time I shot them they appeared in the European magazines.

Out of a conversation with Paul and Gene, they told me about their live album and asked, "Would you be interested in shooting the cover and doing something along the same lines as the Uriah Heep album?" *Uriah Heep Live* came with a booklet with photos of the band. Once KISS saw that they decided to do that with *Alive!* and include a booklet with photos that showed off their live show.

Picture perfect: photo shoot, Michigan Palace, Detroit, May 15, 1975
Fin Costello/KISS Catalog Ltd.

Photo shoot, Michigan Palace, Detroit, May 15, 1975 Fin Costello/KISS Catalog Ltd.

I remember Gene saying to me, "We're a live band—this is about theater; this is about rock-and-roll cabaret."

In terms of an album cover, the idea was to shoot it live at Cobo Hall. I'd already been to Cobo and knew it was a brilliant live venue. We always thought we'd get the cover shot at the concert. They were doing tech rehearsals the previous day [May 15, 1975] at the Michigan Palace, which was a little run-down baroque Victorian theater that was the home to bands like the MC5 and Iggy Pop & the Stooges. That same day they were shooting promo videos for two songs as well ["Rock and Roll All Nite" and "C'mon and Love Me"].

PAUL STANLEY: Those early promotional films were shot real quickly and were nothing more than trying to capture a reasonable facsimile of what we were about. Obviously, we couldn't run around very much and we had to stay stationary for the cameras, but this was not conceptual art, it wasn't anything more than trying to document the band live for overseas purposes. I like those promos. When you realize what was out there at the time it's in a completely different league. Who in 1975 was doing anything that had that kind of personality and visual impact other than Bowie or maybe Alice Cooper? But it still was nothing like what we were doing. It was one individual as opposed to four.

FIN COSTELLO: We were there all day and my plan was to get a poster shot for a Swedish magazine called *Poster*. There was no intention of getting a photo for the album cover. So I put up this yellow background in the middle of the stage in front of the drums and we photographed the band against it. Status Quo were a big British band who had a bit in their show where the three guitarists came close together and did a little dance, which had impressed Gene. It became a sort of in-joke during the shoot. They were doing something with their guitars and I said, "That's a bit like Status Quo." I took the backdrop out, which left the band's stage set. I told them to do the Quo move again, which was holding the guitars together and swinging them back and forth. On the cover of *Alive!* you can see that Quo move with the way Ace is holding his guitar. I kept on making them do it over and over until Paul eventually got fed up and said, "Look, we're not Status Quo, we're KISS" [*laughs*]. In the heat of it the band are just a prop, they're not people, you're just shouting at them to do what you want them to do.

PAUL STANLEY: Obviously, if you look at how Ace is holding his guitar—nobody can play a guitar like that [*laughs*]. But it was a cool picture that really captures the attitude of KISS.

FRANCIS ROSSI (LEAD VOCALIST/GUITARIST, STATUS QUO): Back then I thought KISS's image might put people off, but in fact it enhances them. No one had ever seen anything like KISS before or since. They had the image and you could never destroy it. It's one of the most unique things that came out of rock and roll. It was ahead of its time then and today it kind of fits. KISS could never get torn apart as individuals, so perhaps that gave them strength as a band because they've always got the mask and their image never let them down. They took something and really blew it up. It made the rest of us "rock bands," and they were KISS. It was the complete package, and I thought it was totally brilliant.

FIN COSTELLO: The next day we went to Cobo and I directed the little film, which was shot by John Kelly, a business colleague of Bill Aucoin and Joyce Biawitz's, which showed the band walking from the dressing room to the stage. This footage was projected onto the big screen above the stage before the band went on to build anticipation. I photographed the show and shot every idea that I had, but it turned out that I didn't get the picture that I wanted for the cover. The band in conjunction with Bill ultimately chose the picture that became the cover of *Alive!* They saw much more in the photograph than I did. Also, as you can see from the high angle of the camera, this could not have been taken at a live show, as I would have had to have been suspended above the stage to get that angle.

When I first saw the cover of *Alive!* I thought it was awful, all muddy and blurred, and it didn't look right. Technically, it's just not very good as a photograph. But then it gradually took on a life of its own. It didn't need to be sharp and clean and photographically perfect because it put across the atmosphere of what the band were about. It was a technical failure from a photographer's point of view;

it wasn't a failure in terms of what it did. [But] *Alive!* is probably one of the most successful album covers of the era.

As for the album's back cover, Fin Costello captured the classic enduring image of two excited KISS fans, fifteen-year-old teenagers Lee Neaves and Bruce Redoute, proudly holding their homemade KISS poster inside a packed Cobo Hall.

LEE NEAVES: I first saw KISS at the Fraser Hockeyland arena in Fraser, Michigan, in May of '74, and they were mind-blowing. I was hooked and felt this was a band I wanted to get behind. The next day I told everyone I knew in high school, "Dude, you've gotta see this band called KISS." When we found out that KISS were coming back to town to play Cobo Hall [May 16, 1975], we were beyond excited. We were fifteen years old at the time. The day of the show, my buddies Bruce Redoute and Bob Bommarito said, "Let's make a poster for the show," so we ditched school and worked on the poster.

BOB BOMMARITO (DETROIT KISS FAN): Lee was more of an artist and Bruce and I were the accessories type. So we agreed that he would draw and sketch the faces and Bruce and I would do the lettering and trim.

LEE NEAVES: I did the artwork on a big piece of cardboard in about twenty minutes—the faces and the lettering—and Bruce and Bob did the coloring with colored pencils and magic marker. We put silver glitter in each of the red dots on the poster surrounding the entire image and then I traced around each head with glue and spread glitter on that as well to give it more depth. Then we finished it by putting aluminum foil around the edges, keeping the KISS color scheme of silver and black in place.

BRUCE REDOUTE (KISS FAN PICTURED ON BACK COVER OF *KISS ALIVE!*): We were die-hard rock fans and we made the poster because we were hoping to get noticed. My brother Brian knew this ticket broker and had connections to great seats and we ended up getting tickets sixteen rows back.

BOB BOMMARITO: The night of the show we met at Lee's house and got ready to rock. We had a game plan: roll up the poster and tuck it away in our shirt so security would not hassle us, and get down close to the stage when the lights dimmed.

LEE NEAVES: So we get inside and if you looked around, we were the only ones with a poster.

FIN COSTELLO: That night Bill Aucoin came up to me and said, "Try and get a shot of the big crowd." I'd previously done it with Aerosmith at the Kingdome in Seattle, where we showed the vast crowd. There was a magazine for booking agents and concert promoters called *Performance* and they wanted to run a centerfold of a big crowd at a KISS show, which would convey the idea that KISS was a viable band that promoters should book. So I wandered off into Cobo Hall while the band was finishing putting their makeup on. I wanted to take a shot that showed off the crowd and the scale of the place. I was walking about and was amazed to see teenagers wearing KISS makeup, and I took photos of all that.

BRUCE REDOUTE: It was intermission, and my brother Brian, who was sitting next to us, wanted to bring out the poster. I said, "We should really wait for Lee," but he didn't want to so he ended up pulling it out.

LEE NEAVES: I went to the concession stand to get something to eat and came back to our seats and saw a crowd of people with flashes going off. And as I got closer I saw that it was my buddies Bruce and Bob holding the poster.

BRUCE REDOUTE: Brian and I lifted the poster up and did a 360 there in the sixteenth row, showing it to the audience at Cobo. People went crazy!

FIN COSTELLO: I saw these kids holding a poster and they said, "Are you Fin Costello?" At that time my name was very well known amongst the rock fans, as my work was appearing in *Circus* and *Creem*,

Alternate *KISS Alive!* back cover image with fans Bruce Redoute and Lee Neaves, Cobo Hall, Detroit, May 16, 1975 Fin Costello/KISS Catalog Ltd.

and my camera bag had metal plates with my name on them. They excitedly asked me, "Can you get this poster signed by the band?" I told them I couldn't help them because they were busy getting ready for the show. Then it suddenly dawned on me to get a photo of them holding up their KISS poster. I said, "Come down to the front, I wanna get a shot of the whole theater and I'll put you guys in it with your poster." I had my back to the stage barrier and they were a couple of feet in front of me.

LEE NEAVES: The photographer orchestrated the photo and said, "Put your arm up," so I did.

FIN COSTELLO: I had a big wide-angle lens, composed the shot and took three or four frames, and that was it.

LEE NEAVES: He took a few photos of me and Bruce holding the poster and I didn't think anything of it beyond that. A few months after the Cobo show I'm reading *Creem* magazine and I get to the inner back cover of the magazine and see a black-and-white ad for KISS's new live album and it's a photo of Bruce and I holding the poster! I was like, "What the heck? Dude, that's me!" Sometime after that a friend of ours called me and said, "Dude, did you see the album?" I said, "No, what's it look like?" And he said, "It's awesome. It looks like a live party. You gotta take a look at it." I said, "Well, what's it look like?" And he said, "Dude, you've gotta check it out." After work Bruce and I went to Korvette's, a local department store.

BRUCE REDOUTE: We walked into the record department and we both picked up a copy of *Alive!* and looked at the front cover and started examining it. At that point we didn't even turn it over yet. Then we flip it and we both looked at each other and our jaws dropped. It was *us* on the back cover holding the poster! We high-fived each other and screamed, *"Yeah!"* We couldn't believe it. To see that on the back cover in living color was the ultimate. It was a dream come true.

LEE NEAVES: I ran home and told everyone, "We're on a KISS album!" We were pretty popular before that but that made us stars in high school.

FIN COSTELLO: It would never have occurred to me to use that photograph for the back cover of the album. That was a big surprise for me, but it was perfect.

CAROL ROSS: I submitted photos to Bill [Aucoin] and I believe we all agreed, including the band, to use that photo of the fans holding the poster. And since the fans were such an integral part of the activities of KISS, it made sense to feature them on an album cover.

LEE NEAVES: I feel really proud to be a part of KISStory. Put it this way: to top off your childhood appearing on the back cover of an album by a band that you love is priceless. As an aside, our buddy Bob Bommarito wasn't left out either.

BOB BOMMARITO: If you look closely at the back cover of *Alive!* I'm sitting in a chair, four or five rows behind where Lee was standing.

LEE NEAVES: As for the original poster, we still have it. It's locked away in a dry, safe place.

FIN COSTELLO: We tried to do a similar photo for the cover of Aerosmith's *Rocks* album but it didn't work so we made a poster out of the photographs instead, which was included with the album. I captured lightning in a bottle with that shot of the kids holding the poster. Funnily enough, Chad Smith of the Red Hot Chili Peppers was at that show.

CHAD SMITH (DRUMMER, RED HOT CHILI PEPPERS): I was a total KISS freak from the first record on. I saw KISS for the first time on the *Dressed to Kill* tour at Cobo Hall in '75 when I was thirteen years old. It was the second concert I ever saw. We wound up with tickets in the twelfth row on the aisle. It was the most exciting moment in my life up to that point. My brother would say, "KISS sucks. Led Zeppelin is way better," and I'd respond, "Yeah, but Jimmy Page doesn't breathe fire or spit blood and [John] Bonham's drum riser doesn't go twenty feet in the air" [*laughs*].

So we get to the show and Cobo Hall's sold out. Everybody's smoking weed and we get our buzz on before the show. I turn around and see the guys with the poster and see this photographer taking pictures. I watched the whole thing go down. Little did I know that photo was gonna wind up being the back cover of the record [*laughs*]. When I tell people I was at that show, they say, "Well, you're not on the back cover," and I say, "I know, I was in front of them!" That photo was the perfect depiction of the average Detroit rock fan. The poster is really beautiful and touching in its homemade, primitive, mullet-wearing Detroit working-class kind of way. You look at it and go, "*There's* a time capsule."

As for the show, it was fuckin' awesome. They had one big screen over the top of the stage. When the lights went off, they started off with the recorded intro of "Rock Bottom" and the cameras caught them walking out of the dressing room down the hallway. My mind was so blown. I couldn't believe I was in the same building as KISS.

There were the actual guys, not the ones on my wall or on the records, and they're gonna come out and be twenty-five yards away from me and play all those songs I love! I'm getting goose bumps thinking about it now. The lights go off, the "Rock Bottom" intro starts, and the place goes fuckin' berserk. The noise just drowned out the prerecorded music. They came on and it was so loud, just this sensory overload. Everything about it totally lived up to any expectation I had. I was so blown away that I was breathing the same air as these guys.

So the show ends and my brother's friend, who's this really savvy concertgoer that knew how to get backstage, said, "I know where the stage door is, and we'll wait for the band to come out." So we went up to the stage door and one of the roadies said, "No, the band is gone, but here's some stickers for you." They gave us the backstage pass from the show, which said, "KISS Spring Tour '75." My brother's friend said, "I know they've gotta be here somewhere," so we drove around and saw a limo waiting at one of the farther doors down and no one else was there. We waited there and sure enough, about an hour after the show, the band came out without their makeup, which was a big deal at that time. We ran up to them and I got all of their autographs except for Peter. I remember my pen didn't work and I was freaking out but Gene was very patient waiting for me to get a pen that worked. I still have the pass and there's a bunch of scribbles on it. Dude, it was the greatest night of my life up until that point and it's probably taken a long time to beat it.

No longer did their long-suffering booking agency, ATI, have to beg, borrow, and steal to land KISS an opening slot on a three-act bill. By mid '75, the band was a legitimate concert headliner with solid drawing power nationwide.

PAUL STANLEY: I saw a pattern emerging with us on the road. Every night I'd ask somebody before the show, "How are we doing?" which meant, "What's the attendance?" One night they said, "It's sold out," and then the next night I'd hear the same thing. All of a sudden it was becoming the norm. For me the first realization that things were on an upswing was when we played the Hara Arena in Dayton, Ohio. Before the show I went onstage, looked out through the curtain, and saw this big crowd and said to myself, "My God, this is really happening!"

KISS's headlining show at Detroit's Cobo Hall on May 16, 1975, was a turning point in the band's career.

J.R. SMALLING: Cobo Hall was the first time they'd played to a sold-out crowd and a venue that big as headliners.

RICK MUNROE: It showed us what we were feeling and seeing around the country wasn't a fluke.

PAUL STANLEY: It was happening for us at that time. The roller coaster had gone over the top and we were on the ride. I could sense that we were really on our way.

PAUL CHAVARRIA: From that point on things started to move extremely fast.

JOYCE BOGART-TRABULUS: Going from clicking people into their show at Coventry in late '73 to less than two years later selling out Cobo Hall was incredible. When the twelve thousand screaming fans at Cobo Hall in Detroit held those lighters high, Bill and I started to sob. I'm getting chills thinking about it now. After the show I remember looking at Neil backstage and saying, "Oh my God, we've done it!" That show at Cobo Hall was the realization that there was nothing stopping this group. They were gonna be big.

NORMAN NARDINI (BASSIST, DIAMOND REO): Diamond Reo opened the show the night KISS recorded parts of *Alive!* at Cobo Hall. That still impresses people today when I tell them that. It was the second biggest show I'd ever played in my life, so I was green. We were just guys from Pittsburgh playing original music and we learned a lot that night. We learned we had to bring something more real, simple, and street to compete on the level of bands like KISS.

We happened to stay at the same hotel that KISS did and I didn't realize how big KISS was in Detroit. The hotel was jammed with insane people, many were dressed up like KISS and trying to find them. That insanity was following them everywhere.

GENE SIMMONS: While that Cobo Hall show was pivotal for us, we made one of the biggest blunders of all time that night. Instead of our normal show opener, which was "Deuce," we opened with "Rock Bottom," which had this quiet instrumental introduction. Ace and Paul played the instrumental interlude and the guitars are all out of tune. I'm standing there doing nothing while they're playing because the bass doesn't play on the intro. "Rock Bottom" didn't have a slam-bang beginning like "Deuce" and people were just sitting there like crickets. Thankfully, by the time we got to the third song everything was okay. We realized what doesn't kill you makes you stronger. We also quickly realized you needed to kick 'em in the nuts with a pile-driving opening song. So for the next show "Deuce" was back as the opening song.

VICTOR DAWAHARE (CONCERT ATTENDEE, COBO HALL): In the span of fourteen months I had gone from watching KISS on ABC's *In Concert*, having never heard of them before, to seeing them perform live at the Michigan Palace and then live again at Cobo Hall. At the Michigan Palace, there was so much energy the room could hardly contain it. My friends and I who had attended the show walked around our junior high school the following week shell-shocked. We had witnessed something so special and were blissfully unaware that we would never be the same. We wanted to share them with anyone who would listen, yet at the same time keep them all to ourselves. KISS was ours. On May 16, 1975, we attended the now legendary Cobo Hall show. This wasn't the Palace anymore. Sold-out arena, twelve thousand strong, large video screens, and the same unbelievable, uncontainable energy. We left with mixed feelings. KISS was going to be huge and they would no longer belong to just us anymore—they now belonged to the world.

A month after KISS's triumphant gig at Cobo Hall, the band's co-manager, Joyce Biawitz, a key architect behind the group's breakthrough, severed ties with the group.

JOYCE BOGART-TRABULU$: I think the band felt that there were things that they weren't getting from the label and thought there could be a conflict of interest because I was going to marry Neil. But to be honest, because of my relationship with Neil I was able to get a lot more for the group. I kept Neil interested and energized about what was going on with KISS. I'd say things like, "How exciting would it be if we could do this effect, but Bill and I can't afford to pay for it—can you?" [*laughs*]. And none of this was done behind Bill Aucoin's back. Bill was my partner and always knew what I was going to ask for or do. I ultimately pulled away from managing the band and our management company Rock Steady when I moved to Los Angeles to be with Neil and get married. It was a friendly parting of the ways with Bill and the band. Within a few months I went on to manage Donna Summer.

Long before an album makes its way into record stores, a marketing, promotion, and sales campaign for its release is carefully orchestrated. For a band like KISS, whose striking look was their calling card, creating the perfect album cover to enhance the explosive hard rock thunder pulsing in the grooves of the record inside was key to the band's success. New York–based art director Dennis Woloch was put in charge of preparing the design for KISS Alive!

DENNI$ WOLOCH: *Alive!* was the first of many KISS albums I designed. I did every single album from *Alive!* until *Crazy Nights*. One day Bill came into Howard Marks Advertising and said, "We're thinking of doing a live album; do you want to design it?" And being the young, hip rock-and-roll guy at the agency, I said, "Yes, I do!" *Alive!* was the first album I designed. We had no show business clients at the time.

We were doing diaper services, we were doing Wall Street clients, and we had some industrial clients.

Alive! was not a typical design. They already had the front and back shots picked and they looked great to me. We had the front cover photo bleeding off all four corners and the photo was gonna speak for itself. So in my head 90 percent of the job was already done. I had to pick a typeface and come up with a good-looking layout.

Then they told me it was gonna be a gatefold and I said, "Oh, now I have to design stuff." I came up with the stencil lettering for *Alive!* because that looked like it was impromptu, like it was very rushed. Instead of "side one" or "side two" I came up with "One, Two, Three, Four," almost like a musician counting off a song: "One, two, three, four!" Then in the gatefold, Bill said, "Maybe there should be a message from the band to the fans." I said, "I've got a better idea: let's have them write the notes to the fans in their own handwriting and I'll photograph them so it'll look real personal." He said, "I love it." I knew that the notes would look great just lying there; you could see all the detail and the paper. I knew that would have a tactile feeling about it. I got David Spindel to shoot that. He's a photographer I worked with a million times. I had each member of the band use a different pen and a different kind of paper so it looked like it was personal from them, like they wrote it in their bedroom at night while they were thinking about their fans. As for the content of the messages, some of the band members may have been helped along a bit by our copywriter, Peggy Tomarkin.

Alive! was a turning point in their album production because it's the first one designed by an advertising agency, people who knew marketing and knew the value of how to market, mold, and sell an image. That's what we do in advertising. We take a product and say, "You will have sex tonight if you buy this shampoo" [*laughs*]. It's not true, but you imply it in your commercial and people buy it. So we did that with KISS. If you look inside the gatefold, we have the three previous KISS albums on the inner gatefold sleeve. After hearing

Alive!, sales of the first three KISS albums, which were dead in the water before that, began to sell. Not long after that we repackaged the first three KISS albums as a three-LP set, *The Originals*.

Today, KISS are universally acknowledged as crafty merchandisers. But in 1974 and 1975, merchandising was still unexplored terrain in the music industry. That all changed on the band's KISS Alive! *tour with the introduction of their first piece of merchandise, a tour book. Two short years later, KISS's merchandising machine was in full force, raking in millions of dollars with items ranging from KISS radios to sleeping bags, dolls, and Colorform sets.*

PAUL STANLEY: Our first piece of merchandising was the KISS tour book, which was Bill's idea. It probably came from his theater background—the idea of a tour program or souvenir book from Ringling Brothers. Not too long after that we had belt buckles and T-shirts. Other bands saw it as sacrilege, the idea of a fan club or merchandise. If you're giving a fan an album, why don't you give them a belt buckle if they want that, too? It was born out of that and just grew and grew. Success breeds success, and when people see success they want to be a part of it. Once the merchandise succeeded people started coming to us to license the KISS brand, whether it was the logo or our images.

JOHN SCHER: KISS and Bill Aucoin were a great team. They were really smart guys. KISS not only stretched their talents musically and theatrically but also business-wise. They're probably the best and most successful early models of merchandisers in the music business. They paid much more attention to the T-shirts and the tchotchkes that they were selling to their fans than other acts. Early in their career I remember talking to Gene about T-shirts and he said, "Every kid wearing a KISS T-shirt is a walking billboard for us," and it was true. That really helped build loyalty among their fan base.

CHIP DAYTON (PHOTOGRAPHER): I bought the first KISS album in 1974 and became a fan as soon as I put the needle down on the record and heard "Deuce." I first saw KISS at the Beacon Theatre [in New York, March 21, 1975] with Jo Jo Gunne. As an afterthought I brought my sister's Pentax camera along with a couple rolls of black-and-white film. I was enrolled at C. W. Post College [on Long Island] and was taking a photography course. So I get to the show and start taking photos from the balcony and right up front. Back in those days you were able to get away with taking photos and doing pretty much what you wanted. I shot the show, developed the photos, printed them in the college's darkroom, and mounted them. The photos turned out great. I was blown away. Almost immediately I started thinking, "When can I shoot KISS again?" I also wanted to try and meet them and show them the photos.

I found out they were playing in Boston at the Orpheum Theatre, opening for [the] Hunter-Ronson [band]. At about four o'clock in the afternoon I went to the backstage door and asked one of their roadies where they were staying and he told me, so I went down to their hotel. I walked straight up to the front desk and said, "What room is Paul Stanley in?" and she told me. I get on the elevator and this guy gets on with super-long black hair. We go up one more floor and he gets out. He looked like he could be in a rock-and-roll band so I followed him and asked, "Are you Paul Stanley?" and he said, "Yeah." I said, "I'm Chip from New York. I've got some photos of the band at the Beacon Theatre." I showed him the photos, which were large eleven-by-fourteen prints, and I could tell he was really impressed. He invited me into his room and Peter Criss was sitting on one of the beds. He said, "Hey, Peter, this is Chip from New York, he brought some photos of us at the Beacon Theatre," and Peter began to look at the photos. And like Paul, he seemed really impressed. Later on I went to shoot the band at the Calderone Hall in Hempstead, New York, and I bumped into Lydia Criss. I showed her a huge photo of Gene I'd taken in Boston and she said, "That's a great photo. Can I bring this backstage to Gene?" And I told her, "Sure, you can have it."

A couple of months later I went to see KISS at the Capitol Theatre in Passaic, New Jersey, and I got backstage. I walked into Gene's dressing room and started showing him my photos, including the one Lydia gave him. He said, "Yeah, I have this one. You're the one who took this? This is really good." One thing led to another and I was given a pass to shoot their show on New Year's Eve, December 31, 1975, at the Nassau Coliseum. I took some photos in the audience from about thirty feet away from the stage with a new wide-angle lens that I bought that day.

The buzz at that time was they were gonna do a tour program. I show up at their office with my Kodak Carousel slide projector and portable screen. I started going through these photos of them; they were color slides of KISS from various shows I shot, including New Year's Eve 1975. So Bill Aucoin is looking at the photos and seemed in kind of a hurry. So somewhat impatiently he'd say, "Next! . . . Next!" All of a sudden an image came on the screen, which was a group shot of the band at Nassau Coliseum. Instead of saying "Next!" Bill leapt out of his chair and stood for a good fifteen seconds staring at it. Then he sat back down and says, "Next!" And I'm thinking he liked that one. A week or two goes by and I decided to call Dennis Woloch, the band's art designer, and said, "Dennis, how's the tour book going?" And he said matter-of-factly, "We finished it." I asked, "Did any of my photos make it?" And he said nonchalantly, "Well, you got the cover." And I almost dropped the phone. Here I was a huge fan of the band and was lucky enough to shoot them in concert at a bunch of shows and I got the front cover of their first-ever concert program, which to this day is one of the greatest thrills in my life.

ALIVE AND KICKING

Their first three studio albums had barely made a dent on the Billboard charts; the band's first live album was born out of a pragmatic decision to piggyback on their ascendancy as a mighty force on the concert circuit.

PAUL STANLEY: The disparity of the number of people who were seeing us versus buying our albums was startling. We did a live album because our studio albums weren't selling but the tickets were. Some of our fans would say, "Your albums don't sound like you do." The producers we were working with didn't capture what we were like. We didn't have the capacity at that point to articulate it or the technical ability to make it happen. I never thought any of our first three albums captured the intensity of what the band was going for or was. And it was a problem because people would come to see us and many of them weren't buying our albums.

Record shops could not keep the double-LP KISS Alive! in stock. The album was a milestone in the band's career, capturing the raw insanity and contagious excitement of the band's live performances.

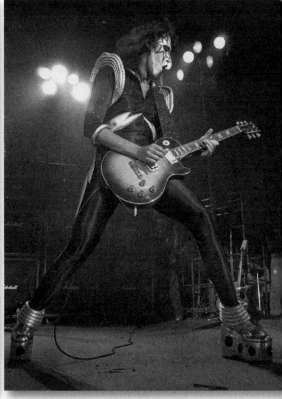

Paul and Ace at the Calderone Concert Hall, Hempstead, New York, August 23, 1975
Photos by Len DeLessio/www.delessio.com

GARY MAJOR: KISS had three albums which weren't all that successful, but their concert tours were gangbusters. A lot of what KISS did you can equate to what went on for years in country music. You had artists permanently out on the road playing shows across the country whether as a warm-up act or headliner.

LARRY HARRIS: They were on the road constantly and had no time to write new material and we didn't have the money to put them in the studio. No rock band had ever come up with a double live album unless they had some hits, and KISS didn't have any hits at all at that point.

MARK PARENTEAU: Not a lot of bands were successful with live albums. Sometimes they were a throwaway to fulfill a commitment to their record company. But *Alive!* was the real deal.

JOYCE BOGART-TRABULUS: *Alive!* captured who they were and what they were about. By the time they came out with *Alive!* they'd covered the waterfront in so many cities and had laid the groundwork for it.

JAAN UHELSZKI: KISS kicked ass live and really fed off the audience. They were galvanized by a good crowd; Paul especially really fed on the adoration. *Alive!* features all their kick-ass songs. Listening to *Alive!*, that visceral, scary, in-your-face thing came across on that album in a way it didn't come across on their previous studio albums.

ROBERT DUNCAN: The earlier albums seemed a little bit tame; they just didn't have the power, punch, or raw sonic energy that *Alive!* had. It was simply a better sounding record. KISS was definitely fun live and you can sense and hear their live energy on that album. They were building an audience, and their marketing finally delivered them to a bigger audience.

Light my fire, Calderone Concert Hall, Hempstead, New York, August 23, 1975
Len DeLessio/www.delessio.com

GARY MAJOR: KISS literally put sweat equity in what they did and it eventually paid off with *Alive!*

MARK PARENTEAU: *Alive!* hit big because KISS was a live act. What captured them best was that energy in front of an audience.

Bolstered by the hit single "Rock and Roll All Nite," the album became the smash hit KISS and their struggling label so desperately needed. KISS Alive! captured the band's commanding presence on the concert stage and established KISS as one of the most popular groups in rock and roll. With a blockbuster multiplatinum album, smash hit single, and string of sold-out shows across the country, KISS had truly hit the big time.

BILL AUCOIN: Actually, we knew about six months before *Alive!* was released that we were destined for success based on the growth of the recognition and airplay the group was getting. I also think that not getting overexposed by the mass media during the first two years allowed KISS to grow slowly and achieve success at their own pace. If they had gotten too much attention at first, they could have been destroyed.

MARK "ZERO" STINNER: Their success happened so fast—it was like a rocket ride. My first shows with them were in March of '75 in a small theater and less than a year later they'd set an attendance record outselling the Rolling Stones and the Who at the Capital Center in DC [November 30, 1975].

GENE SIMMONS: We knew something was going on. We were selling out concerts. We couldn't find groups to play with. We were thrown off of an Argent tour, a Savoy Brown tour. Black Sabbath threw us off their tour. It was a live-or-die situation for Casablanca. They didn't have any hits. But we just did what we did. And we always went against the grain.

BILL AUCOIN: KISS's live performance was so strong and the audience reaction was so positive that I figured if anything could kick the group off, it was a live album. I had a gut feeling that it would work. A live album was completely contrary to the current trend at the time. In the industry, everyone said that live albums hadn't sold for years and they would not sell in the foreseeable future. I was even told that a live album would be the death of the group, and even worse, I was cautioned that the last three albums hadn't sold well, and consequently, a live album of the same material wouldn't sell either. I had no reason to believe I was right except for my own belief and Neil's support. We plowed ahead despite the industry's warning that the live album would be the death blow. *Alive!* was a big success, setting the trend toward live recordings. Everyone did one after that, from Peter Frampton to the Rolling Stones.

GENE SIMMONS: Recording a live album when you really haven't made it was crazy. We hadn't even had a gold record. We just decided that we were gonna do a live album and we were gonna make it a *double* live album. Sonically, *Alive!* is what the band is about. Somehow taking an audience away from our songs makes it a lot more clinical or colder.

BILL AUCOIN: We also decided to do a live album because it was less expensive than recording a studio record. We had never gotten a royalty statement from Casablanca. Neil was going through all sorts of craziness with the company. They had left Warner Brothers. Neil mortgaged his house and asked independent distributors to put money into the company to keep it going. They did that based on the fact that Neil had success when he was at Buddah. Casablanca was really at the end of their rope.

PAUL STANLEY: Casablanca was in arrears on our contract and owed us quite a bit of money. It reached a point where we were looking at other options.

PAUL MARSHALL (KISS ATTORNEY, MARSHALL, MORRIS, POWELL, & SILFEN): Neil was not a good businessman but he was a great promotion guy. Fairly soon after *Alive!* was released, Bill told me to go to Neil Bogart and get the money we were due. Neil and I had a bad fight. You can't decide when you want to pay a band because you don't have the money. That's breach of contract. Not only did I

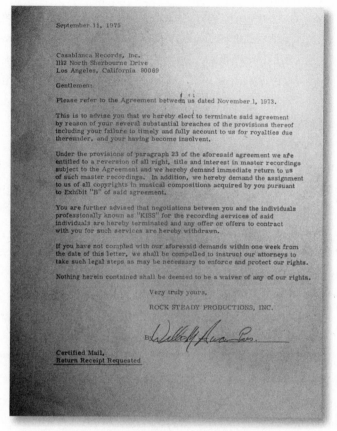

Rock Steady letter to Casablanca Records claiming breach of contract,
September 11, 1975 KISS Catalog Ltd.

want the back royalties we were due but I also leveraged the success
of *Alive!* and told Neil I wanted to make a new deal. Neil was furious
because I'd never had an adversarial relationship with him. I was
very firm and told him, "Take it or leave it." I had to be tough.
Bill was discussing offers with other labels. I remember Bill asking
me, "Can we walk?" And I said, "I think we can walk because they
haven't been paying us royalties." My advice to Bill was to pull them
off the label.

BILL AUCOIN: One of the reasons I used my American Express
card to finance KISS on tour was because the record label couldn't
afford to give us any more money. When I challenged Casablanca

over their nonpayment of royalties, the lawyers revealed that we were suing the label. It became a real war. Neil took offense to that because he had done a lot for us. I adored Neil, and he took it very negatively. Neil felt I was going against him and Joyce was caught in the middle. We were just releasing *Alive!* and I said, "If we don't get things straightened out now we're dead."

PAUL MARSHALL: *Alive!* was breaking and on its way toward becoming a smash album and Casablanca couldn't afford to lose the band. Neil was financially unwise and having trouble keeping the label afloat. Even though I liked him very much, as an attorney, when you know those things you must take advantage of it.

BILL AUCOIN: The word on the street in the record industry was that KISS was starting to break. They were listening to the kids who were saying, "KISS, KISS, KISS . . ." We finally worked it out, but all the other record companies were rushing in saying, "Sign here, sign here!" Doug Morris from Big Tree, which was part of Atlantic, wanted to sign KISS.

BUCK REINGOLD: There's no way in fuckin' hell that any label would have stuck with KISS as long as we did and put as much energy into trying to make them happen. If it was not for Neil Bogart, that group would have been dead in the water.

JOYCE BOGART-TRABULUS: The whole label was behind KISS. No other label would have given them that type of support. Everyone at Casablanca was a KISS fan. They worked tirelessly to help make them a huge success, but it took time. It wasn't gonna happen overnight. Had they signed with Atlantic Records or another label they would have been just another band on the label.

LARRY HARRIS: Neil filed a cease-and-desist order against KISS in the state of New York saying they couldn't talk to another label as they'd break their contract illegally.

BILL AUCOIN: I really had no reason to leave Neil. I just had to straighten out this business end. Neil actually went to the guys and asked them to leave me. He told them that he would manage them and Casablanca would do everything. This was all because I was going against him. But the guys made it clear to Neil that they wouldn't leave me. Basically we had Neil and Casablanca over the barrel.

JOYCE BOGART-TRABULUS: Things got out of hand. Neil respected and adored Bill as well. He thought he was incredibly creative and inspirational. We were all a great team together.

LARRY HARRIS: *Alive!* was a do-or-die album for KISS and for us. We had no money at the time, and if this album didn't take off we would have been in dire financial straits and KISS would have left the label. Thankfully, *Alive!* and Donna Summer started to break around the same time and we were selling a lot of albums.

PAUL STANLEY: When *Alive!* became such a huge success, they came up with the money and paid us what we were owed, and we stayed put with the label.

BILL AUCOIN: We signed a new deal with Casablanca, who paid us a lump sum of what we were owed, and we would go forward.

LARRY HARRIS: It was not easy but Neil scraped together a couple of million dollars and sent Bill the biggest check he'd ever seen in his life.

BILL AUCOIN: We went from literally having no money to getting a check for two million dollars. This was back in '75, when two million was like ten million. All I can remember is staring at those zeros. I sat there and kept counting the zeros. I must have counted those zeros a thousand times.

PAUL STANLEY: The great thing about *Alive!* is that it was a recording that featured and paid tribute to the audience as much as the band. I think that's what people respond to so well with *Alive!* It really captures the live experience in terms of what it felt like in the audience. It was real important to me that the audience not be background because at a KISS concert in some ways the audience is competing with the band [*laughs*]. It's a communal effort. It's like a church revival; it's trying to get everybody to peak together. *Alive!* really spotlights the experience not only in terms of what the band

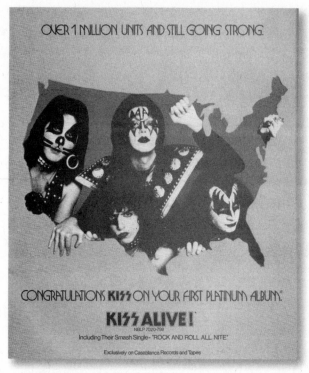

KISS Alive! platinum album trade ad Courtesy of Mark Cicchini

was doing but what the audience was doing. KISS has always been essentially a live band. *KISS Alive!* was a sonic souvenir. Instead of getting the tour book at the show, you got the album. It wasn't something that you listened to as an outsider. The album was designed to be inclusive. When you heard it you felt like you were in the middle of the crowd. It was the first album that captured what KISS was about.

ACE FREHLEY: A lot of guitar players come up to me and say *Alive!* is their rock-and-roll bible. That's how they learned how to play guitar, which I find flattering. If that album bombed we would have been dropped from the label. But I knew the record was gonna be great because I believe the only way to capture KISS is with a live record. At that point our studio albums didn't capture us as well as the live album. I thought I played better live because the audience inspired me.

PAUL STANLEY: *Alive!* was a make-or-break album. We were at a turning point. I remember saying to Bill while we were doing it, "Do you think we'll sell 350,000 copies?" And he said, "Well, that would be great but let's not get our hopes up."

EDDIE KRAMER: Because of KISS's fan base, we thought the album was gonna do okay. Maybe it would sell 250,000, 300,000 copies, which would be very respectable. Then, of course, the album took off like a bloody rocket and did half a million, then a million, two million, and wound up selling over four million copies. Everybody went crazy. *Alive!* sold way beyond our wildest expectations.

PAUL STANLEY: I always had faith in the band. I knew it was going to happen eventually but it was after the first live album that I knew we'd finally broke. It captured what we were doing and we began to see the difference in audience reaction. It was then that we could look out from the stage and see that the place was packed. When it happened night after night we realized that it was not going to let up. We knew what the audience wanted and we were determined to give them what they came to see. We understood the audience because in a sense, we are the audience.

The smashing success of KISS Alive! *was the breakthrough KISS so desperately needed. With KISSmania raging throughout the United States, the band continued touring at a frantic pace. Near the tail end of the* KISS Alive! *tour, KISS made a welcome detour to the Hawaiian Islands, playing a show on February 29, 1976, at the Neal S. Blaisdell Memorial Center Arena in Honolulu. The following evening, three of the band members— Paul, Gene, and Ace—showed some aloha spirit by taking the stage at a tiny club called O'Pehrs for some after-hours jamming with members of a hot local band, Uncle Leo's Rock 'n' Roll Road Show.*

TRENT DOWNING (DRUMMER, UNCLE LEO'S ROCK 'N' ROLL ROAD SHOW): KISS was on the *Alive!* tour and stopped to play a show in Honolulu. I went to see their show and it was amazing. Ken Rosene, the concert promoter who booked KISS, was a good friend of my band, and I was dating his secretary, Lynn Denham. The night after the concert she called me and said, "Hey, Trent, I'm with KISS right now at their hotel. They're gonna stay in Hawaii for a few more days and they want to go to a bar to see a live rock band." O'Pehrs was the only rock-and-roll club to see live bands, and we were the house band; we played there six nights a week. So in her own way she was giving me a heads-up that KISS might drop by. She wanted to make sure if they came by, the club could take care of them because they were big rock stars. She didn't want to drop them into some kind of a madhouse without some prior arrangements to their arrival. I assured her I could make whatever arrangements were necessary. At this point I'm freaking out. I get to the club and tell the owner and he says, "Are you kidding me? If you get KISS to the club I'll take care of everything." I called Lynn and told her what he said and she said, "Great, I'm bringing them by tomorrow night." I assumed they'd come in around midnight since we played every night until three in the morning.

So the next night rolls around, I get to the club around eight thirty and have a drink before we start playing. I'm sitting at the bar sipping Jack Daniels and look out the door and two big, long black stretch limos pull up. Out of the first limousine comes Gene, Paul, Ace, and Lynn. Out of the second limo comes Peter Criss with four groupies. The club wasn't even crowded at this point. Lynn brings them in and these guys are dressed like rock stars. It wasn't their stage attire but the KISS attitude was in full display—black leather pants, platform heels. I meet them and introduce them to the bar owner and he said, "Whatever you guys want, I'll take care of you. We have a table cordoned off over here." And Gene said, "No, I don't wanna sit at a table. I wanna sit next to the band right here at the bar." Paul and Gene pull up a couple of stools and we're bullshitting. Meanwhile, I'm looking at Peter and he's got two chicks on each arm. He makes a quick big circle around the club, comes back to where we're sitting, and said, "I've seen enough, I'm going back to the hotel—bye." So he jumps in the limo and he's gone and out of the picture for the rest of the night. And I'm thinking, "If we can get these guys to jam, there's no other drummer in here but me." I asked Gene and Paul if they wanted to jam and they said, "No, we're only here to hang out and have a good time." While I was sitting with Gene and Paul at the bar, Ace was off playing pool.

So I get up and we started our first set. We played a mixture of cover tunes and originals and avoided playing the KISS songs in our set because we didn't want to play them while they were in the club. We finished our set and took a fifteen-minute break. I go back to hang out with Gene and Paul, and Ace is still playing pool. Now word is starting to get out that KISS is in the club. People were jumping on payphones calling all their friends and the place was packed to the rafters. It got so crowded that we couldn't let any more people in because it was a potential fire code violation.

MICHAEL CORCORAN (MUSIC CRITIC, SUNBUMS): Gene Simmons was trying really hard to pick up the waitress; I remember him doing that whole locked-in-eyes thing with the deepish voice.

TRENT DOWNING: Before we start the second set I'm speaking with Paul and Gene and said, "C'mon guys, let's jam together!" They said, "Well, let's see what Ace wants to do." I let a few more minutes go by and said, "C'mon, let's go, let's do it." So they turned, looked at each other and kind of shrugged, and Gene said, "Okay, let's do it. You guys play a couple of songs and then call us up." So we played a couple of songs and by this time the club is full of energy and excitement. Then our guitar player, Rocky Disopa, said, "We've got a couple of special friends we want to bring up right now. You saw them a couple of nights ago at the [Neal S. Blaisdell Memorial Center] Arena. Will you please welcome from KISS, Paul Stanley and Gene Simmons!"

The crowd went absolutely apeshit and all hell started to break loose because everybody is realizing they're gonna jam. So our bass player walks off the stage because Gene's playing bass and our keyboard player also walks off the stage. So now it's just Gene and Paul, me, and Rocky, our guitar player. We could barely talk to each other because there was so much yelling and screaming going on. I'm thinking, "Great, we've got them on the stage, now what the fuck are we gonna play?" I leaned over to Gene and asked, "What are we gonna play?" And he's like, "Do you know any songs by Free?" And I said, "Yeah, we know 'All Right Now,'" and he said, "Play that." So I yell over to Rocky and said, "'All Right Now.'" He nodded in the affirmative and Paul also nodded as well. I counted it off and we came out of that gate like gangbusters. They ended up playing part of the next three sets with us. By that time Ace had jumped onstage and joined the ruckus.

MICHAEL CORCORAN: They did one song, a slow blues number that they called something like "New York City Blues."

TRENT DOWNING: I still have a list I scribbled down after the show of some of the songs we played: "Brown Sugar," "Johnny B. Goode," "Jumpin' Jack Flash," "Smoke on the Water," and "I Just Wanna Make Love to You." What was really cool was in between one of the sets Gene told me this was the first time KISS had ever played publicly without makeup.

At one point during a break between sets I was at the bar talking to Gene and out of the blue he lifts up his massive black platform boot so his leg is parallel to the floor. He's pointing to a monogrammed gold dollar sign on the top and says, "You see this?" and he points to the gold dollar sign. I replied, "Yeah." He said, "They call me 'money bags.' I made my first million dollars this year." I responded, "That must be nice," and Gene said, "Yeah, it's nice but it's a lot of hard work." Little did I know that the monogrammed dollar sign that Gene shared with me would later be incorporated into what is now known as the copyrighted money bag logo Gene uses to represent his company.

During the break before the last set, I was throwing more songs out at Gene and Paul and they were throwing a couple of tunes at me: "Do you guys know this?" While we're bouncing songs off of each other, I said, "Why don't we play one of your songs?" They looked at each other and I could tell they were thinking that was not a good idea. Then Gene goes, "What songs of ours do you know? And I told him we knew "Strutter" and "Rock and Roll All Nite." He looks back over at Paul and nothing was said between them. Now it's time to start the final set and Gene, Paul, and Ace came right up again. We played some more tunes, and it's fucking pandemonium. We had to end the set early because right in front of the stage was like a mosh pit. The energy and excitement had gone through the roof. I told Gene, "It's getting too crazy in here so we need to end the set with one final song." And he said, "You told me you know 'Rock and Roll All Nite'—let's do it." And we played it and all hell broke loose. I was like, "Goddamn, man, I'm playing with KISS!" I couldn't believe it; it was incredible.

At the end of the night when we ended the set I was in seventh heaven. The set's over and the lights come on. Everybody's crowding around Gene and Paul and Ace for autographs. Some people had copies of the *KISS Alive!* album. They signed a couple of autographs but it had been a long night and they wanted to get out of there. I came out from behind the drums and was smiling at Gene and he cracks this big smile at me and said, "I've gotta tell you, you're a great drummer. I had a great time playing with you tonight." And at that point Paul turns around, shakes my hand, and said, "You were really good. I had a lot of fun." I was just blown away. I walked the band to the limo and by now there were tons of people on the street. They thanked me again, jumped into the limo, and sped off into the night.

Jamming at a local club and enjoying the company of some of Honolulu's most beautiful women—KISS was reveling in the well-earned spoils of their success. But a life-threatening incident almost led the band's prized frontman to an early grave.

RICK STUART: We were in Waikiki Beach and Zero, our pyro technician, and I rented a catamaran, and we really didn't know what we were doing. The guy who we rented it from said, "Stay in this cove area and you'll be fine." We saw the break where you could go straight out to sea and were just tooling back and forth around the cove and then suddenly there's Paul at the end of this little pier and he's waving at us saying, "Hey, come on and pick me up!" We managed to steer ourselves toward the pier and Paul hopped on. So we're all on this catamaran with two little hulls and a sail and we started moving back and forth. Then we saw Bob Davies, who was the band's production manager, and Tony Canal, who was our wardrobe person. The two of them were on a catamaran on the outside of the cove and were out to sea, but Bob was a sailor and knew what he was doing. They were heading toward the break in the cove to come back in and we started heading toward that way to meet up with them.

PAUL STANLEY: None of us knew how to work a catamaran. As we're going out some of our crew was coming back in and they said, "Be real careful, there's riptides out here." I thought we were gonna parallel the shore but we headed straight out to sea.

RICK STUART: The next thing I remember is we passed them by and the current just sucked us right out. At that point we were about a mile out from the shore. But we kept going out and to our right were these giant waves breaking and we started drifting behind them. We didn't have control at this point. The wind and the ocean were taking us where these waves were breaking.

MARK "ZERO" STINNER: We weren't experienced sailors and wound up getting pretty far out in the ocean. The catamaran was bouncing around in the waves and Paul was getting scared that we wouldn't be able to get back to shore.

PAUL STANLEY: I thought, I'm the guy from the *Reader's Digest* stories who's gonna be out at sea for two months eating seagulls. So I jumped off the catamaran, which was really stupid. I jumped off and the catamaran kept going and there was a really strong current. Instead of swimming diagonally with the shoreline I'm trying to fight the tide and swim into shore, which you'll never be able to do.

RICK STUART: I stood there frozen looking at him. We were out to sea and that's my rock star in the water. We threw him a life preserver but it just drifted past him because the water was so choppy.

PAUL STANLEY: I told Rick, "Don't just sit there, jump in!"

RICK STUART: I looked at Zero—"Good luck, I'll see ya"—and I dove in. Man, we were at least two miles out and it was real choppy and rough.

PAUL STANLEY: And now the two of us are drowning.

MARK "ZERO" STINNER: I was still in the catamaran moving in the wrong direction and couldn't turn the thing around and get them.

RICK STUART: Then we started moving into these giant waves, which were breaking on us and smashing us down into the water.

PAUL STANLEY: Surfers are telling us to go fuck ourselves. All they were concerned with was we were in their way.

RICK STUART: They were being really nasty and almost hitting us with their surfboards. It was a pretty panicky situation for both of us. Paul and I both got smashed down into the coral and it felt like someone had sliced my foot open with a razor. Same thing happened to Paul. Turns out we stepped on sea urchins but we didn't know that at the time. Then we moved into a dark, murky area which was a little calmer. My thought was my foot was cut wide open and this was a perfect place for a shark to get us. We were exhausted and fighting to swim in.

PAUL STANLEY: It was humbling because I was looking at the shore and people are playing volleyball and sunning themselves, and I'm dying. It made me aware of how unimportant I am in the world. The world's gonna go on and I'm dead.

RICK STUART: Thankfully, the guy who rented the catamaran saw us and came out in his rescue boat and brought us in. Once we got in the boat we discovered there were dozens of sea urchin spines in our feet and it was very painful. Paul and I were taken to the hospital and we went to the emergency room. The doctor told us the only thing we could do was piss on our feet [*laughs*]. We thought he was fucking with us and trying to screw around with an off-island rock star. But as it turns out it was absolutely true and it's a well-known cure. We got back to the hotel. Paul and I went to our rooms. About ten minutes later my phone rang and it was Paul and he said, "I just pissed in the sink on my foot and it worked" [*laughs*].

It was a very scary experience. Paul and I were lucky to survive. Not long after I remember him introducing me to his parents, saying, "This is the guy who saved my life in Hawaii." And as for me, months later I was still pulling sea urchin spines out of my feet [*laughs*].

THE HOTTEST BAND
IN THE LAND

Released in November 1975, the live version of "Rock and Roll All Nite" ushered KISS into superstardom; it peaked at #12 on the Billboard singles chart in January 1976. Today, more than thirty-five years since its initial release, "Rock and Roll All Nite" remains KISS's quintessential party anthem.

PAUL STANLEY: Neil had met with us at the old Casablanca office on Sherborne Avenue in West Hollywood and said, "You guys need to write an anthem." I had no idea what he was talking about. I asked what he meant and he said, "A song that fans could rally behind that would embody what the band symbolizes, like the Sly & the Family Stone song 'I Want to Take You Higher.'"

GENE SIMMONS: Neil was not a musician, he was a concept guy, and he made us understand what an anthem is. He said, "Something that says who you are and makes you want to raise your fist in the air." And we said, "You mean something like a football kind of song?" I was thinking of a military song like [*singing*] "Off we go into the wild blue yonder . . ." kind of song. He said, "Who are you and what do you believe in? That's what you have to write about." We thought that was an interesting notion 'cause we always liked writing about how we feel and most importantly who we are.

PAUL 5TANLEY: I remember going back to the Continental Hyatt and sitting in my room and singing, "I wanna rock and roll all night and party every day." I just had the chorus and nothing else. The chorus can exist on its own because it's so powerful. It was pretty undeniable. I went to Gene and played it to him.

GENE 5IMMON5: I had a song called "Drive Me Wild," which was a song based on the Stephen King book *Christine* about a car that comes to life and the lights are on in the dark like boobs. "You drive us wild, we'll drive you crazy" was written as poetic lyrical license from the viewpoint of the car.

PAUL 5TANLEY: Gene played me this verse for this song he had and his verses and my chorus fit together seamlessly. It sounded like a perfectly good song. It's a track that the audience had to connect to; that's what made it what it is. It was released as a single and it tanked. It wasn't until the live version came out that it became a hit.

5COTT 5HANNON: Neil Bogart had incredible intuition about what people wanted. When he saw the incredible response from the audience when the band played "Rock and Roll All Nite," he decided to release it as the single.

LARRY HARRI5: "Rock and Roll All Nite" was very well received when they played it live. Despite it not being a success when released as a studio single, we thought it might work as a live single and we were right. If you played the versions of "Rock and Roll All Nite," both studio and live, the live version had so much more energy.

PAUL 5TANLEY: The magic about that song didn't really happen until *KISS Alive!* That song clearly blew the doors open for us. Those were days where radio would grab onto a song and start playing it and there'd be a groundswell, not necessarily always from the record company. Radio stations were playing *KISS Alive!* and they gravitated toward "Rock and Roll All Nite," so we released it as a single.

BUCK REINGOLD: The first batch of singles KISS released weren't radio-friendly but "Rock and Roll All Nite" had all the ingredients for a top-40 hit.

BOB EZRIN: For the first time in their history radio was playing them in heavy rotation. Once people heard that song they connected with the band on a whole new level because "Rock and Roll All Nite" was a pop/rock hit. It wasn't a left-field, strange, twisted, cartoony, unusual piece of music in the vein that people expected from a band that looked like that. Instead, it was very mainstream. That single opened up the market and got people to view them in a different way. They suddenly realized, "This is a pop/rock band that has embraced pop culture and is wearing it like a costume."

MARC NATHAN: We put out the "Rock and Roll All Nite" single with the live version on one side and the studio version on the other. Warner Brothers had just experienced success with Deep Purple's "Smoke on the Water" in a very similar fashion. The studio version of "Smoke on the Water" didn't do well and then it appeared on their live album [*Made in Japan*]. They put out a single with the live version on one side and the studio version on the other. A guy named Bill Tanner was the program director for a very progressive top-40 radio station in Pittsburgh called 13Q and had taken that live version of "Smoke on the Water" and started playing it in night rotation. Warner Brothers put it out, and all of a sudden this top-40 radio station starts playing it and it begins to sell. With KISS, I saw a similar situation happening.

I was the West Coast regional guy, and while Pittsburgh wasn't my territory I had relationships with programmers in other parts of the country. I didn't think that anyone would get upset at me for over-stepping my bounds and reaching out beyond to a program director that I had a relationship with. So I sent a very simple Western Union telegram to Bill Tanner which said, "As you did with Deep Purple's 'Smoke on the Water,' I suggest you check out KISS's 'Rock and Roll All Nite.' Same pattern developing." I was letting him know this was a band that was starting to make moves in concert and at rock radio. Once Bill started playing it, it blew up. It was a real hit record. That's why thirty-five years later you still hear it in hockey arenas and you still hear it on classic rock radio and you still hear it on oldies stations.

The whole idea about hit records that turn into hit acts, you catch lightning in a bottle. KISS had never had a hit before and all of a sudden it was their moment; it was their time and it was their song. The reaction to that song at pop radio was so immediate that the thing just exploded. "Rock and Roll All Nite" is the record that put them on the map to stay.

Look, everybody's gonna take credit for it. I don't necessarily take credit for breaking the record. But I certainly take credit for sending Bill Tanner that telegram and I absolutely know that Bill Tanner was the first major top-40 guy to play the record. All of this happened in a much different era, when radio stations were privately owned and there wasn't the kind of monopolies and duopolies of Clear Channel. Records spread a whole lot differently in the seventies than they do in the twenty-first century. Bill Tanner was a program director who was very well respected amongst his peers. As soon as he took a shot on that record, there were other programmers in the United States with similar backgrounds and their radio stations had a similar demographic slant that they took his lead and ran with it. It didn't take long for the record to become a hit. You put the record on the radio and the phones went crazy and the album sales went crazy and we had a 45 that was selling to kids who weren't album buyers.

DENNIS ELSAS: Radio needed to catch up with the public who were already embracing the band as a live act and "Rock and Roll All Nite" was the perfect song to reflect that.

GARY MAJOR: "Rock and Roll All Nite" was a great song and it sounded like a hit. Timing is everything. Rock-and-roll radio sounds better in the late spring and fall than it does in the winter. That song sounded great over the car radio with the windows down. It's since become the band's national anthem.

EDDIE KRAMER: That song has pure energy and vibe. If you capture that on tape the public will gravitate towards it. Look at Peter Frampton and his album *Frampton Comes Alive*, which was the other massive live album I was involved with. I did two or three albums with him prior to his big live album. That was a setup for the live album. Even though his studio records were good, the live album had a magic that was so compelling, and it's the same thing with KISS. Their live version of "Rock and Roll All Nite" was so compelling. It grabbed you by the nuts.

Gene Simmons's handwritten letter that charts the success of *Alive!* Courtesy of Ross Koondel

Backstage at Cobo Hall, May 16, 1975, Detroit. *Left to right:* Bill Aucoin, Peter Criss, Gene Simmons, Paul Stanley, Ace Frehley, Joyce Biawitz, Neil Bogart. *Sitting:* Concert promoter Steve Glantz.
KISS Catalog Ltd. /Fin Costello

GENE SIMMONS: A message may only be as good as the messenger. So when the right message comes out of the mouth of the right messenger you've got something and it connects, and that holds true for "Rock and Roll All Nite." It was the right song with the right message at the right time. It was the post-hippie social environment. People were bored by their regular nine-to-five jobs and they were looking for an escape, and "Rock and Roll All Nite" had an idyllic "I just want to have a good time while I'm alive" quality that drew people in.

PAUL STANLEY: When I wrote the chorus of "Rock and Roll All Nite" the idea was to write a rallying song, and the message was anthemic. So when you turned that into a song involving twelve thousand people it hit home.

MARK PARENTEAU: "Rock and Roll All Nite" was the first really memorable KISS song that really worked on the radio. And it's still the KISS song that gets the most airplay on classic rock radio stations. In reality, KISS was a phenomenon that made it in spite of radio. They did it on the strength of their live shows and marketing.

JEFF FRANKLIN: The album busted wide open because we'd toured them so much. They caught their own spirit on that record.

LOU GRAMM (LEAD VOCALIST, BLACK SHEEP): When Black Sheep played with KISS they were at the top of their game. Not only was their show great but we liked their songs. For their image and the type of band they were, they crafted songs that were right on the money. After we played we'd go sit in the audience and watch them. They were really exciting. We'd listen, enjoy it, and learn. I learned a lot from them about professionalism and connecting to the audience, which I later tapped into when I worked with Foreigner. Paul would say things that would incite the audience and then kick into another song. Black Sheep had done shows with Peter Frampton, Procol Harum, and Aerosmith. One of the hard rules I learned was no matter how much they love you, don't even consider playing an encore. None of those other bands would allow us to do encores. When we played with Frampton, the plug on the PA was pulled. When we played with KISS, the audience really enjoyed us and the band let us do an encore. KISS was real good to us, and that's something I'll always remember.

NEAL SCHON (LEAD GUITARIST, JOURNEY): In '75 we opened shows for KISS. We opened up for everyone in those days, from KISS to Cheech & Chong to Emerson, Lake & Palmer.

ROSS VALORY (BASSIST, JOURNEY): It sounds like an odd combo to have early Journey opening up for KISS, but in those days those kinds of things happened.

NEAL SCHON: At that time, Journey was pretty much a rock-fusion band. We were listening to a lot of Mahavishnu Orchestra.

ROSS VALORY: I didn't know anything about KISS. All we were told was they were all about theatrics and costumes.

NEAL SCHON: We got to the gig and they were already there in bathrobes putting on their makeup and costumes. I was like, "What is going on here?" [*laughs*]. We did our set and frankly, most of what we were doing went right over the audience's heads. KISS had rabid fans and their audience wasn't easy to play for. Then KISS went on and Gene was spitting blood and blowing flames.

ROSS VALORY: I'm sitting there watching them going [*laughing*], "What the hell is this?"

NEAL SCHON: I didn't quite know what to think.

ROSS VALORY: It was certainly surprising and definitely amusing. And that's the whole idea. I wasn't surprised that KISS made it because of the entertainment value and the uniqueness of it. They were definitely one-of-a-kind, if not the first of a kind.

LESLIE WEST (LEAD GUITARIST, THE LESLIE WEST BAND): My group, the Leslie West Band, opened for KISS at Nassau Coliseum [December 31, 1975]. In the middle of our set some fans started spraying mustard all over the stage. It was like an ice skating rink of mustard [*laughs*]. I did my best not to slip and thankfully we got through our set unscathed, but you could tell that the fans were getting restless and didn't want to wait any longer for KISS to get onstage.

GARY HERREWIG (GUITARIST, ARTFUL DODGER): We did shows with KISS when the *Alive!* album was breaking. Being an opening act wasn't that much fun; you knew you were cannon fodder for whatever the audience wanted to throw at you. But there were shows where we did well. We viewed it as a challenge. But it was like opening for the circus: they wanted to see the elephants and the trapeze and we were just guys with guitars, and we weren't spitting fire and having fireworks come out of our guitars.

GARY COX (GUITARIST, ARTFUL DODGER): In retrospect, deciding to tour with KISS and rushing our second album to do so was probably the worst decision we ever made. The excitement of getting our product in front of such a large audience was tempting, but it would teach us a great lesson. The lesson? Those tours were designed to sell KISS . . . period. The fans don't go to KISS concerts to sit and listen to good songs, get to know the bands. They're coming to see fire-breathing, blood-spitting figures that are bigger than life. KISS delivered and earned their fans every night. When you left the show you were a fully indoctrinated member of the KISS Army.

It reminds me of the 1933 film *King Kong*. There's a scene in the film where the character Jack Driscoll returns to New York with the eighth wonder of the world, and the audience in the movie sits in nervous anticipation of the curtains being raised to see the beast. Then Driscoll shouts, "I give you *Kong*!" and the curtain rises. Every person in the audience was speechless and breathless at what they were seeing. Try being the opening act for King Kong! That would be a good practice tour to get your band ready for KISS.

I remember one night the band getting a really great response from the KISS crowds. I saw Gene and Paul off to my right in the shadows checking out the show, and Paul gave me a thumbs up. After the set I was hanging out backstage just soaking up the after-show atmosphere when down a lit hallway I could see Gene motioning me toward him. He was in full KISS attire standing about seven feet tall. I walked up to him and he says, "Good show tonight." And with that, he grabs me under my arms and lifts me up and around and slams me up to the concrete wall. He gets this demonic look on his face and growls, "Now take that goddamn Nils Lofgren button off your shirt! Who are you trying to sell out there? Artful Dodger or Nils?" He said, "I want to see Artful Dodger on your T-shirts and anywhere else you can put your name." Gene could really get preachy when it came to business. I did take that button off and still have it to this day as a reminder of that time with KISS. He was right after all. There comes a point when you have to stop acting like a fan and start selling yourself out there.

GARY HERREWIG: We had a real connection with Paul and Gene because they liked the kind of power pop music we were doing. Some nights they'd be on the side of the stage watching us, just grinnin' and enjoying it. They weren't cutthroat. One time they came to visit us in the studio when we were recording at the Record Plant, and I remember Paul told me, "Man, I wish we could do the kind of music you guys are doing."

GARY COX: We had played some huge coliseum in some town and after the show I ran into Gene backstage. He said, "I want you to follow me. I want to show you what real money looks like." I can't recall which bandmate went with me, perhaps Steve Cooper, but we followed. In tow were some business guys with briefcases, one of which was handcuffed to the guy's wrist. We enter this big room in the belly of the coliseum and I was stunned at what I saw. A room filled with people sitting around counting mountains, piles, stacks of cash from the show. It was like an opium parlor for accountants. Off to one side I see truck drivers getting paid, ready to roll on to the next town. These guys were in a hurry. It was a machine. There was very little talk—just the sound of money being counted. It was beyond my wildest dreams. And Gene? Well, looking back on it, his fascination with money was beyond the love of money. It was more like an addiction, really. To see Gene in the midst of all that cash was like watching Anthony Hopkins close his eyes and sniff the air in *Silence of the Lambs*.

ROBERT DUNCAN: In a wonderful way, "Rock and Roll All Nite" resists intellectualization and analysis. It's about the gut and leaving your brain at home. I embraced the song's complete lack of pretension. KISS is all pretense and yet at the same time they're more authentic because they're not trying to pretend they're something they aren't. I used to kid that you could hear their New York accent in the singing.

DON WASLEY: It was a very liberating time and that was a liberating song which said what everybody felt.

ROBERT DUNCAN: The song carried this New York–ish aggression. There's nothing louder, more direct, or dumber than "I wanna rock and roll all nite and party every day." If you imagine somebody who does that [*laughs*], that's a headbanger before we identified them as headbangers.

NANCY SAIN: What teenager doesn't identify with rock and roll and partying? If you were a party person that was your song.

KEN BARNES: I think the success of *Alive!* and "Rock and Roll All Nite" aligned itself with the rewards of constant touring, a great single, and the hard work of band, record company, and management. Persistence pays off and they're the proof of that.

GENE SIMMONS: KISS has always been essentially a live band. We've never spent a lot of time in the studio; we just don't have the temperament for it or the patience. That meant the live versions of our songs had a more honest energy and *Alive!* captures that perfectly.

MARC NATHAN: Casablanca was an interesting place to work because they spent money like no other label. I'm not so sure I would have taken the job at Casablanca if I really knew our precarious financial situation. This KISS record ["Rock and Roll All Nite"] and this

Donna Summer record ["Love to Love You Baby"] both came within the first three or four months that I was there. The success of those two singles helped save the label from going under. As it was, even with those hit singles, we still put out far too many records and we still spent far too much money.

In February of '76, with a real hit record under their belts, I was still working for Casablanca but now had moved down to Los Angeles and assumed a national promotions position based in the LA office. Bobby Rich was the program director for B-100, which was the top-40 radio station in San Diego. Despite the success of "Rock and Roll All Nite," there were still some skeptics about the viability of KISS as a pop act. I felt if I took Bobby to the show and he saw how young and passionate the audience was I might be able to convince him to start playing KISS. I was twenty years old, which was very young for a guy to be doing promotion as long as I had been doing it. I'd started four years earlier working for Bearsville Records while I was still in high school. So here I am, twenty years old, and I'm going to a KISS show. This was really my demographic. And the reason I was so sure it would be a good idea to take Bobby to the show was that only five years earlier I was one of those fifteen-year-old kids going to see an Alice Cooper show at the Fillmore East. It was crazy theater. I knew KISS was the next step from going to an Alice Cooper show. You were going to be bombarded with fire and lights. It was unlike anything you'd ever seen.

So we're at the show, and during the band's performance, someone within an eyeshot of where Bobby and I were sitting, some kid decided to do fire-breathing and the fire burst out of his mouth and it singed the hair of the person who was sitting directly in front of him, which caused a huge commotion with security and police. It was an incident that crystallized just how insane the whole KISS experience was. You'd be sitting there one minute and the next minute your hair could be on fire [*laughs*].

Once KISS had a hit record, they were really able to maximize the success of it with the touring and the merchandising. It really set the tone for so many acts that would follow them in the years to come. What it really proved in that era and still proves to this day is that a pop record will make you much bigger than you could ever possibly imagine, and they were able to parlay their hit into a real career. There's always a difference between hit records and hit acts. There's plenty of one-hit wonders that have massive singles that have been as big or bigger than "Rock and Roll All Nite." But very few have been able to parlay that success into album sales, concert tickets, merchandising, and a career that still thrives today.

There's an airplay monitoring service called Mediabase, and within the last seven days there were still 150 radio stations across the United States that played "Rock and Roll All Nite" at least once. "Rock and Roll All Nite," both the studio version and the live version combined, have been played well over 320,000 times since the inception of this monitoring service in 1998. The next most popular KISS song is "Detroit Rock City," which has been played 86,000 times, so that gives you an idea as to the magnitude of that particular song and what it has meant in popular culture.

LARRY HARRIS: Nobody, not the label or the band, were expecting it to be so successful. The album just exploded.

JEFF FRANKLIN: We had suffered major financial losses and thankfully, [three] of our records hit around the same time to save our asses—*KISS Alive!*, *Mothership Connection* by Parliament-Funkadelic, and *Love to Love You Baby* by Donna Summer.

EDDIE KRAMER: That record made them. It saved the record company and certainly kicked KISS's career in the ass and moved it forward. There was no other band like KISS that was able to utilize the core raw elements of rock and roll and combine them into an intelligently put together, very exciting, and very visual show. It hadn't been done before. *Alive!* captured a spirit and captured a vibe that the public wanted to hear. It has a fantastic energy. *Alive!* is still one of the great live hard rock albums of all time.

Paul shows off his first platinum record to a sold-out crowd at Detroit's Cobo Hall, January 25, 1976 Photo by Tom Weschler/www.BackstageGallery.com

JOYCE BOGART-TRABULUS: KISS was Neil's obsession. He believed in them and knew that they were stars. He knew they were gonna happen and when they broke through with *Alive!* it was the ultimate high.

LARRY HARRIS: I came out during an encore at one of their shows at Cobo Hall in Detroit [January 25, 1976] and presented the band with platinum records for *Alive!* They were beyond thrilled. They'd worked so hard for it and finally achieved their dreams. KISS had finally made it.

PAUL STANLEY: Getting a gold album was what I'd aspired to and what I'd worked towards since I was a little kid. That was really the pinnacle to me as far as I was concerned. To get a gold album for *Alive!* meant much more to me than when it went platinum. The success of *Alive!* happened so quickly. That album became gold in the blink of an eye and then went platinum very quickly, and it just kept selling. The doors just broke open.

GENE SIMMONS: *Alive!* stayed on the charts for over sixty weeks. In January of '76 we got a gold album and within another month sales doubled and it became a platinum album. Two months later it was double platinum. Casablanca was literally going broke until the album happened. Getting our first gold record was amazing. It felt like a dream. All of a sudden we had a gold record and bands that we loved were now opening for us. It's one thing being up onstage and seeing KISS fans go out of their minds, but getting a gold record was a stamp of legitimacy by the world. We felt we had arrived.

KISS receiving gold records for *Alive!* backstage at Nassau Coliseum, Uniondale, New York, December 31, 1975 Fin Costello/KISS Catalog Ltd.

36

THE ROAR OF THE GREASEPAINT, THE SMELL OF THE CROWD

The primal energy of their studio records notwithstanding, KISS is meant to be experienced in a concert setting. A KISS show offers pure escapism: a chance to forget your problems or your dead-end job and be swept into a fantasy world of loud guitars and mind-blowing theatrics. The band's juggernaut of sound and spectacle remains an immersive experience for both KISS and its audience.

GENE SIMMONS: When we introduce ourselves with "You wanted the best, you got the best," we are not only proclaiming to the fans that they're about to get a treat but also throwing down the gauntlet for ourselves each and every time we step up on that holy stage.

PAUL STANLEY: Playing live is as much an escape for me as it is for the audience. No matter what's bothering me or what kind of hassles I'm having, when I hit the stage I blot them from my mind. While I'm onstage with KISS, I'm escaping from myself. It does the same thing for the audience. It's fantasy and escape and power and it's

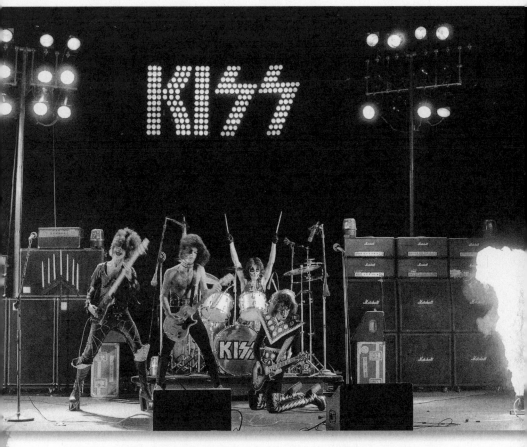

Photo shoot, Beacon Theatre, New York City, March 21, 1975 Len DeLessio/www.delessio.com

no different for them than for me. The people that I really looked up to as performers were Pete Townshend, Roger Daltrey, Robert Plant, and Steve Marriott. There are certain things that you have to do to draw in twenty thousand people. I remember seeing Steve Marriott and it was like being at a church revival. And that to me is the coolest thing you can do—turn it into an evangelical event. I love that whole vibe. It's kind of an electric church, electric temple, electric synagogue.

GENE SIMMONS: We continue to be dedicated to the notion that our fans deserve the best, which is why our shows are always jam-packed with more—more fireworks, more lights, more sound, more special effects.

PAUL STANLEY: Those who are either insane or independent make and walk their own path. I guess the end result determines which category you fall into. Maybe we're a little of both. KISS has always been proud to be different—proud to break rules and make our own. That's our badge of honor. We've never set ourselves up as role models, but if people find inspiration in us, let the past forty years be their battle cry.

We never got into this to be this year's hula hoop. We never got into this to be this year's critical darling. We got into this only because we loved what we were doing. We started out with the idea of doing this forever, and we're still doing it.

ACE FREHLEY: Back in those days we all had lots of laughs together. We were all success-driven, but to what ends I would only find out much later on down the road. Regrets? Yeah, I have a few, too few to mention. Sinatra says it best!

GENE SIMMONS: Gene, Paul, Ace, and Peter are four bums off the streets of New York who had a dream and started following that dream on the yellow brick road and literally found the pot of gold and the answer to all their prayers at the end of the rainbow. KISS's career from 1972 to 1975 is a story of the good, the bad, and the ugly. For the good, we were fortunate enough to have met Ace and Peter, who completed the puzzle and made us whole. Both Ace and Peter were every bit as important as Paul and I in defining the sound and look of the band. The naiveté and the innocence that all four of us had when the band was formed was priceless. That's the memory I'm always gonna take with me. At the beginning, everybody in the band had an "all for one, one for all" attitude. Nobody could pick on us. Nobody could say anything bad about us. You may have disagreements with your family but you all come together if anyone says anything bad about your brother or sister. To this day there's a soft spot in my heart for the Beatles during the period right before *A Hard Day's Night*. When I think about Elvis, eternally the iconic imagery is when he was a young guy in 1956. And when I think about KISS, I always want to think about when Ace, Peter, Paul, and Gene were all young and innocent and believed in the same thing, and that thing was called KISS.

PAUL STANLEY: I look back very fondly at the band's early days. There was a real sense of purity then because all of the outside influences hadn't infiltrated and tainted the good. It was exciting. It was new. Back then we shared everything with each other. We shared our time onstage. We shared women. We shared dreams. It was an elite club of four very special people. In the beginning, whatever differences we had, the magic was not to be devalued or taken for granted. And that's why we were together. Through whatever tensions there may have been, there was a sense that this was special and only comes along once in a great while. Although we all came from different points of view and different backgrounds, in our own way we all wanted the same thing. But at this point it was really still about the four of us and this mountain we all wanted to climb.

Thanks to the unprecedented success of KISS Alive!, *KISS were now officially superstars. After 1976, KISSmania spread across the country, and the group attained elite status as arena headliners and global hitmakers. The KISS phenomenon was in overdrive. A series of multiplatinum releases* (Destroyer, Rock and Roll Over, Love Gun, Double Platinum, Alive II, *and* Dynasty), *solo albums, sold-out world tours, a TV movie, and a mighty merchandising bonanza that raked in hundreds of millions of dollars transformed KISS into one of the seventies' most commercially successful bands.*

Sadly, the original lineup did not last. Drummer Peter Criss would be the first member to depart, in 1980, followed two years later by Ace Frehley. Both embarked on solo careers, and Frehley achieved modest success as a recording and touring artist. Replacing Criss was drummer Eric Carr, while Vinnie Vincent, Mark St. John, and Bruce Kulick each took their turn in the lead guitar slot.

In September 1983, the band did the unthinkable and revealed their faces sans makeup on an MTV special. Bolstered by the well-received albums Lick It Up, Animalize, *and* Revenge, *and the hits "Lick It Up," "Heaven's on Fire," "Tears Are Falling," and "Forever," the group met with considerable commercial success from the eighties through the mid-nineties, albeit nothing like their extraordinary run in their heyday in the seventies. Throughout those post-makeup years, generations of KISS fans, many of whom had never even seen the first lineup in concert, continued to clamor for a reunion of the original band. Their wish was finally granted in 1996, when Gene, Paul, Ace, and Peter reconvened for a massively successful—and lucrative—reunion tour, the studio album* Psycho Circus, *and two follow-up road treks.*

Four decades since they first donned their leather outfits and stepped into their seven-inch boots, four decades since an unsuspecting public first laid eyes on the iconic images of Paul, Gene, Ace, and Peter, KISS is more popular than ever. Today, the band, stewarded by founding members Paul Stanley and Gene Simmons, and with new recruits lead guitarist Tommy Thayer and drummer Eric Singer, soldiers on. Their two studio albums, Sonic Boom *and* Monster, *have been well received, and KISS continues to tour internationally. Yet for many fans, KISS's original lineup is still the only configuration of the band that really matters. KISS's formative years, from 1972 to 1975, laid the foundation for the rock-and-roll glory and worldwide success that followed.*

They say you'll always remember your first kiss. With the life-affirming power of mind-altering rock and roll mainlined into their veins, KISS tore up the rule book and followed their own credo, much to the disdain of their detractors. That burning ambition, unblinkered focus, and unwavering commitment—some would call it naiveté—served them well. Finally making it in the rock-and-roll big leagues—on their own terms—was a sweet, hard-fought victory KISS will never forget. And it all started with four guys who had nothin' to lose.

CAST OF CHARACTERS

GAVINO ABAYA III: A KISS fan who attended and photographed the band at the Hotel Diplomat show in July 1973.

JOHN ALTYN: A KISS fan who attended some of the band's early shows in 1973.

ROD ARGENT: The founding member of 1960s hitmakers the Zombies and 1970s outfit Argent, who scored hits with "Hold Your Head Up" and "God Gave Rock and Roll to You," a song covered by KISS in the 1990s.

SCOTT ASHETON: The drummer for Iggy & the Stooges, who played on the same bill with KISS at New York's Academy of Music on December 31, 1973.

RONI ASHTON: An employee at the Daisy in Amityville, New York, site of some of KISS's earliest shows.

BILL AUCOIN: Besides the band themselves, Bill Aucoin, KISS's manager from 1973 to 1982, was the person most responsible for their success. In the 1970s, his management stable also included Piper, a band led by future rock star Billy Squier, Starz, and New England. His biggest post-KISS success came when he managed Billy Idol. Aucoin passed away in 2010.

JOHNNY "BEE" BADANJEK: The drummer with Detroit hitmakers Mitch Ryder & the Detroit Wheels and 1970s heavy rock outfit the Rockets, who opened shows for KISS on various tours in the 1970s.

RUSS BALLARD: The guitarist, vocalist, and songwriter for the 1970s British outfit Argent. He wrote several songs recorded by KISS, including "God Gave Rock 'n' Roll to You" and "New York Groove."

DOUG BANKER: The concert promoter for Doug Banker Productions, he promoted KISS shows in the 1970s.

KEN BARNES: A music writer for *Phonograph Record Magazine* from 1971 to 1978.

BILL BARNETT: A football player for the Cadillac High School Vikings in 1974 and 1975, he is the current mayor of Cadillac, Michigan.

ROBERT BARRETT: Attended KISS's Palisades, New York, library benefit in May 1973.

VIRGINIA BARRETT: One of the organizers of KISS's Palisades, New York, library benefit in May 1973.

JAY "HOT SAM" BARTH: KISS's front-of-house sound engineer from 1974 to 1976.

JULES BELKIN: An Ohio-based concert promoter with Belkin Productions from 1966 to 2001, he booked KISS on various tours beginning in the 1970s.

DAVE BELL: The lead singer of Canadian band Barbarossa, who were the headlining act for two shows on KISS's February 1974 tour of Canada.

PATTY BENJAMIN: The daughter of Sid Benjamin, owner of the Daisy, the site of KISS's earliest club gigs. She saw the band perform many times at her father's club.

RICHARD BENJAMIN: The son of Sid Benjamin, owner of the Daisy in Amityville, New York.

SID BENJAMIN: The owner of the Daisy in Amityville, New York, the site of some of KISS's earliest club gigs. He passed away in 1988.

TERRANCE BERT: A music photographer who photographed the onstage pie fight between KISS and Rush at the end of KISS's tour in June 1975.

HAROLD C. BLACK: A multi-instrumentalist (harmonica, congas, and tambourine) for Teenage Lust, who performed on the same bill with KISS at New York's Academy of Music on January 31, 1973.

IRA BLACKER: The co-owner of the ATI booking agency from 1968 to 1974; the agency handled KISS's early tours.

ERIC BLOOM: The lead vocalist and guitarist in Blue Öyster Cult, a band that bridged hard rock and the macabre and forged a remarkable four-decade career, tallying up radio hits like "Don't Fear the Reaper" and "Burning for You." BÖC opened for KISS on the *KISS Alive!* tour.

NEIL BOGART: A veteran music industry mover and shaker who worked at MGM Records, Cameo-Parkway, and Buddah Records, he was deemed a promotion genius. KISS was the first act signed to his label, Casablanca Records, which also launched the careers of Donna Summer, the Village People, Parliament-Funkadelic, Angel, and others. Neil passed away in 1982.

JOYCE BOGART-TRABULUS: With partner Bill Aucoin, she was comanager of KISS from 1973 to 1975. In 1976, she married Casablanca Records founder Neil Bogart. Today she serves on the board of directors for the Bogart Pediatric Cancer Research Foundation.

BOB BOMMARITO: A Detroit KISS fan who attended the band's Cobo Hall show in May 1975, one of the shows taped for *KISS Alive!*

MICK BOX: The guitarist for 1970s British hard rock outfit Uriah Heep. KISS opened shows for the band in 1974 and 1975.

DAVE BRINES: The head football coach of Cadillac High School's Cadillac Vikings in 1974 and 1975.

JOEL BRODSKY: A renowned music photographer who shot

album covers for KISS's debut as well as for the Doors, Van Morrison, MC5, the Stooges, and others. He passed away in 2007.

RUSTY BURNS: The lead guitarist in the 1970s Southern rock band Point Blank, which opened for KISS on various tours in the 1970s.

GEEZER BUTLER: The bassist and founding member of Black Sabbath, widely regarded as the pioneers of heavy metal. KISS opened a show for Black Sabbath in December 1975.

DAVID EDWARD BYRD: The graphic artist responsible for creating posters for Bill Graham's Fillmore East venue and the Rolling Stones' 1969 world tour. He designed the Casablanca Records logo and assisted during the photo shoot for KISS's first album.

MICK CAMPISE: An original member of KISS's road crew from 1974 to 1976.

ERIC CARMEN: The lead vocalist and guitarist of the influential 1970s power pop band Raspberries. That band was a major influence on Paul Stanley, who was inspired by the group's top-5 hit "Go All the Way" when writing the opening riff that begins "Deuce," a song from KISS's debut album.

PAUL CHAVARRIA: One of KISS's original roadies and bass tech from 1974 to 1980.

LYN CHRISTOPHER: An artist whose 1973 self-titled album was released on Paramount Records. Gene Simmons and Paul Stanley contributed backing vocals to several tracks.

DICK CLARK: The music legend—impresario, *American Bandstand* host, music industry entrepreneur. He was also an early champion of KISS, booking the band's first TV appearance on his show *In Concert*, which aired in March 1974. Clark passed away in 2012.

MILISSA CODDEN: A cheerleader for the Cadillac High School Vikings from 1975 to 1977.

MARIA CONTESSA: The designer of KISS's first set of costumes.

ALEX COOLEY: A Georgia-based concert promoter with Alex Cooley Presents, he promoted numerous KISS shows in the 1970s.

ALICE COOPER: The theatrical rock visionary, he was a major inspiration for KISS. He attended the February 1974 launch of KISS's label at the Century Plaza Hotel in Los Angeles.

MICHAEL CORCORAN: The music critic for Hawaii music magazine *Sunbums* from 1975 to 1977, he was in the crowd and witnessed KISS's after-hours jam session at a Honolulu club during the *KISS Alive!* tour.

STAN CORNYN: Executive vice president of Warner Brothers Records who oversaw the day-to-day launch for KISS's debut album.

STEPHEN CORONEL: A childhood friend of Gene Simmons, he arranged the first meeting between Simmons and Paul Stanley. He's a onetime member of Simmons and Stanley's band Wicked Lester. While playing in that band, Simmons and Coronel cowrote the KISS songs "Goin' Blind" and "She."

FIN COSTELLO: Acclaimed Irish rock-and-roll photographer who took the classic front- and back-cover images for KISS's breakthrough album, *KISS Alive!*

BOBBI COWAN: Longtime music publicist who handled KISS's Casablanca Records February 1974 launch while working for the PR firm Gibson & Stromberg.

GARY COX: A guitarist in 1970s power pop band Artful Dodger, who opened shows for KISS on their *KISS Alive!* tour. He passed away in 2012.

MARSHALL CRENSHAW: Acclaimed guitarist and singer/songwriter, he is best known for the 1982 hit "Someday, Someway." His 1970s band, Astigafa, opened one show for KISS on the *Dressed to Kill* tour.

JOEY CRISCUOLA: Peter Criss's younger brother, he tagged along with Criss when he first met Gene Simmons and Paul Stanley outside New York's Electric Lady Studios. He also attended many early KISS shows.

LYDIA CRISS: In 1970, Lydia Di Leonardo and Peter Criss were married; they divorced nine years later. She attended and photographed many of KISS's early shows.

PETER CRISS: Founding member and drummer of KISS, he left the band in 1980 and rejoined in 1996 for a highly successful reunion tour and album. He departed the band once more in 2004, and three years later released the solo album *One for All*.

BURTON CUMMINGS: The lead vocalist of popular Canadian hitmakers the Guess Who, who scored countless hits in the 1970s, including "No Time," "Share the Land," "No Sugar Tonight," "American Woman," Undun," and "Star Baby." He attended Casablanca Records' Century Plaza launch in February 1974.

BOB "NITEBOB" CZAYKOWKSI: The New York Dolls' sound engineer from 1973 to 1975. Following his stint with the Dolls, he worked on the road for Aerosmith.

JIM DANDY: The lead vocalist of Southern rock outfit Black Oak Arkansas, who were the headlining act for various tour dates with KISS in late 1974.

VICTOR DAWAHARE: A fan who attended KISS's May 1975 Cobo Hall show that was taped for the *KISS Alive!* album.

CHIP DAYTON: Rock photographer and avid KISS fan who photographed the band from 1974 onward. A photo by Dayton appears on the cover of the band's first tour book.

SEAN DELANEY: The band's creative consultant and choreographer, he was also their original tour manager, cowrote many KISS songs, and produced Gene Simmons's 1978 solo album. Delaney passed away in 2003.

RON DELSENER: A New York concert promoter for Ron Delsener Presents. He promoted many KISS shows, beginning with their March 1975 stint at the Beacon Theatre.

MICHAEL DES BARRES: The lead vocalist of UK rock outfit Silverhead, who performed on bills with KISS in early 1974. He went on to enjoy success as a member of Power Station and as an actor.

WARREN DEWEY: The engineer for the band's first two albums, *KISS* and *Hotter Than Hell.*

DENNIS DEYOUNG: The former lead vocalist, keyboardist, and songwriter with popular Midwest rock band Styx, who opened shows for KISS on their *KISS Alive!* tour.

BUCK DHARMA: The lead guitarist for Blue Öyster Cult, a band that bridged hard rock and the macabre and forged a remarkable four-decade career, racking up radio hits such as "Don't Fear the Reaper" and "Burning for You." BÖC opened for KISS on the *KISS Alive!* tour.

ANDY DOBACK: Attended KISS's early shows at Coventry in 1973.

NEAL DOUGHTY: A founding member and keyboardist of REO Speedwagon, who performed on various bills with KISS in 1974 and 1975.

TRENT DOWNING: A drummer in Honolulu club band Uncle Leo's Rock 'n' Roll Road Show. He jammed with KISS at an after-hours club show during the *KISS Alive!* tour.

ROBERT DUNCAN: Managing editor of *Creem* from 1975 to 1976 and a staunch early supporter of the band. He is also the author of *KISS*, the first book ever published about the band.

DENNIS ELSAS: The music director at WNEW-FM from 1972 to 1976. He was one of the first DJs to play KISS on the radio.

BOB EZRIN: A legendary producer who oversaw production duties on three KISS albums: *Destroyer, (Music from) The Elder*, and *Revenge.* He's also revered for his seminal work with Alice Cooper and Pink Floyd.

JAY FERGUSON: The founding keyboardist of Jo Jo Gunne,

who played on bills with KISS in 1975. He later wrote the theme song for the popular NBC television series *The Office*.

MORGAN FISHER: The keyboardist with Mott the Hoople, who lit up the charts with their hits "Roll Away the Stone," "All the Way from Memphis" and David Bowie's smash hit "All the Young Dudes." Mott opened shows for KISS in 1975.

BRUCE STEPHEN FOSTER: Grammy Award–nominated songwriter and solo artist who provided rollicking piano on "Nothin' to Lose," KISS's first single. He has worked with Cher, Gladys Knight & the Pips, Status Quo, and Bon Jovi's Richie Sambora.

JIM FOX: The drummer with popular 1970s Ohio power trio James Gang, who played on various bills with KISS in 1975.

RIK FOX: One of the earliest KISS fans. He visited the band while they rehearsed in their loft at 10 East Twenty-third Street and was also a habitual attendee at key early shows at Coventry and Hotel Diplomat.

JEFF FRANKLIN: The owner of ATI booking agency from 1968 to 1980. The agency booked KISS on early national tours. A close friend and confidant of Neil Bogart, he helped fund the launch of KISS.

ACE FREHLEY: A founding member and lead guitarist of KISS. He split from the band in 1982, rejoined in 1996 for a successful reunion tour and album, and participated in the group's farewell tour before leaving again to pursue a solo career. Frehley continues to tour and record; his most recent album, *Anomaly*, was released in 2009.

LOU GABRIELSON: A fan who attended shows at the Daisy in Amityville, New York, site of KISS's earliest club gigs.

SKIP GILDERSLEEVE: A Rush roadie from 1975 to 1997, he was on board during the KISS/Rush shows of 1975.

RANDY GIRARD: The drummer for Canadian rock band Joe, which opened for KISS in 1974.

STEVE GLANTZ: A Detroit-based concert promoter with Steve Glantz Productions. He promoted KISS's May 1975 Cobo Hall show, which was taped for the *KISS Alive!* album.

LOU GRAMM: The lead vocalist in Black Sheep, a band that opened shows for KISS in 1975. Gramm went on to enjoy major success as a founding member of 1970s hard rock giants Foreigner.

ALAN GRATZER: The former drummer for 1970s hitmakers REO Speedwagon. The band opened shows for KISS in 1974 and 1975.

BOB GRUEN: Legendary rock photographer who captured images of KISS throughout their career. He also photographed the cover of the band's third album, *Dressed to Kill*.

HARRY HAGSTROM: Played for the Cadillac High Vikings football team from 1974 to 1975.

TOM HAMILTON: A founding member and bassist with popular 1970s Boston hard rock sensation Aerosmith, who headlined several shows with KISS in 1974.

SUSAN HARP: Attended the KISS show in Calgary on their February 1974 tour of Canada.

LARRY HARRIS: Co-owner, senior vice president, and managing director of Casablanca Records, he was key in helping launch KISS's career.

SHAYNE HARRIS: The drummer with Luger, a band that opened for KISS at the Hotel Diplomat in August 1973.

LEONARD HAZE: The drummer with hard rock outfit Yesterday & Today, who opened shows for KISS on the band's *Hotter Than Hell* tour.

GARY HERREWIG: A guitarist in the 1970s power pop band Artful Dodger, who opened shows for KISS on their *KISS Alive!* tour.

DAVE HILL: The lead guitarist with British glam rockers Slade. Slade's anthemic sound, stage show, and outrageous look had a seminal influence on KISS during their formative years. The band's first hit, "Rock and Roll All Nite," was inspired by Slade. They opened shows for KISS on the *KISS Alive!* tour.

NODDY HOLDER: Slade's lead vocalist, guitarist, and songwriter. Slade's anthemic sound, stage show, and outrageous look had a seminal influence on KISS during their formative years. The band's first hit, "Rock and Roll All Nite," was inspired by Slade. They opened shows for KISS on the *KISS Alive!* tour.

MICHAEL HUBLER: Vice president of the SAIT (Southern Alberta Institute of Technology) student association, which helped promote a show on KISS's February 1974 tour of Canada.

ANNEMARIE HUGHES: She and fellow early band supporter Rik Fox were among KISS's first fans. She attended early shows at Coventry, the Daisy, and Hotel Diplomat.

KEITH "KJ" JAMES: DJ at CHED-AM in Edmonton who conducted KISS's first radio interview on their February 1974 tour of Canada.

DAVID JOHANSEN: Johansen is the lead vocalist of influential punk rock band the New York Dolls, a band that performed shows with KISS in '74.

RON JOHNSEN: The producer of Gene Simmons and Paul Stanley's pre-KISS band, Wicked Lester, who recorded an album for Epic Records that was ultimately shelved. He also assisted in the early launch of KISS.

KENNY KERNER: Worked with the likes of Badfinger, Gladys Knight & the Pips, and Stories, who scored a number-one record with "Brother Louie." Kerner coproduced the first two KISS albums, *KISS* and *Hotter Than Hell*.

SPENCER KIRKPATRICK: The guitarist for Hydra, who opened shows for KISS on their *Hotter Than Hell* tour.

IVAN KRAL: The guitarist with Luger, a band that opened for KISS in August 1973 at Hotel Diplomat. He later became a member of the Patti Smith Group.

EDDIE KRAMER: Legendary producer for Jimi Hendrix, Led Zeppelin, Humble Pie, and others, he produced the first KISS demo and the band's 1975 breakthrough *KISS Alive!*, as well as their albums *Rock & Roll Over, Love Gun, KISS Alive II,* and *KISS Alive III.*

KENNY KRAMER: A comedian who was the inspiration for the Cosmo Kramer character on the popular TV series *Seinfeld.* He was the opening act for a single KISS show in late 1974.

BOB KULICK: A musician who originally auditioned for the lead guitar position in KISS. A close friend and confidant of Paul Stanley, his six-string work appeared on KISS albums *KISS Alive II, Killers,* and Paul Stanley's 1978 eponymous solo album. His brother, Bruce, joined KISS in 1984.

JIMI LALUMIA: A writer for the 1970s music magazines *Words & Music* and *Rock.*

DAVE LAURENT: Played for the Cadillac High Vikings football team from 1974 to 1975.

JOHN LAURENT: The principal of Cadillac High School from 1969 to 1978.

JIM LEA: The bassist and songwriter with Slade. Slade's anthemic sound, stage show, and outrageous look had a seminal influence on KISS during their formative years. The band's first hit, "Rock and Roll All Nite," was inspired by Slade. They opened shows for KISS on the *KISS Alive!* tour.

GEDDY LEE: The bassist and lead vocalist with the popular Canadian hard rock trio Rush. They opened over fifty shows for KISS in 1974 and 1975.

ALEX LIFESON: The lead guitarist with popular Canadian hard rock trio Rush, who opened over fifty shows for KISS in 1974 and 1975.

LEW LINET: The manager of Gene Simmons and Paul Stanley's pre-KISS band, Wicked Lester, and KISS's original manager.

Billy Lourie: Attended KISS shows at the Daisy, site of the band's earliest club gigs.

Dave Lucas: A concert promoter and co-owner of Sunshine Promotions from 1974 to 1997, which promoted many KISS shows in the 1970s.

Gary Major: The music director for WKLO in Louisville from 1973 to 1979.

Jim Manfre: The assistant manager for Disc Records in Schaumburg, Illinois, site of "The Great KISS-Off" finals.

Paul Marshall: A partner at Marshall, Morris, Powell & Silfen, he handled KISS's legal affairs from 1974 to 1994. He passed away in 2012.

Nydia "Liberty" Mata: A percussionist with the all-female rock group Isis. They opened for KISS at Coventry in December 1973.

Bobby McAdams: A longtime friend and confidant of Ace Frehley. He was a regular visitor at the KISS loft and attended early club shows in 1973.

Dan McCafferty: The lead singer of the Scottish hard rock band Nazareth, best known for the hits "Hair of the Dog" and "Love Hurts." They played shows with KISS on the first album and *Dressed to Kill* tours.

Jim McCarty: The guitarist in 1960s hitmakers Mitch Ryder & the Detroit Wheels and 1970s heavy rock outfit the Rockets, who opened shows for KISS on various tours in the 1970s.

Kathi McDonald: A blues and rock singer who worked with the likes of the Rolling Stones, Joe Cocker, and Leon Russell. She was promoting her 1974 debut, *Insane Asylum*, when she opened shows for KISS in the spring of 1974.

Mike McGurl: KISS's first tour manager; he worked with the band from 1973 to 1976.

Bob Merlis: The publicity manager for Warner Brothers

Records, he oversaw publicity efforts for KISS's debut album and arranged the group's Fillmore East press launch in January 1974.

STAN MIESES: A writer for the *New York Daily News* who was perhaps the first writer for a major publication to review early KISS performances.

JON MONTGOMERY: Lead vocalist with Street Punk, who opened for KISS in August 1973 at the Hotel Diplomat.

RONNIE MONTROSE: The legendary guitarist for San Francisco hard rock act Montrose. They opened shows for KISS on their *KISS Alive!* tour. He passed away in 2012.

RICK MUNROE: A member of KISS's original road crew, he served as their lighting director from 1974 to 1977.

NORMAN NARDINI: The bassist with Diamond Reo, who were the opening act for KISS's May 1975 performance at Detroit's Cobo Hall, one of the shows recorded for their *KISS Alive!* album.

MARC NATHAN: Regional promotion director for Casablanca Records from 1975 to 1976. He helped break the "Rock and Roll All Nite" single and *KISS Alive!* album on radio.

LEE NEAVES: A Detroit teenager and KISS fan captured in the photo on the back cover of the *KISS Alive!* album.

DAVID NEFF: The drummer for Double Yellow Line, who served as the opening act for KISS's Cadillac High School show in the fall of 1975.

JIM NEFF: Onetime assistant football coach of the Cadillac Vikings, he was instrumental in bringing KISS to Cadillac, Michigan, for the landmark promotional event in the fall of 1975.

DONNIE NOSSOV: The bassist in Street Punk, who opened for KISS in August 1973 at Hotel Diplomat; he went on to play bass on records by Pat Benatar and John Waite.

TED NUGENT: A member of Detroit's Amboy Dukes and a popular solo artist, Ted Nugent opened shows for KISS on their *Dressed to Kill* tour.

JOHN O'DANIEL: The lead vocalist with 1970s Southern rockers Point Blank, who opened shows for Kiss on the *Dressed to Kill* and *KISS Alive!* tours.

PETER "MOOSE" ORECKINTO: A member of KISS's original road crew, he was a roadie and sound mixer and handled theatrical pyrotechnics from 1973 to 1976. He nearly lost his hand in a pyrotechnic accident in late 1974.

MARK PARENTEAU: Music director and afternoon DJ for Detroit radio station WABX-FM from 1969 to 1975. He was an early radio supporter of KISS.

COLIN PATTENDEN: The bassist with Manfred Mann's Earth Band, the headlining act during various shows on KISS's 1974 tour.

ERIC PAULSON: Vice president and general manager of Pickwick International Distribution from 1973 to 1983, which handled record distribution for KISS.

TOM PECK: A musician who auditioned for the lead guitar slot in the original KISS lineup.

JOE PERRY: A founding member and lead guitarist of popular 1970s Boston hard rock act Aerosmith, who headlined several shows with KISS in 1974. In December 2003, Perry became the first rock star to jam with KISS at shows in Oklahoma City and Los Angeles.

BINKY PHILIPS: A high school friend of Paul Stanley, he played lead guitar for the Planets, who opened for KISS in July 1973 at the Hotel Diplomat. He also attended historic early KISS performances and recording sessions.

MARK POLOTT: Saw KISS perform at Coventry, the site of the band's first live performance on January 30, 1973.

IGGY POP: The lead vocalist and frontman for Iggy & the Stooges. They performed on the same bill with KISS at New York's Academy of Music on December 31, 1973.

FRITZ POSTLETHWAITE: KISS's onstage audio engineer from 1975 to 1976.

ANDY POWELL: The guitarist and vocalist with Wishbone Ash, who headlined shows over KISS on the *Hotter Than Hell* tour.

DON POWELL: The drummer with Slade, the popular 1970s glam rockers. Slade's anthemic sound, stage show, and outrageous look had a seminal influence on KISS during their formative years. The band's first hit, "Rock and Roll All Nite," was inspired by Slade. They opened shows for KISS on the *KISS Alive!* tour.

MIKE QUATRO: The keyboardist and frontman of Michael Quatro Jam Band, who played shows with KISS in 1974.

PATTI QUATRO: The lead guitarist of the all-female rock band Fanny, KISS's label mate on Casablanca Records.

SUZI QUATRO: Glam rock bassist and singer who headlined two shows over KISS in the spring of 1974 at Detroit's Michigan Palace.

DEE DEE RAMONE: The bass player of the Ramones. He saw KISS perform at a Bleecker Street loft party in May 1973. He passed away in 2002.

JOEY RAMONE: The Ramones' lead vocalist. He saw KISS perform at Coventry in 1973. KISS later covered the band's "Do You Remember Rock & Roll Radio?" on the 2003 Ramones tribute album *We're a Happy Family: A Tribute to the Ramones*. He passed away in 2001.

JOHNNY RAMONE: The Ramones' guitarist. He passed away in 2004.

MARKY RAMONE: Joining the Ramones for their *Road to Ruin* album, he replaced Tommy Ramone on drums.

TOMMY RAMONE: The original drummer of the Ramones. He attended KISS's early shows at Coventry.

MARK RAVITZ: The New York stage designer who created the first KISS stage sign. He also oversaw the design of KISS's stage show for their first national tour as well as the *Destroyer* and *Rock and Roll Over* tours.

PAT REBILLOT: The pianist for the Pat Rebillot Quintet, who performed on the same bill with KISS at a Palisades, New York, library benefit in the spring of 1973.

BRUCE REDOUTE: A Detroit teenager and KISS fan who appears in the photo on the back cover of the *KISS Alive!* album.

DINA REGINE: New York photographer who shot unseen photos of the band at Hotel Diplomat shows during the summer of 1973.

BUCK REINGOLD: Vice president of national promotion for Casablanca Records, 1974–1976; he was a key to KISS's commercial breakthrough with the "Rock and Roll All Nite" single and the *KISS Alive!* album.

SAM RICCARDO: A Philadelphia-based promotions manager for the music chain Record Museum from 1974 to 1975.

RICK RIVETS: A guitarist with the Brats, a band that opened for KISS at Hotel Diplomat in July 1973.

RICHARD ROBINSON: A writer for the 1970s magazine *Rock Scene*, a New York–based publication that covered KISS early on.

CAROL ROSS: As vice president of the music division at PR firm Rogers & Cowan, she oversaw all of KISS's early press campaigns and was instrumental in engineering national press coverage of the band's Cadillac High School visit in the fall of 1975. She later established the PR firm The Press Office and continued to work with KISS. She also handled high-profile acts like Paul McCartney & Wings and Billy Joel.

FRANCIS ROSSI: The lead vocalist and guitarist in the popular British rock outfit Status Quo. The band opened various shows on KISS's *Dressed to Kill* tour.

GERALD ROTHBERG: The publisher of *Circus*, the national rock magazine, from 1969 to 2004. He was an early press champion of KISS, covering the band extensively.

TODD RUNDGREN: As a solo artist and member of Utopia, he scored major hits with "Hello It's Me," "We Gotta Get You a

Woman," "I Saw the Light," and "Can We Still Be Friends?" He was in the audience for KISS's first major New York show at the Academy of Music on January 31, 1973. "Open My Eyes," a proto-power pop track by his 1960s band The Nazz, inspired Paul Stanley in the writing of "Love Her All I Can," a song that appears on the band's third album, *Dressed to Kill*.

JOYCE SACCO: The ex-wife of Wicked Lester producer Ron Johnsen. She saw an early KISS show in the summer of 1973 at a loft party on Bleecker Street.

NANCY SAIN: National secondary pop promotion director for Casablanca Records in the mid-seventies, she assisted in promoting the *KISS Alive!* album and "Rock and Roll All Nite" single.

JOHN SCHER: A concert promoter for Metropolitan Talent since 1971, he has promoted many KISS shows since the 1970s.

NEAL SCHON: A founding member and lead guitarist in the popular rock band Journey. The band opened shows for KISS on their *Dressed to Kill* tour.

NORMAN SEEFF: An acclaimed South African–born photographer, he made his mark shooting the likes of the Rolling Stones, the Band, Fleetwood Mac, the Eagles, Miles Davis, Van Halen, and countless others. His work appears on the front and back covers of KISS's second album, *Hotter Than Hell*.

BOB SEGER: A 2004 inductee into the Rock and Roll Hall of Fame, he is celebrated as one of rock's most talented artists, penning such rock classics as "Ramblin' Gamblin' Man," "Turn the Page," "Night Moves," "Hollywood Nights," and "Rock 'N Roll Never Forgets." Bob Seger & the Silver Bullet Band performed on bills with KISS in the 1970s.

SCOTT SHANNON: Program director and on-air personality at WMAK-AM, Nashville, from 1969 to 1974, he suggested KISS record a cover of Bobby Rydell's "Kissin' Time," which then appeared on their self-titled debut.

FRANK SHUFLETOSKI: A Canadian photographer who shot previously unseen images of the band on their February 1974 Canadian tour.

KIM SIMMONDS: The lead guitarist of British blues/rock pioneers Savoy Brown. The band headlined shows over KISS on their first national tour.

GENE SIMMONS: A founding member of KISS and the band's lead vocalist, bassist, and songwriter.

J.R. SMALLING: A member of KISS's original road crew who also served as their stage manager from 1974 to 1976. His robust voice is heard on *KISS Alive!* bellowing out their classic stage intro, "You wanted the best and you got it, the hottest band in the land . . . KISS!"

CHAD SMITH: The drummer with the Red Hot Chili Peppers, Smith is a die-hard KISS fan who attended the band's May 1975 show at Cobo Hall, one of several concerts taped for the *KISS Alive!* album.

JOE SMITH: A veteran record company executive, he was president of Warner Brothers Records from 1972 to 1975 and oversaw the label launch of KISS's first album.

EDDIE SOLAN: KISS's original soundman and a roadie from 1973 to 1974. A close friend of Ace Frehley, he shot previously unseen images of KISS inside New York's Bell Studios while they were recording their first album.

CAROL GULOTTA SOTTILI: Saw KISS perform at the Daisy in Amityville, New York.

PAUL STANLEY: A founding member of KISS and the band's lead vocalist, guitarist, and songwriter.

BILL STARKEY: The founder of the KISS Army, which was formed in 1975 in Terre Haute, Indiana.

MARK "ZERO" STINNER: KISS's special effects director from 1975 to 1976.

GARY STROMBERG: As co-owner of Gibson & Stromberg

Public Relations, he oversaw the Casablanca Records' Century Plaza launch in February 1974.

RICK STUART: KISS's director of security from 1975 to 1976.

PAUL SUB: The owner of Coventry, the Queens, New York, club that was the site of KISS's first gig on January 30, 1973.

DONNA SUMMER: A visionary disco artist signed to Casablanca Records. She was later managed by onetime KISS manager Joyce Bogart-Trabulus and also sang background vocals on Gene Simmons's 1978 solo album. Summer passed away in 2012.

STEVE SYBESMA: A concert promoter and co-owner of Sunshine Promotions from 1974 to 1997. They promoted many early 1970s KISS shows.

SYLVAIN SYLVAIN: The guitarist in influential punk rock band the New York Dolls. They performed shows with KISS in 1974.

NEAL TEEMAN: Paul Stanley's friend and bandmate in the pre-KISS band Uncle Joe. He was there when Gene Simmons and Paul Stanley met for the first time. Later, he was an uncredited second engineer on the *KISS Alive!* album.

ANN TONETTI: One of the organizers of the Palisades, New York, library benefit KISS played in the spring of 1973.

RICH TOTOIAN: National promoter director at Windfall Records from 1971 to 1973. He attended a KISS show at Hotel Diplomat in the summer of 1973.

MARTIN TURNER: The lead vocalist and bassist with Wishbone Ash, who were the headlining act for various shows on KISS's *Hotter Than Hell* tour.

JAAN UHELSZKI: A music writer for *Creem* and one of KISS's early press supporters. Her classic 1975 *Creem* feature, "I Dreamed I Was Onstage with KISS in my Maidenform Bra," chronicles her experience performing onstage with KISS in Johnstown, Pennsylvania, on May 17, 1975.

HOWARD UNGERLEIDER: The tour manager for Rush since 1974. He was on hand for the KISS/Rush tours of 1974 and 1975.

JOE VALENTINE: A guitarist with local New York band Rags, he saw several early KISS shows at Coventry.

ROSS VALORY: A founding member and bassist of popular rock band Journey, who opened shows for KISS on their *Dressed to Kill* tour.

JOHN VAN HAMERSVELD: A graphic designer and illustrator whose impressive album cover design work includes the Beatles' *Magical Mystery Tour*, the Rolling Stones' *Exile on Main Street*, and KISS's *Hotter Than Hell*.

PAT VEGAS: Best known for the 1974 hit "Come and Get Your Love," he was the bassist in Redbone, a band who headlined over KISS in early 1974.

DON WASLEY: Vice president of artist development for Casablanca Records from 1975 to 1980. He lent his business and marketing savvy to KISS before they scored a hit with their *KISS Alive!* album.

ERIC WEINSTEIN: A KISS roadie in 1974, Weinstein also worked for Patti Smith and Blue Öyster Cult. He went on to produce the popular HBO series *Entourage*.

FRANK WEIPERT: A Canadian concert promoter for Audience Concerts, which promoted the third show on KISS's February 1974 Canadian tour.

TOM WERMAN: In the early 1970s, he was the assistant to the director of A&R at Epic Records. He was in attendance at an early label showcase at KISS's East Twenty-third Street loft before Ace Frehley joined the band. He went on to become a successful music producer, working with Cheap Trick, Ted Nugent, Molly Hatchet, and Mötley Crüe.

KEITH WEST: The lead vocalist of the Brats, who opened for KISS at the Hotel Diplomat in July 1973.

LESLIE WEST: Legendary lead guitarist and frontman for the early 1970s hard rock trio Mountain. Mountain's "Theme for an Imaginary Western" influenced the writing of "Goin' Blind," a song that appears on KISS's second album, *Hotter Than Hell*. The Leslie West Band opened shows for KISS in 1975.

MICHAEL WHITE: A Canadian concert promoter for Scenemaker Productions, which promoted shows on the first two dates on KISS's February 1974 Canadian tour.

JAMES WILLIAMSON: The guitarist for Iggy & the Stooges. The band performed on the same bill with KISS on December 31, 1973, at New York's Academy of Music.

RICHIE WISE: Worked with the likes of Badfinger, Gladys Knight & the Pips, and Stories, who scored a number-one record with "Brother Louie." Wise coproduced the first two KISS albums, *KISS* and *Hotter Than Hell*.

DAVE WITTMAN: The engineer for KISS's first demo, he also engineered a number of KISS albums, including *Dressed to Kill*, *Killers*, *Creatures of the Night*, *Lick it Up*, and *Animalize*.

DENNIS WOLOCH: KISS's art director and designer from 1975 to 1988. His earliest work with KISS was for their *KISS Alive!* album and tour book.

NEIL ZLOZOWER: The renowned rock photographer captured the band in February 1974 for their first TV appearance on Dick Clark's *In Concert*.

ACKNOWLEDGMENTS

Paul and Gene would like to thank the fans who helped make it all happen.

Ken would like to thank: Paul Stanley, Gene Simmons, Ace Frehley, Peter Criss, Bill Aucoin, Margie, Tim and Samantha Adamsky, John Altyn, Denny Anderson, Mark S. Anthony, Terrance Bert, John Bionelli, Joyce Bogart-Trabulus, Tim Bogart, Rob Bonfiglio, Jim Bullotta, Scott Camarota, Mick Campise, Alex Castino, Jim Ceravolo, Mark Cicchini, Fin Costello, Lydia Criss, Victor Dawahare, Chip Dayton, Len DeLessio, Delmar T. Oviatt Library at California State University–Northridge, Bill DeMild, Robert Duncan, Brad Estra, Bob Ezrin, Jonathan Fenno, "Bazooka" Joe Fields, Rik Fox, Jay Gilbert, Julian Gill, Leo Gozbekian, Charles Hannah, Larry Harris, Shayne Harris, Rich Herschlag, Louis Hirshorn, Bernie Hogya, Jeremy Holiday, Spring Houston, Chris Huckle/*Cadillac News*, AnneMarie Hughes, John Humphrey, Tom Jermann, Ron Johnsen, Susan Katila, Carol Kaye, Elliot Kendall, Andrew Klein, Jason Knox, Ross Koondel, Eddie Kramer, Bethany Larson, David Leaf, Leah Lehrer, Keith Leroux, Dennis Martin, Jeffrey Mayer, Mike McGurl, Joe Merante, Andrew Miller, Terry Munro, Miwako Murakami,

David Naccarelli, Ralph Naccarelli, Marc Nathan, Jim Neff, Peter "Moose" Oreckinto, Bill Parsons, Maria Perez, Binky Philips, Ron Pownall, Brian Rademacher, Ros Radley, Bill Randolph, Dina Regine, Sam Riccardo, Mike Rinaldi, Manny Rosa, Carol Ross, Jon Rubin, Jeff Schwartz, Norman Seeff, Matt Seward/*Cadillac News*, Carol Sharp, Carol Paula Sharp, Jim Sharp, Dale Sherman, Frank Shufletoski, Daniel Siwek, David Slania, J.R. Smalling, Brad Smith, Dean Snowden, Laura Sokolosky/Cinetech, Eddie Solan, Bill Starkey, Mark Stockwell, Steve Strauss, Jeff Suhs, Meghan Symsyk, Rex Tennant, Tommy Thayer, Jaan Uhelszki, Stacey Virta, Tim Wargo, Donny Webb, and Herman, Buddy, Chachi, the Jeep, and Clarice ("Miss Mae") and Mr. Zero ("the Zeep").

Mighty kudos to Jim Bullotta for his creative web design and digital marketing expertise.

A standing ovation to my agent, Dave Dunton, for his support and encouragement.

Big props to my editor, Denise Oswald, for her hard work in finessing and helping shape and tame this beast of a manuscript.

Special thanks to Jeremy Holiday for his editorial assistance and friendship.

My gratitude to Ros Radley for his invaluable help as photo research assistant and with photo editing.

And to my mom, Carol Sharp, my eternal thanks and love for teaching me to think big and follow my dreams.

NOTES

All original interviews were conducted by Ken Sharp. The following citations are for the quotations used in the book.

3. 10 EAST TWENTY-THIRD STREET
26   "I was always into Phil Spector": Harvey Kubernik, "Kiss and Tell," *Melody Maker*, February 15, 1975, p. 47.
34   "I always felt I had something": Frank Rose, "Invasion of the Glitter Goths," *Circus*, April 8, 1976, p. 28.

4. LARGER THAN LIFE
41   "Before KISS, I played every club in New York": Richard Robinson, "Kiss: They Love to Put Out," *Hit Parader*, July 1976, p. 29.
42   "We are an extension of everything that came before us": Scott Cohen, "A Trip Through the Looking-Glass with Rock's Greasepaint Flashers," *Circus Raves*, July 1975, p. 64.
43   "We started wearing makeup when Alice [Cooper] took it off": Elliot Cohen, "The Age of KISS," *The Aquarian*, July 28–August 18, 1976, p. 19.

7. DAISY DAZE
70   "I trusted Lew's taste and I wasn't wrong": Carol Gulotta, "First KISS," *Newsday*, September 4, 1977, p. 13.

8. LIPSTICK KILLERS
85   "What you've got to admire KISS for is staying power": Dale Sherman, *Black Diamond* (Canada: CG Publishing), 2009, p. 65.

10. ROCK STEADY

124 "There were two reasons why I got involved with KISS": Frank Rose, "Invasion of the Glitter Goths," *Circus*, April 8, 1976, p. 24.

11. ALL THE WAY

135 "I always wanted to be an entertainer": Todd Everett, "Roll Back the Roulette Tables, Rick; Rock & Roll Has Come to Casablanca," *Circular*, January 21, 1974, p. 1.

136 "We had about twenty chart records that year": ibid., p. 2.

137 "I tried to live that down for a few years": ibid.

137 "I had Casablanca in my head": Linda Deutsch, "Neil Bogart Strikes Gold in the Record Business," *Milwaukee Journal*, May 31, 1977, p. 49.

138 "I got myself a business manager": Everett, "Roll Back the Roulette Tables, Rick," p. 3.

139 "I was really into *Casablanca*": Anthony Cook, "Play It Again, Neil," *New West*, October 10, 1977, p. 40.

140 "People ask me what kind of music I'm looking for": Everett, "Roll Back the Roulette Tables, Rick," p. 3.

144 "When I first saw them their music hit me like a bolt of lightning": no author listed, *KISS* first album bio, 1974, p. 2.

144 "They're everything I've been looking for in a band": Everett, "Roll Back the Roulette Tables, Rick," p. 3.

12. ON THE ROAD TO CASABLANCA

145 "Casablanca is a company that is owned by myself": Todd Everett, "Roll Back the Roulette Tables, Rick; Rock & Roll Has Come to Casablanca," *Circular*, January 21, 1974, p. 3.

145 "We run the promotion of a record the same way you would an army going to war": Anthony Cook, "Play It Again, Neil," *New West*, October 10, 1977, p. 40.

146 "KISS was the first group we signed": Nick Nichols, "Overnight Sensation or Classic Success Story," *Cashbox*, March 6, 1976, p. 16.

146 "I've never been into hard rock until recently": Harvey Kubernik, "Kiss and Tell," *Melody Maker*, February 15, 1975, p. 47.

147 "When we started with KISS people thought we were crazy": Linda Deutsch, "Neil Bogart Strikes Gold in the Record Business," *Milwaukee Journal*, May 31, 1977, p. 49.

14. GREAT EXPECTATIONS

200 "As a new company we didn't have much time to break them": Ed Harrison, "Number One with a Star: The Inside of Making a Hit Record," *Billboard*, May 21, 1977, p. 44.

15. "PUT YOUR TWO LIPS TOGETHER . . ."

208 "No matter where the group went": no author listed, *KISS Alive!* press announcement, 1975, p. 1.

209 "We were pouring a lot of money into the band": Wes Strick, "A KISS Is Still a KISS," *Rock*, November 1976, p. 51.

20. HAVE ROAD, WILL TRAVEL

285 "All rock audiences want two things": Dan Nooger, "Big Bands Hate Us 'Cause We Steal Their Audiences," *Circus*, March 1975, p. 41.

23. ROAD WARS

339 "No matter when we go on": Dan Nooger, "Big Bands Hate Us 'Cause We Steal Their Audiences," *Circus*, March 1975, p. 41.

24. THE "DARTBOARD TOUR"

362 "It's nice for a band, other than a Japanese group": Harvey Kubernik, "Kiss and Tell," *Melody Maker*, February 15, 1975, p. 47.

28. POWER PLAY

395 "Sure it was tough to try to establish our company and break a new group at the same time": Nick Nichols, "Overnight Sensation or Classic Success Story," *Cashbox*, March 6, 1976, p. 16.

29. MEDIA BATTLES

418 "To build an artist you have to build a following": Linda Deutsch, "Neil Bogart Strikes Gold in the Record Business," *Milwaukee Journal*, May 31, 1977, p. 49.

32. ON THE SKIDS

457 "It was a year of total disaster, other than KISS": Anthony Cook, "Play It Again, Neil," *New West*, October 10, 1977, p. 40.

463 "I made up my own term for these guys": Frank Rose, "Invasion of the Glitter Goths," *Circus*, April 8, 1976, p. 27.